POSTCOLONIALISM, MULTITUDE, AND THE POLITICS OF NATURE

On the Changing Geographies of the European North

Ari Aukusti Lehtinen

University Press of America,® Inc.
Lanham · Boulder · New York · Toronto · Oxford

University Press of America,® Inc.
4501 Forbes Boulevard
Suite 200
Lanham, Maryland 20706
UPA Acquisitions Department (301) 459-3366

PO Box 317
Oxford
OX2 9RU, UK

Printed in the United States of America
British Library Cataloging in Publication Information Available

Library of Congress Control Number: 2005938641
ISBN-13: 978-0-7618-3417-5 (paperback : alk. paper)
ISBN-10: 0-7618-3417-6 (paperback : alk. paper)

™ The paper used in this publication meets the minimum requirements of American National Standard for Information Sciences—Permanence of Paper for Printed Library Materials, ANSI Z39.48—1984

Contents

Part III. Conclusions

Preface and Acknowledgments

Human-induced climatic change is estimated to have a thorough impact on arctic regions and coniferous northwoods due to global warming and melting of ice sheets. The latest prognoses convince that the ecological characteristics of the North are widely threatened. Traditional modes of living and sources of livelihood are also at risk of disappearing. Forests are more likely to be hit by hazards such as storms and insect infestations. Reindeer herding will face the hardening snow conditions. Polar bears, the symbols of the arctic North, are under serious risk of becoming extinct in the coming decades.

Lands and lifemodes in Northern Europe are to be transformed accordingly. It is for example common today in my home region in North Karelia, eastern Finland, to worry about the shortening of the periods of snow cover. North Karelia has annually about 160–170 snowy days, but the present century is estimated to limit the number below one hundred.

Many glaciologists have, on the other hand, warned the Northern Europeans about the consequences of the probable weakening of the Gulf Stream in the North Atlantic as a result of climatic warming. The Gulf Stream has served as an ecological confirmation of the relatively mild climate in Scandinavia, compared for example with much colder Alaska at the same latitudes, but now the melting Arctic is feared to change the course of the stream. Radical changes in this respect can lead to expanding ice sheets and thus toward a new Ice Age. This vision would bring each year 365 days of snow cover to North Karelia.

The climatic change in Northern Europe will in any case result in a rising importance of ecological and cultural buffer zones in the most risky areas. Sea shores and mountain regions are of particular concern, as are the forested lowlands. The wealth of conifer species is to be afflicted with the change, and thus also the general ecological character of the northwoods would go through serious transformations. All this will affect deeply the human communities and sources of living.

The Greenbelt of the conifer-dominated forests on the border between Finland and Russia is one of the key buffer zones in Northern Europe. It is a local guarantee for the forest species to adjust to the gradual global changes. The corridor of forests would let the species move north or south, depending on the signals of the surroundings. The Belt is also seen as an ecological link between the heartlands of Russian taiga and the more fragmented forests of Finland and Scandinavia. The geopolitically closed border served as an east-west corridor for species of flora and fauna during the Cold War, but this contact became threatened in the post-Soviet years by ecological fragmentation caused by intensified economic activities close to and across the border. This transition is a telling example of the complexity of the Greenbelt. The lowering economic border erected an ecological one: the gateway to forest species is at risk to be closed.

The Finnish-Russian Greenbelt, also known as the Fennoscandian Greenbelt, is the focus of the case studies in this volume. The geographical scope is, however, two-fold. The first chapters explicate the specific study approach formulated within the context of Nordic human geography, to be applied in the later chapters to the Greenbelt conditions. The methodological choices are developed through the case studies but they also offer tools for critically evaluating the Greenbelt decisions and politics.

The dialogic character of the volume invites the reader to co-follow the paths of Nordic geographies (as academic practices) and Greenbelt geographies (as societal practices) in a critical comparative manner. The particular lines of Nordic geographical thinking are presented here in close connection to the respective Anglo-American and Continental European debates in geography. On the other hand, the Greenbelt studies illustrate in detail the lands and lives of the people settled down close to a border that forms a multicultural meeting place to Finno-Ugric, Scandinavian and Slavic cultures and is a contact zone for two branches of Christian churches, namely the Orthodox and the Lutheran. The specific border conditions between Finland (or, the European Union) and Russia reveal an array of cultural, economic, environmental, political and epistemic divides, and only a few comparative settings can be found in the Western world. The border zone between Mexico and the United States is one of the few comparable examples of the drama and the dynamics of a contact field across radically diverging cultures.

The Nordic part of the research has been carried out in several study periods in Copenhagen, Helsinki, Joensuu, Oslo, Roskilde and Uppsala. The Greenbelt travelogue is similarly grounded on numerous visits and field excursions to the Greenbelt communities in North Karelia, Russian Karelia (Petrozavodsk, Suojärvi, Kostomukhsa, Viena), St. Petersburg and the Barents Region (Murmansk, Finnmark, Norrland, Upper Lapland). The study periods were financed by the Academy of Finland (in 1992 and in 2000–2001), Danish Ministry of Education (in 1989–1990), Swedish Council for Planning and Coordination of Research (Forskningsrådsnämden, in 1992–1993), Norwegian Academy of Science and Letters and Centre for Advanced Study in Oslo (Senter for Høyere Studier ved Det Norske Videnskaps-Akademi, in 2002–2003). In addition, the Finnish Cultural Foundation (Suomen Kulttuurirahasto) supported the final stage of editing the manuscript. I owe a large debt to all these institutions.

The Nordic and Greenbelt excursions have been guided and accompanied by a number of friends and scholars who have helped in interpreting and reflecting upon the multitude of the geographies of the North. The summaries of this volume owe much to co-inspiration (in different stages of journeying) with Jørgen-Ole Bærenholdt, Thomas Beckley, Sune Berger, Eeva Berglund, Gabriel Bladh, Jacquelin Burgess, Anne Buttimer, David Demeritt, Steen Folke, TiiaRiitta Granfelt, Aleksei Grigoryev, Pekka Haavisto, Yrjö Haila, Frank Hansen, Raimo Heikkilä, Kaija Heikkinen, Anders Hjort-af-Ornäs, Tiina Hokkanen, Marjatta Hytönen, Jouni Häkli, Gregory A. Isachenko, Michael Jones, Jarmo Kortelainen, Tarmo Koskinen, Juha Kotilainen, Christer Krokfors, Matti Kärkkäinen, Pekka Laaksonen, Santeri Lesonen, Sarah Lloyd, Anders Lundberg, Don Mitchell, Markku Nieminen, Oula Näkkäläjärvi, Venke Olsen, Kenneth Olwig, Anssi Paasi, Samu Pehkonen, Tiina Peil, Elisa Peter, Nadezhda Polevtsikova, Maire Puikko, Jarmo Pyykkö, Kaisa Raitio, Pertti Rannikko, Jussi Raumolin, Gulnara Roll, Teijo Rytteri, Olli Saastamoinen, Klas Sandell, Bjørnar Sæther, Virpi Sahi, L. Anders Sandberg, Andrew Sayer, Gunhild Setten, Kirsten Simonsen, Kari Stuberg, Maria Tysiachniouk, John Westerholm, Mats Widgren, Sakari Virtanen, and many others. I am grateful for the collaborative effort.

I am also deeply indebted to Sisko Porter for carefully correcting my English and pointing out the "verbal stones" page by page. English is not a language closest to me, but in this process I have gradually learnt to like the way it encourages toward fluent articulation. I am convinced that the final result is readable by all who have an interest in the riches of the local-global North. The processing of the Figures and the technical layout were carried out by Timo Pakarinen and Janne Kuivalainen, who also deserve warm thanks.

A few chapters of this volume are revised versions of earlier publications. "*Samhällsgeografi* and the Politics of Nature" (originally published in *Voices from the North*, eds. Kirsten Simonsen and Jan Öhman, 2003), "Coping with the Borders" (originally published in *Politics of Forests*, eds. Ari Aukusti Lehtinen, Jakob Donner-Amnell and Bjørnar Sæther, 2004) and "On the Edge" (originally published in *Encountering the North*, eds. Frank Möller and Samu Pehkonen, 2003) are published by permission of Ashgate. "Politics of the Margin" (originally published in *Fennia* 178, no. 1, 2000) and "Rescaling the Northwoods" (originally published in *Fennia* 180, nos. 1–2, 2002) are reprinted by permission of the Geographical Society of Finland. "Provincialism in a Frontier Community" (originally published in *Nordia* 27, no. 1, 1998) is included here by permissions of the Geographical Society of Northern Finland and Teijo Rytteri, the co-author of the original article. "Wilderness Politics and *Erämaa* practices" (originally published in *Dieđut*, no. 3, 2004) is republished by permission of the Nordic Sámi Institute. The permissions to present copyrighted quotations and illustrations are pointed out in connection with the respective citations.

Ari Aukusti Lehtinen
Joensuu, Finland
February, 2005

Cover photos top to bottom:

Hugo Simberg's *Halla* (1895) visualizes in a chilling way the dreaded moment of freezing in the agrarian North. *Halla* is reproduced by the permission of the Finnish National Gallery.

The painting on Martti Kitunen (1747-1833) and bear hunting by Alfred Wahlberg and J. W. Wallander is reprinted by the permission of the Swedish National Museum.

The drawing by Vihtori Ylinen (1915) is one of the *Finnish Paintings of Enlightenment:* it opens a view over Lake Tavajärvi in Russian Karelia, south of Paanajärvi National Park. The drawing is published by the permission of the Finnish Kuvasto.

An aerial view on Finnish mirescapes is reproduced by the permission of the Finnish Land Survey.

Part I. Introduction

1.

Postcolonial North?

Through ages, the European North has served as a specific source of inspiration for researchers and travelers, and especially for geographers. The written and celebrated past of the Arctic is a heroic one and it has also functioned as a central cause for the initial institutionalization of geography as an academic discipline in the Nordic countries.

The return of Nils Adolf Erik Nordenskiöld to Stockholm in 1880, after the pioneering sail across the Northeast Passage, was the event to raise public interest in the Arctic and it also motivated the Nordic countries toward more organized and systematic inventories of the far North. The Swedish Society of Anthropology and Geography (*Svenska Sällskapet för Antropologi och Geografi*), founded in 1877, began to publish *Ymer* in 1881 and the journal soon grew into an important forum for arctic research. Lund, Uppsala, Gothenburg and Stockholm received their first professors of geography in a short period at the turn of the century, which was undoubtedly a sign of the growing societal interest in locating Sweden centrally on the map of modern science regimes. Geography was during those days the science of expansion, and in Sweden, as within the rest of the Nordic countries, the primary focus for territorial curiosity was the North.[1]

In Norway, the Geographical Society was founded in 1889, after the return of Fridtjov Nansen from his expedition to Greenland. The founding idea of the Society was to support geographical voyages of discovery and spread information about the explorations to the broader public. The early professional geography was part of the construction of nationalistic framework for the emerging (nation)state of Norway but it was also integrated into the expansionistic politics of the country. Polar research was part of the national identity-building and industrial-territorial extension. Military leaders, diplomats and entrepreneurs were common visitors to the first meetings of the Norwegian Society of Geographers.[2]

The success of Nordenskiöld was also noticed in Finland, and the necessity to participate in the competition over the North became evident. In Finland, as in the western neighbors, the expeditions northward were regarded both as a tool for solidifying the national cultural existence and a means for optional territorial expansion. The provincial country, then under the Russian Empire, could show her vitality by these symbolic activities. Zoologist J.A. Palmen, who for several years had analyzed the bird observations of Nordenskiöld's Vega voyage, soon made plans for a Finnish expedition to the Kola Peninsula in Northwest Russia. The Kola expedition took place in summer 1887 and it had a decisive impact on the foundation of the Finnish Geographical Association (*Geografiska Föreningen i Finland*) in winter 1887–88. Palmen was one of the founders of the Society and also its secretary for the first 29 years.[3]

In Denmark, the Royal Geographical Society had been established already in 1876 and one of the main interests of the Society was focused on Greenland, the vast northern island currently connected to Denmark as an independent administrative unit with home rule. Greenland research intensified in Denmark during the post World War II decades, and especially since the 1980s in the context of North Atlantic studies. The North Atlantic is still in the early years of the 21st century a strained question to the Danes, surfacing for example in the debate on the relations between the mainland and the Faroe Islands. The celebrated and widely read novel *Smilla's Sense of Snow (Frøken Smillas førnemmelse for sne)* by Peter Hœg[4] intensely elaborates Denmark's difficult relation with her colonial-territorial past in the North Atlantic.

Today's geography of the European North is inevitably less heroic and often rather critical of the early master narratives of expansive modernization. The North, however, continues to have the role of inspiration in geography. The last decades have witnessed several new orientations northward by geographers and colleagues within the related disciplines. The North has been approached by a broad variety of renewed motives and ideas, taking shape for example in critical ecopolitical, cultural-economic and ethnoecological reorientations.

The early geography of expansion turned into a multitude of complementary approaches during the late 20th century, increasingly motivated by a sensitive rearticulation of the specific time-space geographies of the North. Imperial spaces of mapping were replaced by zones of cross-border interaction, lands of otherness re-emerged as multicultural realms with shared heritage, and modern territorial divisions confronted the layers of mythopoetic landscapes. Both the motives and the perspectives of the research diversified. The Northern landscapes of geographers became elastic and diffuse, comprehensible only from pluralistic and mobile positions. The North of the geographers emerged as a critical voice from the margins. It grew into an invitation to reciprocal learning, an existing alternative to the dominating standards of the West (or South, when seen from the North). Furthermore, the North became a connection to pre-Christian belief traditions: today it symbolizes for many the contact to early ancestors and their worldviews.

The ongoing diversification of the academic geographies of the North has, however, had only limited success in gaining firm ground in the North. The theoretical sophistication has enabled us to construct a deeper picture of the North but, at the same time, it has kept professional geographers rather paradoxically in the role of foreigners in the daily spheres of living in the North. The motives and legitimacy of research have especially been questioned. Despite the immanent critique and radical renewal of the early colonial approaches, the *avant-garde* of postcolonial academic geography has been unable to construct a satisfactory correspondence between the academic landscapes and the everyday life worlds of the Northern peoples. The elegant discourses and diverse maps of meaning constructed by the researchers have largely remained alien to the everyday means of orientation and communication among the local folks.

The Northerners have, on the other hand, been able to develop their own forums of internal correspondence and this has largely taken place both in spite of and due to the pressures from the outside. The internal dynamics has sometimes even been fueled by the adjustment demands from the South. These forums have co-forged geonarratives and personal geographies of their own. This source of geo-inspiration, emerging from inside the life worlds of the North, has gained only marginal interest among the professionals in geography. The North has remained alien to her academic students and this, if anything, is a place for scholarly self-reflection. How to rethink the discipline of geography in order to reach the credibility and legitimacy in the North? How to avoid the traps of elitism? How to become free from the strains of (post)colonial annihilation?[5]

This is the starting point and the basic question of this volume. The argument is that geographical imagination is deeply present in the North, and profoundly represented by the Northerners themselves, and this needs to be considered a source of critical self-reflection and inspiration to academic geographies. This challenge is met here in the form of excursions along the Greenbelt of the Finnish-Russian border; by landing on northern mirescapes, visiting forest villages and indigenous Sámi communities, and journeying through the Euroarctic wildernesses. The case excursions introduce the Greenbelt in different spatial scales ranging from the life worlds of the border settlements up to the forums of international forest-industrial operations.

The research approach applied and developed in this volume links the human geographical renewal (in humanity-nature studies) to the wider spheres of intellectual and political environmental reorientations. Historically, as is shown in the proceeding pages, the key questions of geography have been indelibly related to the development of environmental ideologies and practices, and the present state of affairs is no exception to this rule. The various portraits of geographers influencing, and becoming influenced by, the changes in environmental concerns are assessed, and this discussion forms the general background whereupon the main historical routes to the present critical socioenvironmental updating become explicable.

This volume argues that the formulations and interpretations of Western environmentalism have gradually reached a broadly agreed uniform shape, and only recently this unification has met profound criticism. The critical turn is in many ways linked to the emergence of new socioenvironmental approaches that share the intellectual background with multicultural and (post)colonial views in the academic world and beyond.

The protagonists of this intellectual renewal have, however, met difficulties in identifying themselves as critical commentators of the ongoing geopolitical production of environmental risks and injustices. The sophisticated reassessing of the foundations and historical turns of environmentalism has, as is argued in this volume, in practice offered a popular means to scholars to promote their own positions in academic markets. The renewed rules of academic efficiency, bound to citation indexes and abstract impact factors, have also encouraged the narrowing of the societal scope of Western environmentalism. Whereas several of the pioneers of environmentalism, such as Georg Perkins Marsh (1801–1882) and Carl Ortwin Sauer (1889–1975), were for example famous for their multilingual skills, the current critical generation is largely satisfied with the rapid anglophonization of the "environmental order." Several of the speakers of the younger generation of critical environmentalists, inspired by multiculturalism, have therefore in their practical scholarship served as promoters of the harmonization of environmental thinking.

The Generations of Environmentalism

In their collection on *Liberation Ecologies*, geographers Richard Peet and Michael Watts argue that the political ecology of the late 1970s and 1980s was "markedly different from that of the first environmental wave of the 1960s, which was dominated by Darwinian and Malthusian thinking and simple organic analogies."[6] For them, political ecology is part of a larger renewal rooting from the critique of ecological anthropology and cultural ecology that initially gained currency during the "first wave" and drew attention to the adaptive capacities of indigenous peoples. The second phase of environmental activism had to react to the dramatic changes in global politicoeconomic and environmental conditions and it profoundly modified the motives and approaches. The new phase, according to Peet and Watts, grounded its argument on the alarming recognition of the deepening human-induced modifications of the global environment and it was broadly characterized by the rise of green movements worldwide. The authors update on this ground the challenges of the political ecology movement to meet the conditions of the late 20th century.

In a manner similar to Peet and Watts, the launch of modern environmental awareness is often located in the 1950s or early 1960s. This view repeatedly identifies the initial formulations of the environmental awakening with the influential speeches of the Princeton Symposium on Man's Role in Changing the Face of the Earth in 1955[7] or, alternatively, with the publication of *Silent Spring* by Rachel Carson in 1962.[8] In addition, researchers of environmental politics tend often to begin their historical counting from those days, as do John S. Dryzek, David Downes, Christian Hunold, David Schlosberg and Hans-Kristian Hernes in their comparative analysis of environmentalism in Germany, Norway, the United States and the United Kingdom. For them, environmentalism is emblematic of the late 20th century social movements in its post-materialistic commitments and, therefore, they "look at the history of the movements since the 1960s, showing how and why the movement took shape in the very different ways in four very different states".[9]

It seems to have become largely accepted within this discursive realm that environmental critique finally began in the 1950s and 1960s. The emphasis of this time span is often colored with personal recollections and memories that stand as witness to a strong presence of a biographical element. Commentators willingly identify themselves as an integral part of the historical change. Michael Watts makes confessions of this type while sketching connections between the early radicals of the "68 generation" and the radicals of the "post Seattle 1999 generation". Watts states that the Seattle activists, i.e. the NGO network criticizing the governance of the world regulatory agencies, are "echoing the spirit and carnivalesque street practices of 1968." For him, the political repertoires were "right out of the 1968 handbook" and he also concludes that "Seattle was Berkeley gone global—a multitude against Empire."[10] This remark refers to the biopolitical views of literature theorist Michael Hardt and political philosopher Antonio Negri in their global vision on Empire-building and its criticizers.[11]

Similar personal attachment surfaces in Andrew Jamison's self-reflective journeying from the United States to Sweden in his search for an "ecological society." Jamison's "green knowledge" was composed in the 1950s and 1960s and thereafter reformulated through stages of institutionalization, politicization, professionalization, integration and internationalization.[12] For him, Sweden gradually in the 1970s turned into a model of environmentalism, as the country was the first in the world that had established a state agency having an overall responsibility for environmental issues (in 1967), and its parliament was the first to pass a comprehensive law on environmental protection. For Jamison, who is an expert on science and technology theory, the "making of green knowledge is our story." This story is full of views from inside the movement and it especially concentrates on the development of the cognitive praxis of greening. Jamison writes from Sweden:

> *Det var under perioden precis efter andra världskriget som det traditionella naturvårdsintresset började förändras till en ny sorts miljömedvetenhet. Man brukar anse att denna medvetenhet växte fram på 1960-talet, främst inspirerat av Rachel Carsons* Tyst vår *men den började utformas mycket tidigare av några ledande personer inom naturskydds-rörelsen, speciellt i USA och Storbritannien.*[13]

> Soon after World War II the traditional nature conservation began to develop toward a new environmental awareness. It is widely agreed that this awareness took shape in the 1960s, much inspired by *Silent Spring* by Rachel Carson, but it in fact became formulated much earlier by a few leading figures of nature conservation, especially in the USA and Great Britain. (Translated from Swedish by the author)

Jamison then mentions for example Julian Huxley, Fairfield Osborn, Joseph Wood Krutch, David Brower, William Douglas and Ansel Adams as among those leading the modern environmental awakening.

The 50-year view on environmentalism's past is not then the only time horizon underlined in the historical interpretations of environmentalism. Another and similarly popular time span is approximately 150 years old. This history identifies the first years of modern environmentalism with the days when the early classics of modern environmentalism were published. One of the most celebrated pioneers of this history is George Perkins Marsh, a cosmopolitan polyglot from Vermont, who by his *Man and Nature—or Physical Geography Modified by Human Action* from 1864 is often named as the first to introduce critical environmental thinking and nature conservation in a broad (inter)cultural context. Historical geographer David Lowenthal agrees with Lewis Mumford, the influential criticizer of civilizations, who assessed in the 1930s that *Man and Nature* was indeed "the fountainhead of the conservation movement." Lowenthal further comments how today, thus in the 1960s, "Marsh's insights are virtually taken for granted." Marsh's radical aim was to show how profoundly humanity had changed the environment and he also sketched concrete means for redirecting the human role, including nature conservation measures. His global view was based on extensive traveling and multilingual readership. According to Lowenthal, Marsh read "omnivorously and rapidly" in twenty languages.[14]

Environmental historian Donald Worster also emphasizes the importance of Marsh's book and underlines that "not until Marsh took up the question in the 1860s did anyone manage to gain a comprehensive view of the environmental upheaval worked by the economic and demographic revolutions."[15] Worster is deeply concerned about the human-induced environmental degradation since the publication of *Man and Nature* but he also highly appreciates the value of the deepening understanding of environmental issues. He for example constructs and repeatedly refers to a chain of influential scholars who have carried on the "critical wave" and devoted much of their efforts to environmental changes. He mentions such colleagues as Ernst Friedrich, John Muir, Giffort Pinchot, Paul Sears and Carl Sauer, and further continues by listing several of the key writers inspired by the Princeton Symposium and *Silent Spring*.[16] These include Jean Dorst, Paul Erlich and Dennis and Donella Meadow.

The longer history of environmentalism is undoubtedly a necessary precondition for the green awakening of the most recent decades.[17] The younger critical scholars have appreciated in general the traditional formulations but also questioned them as being elitist and therefore ignorant of societal tensions or falling into naïve material environmentalism.[18] Geographer David Demeritt for example criticizes those environmental historians, such as Richard White, Timothy Silver and William Cronon, who in a dualistic manner situate the histories of natives and Europeans in the American past into landscape cross-sections from different periods of time. Demeritt states that this tends "to freeze the many different temporalities of human and natural activity in a singular temporal rhythm of explanation."[19] Demeritt also questions the tendency of environmental historians to rely upon ecological science for explanatory concepts such as ecosystem and equilibrium that organize their narratives. For example, according to Demeritt, Worster's[20] "homeostatic nature and capitalistic disturbances of it are constituted by a thoroughly romanticized aboriginal past of ecological peace and harmony." Demeritt shows in a similar manner how William Cronon's[21] metaphor of ecosystem finally "slips away from the figurative bounds of metaphor and claims to be the world itself." Thus, Demeritt argues, in concrete historical case analyses Cronon's ecology turns into the living thing itself.[22]

Geographer Noel Castree further deepens Demeritt's critical stance in his search for "post-environmental ethics." He is particularly concerned about risks of essentialism in current environmentalism. For him, environmental essentialism entails the belief that material entities have discrete and enduring properties, and they are thought to carry immutable and autonomous qualities. Castree critically examines the ethics of environmental "othering" and draws his alternative solution from the more recent hybrid research—which emphasizes socioenvironmental fabrications and culture-nature associations—and asks for increased sensitivity to "the contingent material specificities" while making ethical claims. According to him, particular attention in environmental research needs to be paid to relational dependencies and situational variation.[23]

These critical commentaries function as important intergenerational progress reports. They identify the biases of the past and serve as guides forward in socioenvironmental thinking. The progress in environmentalism has, however, resulted in partial setbacks and paradoxes. For example, the criticism of the younger generation of multiculturalists, explicitly sensitive to situational variation, often in practice tends to turn into a one-sided canonization of the anglophonic renewal. This is witnessed in the bibliographic references often systematically ignoring non-English publications. "Wave thinking" similarly shadows the actual polycentric and multidimensional dispersions of environmental concerns and movements. The much-criticized elitism of the early environmentalists also seems not to have helped the latecomers to avoid cross-cultural ignorance of cultural differences. The multilingual past of the aristocrats has developed into monolingual self-satisfaction; unwillingness to jump across lingual borders between environmental cultures. Finally, and consequently, the theoretical sophistication and informational advance in Western environmentalism seem to lack correspondence to the actual environmental (geo)politics run by the leading regimes of the West. The academic discourse has largely developed as though uncontaminated by the "dirty reality" of (post)colonialism.

Whose histories of environmentalism do we lean on? Whose is the green knowledge Andrew Jamison co-forges with his colleagues? Which debates does Noel Castree refer to and push forward as key constituents of environmental updating? How long can we let ourselves be satisfied with the academic progress that is purified to fit certain discursive dominations, elite lists of key innovators and nicely lengthening records of scientific publications? What if our progress reports only contribute to academic regime-building, and what if the progress reports out there in the environmental (geo)politics appear for us only as interesting cases to study or illustrative examples for further theoretical elaboration? What if the scholarly sophistication that carefully counts the signs of environmental essentialism only serves as a justification for not taking environmental risks seriously?

The remarks and questions above underline the major challenge in Western environmentalism. The lively traditions have during the last decades increasingly been dedicated to and governed by those scholars who prefer the US-centered depiction of the past. Occasional excursions to non-English Europe or other continents serve as exotic side-steps only confirming the main order. This means the contributions to environmental renewal and their collegial co-evaluations are compressed into one monolingual and standardized networking of international academic publishing.[24] Might this be connected to the logics of the Empire in globalization that Michael Watts referred to above?

The introductory part of this volume describes some key contours of the polycentric and multicultural development of Western environmentalism and relates these to the recent rise of highly politicized environmentalism, especially environmental justice concerns. The "justice activists" are seen here as the latest turn in environmental renewal and it is also regarded as the movement that has thoroughly challenged the dominating categories of environmentalism. First, I briefly present the main historical variations of environmentalism within the West, both in terms of theoretical renewal and in the realm of societal practices. The Northern European articulation of justice is specified on this historical basis and compared with the US-centered interpretation of the debate. The main dimensions of environmental justice will be thereafter sketched, as they have emerged from within the specific Northern European and Nordic settings.

Toward Local-Global Environmentalism: Variations within the West

Global environmental concern—from Stockholm 1972 via Rio 1992 to Johannesburg 2002—has resulted in numerous regional and local applications, and similar progress can also be noticed in special fields, stretching from the red lists of endangered species to certificates of green trade. The local-global environmental turn has, however, met serious opposition. Accusations of expert domination, ideological bias, technocratic reductionism, ecological imperialism and green developmentalism have surfaced, both from outside and from within environmental groups and organizations. Internal criticism has become most influential as it has forced environmentalists to rethink their own identification and position in the other end of the general antagonism between conservationists and developers. In the Third World context, proponents of the political ecology approach have provided the most extensive critique of mainstream environmentalism by questioning the relevance of tracing isolated and technical problems and solutions, whereas in the West the environmental justice movement has intensely criticized the social ignorance of environmentalists.[25]

The development of environmentalism seems to have in general strengthened the role of scientific ecological expertise in the identification of environmental problems and also the ranking of the credibility of co-actors.[26] Ecological expertise is increasingly accepted as the guiding knowledge-technology in environmental management and it takes place at the cost of traditional and lay understanding of nature. It has, among other things, resulted in communicative problems: the vocabulary of experts often crucially differs from the lay modes of communication. The programs of nature conservation and environmental regulation repeatedly violate the lay sense of justice. Due to the globalization of environmental concern, the question of justice is thus frequently faced. Whose environments are conserved? Whose expertise is prioritized? Who has the skills to participate in the formulation of goals? With whom do we negotiate? How do we identify the consequences of the decisions?

Due to globalization, and the following intensification of contacts across major cultural borders, variations in the historical development of the sense of justice have emerged as matters of conflict. Tensions in environmental appreciation are central to understanding the current forms of cultural confrontations, ranging from contested spatial groupings in urban milieus to the defence of home forests by indigenous folks, and extending across all the spatial scales, from local "hot spots" to global contests of the leading geopolitical blocs.

The interfaces of justice are deeply rooted in cross-cultural communication, both at the axis of global North-South and within the East-West relations. As a result of centuries of Western colonialism, including its current neo and post versions, the histories of oppression, domination and injustice are interrelated across the globe. The long colonial past is a burden carried among global cultural areas.

The tensions in interpreting the principles of justice have repeatedly emerged also in the West, both in the arenas of trade and geopolitics as well as in environmental politics. The transatlantic negotiations on genetic food manipulation, for example, have progressed slowly and painfully and it is due to the overall critical atmosphere in regard to GM industry in Europe. Concerns about highly modified food products are widespread in the European Union, which is bound to the severe continental food crises of the 1990s. The handling of animals in the food industry—both on the farms and when transporting living meat—has also brought up the question animal justice.[27] The risks of high-tech processes have become evident almost everywhere, even in our kitchens (in the form of new health risks), and this has fueled the debate on unjust results of tightening technological dependencies, both locally and across the global divides.

The transatlantic disagreement has also become manifested in the attitudes toward the role of the United Nations in the coordination of global socioenvironmental crises. The broadly shared opinion in continental and Northern Europe has underlined the importance of UN-centered cooperation in conflict resolutions and large-scale natural hazards, whereas in the USA the willingness to develop US-led coalitions has gained strong support. This has become a heated question in interventions and aid operations in all the continents, especially in the Middle East, Southeast Asia and Sub-Saharan Africa. The war in Iraq sharpened the disagreement in the early years of the 20th century and the emergency aid efforts to the victims of the Asian tsunami in Yule (Christmas) 2004 also were delayed by the confusion of the labor division in organizing global aid.

The specific way of reacting in Europe to large socioenvironmental crises needs to be related to the most recent environmental history of the continent. The crises at the "home front" have profoundly modified the senses of justice in "old Europe." The explosion of a nuclear reactor in Chernobyl in 1986 dramatically reminded us about the vulnerability of the technological age and it also revealed the alarming risks embedded in industrial culture.[28] During the late spring weeks of 1986, radioactive clouds menaced Europe, following the main wind directions and thus not respecting any jurisdictional borders or varying state commitments to nuclear energy. The challenge to shelter oneself from the "hard rain" largely unified people, but the individual protection measures varied according to the ability or willingness to change one's daily routines bound for example to employment histories, variations in wealth and health settings, risk awareness, home place attachment and age identification. The catastrophe also sharpened the claims for critical and ethical reflection concerning our duties toward those innocents suffering from our errors, including the coming generations.[29]

It became broadly evident how the programs of technological modernization were based on organized irresponsibility. The age of nuclear power is widely accepted as a transition period in energy production, and this argument is repeatedly used as a justification of its continuance. This was the case for example in Finland in the spring of 2002 when the National Parliament accepted the industry's application to build one more nuclear reactor to meet the constantly rising energy demand.[30] The transition debate was somehow able to ignore the fact that the generations to come will face the necessity to deal with our nuclear waste from generation to generation. The increase in radioactive pollution also becomes part of our own and our children's health records. Nuclear energy is a political, technoeconomic and moral question but it also is a frame condition without escape. It is, therefore, an example or model of intergenerational (in)justices: in good and bad, we have to learn to live with the path-dependencies manufactured by those before us.

Chernobyl left a mark on the European environmental consciousness and the concern about the direction and justification of modernization grew in importance. The critique of enlightenment, so richly formulated by the Frankfurt School social researchers Max Horkheimer and Theodor Adorno,[31] was found again and re-read by those who could not agree with the popular postmodern promises, aiming at freeing us from the historical worries of the modern.[32] The old century ended with insecurity in Europe. The *Risikogesellschaft* (The Risk Society) had emerged as a continuation to, and a reminder of, the earlier traumas of the continent: the emergence of the risk society further confused the Europeans still suffering from the deliriums of the colonial-imperial past, and it brought back the nightmares of the World Wars and the Holocaust. The risk society pushed the ambivalent missions of enlightenment and progress into a "Millennial end" in Europe. Finally, nature—the material sphere of our earthly being—was thoroughly contaminated, both the one surrounding us and the one in the form of intimate embodied experience. The natural realm, which had been carefully othered in the margins of Europe, returned in the form of radioactive rains, ecosystemic accumulations and new health risks. The boomerang of nature followed the logic the othered Third World had earlier landed on the hearth of the continent. Pure Europe was again challenged.[33]

Increasing contacts across the globe in the form of telecommunication, trade and tourism have in addition radically challenged the European worldviews based on clear territorial divisions. From the war on oil and provincial autonomy in Biafra in the late 1960s to the crises of the early 21st century (in Africa, Near/Middle East and Asia), the territorial geopolitical grouping of the world has become increasingly difficult. The TV images of malnourished children from the war in oil-rich Biafra, killing one million individuals in four years, dramatically affected the breaking of the old geopolitical maps as the reporters gradually unveiled the Western oil interests behind the war. This took place with the help of television, in our living rooms. The growing streams of global marketing and tourism have both in good and bad thereafter continued to shrink and re-divide our world. The tsunami in Asia in December 2004 forced the world to notice the growing presence of Europe on the opposite side of the earth and it also brought, in a terrifying manner, the families of the victims here and out there closer together.[34]

The environmental history of the late modern (and local-global) Europe helps us to understand the way the Europeans tend to deal with socioenvironmental comingling, such as problems with human and animal rights, quality of food, rural and fringe areas, ethnic minorities and ecological hazards and strains. The past is present either in the form of local-global ethical re-thinking, or alternatively, clothed in protective security measures inside the (illusory) "Fort Europe." This tension forms the core of the debate on the constitutional renewal of the European Union. The vision of a strong federal bastion strikingly contrasts with the idea of polyvocal and democratic co-jurisdiction. The question is at bottom how and with which motives the communities of justice are practically defined? The ongoing local-global socioenvironmental crises force us constantly to rethink our sociospatial identifications.

Seen from Europe, the historically forged sense of justice on the other side of the Atlantic Ocean looks strikingly familiar—and different. The roots in enlightenment and colonial modernization are largely shared, but the outcomes vary in detail. The specific environmental justice issues are today run within two main forums in the USA. They are routinely taken care of by law experts in courtrooms while the societal renewal and the formulation of critical alternatives are manufactured by the activist networks worrying about local-global injustices.[35] The historical awareness of the interethnic violence behind the founding of modern Americas is thoroughly present in the work of (pragmatic) experts and (forward-looking) activists. There is no escape from the past.

The European colonization of the "New World" turned into a cruel genocide of the first nations. The frontier of the settlers progressed through the wilderness and this was considered synonymous with the dawn of civilization.[36] The famous melting pot of North America was later forged with similar violence, originally launched by the transatlantic slave trade and finally turning into internal ghettos colored by deep recollections of unfair divisions of welfare.[37] Environmental justice issues in the USA turn therefore frequently into questions of environmental racism. The evidence telling that environmental risks and illnesses tend to accumulate on people of color starkly reminds the US citizens of the violent ethnohistory of the continent.

In the USA, the Environmental Justice Movement was initiated in 1982 in Warren County, North Carolina, due to demonstrations against toxic waste dumping near a neighborhood of colored people. The movement emphasized from the beginning that environmental crises cannot be solved without unraveling the practices maintaining societal and cultural injustices. Many of the traditional environmental organizations, such as Earth First!, Sierra Club and National Wildlife Federation, were in particular targeted by this critique.[38]

The US debate on environmentalism and justice progressed via profound confrontations, which clearly reflects the loaded historical nature of the issue. Racial and other social tensions are often intentionally avoided by dedicated nature conservationists and this undoubtedly reflects the main lines of the whole tradition, originally established and later confirmed in the battles for nature parks and wildernesses. The motives of conserving nature in its most original state directly reflects, as forest ecologist Larry Lohman has argued, the societal status of the conservationists. According to him, the history of the idea of nature is part of the history of the white middle class that defined nature as an aesthetic landscape viewed from a distance. Purified and thus white areas of nature represent the areas of white power. The indigenous first nations were therefore forced to leave their homelands conflicting with the proposed national parks of Yellowstone and Yosemite.[39]

The history of untouched nature, fully developed in the 19th century USA, parallels with the histories of the European North. The indigenous Sámi groups have witnessed the historical colonial pressure in the Nordic countries, originally in the form of (more or less) innocent scientific expeditions and mappings run by those coming from the Nordic South but later developed into full-scale exploitation of natural resources. These programs were later accompanied by establishing nature parks and wildernesses in the Upper North, also introduced from the outside. The present debates on indigenous land rights and regional autonomy thus repeatedly turn into reminders of the unjust past of the Nordic North.[40]

The Nordic history of environment and justice to a great extent shares the European continental root. The devastation of the "pagan rites" of the locals by Christian missionaries, the forceful drawing of state borders across the traditional communal lands and the loads of the *Risikogesellschaft* (such as radioactive pollution since the Soviet nuclear weapon tests in Novaya Zemlya in the 1960s) have all become deposited as central memory layers of Nordic environmentalism.[41] The invaders pushed the indigenous Sámi groups to the northernmost mountains, and this history repeatedly surfaces in the negotiations on land rights and territorial governance in the North. The colonial past of the Nordic countries is also a reminder of the history of the whole continent: the histories of Europe are written by the colonial winners, and therefore the narrations of the lost and minor folks are only rarely commemorated. This state of affairs offers, however, the Sámi a particular status as the only indigenous group that has been officially recognized in today's European Union.[42]

The peasant settlement of the Nordic North gradually produced a specific regional administration, namely *landskap* meetings which were gatherings of the village representatives from a larger area, such as a river valley. The meetings and representations grew into regular practices with jurisdictional power.[43] This was, for example, the way to agree on hunting lands between the villages. The hunting rules also favored shared responsibilities within the villages: the quarry was divided among the villagers according to certain principles (*erät/* shares), which aimed at ensuring the survival of all the inhabitants of the village. In addition, the traditional immemorial public right of access to lands beyond anyone's backyard (*jokamiehen oikeus; allemansrätten*) was, and still is, grounded on the idea of common resources. Forests and lakes outside the farms and villages are open to anyone obeying certain rules that secure the undisturbed state of the lands and resources.

In the Nordic North, the deep history of the *erätalous* system (roughly: wilderness economy) is still traceable in the appreciation of the old customs and common laws. This mentality also includes a respectful attitude toward those features in the landscape that carry the past meanings. Sacred rocks, lakes, hill tops and trees serve as containers of memory. The premodern landscape of the Nordic North can still be identified, often by accidental findings or through intuition, in the form of "appreciations" read from the remnants of our ancestors' topographic and architectural signs and messages. It thus becomes visible from below—via appreciations of the sacred—which is just the opposite to the modern landscape which opens from above, for example from a mountain peak, and reveals the contours of the land below our feet, as if prepared to be drawn under visual or territorial control.[44]

The traditional Nordic peasant life-mode contained, however, no suprahistorical wisdom of co-living with nature and the neighbors. The annual cycle of life in the North was based on the success of farming and hunting, both of which guided toward long-term thinking and sufficient measures. Survival crucially depended on the length and diligence of the working days, both in summer and winter. The signs of land cultivation broadly served as signposts of culture even though the wildernesses also carried cultural signs, helping the co-living within and off the surrounding nature. The Crown gradually became active in supporting the peasant life-mode of the frontiers, as the pioneers were regarded geopolitical actors confirming the territorial rule of the state. The Great Land Partition, which took place in Sweden-Finland in 1750–1950, similarly strengthened the efforts to further cultivate the wildernesses. Common forests around the villages and farms were divided according to the size of the farm: the major farms received the largest forests. In the course of time and with the higher pricing of timber resources, the old habit of forest clearing without replanting was criminalized. Forests and forest owners became gradually the suppliers for the expanding paper industry. The idea of sustained-yield forestry, following the German innovation, was widely applied in the Nordic forest regulation. The sustainability of forestry in the late 19th century was conditioned by expansive official control of forest utilization, to be later followed by an authoritarian coordination of annual timber harvesting.[45]

The Nordic traditions were thus based on the expansive and intensifying utilization of the surrounding resources. Nature was regarded both as a source of wellbeing and an ever-present constraint for those living in and off it. The long winters could only be endured by having a respectful attitude toward the surrounding nature and fellow farmers. The villages and the *landskap* governance were developed to take collectively care of the continuity of nature and culture. The peasant community included human and non-human actors.[46] Communication with *erämaa* natures took place with the help of traditional knowledge and habits based on the deep respect of the signs of nature, including its spiritual guardians. This was the way to prohibit over-exploitation, long before and during the Christianization and Westernization of the Nordic North. The modernization of the North largely followed the external adjustment demands, and the new era gradually strengthened the understanding of human communities as distinct from their natural counterparts and it brought along tools for expanding control over the natural "other."[47]

Local communities of the North gradually fell into crises due to rising export demands and subsequent reorganizations of community relations. New (translocal) interest groups were born around the export actors and the new divisions of labor also reorganized and divided the old communities. Some benefited from the new practices while others suffered and became marginalized. The mentality of diligence was strengthened hand in hand with the export income but, on the other hand, the community responsibility, including the duties toward the natural realm, was left to erode—only to be later taken care of by the emerging Nordic welfare state. The contact to traditional values was thus never fully lost in modernization. The old appreciations are for example still present in those Nordic voices that are critically weighing the ethical risks of straightforward globalization in human rights forums and environmental cooperation.

The Nordic renewal can in general be seen as a reaction to a wide array of socioeconomic, regional, ideological, ethnic, intergenerational, class and gender-based tensions in environmental change but also as a critical reaction to the old but still dominating paradigms of environmentalism introduced from the West, namely those rooted to sustained-yield thinking and nature park promotion. The proceeding chapter describes the historical transformation of the Nordic socioenvironmental thinking by focusing on the practical mixtures of domestic and imported innovations. The analysis follows those features that bear witness to culturally distinctive modes of facing the challenges of modernization. Special interest is cast on the application of continental European and Anglo-American models (of coping with socioenvironmental matters) in a Nordic context.

Notes

1. The North refers here to several sociospatial extensions, ranging from the specific Arctic North (covering the territorial administrative units—countries, states, provinces, *landskap, oblastii, maakunnat,* etc.—that mostly exist north of the Arctic Circle) to the global North (as the dominating part of the global North-South setting). The expression European North, which is also placed in the subtitle of this volume, indicates both the Nordic countries and Northwest Russia. The North is in general used relationally in this study, in connection to its opposite, the South. The exact definition of the concept is therefore context-dependent, understandable only in relation to the discursive continuum explicated case by case. See further elaboration of the multiscalar North in the chapter on *Samhällsgeografi* and the Politics of Nature. An informative analysis of the importance of Swedish scientific expeditions northward during early industrialization is in Sverker Sörlin, *Framtidslandet. Debatten om Norrland och naturresurserna under det industriella genombrottet* (Stockholm: Carlsson Bokförlag, 1988). The role of geography as the science of expansion is discussed in Sörlin, *Framtidslandet*, 120–27.
2. Ann-Cathrine Åquist, "Idéhistorisk översikt," in *Traditioner i Nordisk kulturgeografi,* eds. Bjørn T. Asheim, Sune Berger, Frank Hansen, Perttu Vartiainen and Ann-Cathrine Åquist (Uppsala: Nordisk Samhällsgeografisk Tidskrift, 1994), 1-13; Teuvo Pakkala, "Kaksi viimeistä naparetkeä," in *Namsarai*, ed. Anneli Kajanto (Helsinki: Suomalaisen Kirjallisuuden Seura, 1999), 46-56.
3. Two associations were initially founded in Finland, namely the Finnish Geographical Association in winter 1887-88 (the Swedish title of the Association: *Geografiska Föreningen i Finland*; the Finnish title: *Suomen Maantieteellinen Yhdistys*) and the Geographical Society of Finland in summer 1888 (in Swedish: *Geografiska Sällskapet i Finland*; in Finnish: *Suomen Maantieteellinen Seura*) but these merged in 1921 under the title of the latter. See Kalevi Rikkinen, *Suuri Kuolan retki* (Helsinki: Otava, 1980), 171-74; Kalevi Rikkinen, "Ragnar Hult and the Emergence of Geography in Finland, 1880-1900," *Fennia* 166, no. 1 (1988), 3-192.
4. Peter Hœg, *Frøken Smillas førnemmelse for sne* (Copenhagen: Rosinante/Munksgaard, 1992).

5. By (post)colonialism I refer to those heritages deposited in our ways of thinking (and doing), rooting from the era of early colonialism but persistently (and partly implicitly) alive in our present. The (post)colonial worldview is here seen as the initial phase of critical self-reflectivity in the West (or, in the South, when seen from the circumpolar North) and within the interrelations between the West and the "othered rest." It is the early stage of weeding out, or unlearning, the colonial content in our societal practices. Drawing a strict line between the colonial and postcolonial eras is derivatively seen here as a premature demarcation between the past and the (purified) present. It is for this reason I place the prefix of post in parentheses. Geographer Derek Gregory has tellingly described the gradual process of becoming increasingly aware of the colonial presence and "my own otherness" during his inspiring (auto)biogeographical voyages, see Derek Gregory, *Geographical Imaginations* (Oxford: Blackwell, 1994). See also an application of (post)colonialism into Arctic conditions, Juha Ridanpää, "Postcolonialism in a Polar Region," *Nordia*, 27, no. 1 (1998), 67-77, where he refers to postcolonialism both as "a form of social criticism, an emancipatory way of criticizing an unevenly developed world" and as "a continuity of preoccupations throughout the historical process initiated by European imperial aggression."

6. Richard Peet and Michael Watts, eds., *Liberation Ecologies. Environment, Development, Social Movements* (London: Routledge, 1996), 4.

7. William L. Thomas, ed., *Man's Role in Changing the Face of the Earth* (Chicago: The University of Chicago Press, 1956).

8 Ilmari Hustich, ed., "Symposium on Man's Influence on Nature in Finland," *Fennia* 85 (1960); Sörlin, *Framtidslandet* 1988, 19; Andrew Jamison, "Miljörörelsens upplösning och skapandet av den globala miljödebatten,"*VEST. Tidskrift för Vetenskapstudier* 6, no. 3. (1993), 55-76; Pertti Rannikko, "Local Environmental Conflicts and the Change in Environmental Consciousness," *Acta Sociologica* 39 (1996), 57-72.

9. John S. Dryzek, David Downes, Christian Hunold, David Schlosberg and Hans-Kristian Hernes, *Green States and Social Movements. Environmentalism in the United States, United Kingdom, Germany and Norway* (Oxford: Oxford University Press, 2003), vii.

10. Michael Watts, "1968 and all that...," *Progress in Human Geography* 22, no. 2 (2001), 179. The Seattle activists is one label for those civic concerns and initiatives (against the tightening global governance of transnational corporations and agencies) that were initially introduced to broader publicity in Seattle in November-December 1999. In Seattle, the demonstrations were directed against the secrecy of the Ministerial Meeting of the World Trade Organization. During the following years, the large civic demonstrations took thereafter place wherever the global politicoeconomic elite had their meetings, for example in Gothenburg (Sweden) and Genoa (Italy) in summer 2001. The terrorist attacks on the World Trade Center and the Pentagon in September 2001 had, however, a profound impact on the movement and thereafter the global critical voice has been channeled differently, in a less aggressive manner, for example via Global Social Forums.

11. Michael Hardt and Antonio Negri, *Empire* (Cambridge, Ma.: Harvard University Press, 2000).

12. Andrew Jamison, *The Making of Green Knowledge* (Cambridge, Cambridge University Press, 2002), 2-8.

13. Jamison, "Miljörörelsens upplösning och skapandet av den globala miljödebatten", 57-58.

14. Lewis Mumford, *The Brown Decades: A Study of Arts in America* (New York: Harcourt Brace and Co., 1931), 78; David Lowenthal, "Introduction," in *Man and Nature—or Physical Geography Modified by Human Action* (Cambridge, Ma.: The Belknap Press of Harward University Press, 1964), ix-x. Originally published in 1864 by Charles Scribner, New York.
15. Donald Worster, ed., *The Ends of the Earth* (Cambridge: Cambridge University Press, 1988), 14.
16. Thomas, *Man's Role in Changing the Face of the Earth*; Rachel Carson, *Silent Spring* (Boston: Houghton Mifflin, 1962).
17. The longest of the "environmental waves" (of which we have written documents) was launched by preSocratic philosophers in Ancient Greece. Many of the key figures of modern environmentalism refer to this early history. For example Georg Perkins Marsh, *Man and Nature—or Physical Geography Modified by Human Action* (Cambridge, Ma.: The Belknap Press of Harward University Press, 1964, orig. 1864.); Clarence J. Clacken, *Traces on the Rhodian Shore. Nature and Culture in Western Thought from Ancient Times to the End of the Eighteenth Century* (Berkeley: University of California Press, 1967); Max Oelschlager, *The Idea of Wilderness. From Prehistory to the Age of Egology* (New Haven: Yale University Press, 1991); and Simon Schama, *Landscape and Memory* (London: Fontana Press, 1995) elaborate on these roots from different angles. The later versions of environmentalism owe much to these roots, as Glacken (*Traces on the Rhodean Shore*, vii) convincingly emphasizes. The ancient horizon is, however, beyond the scope of this volume because it mainly concentrates on the critical assessment of (late) modern environmentalism.
18. Peet and Watts, *Liberation Ecologies*, 3-5. See also Ari Aukusti Lehtinen, "Northern Natures. A Study of the Forest Question emerging Within the Timber-line Conflict in Finland," *Fennia* 169, no. 1 (1991), 63-64; David Demeritt, "The Nature of Metaphors in Cultural Geography and Environmental History," *Progress in Human Geography* 12, no. 2 (1994), 431-60; Noel Castree, "A Post-environmental Ethics?," *Ethics, Place and Environment* 6, no. 1 (2003), 3-12.
19. Demeritt, "The Nature of Metaphors in Cultural Geography and Environmental History," 167.
20. See especially Donald Worster, *Nature's Economy* (Cambridge: Cambridge University Press, 1977).
21. Demeritt, "The Nature of Metaphors in Cultural Geography and Environmental History," 174. Here Demeritt refers in particular to William Cronon, *Nature's Metropolis* (New York: W.W. Norton, 1991).
22. Demeritt, "The Nature of Metaphors in Cultural Geography and Environmental History," 174.
23. Castree, "A Post-environmental Ethics?," 3-10.
24. Anthony D. King, "Opening up the Social Sciences to the Humanities: A Response to Peter Taylor," *Environment and Planning A* 28 (1996), 1954–59; Javier Gutiérrez and Pedro López-Nieva, "Are International Journals of Human Geography really International?," *Progress in Human Geography* 25, no. 1 (2001), 53-69; John Rennie, Armando Boniche, Yeong Kim and Patrick Li Li, "Cultural Globalization, Global English, and Geography Journals," *Professional Geographer* 53, no. 1 (2001), 1-11; Maria-Dolors Car-

cia-Ramon, "Globalization and International Geography: The Questions of Languages and Scholarly Traditions," *Progress in Human Geography* 27, no. 1 (2003), 1-5; Jussi Jauhiainen, "Publish or/and Perish in Geography," *Nordia Geographical Publications* 32, no. 2 (2003), 39-46.

25. Joan Martinez-Alier, *The Environmentalism of the Poor* (Cheltenham: Edward Elgar, 2002).

26. Ari Aukusti Lehtinen and Pertti Rannikko, eds., *Oikeudenmukaisuus ja ympäristö* (Helsinki: Gaudeamus, 2003).

27. Anne Buttimer, "Circuits of Calories: Flows of Food and Energy in Germany, Ireland, the Netherlands and Sweden 1960-1990," *European Review* 4, no. 3 (1996), 193-214; Anne Buttimer, Landscape and Life: Appropriate Scales of Sustainable Development," *Irish Geography* 31, no. 1 (1998), 1-33; Scott Lash, Bronislaw Szeszynski and Brian Wynne, *Risk, Environment and Modernity* (London: Sage, 1996); Barbara Adam, *Time-scapes of Modernity* (London: Routledge, 1998); Wolfgang Sachs, Reinhard Loske and Manfred Linz, *Greening the North. A Post-industrial Blueprint for Ecology and Equity* (London: Zed Books, 1998); Alice Dawson, "The Problem of Pigs," in *Geography and Ethics*, eds. James D. Proctor and David M. Smith (London: Routledge, 1999), 193-206.

28. Ulrich Beck, *Risikogesellschaft. Auf dem Weg in eine andere Moderne* (Frankfurt am Main: Suhrkamp, 1986); Ulrich Beck, *Gegengifte. Die organisierte Unverantwortlichkeit* (Frankfurt am Main: Suhrkamp, 1988).

29. Jürgen Ossenbrügge, *Umweltsrisiko und Raumentwicklung* (Berlin: Springer Verlag, 1993); Scott Lash, "Refleksiivisyys ja sen vastinparit: rakenne, estetiikka, yhteisö," in *Nykyajan jäljillä*, eds. Ulrich Beck, Anthony Giddens and Scott Lash (Tampere: Vastapaino, 1995), 153-235; Steven Yearley, "Dirty Connections: Transnational Pollution," in *A Shrinking World?*, eds. John Allen and Chris Hamnett (London: Open University, 1995) 143-82.

30. Ari Aukusti Lehtinen, "Ympäristö, yhteisö ja oikeudenmukaisuus," in *Oikeudenmukaisuus ja ympäristö* eds. Ari Aukusti Lehtinen and Pertti Rannikko, (Helsinki: Gaudeamus, 2003), 9-31.

31. Max Horkheimer and Theodor Adorno, *Upplysningens dialektik* (Gothenburg: Röda Bokförlaget, 1944/1981).

32. Watts, "1968 and all that...;" Juha Siltala, *Valkoisen äidin pojat* (Helsinki: Otava, 2000), 9-28.

33. David Sibley, *Geographies of Exclusion* (London: Routledge, 1995); Hardt and Negri, *Empire*.

34. Ken Saro-Wiva, *A Month and a Day. A Detention Diary* (London: Penguin Books, 1996); Piers Blaikie, Terry Cannon, Ian Davis and Ben Wisner, *At Risk. Natural Hazards, People's Vulnerability, and Disasters* (London: Routledge, 1994).

35. Julian Agyeman, "Constructing Environmental (In)justice," *Environmental Politics* 11, no. 3 (2002), 31-53.

36. William Cronon, *Changes in the Land: Indians, Colonists, and the Ecology of New England* (New York: Hilla and Wang, 1982).

37. Susan Georg, *Velkabumerangi* (Tampere: Vastapaino, 1995), 162-95.

38. David Harvey, *Justice, Nature and the Geography of Difference* (Oxford: Blackwell, 1996); James Proctor, "The Social Construction of Nature," *Annals of the Association of American Geographers* 88, no. 3 (1998), 352-76; Nicholas Low and Brian Gleeson, *Jus-*

tice, Society and Nature (London: Routledge, 1998).
39. Larry Lohman, "Mitä rasismilla on tekemistä meidän kanssamme?," *Muutoksen Kevät* 23 (2002), 24; See Neil Smith, *Uneven Development* (Oxford: Basil Blackwell, 1984) for a rich historical argument behind Lohman's remark.
40. Ari Aukusti Lehtinen, "Mnemonic North: Multilayered Geographies of the Barents Region," in *Encountering the North. Cultural Geography, International Relations and Northern Landscapes*, eds. Frank Möller and Samu Pehkonen (Aldershot: Ashgate, 2003).
41. Sörlin, *Framtidslandet*; Ilmo Massa, *Pohjoinen luonnonvalloitus* (Helsinki: Gaudeamus, 1994); Gabriel Bladh, *Finnskogens landskap och människor under fyra sekler* (Karlstad: University of Karlstad Publications, no. 11, 1995).
42. Michael Hechter, *Internal Colonialism* (Berkeley: University of California Press, 1975); J.A. MacCulloch, *The Religion of the Ancient Celts* (London: Constable, 1992, orig. 1911); Sanna Valkonen, "The Saami Identity and the Politics of Recognition," in *Arctic Governance*, eds. Timo Koivurova, Tanja Joona and Reija Shnoro (Rovaniemi: Juridica Lapponica no. 29, 2004), 97-113.
43. Hal Koch and Alf Ross, *Nordisk demokrati* (Copenhagen: Westermanns Forlag, 1949); Kenneth Olwig, "Recovering the Substantive Nature of Landscape," *Annals of the Association of American Geographers* 86, no. 4 (1996), 630-53.
44. Olwig, "Recovering the Substantive Nature of Landscape," Allen Abramson, "Mythical Land, Legal Boundaries: Wondering about Landscape and Other Tracts," in *Land, Law and Environment*, eds. Allen Abramson and Dimitrios Theodossopoulos (London: Pluto Press, 2000), 1-30.
45. Ari Jokinen, "Stand/ardization and Entrainment in Forest Management," in *How Nature Speaks: The Dynamics of the Human Ecological Condition*, eds. Yrjö Haila and Chuck Dyke (Durham: Duke University Press, 2005), forthcoming.
46. Arne Naess, *Ekologi, samhälle och livsstil* (Stockholm: LTs Förlag, 1973/1981); Mike Smith, *An Ethics of Place* (Albany: State University of New York Press, 2001), 164-168.
47. Ari Aukusti Lehtinen, "Modernization and the Concept of Nature: On the Reproduction of Environmental Stereotypes," in *Encountering the Past in Nature*, eds. Timo Myllyntaus and Mikko Saikku (Athens: Ohio University Press, 2001), 29-48.

2.

Under German and British Influence: Nordic Socioenvironmentalism

> [Die Raubwirtschaft] *greift so heftig in die Natur ein, dass die natürliche Ausstattung des betroffenen Ortes geschmälert wird. Dabei kann dieser Eingriff ohne wesentliche Folgen bleiben, oder man geht ihnen aus dem Wege (einfache Raubwirtschaft), oder aber es wird ein Notstand der raubwirtschaftenden Bevölkerung hervorgebracht (charakterisierte Raubwirtschaft).*[1]

> *Raubwirtshaft* [Extractive economy] transforms natural conditions of certain areas to such an extent that the physical regenerative mechanisms weaken. The transformation does not necessarily lead to any profound social changes, or these are eliminated (plain *Raubwirtshaft*), or it can turn into a risk for people (characteristic *Raubwirtshaft*). (Translated from German by the author)

Geographer Ernst Friedrich published in 1904 a critical article on *Raubwirtschaft*, or the destructive agency of humanity in the biosphere, that aimed at broadening the scope of environmental economics in Germany. The long tradition of developing general technical criteria to nature-based exploitation was now extended to cover also global sociocultural aspects in a comparative manner. The concept of destructive exploitation refers, according to Friedrich, to those utilization practices that threaten the resource-specific or local endowment potentials. Friedrich's important remark distinguished two types of extractive practices. Plain *Raubwirtshaft* covers those features that provoke no human distress, whereas characteristic *Raubwirtshaft* points to environmental change that tends to marginalize certain human groups. He thus underlined the social distribution of consequences in human-induced environmental change.

Friedrich aimed at renewing the tradition that had been developed in the German-speaking Central Europe since the mid-18th century. Forestry scientists had initiated a research program that is known as the sustained-yield paradigm. The tradition, forged by such scholars as Georg Hartig, Johann Heinrich Gotta, Johann Hundeshagen and Friedrich Pfeil, was built upon a quantitative approach to measure and regulate the exploitation of forest resources on a sustainable basis. The innovation was initially grounded on large subdivisions of forests to be managed by clear-cuttings, whereas the later development of the model emphasized increasing variation of logging areas and selection of trees. The model was also instrumental in the unification of the fragmented fiscal administration of *Kleinstaaten,* and the new approach became therefore known as cameral sciences due to its practical link to modern state-building.[2]

The sustained-yield tradition gained followers during the 19th century, especially in the German colonies but also in the forested countries of Northern Europe where the results of intensive tar production and slash-and-burn cultivation had gradually brought up the question of controlling the lay utilization of forest resources. The description of the state of the Finnish forests in 1859 by Edmund von Berg, the chief forester of the state of Saxony and director of Tharand Forest Academy, had for example a decisive impact on the solidification of Finnish forest administration. von Berg's critical remarks on the forest devastation and proposals for improvements given to the Senate of the Grand Duchy of Finland led to the establishment of the National Board of Forestry (later to be known as the Finnish State Forest Service) in 1859 and the enactment of the first forest law in 1886. The main motive behind the new legislation was the prohibition of further devastation of forests by the peasants, but the law also contained an idea of integrating the common forest lands under the state's possession.[3]

Following the German model, the Finnish forest administration was established as the holder and guardian of forest property. The primary aim was to control the utilization of private forests. Sustainable forestry was considered threatened by the actions of the peasants. The agrarian forest practices were to be guided along the lines of reasonable and forward-looking wood production. The main motivation of the state forestry was to control and protect national property. Nature conservation was thus seen as an inseparable part of the national forest administration.

The introduction of the German model met broad opposition in Finland, especially among the peasants who had for long developed their own individual solutions in forest use. In Sweden,[4] on the contrary, the German influence became an issue of heated debate between two schools of professional forestry. The early method of standardized clear-cuttings by subdivisions of forests was gradually replaced by a softer method of selective cuttings. The change reflected the development of the respective debate in the 19th century Germany. Forest-industrial developers were most critical of the softening that was seen as limiting their space of operations.

Forester Uno Wallmo's powerful initiative in 1897 to integrate ecological and aesthetic values into Swedish forest management was largely considered unrealistic among the industrialists. Wallmo's interpretation of the German sustained-yield model guided him to promote those methods that followed nature's own dynamics, including selective cuttings. He valued the forests as such high and also expressed the fear that instrumental and shortsighted loggings would in a longer run result in lack of forests in Sweden.[5] Despite the strong fronting against Wallmo, the model of diverse and uneven-aged forests gained popularity in forest management. Forest regeneration law took force in Sweden in 1903 and the principle of sustained-yield was from then on applied by emphasizing selective cuttings and natural regeneration.[6]

The late 19th century witnessed, however, a new opening in nature and forest conservation in the Nordic countries. The main figure behind the new initiative was Nils Adolf Erik Nordenskiöld (1832–1901), the celebrated pioneer of the Northeast Passage, who in his influential speech in Stockholm in 1880 promoted the idea of establishing national parks:

> *För hvarje dag blir det inflytande, det senaste århunradets stora uppfingar utöfvat på den natur, som omger oss, allt mer märkbart. Den aflägsnaste landsbygd genomkorsas snart af jernvägar och telegrafer; sågverk och andra verkstäder af mångahanda slag anläggas långt i ödemarken och samla en talrik befolkning i urgammal bygd; odlarnes arbete belånas, sedan åkerbruket blifvit fotadt på vetenskapliga grunder, med en riklig äring äfven der jorden förut ansetts värdelös; sjöar sänkas, kärr och myrar uttorkas, skogen afverkas, nya skogsparker planteras och gammal fritt vuxen skog kommer snart att anses som ett lika säkert tecken på dålig skogshushållning, som naturliga ängar på dålig ängsskötsel och svedjning på dåligt åkerbruk.*
>
> *I en framtid, som sannolikt ej år långt aflägsen, skall det därför blifva svårt att få en fulltonig föreställning om den natur, med hvilken våra stamfäder hade att kämpa deras första strid, som närt nordbons aldrig kufvade frihetskärlek och fostrat dess djerfva krigareskaror, som utgjort det vidsträckta museum der alla forskare och konstnärer börjat sina studier, som bildar grundtonen i våra skalders sånger, i våra fäders och vår egen lifsåskådning.*
>
> *Nordens länder ega vidstäckta områden kronojord. Mångenstådes lemnar denna föga eller ingen afkastning och utan nämndvärd uppoffring kunde derför en lämplig sträcka utväljas och förklaras för Rikspark, der skog och mark och sjö skulle få stå alldeles orörda, der träd ej finge fällas, snår ej rödjas, gräs ej afmejas, och der alla djur, som ej vore verkliga skadedjur, året om kunde gå trygga för jägarens lod. Vården om en sådan park finge således ej utsträckas*

utöfver skydd mot åverkan, obetydliga väganläggningar och nödig öfverupp-sigt. Den behöfde derför ej medföra någon nämnvärd kostna.[7]

The great inventions of the last century increasingly transform our natural environments. Railroads and telephone lines soon extend over the remotest areas. Sawmills and other industrial units are founded in the wildernesses, and folks resettled accordingly. Farm work is changing on scientific grounds, and marginal lands become integrated in production; lakes are lowered, peatlands drained, forests logged and new tree plantations established. The remaining old-growth forests are seen as signs of poor forest management and thus seen as belonging to the same category of resource misuse as natural meadows and slash-and-burn cultivation.

It will soon become difficult to imagine the natural landscape that was the primary challenge to our ancestors. It will become impossible to face the conditions where they learnt the love of freedom and brought up their brave soldiers. We currently witness the disappearance of the source of inspiration that has been so important to all the scientists and artists and has been the undertone in the songs of our rune singers and poets.

Vast lands belong to the Crown in the Nordic countries. Some parts of these lands could therefore easily be founded as Crown parks where forests, soil and lakes could remain completely untouched; where no trees could be cut, no meadows or groves disturbed by humans, and where all the wild animals could live free from the risk of being shot. Crown parks should be protected from any kind of harvesting or unnecessary constructions. This solution would therefore not demand any investments worth mentioning. (Translated from Swedish by the author)

Nordenskiöld's Crown park proposal addressed the needs of nature conservation in all the Nordic countries. He referred to the signs of industrial progress, present almost everywhere in Nordic nature, soon obscuring the future generations' views on the original lifeworlds of their ancestors. For him, conserved areas of pristine nature served as memoirs of early settlements with their indigenous relations with nature. Crown parks—*riksparker* in Swedish—thus needed to be established to commemorate the origins of the people of the North. The lands, forests and waters were to be preserved both as natural areas and national heritage.

The speech by Nordenskiöld in Stockholm in 1880 thus introduced an alternative to the German innovations favored by the leading forest professionals. The promotion of Crown parks was explicitly linked to the building of national heritage. Nordenskiöld's initiative was motivated by an idea of creating natural areas where one could experience the atmosphere of an outdoor museum. The patriotic vision of nature as the basis for the formation of national integration was a central theme for Nordenskiöld, and it clearly echoed the US outlines in Yellowstone and Yosemite. His idea of nature was a relatively static and conserving one, as though beyond societal interests, and it largely excluded the purposes of economic benefit.[8]

The idea of nature conservation Nordenskiöld was leaning on had earlier become popular in the USA, but initially it was not of US origin. The Crown park model had already been formulated in Medieval Europe, especially in France and Britain, where the Royal Forests were introduced as territories privileged for "wild beasts and foules of forests, chase and warren, to rest and abide in, in the safe protection of the King for his princely delight and pleasure."[9] The Royal parks were hunting grounds delimited by royal decree. Hugo Conwentz (1855–1922) later developed the ideas of park conservation in Central Europe but the innovation spread also to the Colonial India under the program of protecting the Empire's forests, and it was later applied in the British colonies in Africa, Australasia, and North America. The original Empire model in nature conservation gained strength along the development of scientific ecology, and it became widely applied in the countries of the Commonwealth.[10]

According to the historian Gregory Barton, modern environmentalism indeed posed environmental problems and solutions as a means of constructing the state. This took generally place under the banner of government reservations, fire protection and revenue-enhancing forests.[11] As was argued above, similar imperial aims of state control emerged also in the German-influenced countries and colonies during the 19th century, even though the practical method was different. The German idea of forest conservation was seen more as a guide toward sustained yields, whereas the British one aimed at establishing Royal reservations and nature parks.[12]

Both the German and British traditions developed well during the early 20th century in the Nordic countries and provinces. The first Nordic national parks were founded in 1909 in Sweden, to be followed by several other parks during the coming decades. The initial process followed the programmatic vision of Nordenskiöld, and it was colored by nationalistic and national-romantic visions. The parks were seen as symbols of the nation and they served mostly scientific, cultural and aesthetic aims of those living in the more urbanized parts of the country. In Finland, *Societas pro Fauna et Flora Fennica* sent a proposal to the Senate in 1917 for a nature conservation law which took force in 1923. The nature conservation law enabled the establishment of national parks, but only after long and intense political debate the first national parks were founded in 1938. Norway got her first national park in 1962, but it was already in the late 19th century that the Norwegian Mountain Touring Association, founded in 1868, made proposals to preserve unique waterfalls and establish national parks. Danish Conservation Society and the Nature Conservation Act, both launched in 1917, prioritized from the beginning public access rights on private lands, and the establishment of nature parks has therefore not gained popularity. Denmark has had its own particular concern in the Nordic context in transforming the heaths and wetlands as wastelands into areas of protection and recreation.[13]

The societal and industrial innovations of economic liberalism, transportation, steam sawing and mechanical and chemical pulping gradually confirmed the role of forest exploitation as the economic backbone of the more forested areas of the Nordic countries. The strengthening of private forest ownership, extensive scientific forest inventories, the development of sustained-yield management and active export orientation of the wood-processing industry all together shaped the environmental contours of the countries. The export orientation of the expanding forest industry influenced the formation of a specific Nordic "wood order" and countries were broadly organized into manufacturing cores and forest peripheries.

In Norway, who got her independence from Sweden in 1905, the long and steady growth of the forest industry covered the first half of the 20th century. The success was based on the fine qualities of Norwegian spruce growing abundantly near the major export harbors of the Atlantic Ocean. The trend turned, however, into a relative weakening in the 1950s due to the development of other economic sectors such as engineering and the oil industry. In Sweden, the frontier of timber extraction reached the northernmost provinces and mountain forests during the late 19th century. The volumes of timber floating down the northern rivers grew rapidly, and especially the high-quality and large-diameter pine gained currency. Norrland's development in northernmost Sweden, known as *Norrlandsfrågan*, brought up the question on the ownership and exploitation rights of the natural resources of the far North, especially forests but also hydropower, iron ore and peatlands. The main tension in the debate stretched between two opposing groups: industrial developers demanded full access of companies to natural resources, whereas local farmers defended their authority over the lands. The confrontation was ideological in many ways, having a crucial impact on the establishment of the political parties in the whole country. The Social Democratic solution to the *Norrlandsfrågan* introduced state authorities and state companies as balancing actors of the Swedish North.[14]

Finland was introduced during the interwar years (1920s and 1930s) to international markets as an exporter of forest products. The growth of the pulp and paper industry was "trickling down" even to the backwoods and spreading welfare over the whole country. The industrial centers absorbed and employed all the labor in their fringe areas. Logging was carried out during the winter seasons in the backwoods, and it offered additional income to the farmers. This period of fast industrial development with evenly rising economic activity and wellbeing, only slightly affected by the Western economic collapse of the 1930s, cemented the position of the forest industry as the economic core of Finnish society. As a result, the national benefits were largely associated with the prosperity of forest companies. Finland became a forest-sector society.[15]

During those years, before World War II, no broader disagreement existed in the Nordic countries between the park conservationists and the sustained-yield advocates. Economic welfare based on industrial progress was, on the contrary, seen as a means toward nature conservation. In Finland in particular it was popular among the nature conservationists to think that only by becoming richer could the state afford to leave some natural areas outside industrial use. Sweden could afford an extensive network of 16 national parks during the first half of the 20th century and this development cast increasing pressure on her Nordic neighbors.[16]

A polarization between forest managers and conservationists, however, surfaced in the post World War II decades. This was primarily due to the intensification of forestry methods bound to large-scale clear-cuttings. The expansion of industrial forestry to pristine backwoods also fueled the disagreement.

In the 1950s, clear-cuttings broadly substituted for the practices of selective loggings (or forest thinning) as well as the seedling tree and protection-forest methods. The intensification was legitimated by the development of the forest inventories, revealing the problem of underutilized timber resources. The annual increment of wood, calculated by cubic meters, was much ahead of the level of loggings, and this served for the new postwar generation of forest professionals as a sign of unused economic options.[17]

The general changes in environmental values undoubtedly had an impact on the growing criticism of industrial forest exploitation. The early environmentalism of conservationists turned into critical political environmentalism, or socioenvironmentalism (see chapter 3), which gradually broadened the participatory basis of the debate. Scientific authority was not the only means to push forward environmental argumentation. Negative environmental changes close to industrial centers were clearly perceivable by lay people and this tended to democratize the concerns that were earlier mainly expressed by professionals and certain hobby circles.

The intensification of forest exploitation thus paved the way to a new generation of environmentalists, now in opposition to the forest professional interests. This setting was one of the motives for the 1959 National Symposium on Man's Influence on Nature in Finland, which followed the idea of the Princeton Symposium in the USA in 1955, now in a Finnish context. Geographer Ilmari Hustich (1911–1982), one of the initiators of the Finnish symposium, was the central figure to inspire the societal visibility of Finnish environmentalists in the post World War II period. The confrontation of industrial forestry and the new environmental movement was unavoidable in the 1960s. The concerns of the movement were initially limited to aesthetic-ecological and local overacts of industrial wood exploitation but soon they expanded to include the whole chain of wood processing.[18]

The confrontation was further exacerbated in Sweden and Finland by the decisions made in energy politics. In both countries, the industrial solution emphasized the nuclear power technology as the future solution to energy shortages. Due to hydropower potential and expanding oil industry, Norway could choose another path. In Denmark in the 1970s, the antinuclear opposition could convince the politicians that alternative energy sources, for example modern windmills, off-shore tidal waves and biogas, could satisfy the country's energy needs in the future.

Sweden became involved already in the 1950s in nuclear energy strategy, resulting finally in the 1980s in 12 reactors in five locations and covering almost half of Sweden's energy needs. The 1970s were the first decade of profound energy-political tensions in Sweden. Numerous nuclear power plants were under construction when the Social Democrats in the mid-1970s dramatically lost their leading position as the party in governmental power (since 1932). The agrarian Centre Party took the lead for a while by emphasizing renewable energy sources and aiming at compromises with nuclear actors. The global oil crisis of 1973 had also forced the central industrial stakeholders to critically reassess their energy strategies. Rapidly rising costs of energy motivated a search for technological and societal alternatives. For example, the traditional fuel value of timber returned to the debate. Swedish nuclear energy program was thus severely challenged despite the fact that several reactors were under construction.[19]

In Finland, Teollisuuden Voima, an enterprise founded by the leading industrial actors, built two nuclear reactors in the 1970s on the western coast of Finland. The forest industry was well represented in the establishment of industrial nuclear strategy even though the sector was then rather self-sustained in energy consumption. The role of the forest-industry in nuclear energy politics reflected the vested industrial interests in the politicoeconomic life of Finland. The private nuclear program followed the example of the state enterprise, Imatran Voima, which had slightly earlier decided to build two reactors on the southern coast. The decisions were made without a democratic voice or broader societal discussion.[20]

The protagonists of the nuclear energy strategy in Sweden met serious drawbacks in the 1980s. In the referendum on nuclear energy in 1980, the majority voted for the gradual phase-out of nuclear power. The phase-out was adopted as the official goal. The antinuclear message was further strengthened by the socioenvironmental and political consequences of the reactor explosion in Chernobyl in 1986.[21]

The major socioenvironmental reactions of the 1970s and early 1980s against the industrial programs were based on alternative experiments in regional policy and research. "Development from below" was in high currency among the official regional strategists, and a new phase of rural development based on active village committees was launched. Several semi-official ecopolitical experiments were also started in the early 1980s in the resource peripheries.[22] New alternative groups raised criticism of the professional and specialized policy practices and highlighted the democratic shortcomings in decision-making. General demand advocated the opening of the channels for concerned citizens to take part in societal goal formulation.[23] In forest policy, this development questioned the historical division of labor, which had privileged the forest professionals and excluded the voice of the lay people from decision-making.

It finally became widely evident that in forest-related politics the former allies (foresters and conservationists) were entrenched in opposite environmental camps. The environmentalists had lost their confidence in the state of forestry and also the laymen had awakened to question the intensive wood exploitation and processing based on sustained-yield calculations and one-sidedly privileging the needs of the export-dominating forest industry. The official controlling power in forest management had in a space of 100 years lost much of its societal authority, and the concerns about the state of the forests under industrial forestry were increasingly shared by the public.

The polarization between industrial (sustained-yield) and alternative (sustainable development) approaches in resource exploitation continued in the 1980s and 1990s. On the one hand, environmental awareness had gradually broadened from traditional ecological demands to more general (eco)political concerns. The establishment of the Ministries of the Environment (in the 1970s and 1980s) and the prominent launch of Green parliamentary groups and parties (in the 1980s) had gradually confirmed the institutionalization of environmentalism in the Nordic countries. On the other hand, antiparliamentarian civic actions continued, now around a wide spectrum of local-global issues, ranging from food ethics and human and animal rights to globalization critique. The civic activism explicitly aimed at further politicizing socioenvironmental issues that were often related to concrete environmental justice concerns.[24]

The antinuclear turn in Sweden resulted finally in a closure of the first reactor in Barsebäck in 1999, near the border of Denmark. Another reactor in Barsebäck was run down in summer 2005. In Finland, on the contrary, the Parliament accepted in 2002 the industry's application to build the fifth nuclear reactor, to be located beside two other reactors in Olkiluoto on the western coast of the country. The decision was made after a heated energy debate dividing the country into two opposing camps.[25]

The industrial regime went through a profound transformation in the last two decades of the 20th century as the Nordic forest-industrial activities became characteristically international and global. This took place in the form of active investments abroad and through mergers and acquisitions, and it resulted in tightening competition for the existing resources, both material and immaterial. The leading forest companies became continental European corporations actively searching for global transcontinental positions in Russia, Southeast Asia and on the other side of the Atlantic Ocean. Forest-industrial globalization in general underlined the need to deepen the awareness of cultural differences between continents and across the local-global divides, both in official forums and within non-governmental activities.[26]

The phases of Nordic environmental orientation have thus offered both professionals and lay people an array of tools for monitoring and reacting to environmental damage. Despite the periods of lay activism and civic demonstrations, environmental experts and authorities have largely been able to maintain their prior role in Nordic environmental renewal. The early elitism of environmentalism, initially connected to upper-class nature conservation and scientific interests, has in a way returned after the years of broadening public concern. The return has been most visible in conservation measures based on biodiversity concerns and in technically advanced environmental governance. The followers of both the German and the British traditions have in other words been able to keep and renew their authoritative approaches and they have also succeeded well in their respective regime-building. It is, however, possible to distinguish from this historical ground some specific Nordic features of forest-based welfare, coemerged as part of the local-global reorganization of socioenvironmental concerns at the turn of the millennium.

The Nordic Wood Order and the Welfare Model

All the major Nordic forest companies launched their globalization strategies during the 1990s. Stora (from Sweden) and Enso (from Finland), both among the ten largest forest companies in the world, announced in 1998 a merger strategy which led to a new major expansion, namely the purchase of Consolidated Paper, in the USA in 2000. The new Stora Enso became well entrenched in newsprint and magazine papers, as well as in board production and sawing. Similarly, UPM (from Finland) diverged from its exclusively European strategy in 1997 and grew into an important actor in Southeast Asia and in the USA, especially in magazine papers. Norske Skog (from Norway) announced in April 2000 a major move: by purchasing Fletcher Challenge Paper (from New Zealand) Norske Skog became the second largest in global newsprint production. The purchase was, as was underlined in the media, the biggest ever in the economic history of Norway. This development brought new elements into forest markets and also forced the Nordic countries, as the home countries of the companies, to reconsider their relationships to these international actors. It became clear that the interests of the companies had distanced from the interests of their background societies.

The expansive companies can in general compensate for the limits in the operational spaces in their home countries by strengthening the production volume and marketing abroad. From the viewpoint of the home countries and provinces, the relative weakening of the production basis turns easily into risks within the export options and, as was witnessed during the early 1990s in the Nordic countries, into national and regional economic recessions and welfare crises.[27] The problem of welfare development, emerging due to a new confrontation of the interest between the state and its dominant export actors, is evidently an example of the client state setting introduced by L. Anders Sandberg in the Eastern Canadian context.[28] The activities of the client are to a large extent conditioned by the interests of the companies dominating its export operations. The state or the province, as a client of the company, finds itself in between unstable trading conditions, debt difficulties and export determinations.

The 20th century witnessed Finland becoming a forest-sector society. It was a success story but not without serious socioenvironmental side effects both at the level of national economy as well as within the forest provinces of Lapland, central and eastern Finland.[29] In Sweden, the broader economic spectrum helped the country to avoid the client state risks, but the most forested provinces (Norrland and Värmland) faced the pressures of company rule.[30] In Norway, the forest sector was in the early years of independency a key factor for the country's development, but as a result of a significant broadening of the economic activities since the 1950s the problems have become limited to certain localities in southern and central Norway, namely Hedmark, Buskerud, Ostfold and Nord-Trondelag.[31]

The Nordic model of forest-based development led in the late 20th century to a deep economic recession. The forest provinces suffered in particular from severe regional economic setbacks. The motorization of forestry and the automatization of wood processing resulted in growing unemployment. In Finland, for example, the national unemployment increased to 17 percent (ca. 430,000 persons) in 1995, but the forest companies could nevertheless in the same year announce new records in production and export activities.[32]

The successes and crises of the past have in general brought along particular sensitivity to Nordic forest politics. Forest companies have learnt to be careful with the demands of private forest owners. Family-owned private forest land constitutes on average two-thirds of the total forest area in the Nordic countries. For this reason, forest policy became a game of three: the companies, the state and the private forest owners could agree upon income distribution. This has not been the case in other parts of the conifer-dominated northwoods. Private forest owning has been, for different historical reasons, marginal both in Canada and in Russia. The key characteristics of the Nordic forest model, including also variations between the countries, are described now by paying attention to the articulation of socioenvironmental concerns in local, state and company contexts. The explication helps us to trace the concrete consequences of the ongoing globalization in forest localities, companies and countries.

Translocal Forests

The question of uneven development in wood processing becomes a concrete livelihood issue in those, often peripheral, regions of countries where forests are the dominant resource. In the Nordic forest model, the voice of those in the peripheries has mostly been limited to forest owners and their organizations. As part of the forest-based modernization, the rest of the local community has become excluded from the decision-making in forest policy. The land and resources are exploited according to external functional needs, by conditions set from outside the local communities.[33]

Rural researcher Sarah Lloyd,[34] while analyzing the erosion of local forest power in Jokkmokk, northern Sweden, describes how over the second half of the 20th century the forest industry had distanced itself and become disembedded from the local socioeconomic space. According to her, it happened in the form of steadily worsening local employment opportunities, followed by decreased income to the municipality from the forest sector. Several of the companies operating in the region no longer had physical offices located in the municipality. After witnessing decades of bankruptcies and new starts of the main local sawmill run for example by such companies as Sarek Wood and Jokkmokks Trä AB, the common attitude was in the late 1990s that the market relationships were by far arrogantly dominating and controlling the interactions to the detriment of reciprocal or associative relationships.

Lloyd identified two different maps of local forest power in Jokkmokk. First, the local municipal and industrial leaders considered the sawmill fundamental in the livelihood of the municipality, and their investment decisions were made according to this belief despite the hard facts of translocalization within the wood processing. On the other hand, the lay people, while feeling that they had little access to the decision-making power, saw no fundamental value in the continuity of the local wood processing. An appreciation for the recreation values of the forests and the new internet-based entrepreneurship seemed, instead, to condition the ordinary people's future prospects. The contours of the lay map told in general that "the municipality and the region have been unjustly cheated out of the riches of the natural resources; hydropower, forests and iron ore exported from the north for the benefit of the Swedish state treasure located in Stockholm." The map told also that "the companies were in debt to the municipality and the community of Jokkmokk for the destruction of the natural environment caused by the resource exploitation."[35] Lloyd's remarks are in no way rare or extraordinary. Similar summaries are repeatedly drawn in the analyses of the local resource-based communities in the northern peripheries.[36]

It has become evident that, while freeing themselves from the ties to their earlier home localities, the translocal companies have grown increasingly dependent on the networks of state-related and international partners. They have become embedded in a constantly widening "discursive regulation" of numerous country-specific and international stakeholders, including state actors expecting tax revenues and domestic investments, forest owners with demands on timber prices, employees in need of salary increases, environmental groups asking for eco-efficiency, indigenous populations expecting respect of their land rights and, of course, the ranks of shareholders and consumers with their diverse demands. This is the network through which requirements for broader socioenvironmental responsibility and participation in forest forest-industrial cooperation have been taking shape in globalization.[37]

Translocalization lays thus much responsibility on the actors of the network connected to the main companies. It depends on the strength of the network pressure how the companies behave within the new arenas of cooperation and especially how they integrate old and new localities to their strategies. Norske Skog, Stora Enso and UPM have for example been forced to face the discursive pressure of their new partners and this has had an effect on their location strategies and processing design. A good example is also Jaakko Pöyry, the consulting engineering company from Finland, which in the 1990s received intensive criticism of the Master Plans it had prepared together with several of its client countries in the Tropics. The criticism came both from the civic action groups in the target countries and the action groups in the home country of the company.[38]

Green Regimes

The Nordic model of forest-based development has broadly been a successful one, even though it was a central mechanism behind the severe economic recession and unemployment that especially hit the forest provinces in the 1990s. The success talk could still, after the deepest recession, be defended by emphasizing the indirect "multiplier effects" and "derivative impacts" of the forest-industrial activities, as was done in Finland.[39] According to this view, if the direct impacts on employment and welfare are invisible or even negative, the indirect ones are in turn considered crucial. This viewpoint underlines the rising level of overall economic activity caused by the intensification of forest utilization and wood processing. However, the domination of the leading export sectors, supported by an array of state subsidies, caused also much economic trouble and political tensions between industrial actors. Domestic and alternative sectors were in general left to suffer from the export priorities.

Finland is perhaps the most extreme case in this type of regime-building by the state and leading forest companies. The country matured into economic independency as a mass producer of pulp and paper, which meant that the forest industry, with all its societal strength, could gradually make Finland a client to itself.[40] The country became tied to those economic clusters that favored and reinforced the central position of the forest industry. Finland naturally benefited in many ways of this setting but, on the other hand, it could see no alternative but support the exporters of pulp and paper. In comparison, Denmark became during those decades the leading producer and exporter of wooden furniture in Northern Europe, not Finland, the country where in the 1990s on average one-third of the goods exported were wood products.[41]

The pressure for economic diversification in Finland finally grew big enough to burst out in the form of information and communication technology (ICT). The general process was not exceptional in the Nordic or Western context but the shape and pace it took were: the "Green Kingdom"[42] of the deep northern forests rapidly turned into a "Nokia Land", an advanced ICT country with an emphasis in fluent electric communication skills. Paper production with its capital-intensive machinery was challenged during the 1990s by the expansion of new technology based on the paperless modes of communication. The export share of forest goods dropped in Finland from 34 to 26 percent in a five-year period (1995–2000).[43] The change was dramatic in production but also at the level of everyday life. A major shift toward new industrial agglomerations in Finnish regional economic infrastructure was witnessed and a new networking of social life took place via mobile phones and in connection with the www world. The new high-tech activities gained a strong position in Finland by thoroughly permeating the modes of living and production. The restless local-global reorganization of production and consumption patterns within the ICT sector has, however, added volatility and insecurity in the socioeconomic development, and a similar trend has been documented in the sphere of families: rising costs of telecommunication have brought along problems in individual budget planning, especially among young generations.[44]

These shifts in production and consumption patterns bring along new options and risks to the northern frontier settlements and wildernesses. The trend is clearly that northern and eastern Finland, together with the rest of the Nordic North, have to be adjusted to the role of the Greenbelt of Northern Europe, and this development can evoke persistent uncertainty in many places, as was witnessed in Jokkmokk. These trajectories are indelibly connected to the shrinking space of strategic alternatives in the forest peripheries. From a historical perspective, to summarize the argument above, the Green Kingdom, or regime, of the North has actively forged such a setting for itself.

Good and Bad Companies

As has become already evident, even the transcontinental companies are not free of risks caused by value changes within the world markets and among the consumers. Wrong moves in their specific activity contexts can turn into severe market losses. Again, the Finnish case is worth examining. The Finnish forest companies have mostly been conservative actors relying on the technological innovations that confirm their entrepreneurial security. The solutions found useful in the past are favored. The companies have tended to invest in production capacity that supports the past division of labor. The changing market conditions, including intercultural and socioenvironmental adjustement demands in globalization, have remained peripheral while sketching new plans, if compared with the role and effect of technological innovations and applications. This has resulted in periods of overcapacity and fluctuations in price levels in the markets.[45]

During the recent years, the companies have, however, faced the signal to slow down the speed of capital allocation. The pressure has come from international investors who easily react to the risky moves of the firms by selling their shares. This in turn causes a fall in stock prices. The setting is crucial to an industry that is capital intensive and in which overinvestment has been a repeatedly-faced problem. Overcapacity becomes reflected as fluctuations in price levels and profitability, which is worrying to the investors. This is contrary to the earlier Finnish national context, which less critically supported expansive investment strategies.[46]

The companies have also met difficulties in reacting to new environmental demands and innovations, which is partially due to the strengthening role of professional shareholders in the forest industry. The signals from the stock markets have not encouraged the companies to become active in fields not clearly connected to profit-making. There are also country and company-specific variations in environmental performance. Finnish and Norwegian companies have been slow to consider the new socioenvironmental pressures as an instrument with which to renew the market strategies and governance. The Swedish forest sector has broadly applied the green recipe of FSC (Forest Stewardship Council) certificate, whereas the Finnish and Norwegian partners have applied the Pan European Forest Certification (PEFC) criteria, which in practice tend to guarantee that the forestry methods in use have already been sustainable. Finally, of course, the main consumers of paper products have the vote, and the experiences tend to support the Swedish solution of a more proactive formulation of environmental strategies.[47]

The future of the Nordic forest companies is in general related to their sensitivity to the new challenges of integration and innovation in Europe and globally. The most promising future prospects within the EU are connected to the economic clusters of the information technology, welfare and the environment, but also the traffic and energy clusters seem to have good options. The unforeseen fluidity of the economic activity context in Europe has roused the forest industry, which is capital-intensive by nature and demands long-term strategic thinking. The sector has, however, been able to respond relatively fast by narrowing the spectrum of core products and by actively searching for global economics of scale.[48]

The leading Nordic companies still primarily rely on standard production, both in Europe and globally. This means growing risks in Europe but also fierce competition with the producers in the Tropics. To avoid the worsening comparative advantages, acquiring a firm presence in the Tropics has therefore emerged as an alluring move. An alternative for this would be a more regional and selective strategy, aiming toward a gradual rise in the level of refining in the "old" production units. Some smaller companies have taken this path. The latter alternative is naturally less interesting for those aiming at a high ranking on the list of the world's biggest forest companies even though, from a regional perspective, the local specialization could be easily justified.

The Six Senses of Nordic Justice

The historical explication of the Nordic challenges, being inspired by and also inspiring international cooperation, serves here as the framework from within to elaborate on the key questions of Nordic socioenvironmentalism in today's local-global world. As has become clear, most customary practices have gradually become marginalized and outdated during the centuries of Nordic modernization. Some of them have, however, survived as remnants from the past, modified and modifying the later codifications of ethical socienvironmentalism and senses of justice. The continuous cultural co-inspiration of ethical communities and networks has produced a multitude of sociospatial associations we witness today as integral constituents of the late modern world. Some of these associations have in time grown into spatial socioenvironmental regimes finally connected to translocal networks of globalization. Others have remained in the margins.

This type of hybrid reorganization is present in the current discourses on (ethical) sensitivity and willingness to assess the reasons and outcomes of the societal distribution of environmental "goods and bads," The cultural reflection of these ethical dependencies is central to the understanding of the current forms of local-global socioenvironmental justice. The following Nordic articulations of justice have been valued as worth developing and they have therefore gradually become characteristic elements of Nordic globalization critique.

Landskap *Traditions and the Fate of the Local*

The sensitivity to regional representativeness, originally formulated within the framework of traditional *landskap* organizations, is today present in the ethical assessment of the consequences of translocalization. The still ongoing intensive urban concentration of the Nordic settlement structure has shaken the foundations of major cities and silenced many of the frontier villages in the rural fringes. "Topocides"[49] are common in the rural regions silenced by out-migration but they are as evident in the large cities targeted by crude redevelopment caused by pressure of overpopulation. Places and place identities are under constant redefinition and this is reflected in the erosion of attachment to local alternatives, especially among the younger generations.[50] The alluring (individual) options of translocal identities underline the fluid character of society, and this tendency questions the feasibility of local socioenvironmental associations. Participating in the space of flows is easily seen as synonymous to a dynamic and forward-looking lifemode and, within this view, local dependencies are considered signs of stagnancy. This division is today apparent for example in Finland between the networks basing their communication in English and the domestic forums satisfied with Finnish.[51] The setting reminds the Finns of the era of the Swedish Crown in Finland (from the 14th century till 1809), establishing a Swedish-speaking elite running the key areas of society up to the 20th century.

Nordic forest localities at the frontier have mostly aimed at following the dynamic path, and often it has resulted in hardships explicated above in connection to Jokkmokk. Authorities have found it necessary to develop their communities into flexible (post)industrial regimes racing to find a place in the fluid networks of globalization. Local cultures and natures have been in this setting either ignored or developed into market attractions. In places, however, a renaissance of *landskap* values can be witnessed and this phenomenon can be understood both as a counter-reaction to pure place marketing and a sign of popular support of local strategies grounded on the histories of their own. Numerous coastal settlements, river valleys and wilderness villages, initially shaped by the waves of early industrialism, have therefore become increasingly commemorated as locations of socioenvironmental heritage.[52] A divide between those localities that trust in dynamic modernization and those localities that show their respect to the past can sometimes be identified. Local outcomes and compromises depend much on the power geometrics and lay attitudes characterizing the local regime formation. The Greenbelt localities in eastern Finland belong mainly to the latter group of dynamic redevelopers. This is documented for example in the radical break with the values of the forest past and in the disappearance of the old wooden towns in the region since the 1960s (see chapter 4 and especially Fig. 4.2).[53]

Care Across Generations

The future generations stand today in the mainstream of the popular sustainability debates but much less attention has been paid to the rights of the past generations. We face the past generations in the spatial organizations and architectural details of our daily spheres of living, and this heritage is contested every time we make decisions concerning local redevelopment. Memories are vital to our identity constructions, and one cannot ignore the physical milieus as principal containers of these memories.[54] When redeveloping historical places, we redevelop ourselves. We can thus wonder whether sustainability is at all meaningful without co-appreciating the rights of both the past and future generations.

The family-based intergenerational ties have gradually loosened in the course of modernization, and in the Nordic welfare state both children and grandparents have found institutional day-care of their own, such as kindergartens and retirement homes. The change is dramatic in historical terms. Before the literary forms of communication, the oldest in the communities were those who knew the most. They were the messengers of the past and respected accordingly. The questions of ethics, responsibilities, cooperation and fair decision-making were based on traditions and the aged ones had a central role as intergenerational translators and interpreters. The oldest of the (extended) families had also a key role in transmitting their knowledge to their grandchildren.

The exclusion of youth and elderly people is increasingly criticized in today's political and planning practices in the Nordic countries. Several municipalities in different parts of the Nordic countries have consequently started neighborhood planning projects to integrate the marginalized age-groups and generations in decision-making.[55] These projects thus lean partially on the past traditions (of extended families) and they aim at introducing planning mechanisms that are sensitive to intergenerational senses of justice within the spheres of neighborhoods and other socioenvironmental networks. This renewal is still in an experimental phase and it has not become institutionalized anywhere in the continuum of local-global decision-making.

Gender Bias and the "Glass-roof" Politics

The gender-sensitive dimension of the Nordic debate on socioenvironmental justice has paid particular attention to those pressures and risks that are unevenly divided between women and men.[56] The problem has surfaced for example in the debate on specific spatial risks for women in city conditions. Urban environments carry different signs for men and women, and their "reading" varies much on a diurnal and annual basis. Studies on gender divisions within public spaces, downtown subcultures, city greeneries and traffic milieus have offered us plenty of material for recognizing the unjust urban relations between the two genders,[57] and this updating has called for increasing security guarantees in urban routines.

The question on gender and environment emerges not only at the street level but it is as alarming in the macrogeometrics of resource politics. Environmental decision-making, in connection to nature exploitation and conservation, has traditionally been male-dominated in the Nordic countries, and only slowly and occasionally has the "glass roof" been broken, and women thus been chosen to the high managerial levels of key corporations.[58] According to Ville Hallikainen, a Finnish wilderness researcher, it is rare and still accidental to find anyone prioritizing female "existence values" of wilderness (vis-á-vis "utility values") based on such motives as seeking for peace, quiet and relaxation.[59] Leena Vilkka, a Finnish environmental philosopher, comments that her ideas of the intrinsic values of the indigenous fauna of the North, such as wolves and bears, have made her an *outo lintu* ("strange bird") in the Finnish wilderness world still rather exclusively inspired by the masculine histories of hunting or adventurous hiking.[60]

Economic Polarization and Beyond

The class-based viewing of socioenvironmental justice concerns brings up the question of income distribution in corporate decision-making. The Nordic model of paper production has secured a rather even regional distribution of economic benefits, and it is due to the respectively strong status of family forest owners, widely scattered across the forest provinces.[61] The gradual historical establishment of the negotiation routines between the main corporate partners—the state authorities, the industry and the private forest owners—has, however, resulted in severe structural biases in forest-industrial practices, favoring pulp and paper production, and shadowing such branches as mechanical wood processing and non-timber economies.

In Finland, the postwar history of devaluations of the Finnish mark manifests most clearly the uneven position of forest interests. The strong export regime became established by decisions made by the main corporate actors benefiting the most from the development. The deep recession in the early 1990s, however, forced the forest sector to reassess its corporate strategies. The national recipe was largely renewed by the post-recession expansion of the information technology cluster, but in general the rise from the crisis strengthened the (early) modern class division, now stretched between the nobility of the financial-managerial elite and the fragmented majority of social outcasts with poor employment prospects. The Finnish and other Nordic forest-industrial actors have, under the pressure of international socioenvironmental regulation, tried to strengthen their performance as responsible corporate citizens, but the signals from the side of international shareholders have effectively counterbalanced these efforts.[62] The companies have reacted in various ways to the tension between traditional values and new investor-led values, while the general trend in Nordic globalization has been toward shareholder sensitivity.

Ethnoenvironmental Reorientation

The most difficult and still unsolved historical crime in respect to ethnoenvironmental matters in the Nordic countries is linked to the fate of the stateless Sámi peoples under the pressure of the newcomers from the Nordic South. The majority of the Sámi live in their home areas in the northernmost margins of the Nordic North, but the main cities of the Nordic South have also become centers of Sámi culture. The post World War II decades witnessed also a significant multiethnic immigration of non-Europeans to the capital city regions of Scandinavia, which meant a thoroughgoing modification of ethnoenvironmental relations.[63] In Finland, moreover, the historical interface location between the East (Russia) and the West (Scandinavia) has become reflected in some intercultural difficulties, especially in terms of the Swedish-speaking communities on the Baltic Sea coastline, the Orthodox fringe in the eastern part of the country, and in relation to the more recent increase of the Russian-speaking groups in the larger urban concentrations.[64]

The gradually rising awareness of the existence of ethnoenvironmental tensions, and the subsequent development of intercultural coping strategies, has become one of the dividing questions in the further development of the Nordic welfare society. Atmospheres of tolerance vary and so does the support to the political parties that are committed to defending the principles of the welfare state. The interethnic drawbacks are common today throughout the Nordic countries and racism is an indelible part of the everyday, both in the northern municipalities with the significant Sámi settlements as well as in the urban multiethnic neighborhoods. The question is about basic human and environmental rights. The Nordic Sámi question stands as proof of how the unsolved pasts turn into traumatic memories. The rectification of the past injustices has become the most painful of all ethnoenvironmental issues in the Nordic North. No real co-governing grounded on shared confidence can take place without solving the foundational disagreements. How to reinstate indigenous land rights? How to compensate for the colonial errors of the past? It is increasingly understood that only by answering such historically grounded questions, and thus sketching ethical road maps toward postcolonial politics of nature, can we make environmental justice issues concrete and fully meaningful to those oppressed through centuries. The

Sámi question roots in the historical construction of the territorial extensions of the Nordic states and therefore it is the most painful (post)colonial challenge to the Nordic countries, now under the pressure of international human rights conventions of the International Labor Organization (ILO) and the United Nations (UN).

Non-human Rights and Interspecies Ethics

The environmental justice debate became significantly enriched in the 1990s by animal rights concerns, both in the Nordic countries and elsewhere in the West. The protagonists of animal justice actively search for biocentric positions and defend the intrinsic values of nature. Biocentrism is, however, a thoroughly problematic and disputed approach, repeatedly criticized for disregarding the anthropocentric commitments of which we humans cannot free ourselves.[65] According to the critics, actors of nature can only speak through the human actors defending nature or, more accurately, defending the interests understood by human actors as nature's own. This view does not question the need to further broaden the human care across the spheres of the natural realm, rather it says that there is no way for humans to relocate themselves outside humanity, for example into the regimes of nature constructed as something pure and original.

Following the critics of biocentrism, the crime against animal rights appears as a violation against those defending animals, and thus it is an act that annihilates the co-association of certain actor-activists of nature. The question of justice thus becomes interpreted as a tension between various socioenvironmental co-associations of culture-nature. Consumers boycotting industrial meat, for example, can cause changes in (the nature-culture co-association of) animal husbandry. Measures aiming at protecting the global biodiversity are similarly rooted in the historical construction of the biodiversity concern and therefore they can only be understood as part of the expert discourse on conservation ecology and not so much in relation to the specific practices of nature varying in space and time.[66] Protecting wolves as part of the continental megafauna in the European Union turns into a question of injustice among the reindeer herders of the Nordic North who consider wolves as a threat to their source of living. The prey-predator relationship between reindeer and wolf takes the shape of a tension between reindeer herders and EU governance.

Two radically differing definitions of nature explain much of this confrontation between the reindeer herders and the European Union. The late modern politics of wilderness, or *Urwaldpolitik* (in German), has favored conservation and recreation measures, whereas the northern *erämaa* (wilderness in Finnish) is a central part of the system of nature-based livelihoods, or *erätalous* practices. The main Sámi languages have, moreover, no close equivalent for the word wilderness, because for the Sámi the surrounding lands in the Nordic North are part of their everyday lifeworld. The tension in local-global politics of nature has in this setting become problems of intercultural translation. The view from the North emphasizes on customary grounds that the rights of humans and the rights of nature are indelible. The routines of justice are therefore preferably derived from the local past and only thereafter adjusted to the criteria formulated in the centers of the South.

The six dimensions of socioenvironmental justice formulated above should not be taken as a complete list of the tensions to keep in mind when working with equity issues integral to local-global change in the Nordic North. No attention is paid for example to the everyday challenges of the disabled facing the taken-for-granted standards of those of us considered "normals." Rather, the list serves as an example of how the Nordic actors and communities have tried to integrate multicultural ethics into environmental practices. It also shows how to identify and avoid translocal violations of justice in resource exploitation, nature conservation and bioprospecting. The six dimensions, gathered from the rapidly evolving and fragmented Nordic literature on socioenvironmental matters, also function as raw material from where to formulate a concrete research design (see chapter 3) sensitive to the multicultural variation of the Greenbelt.

The Nordic versions of socioenvironmental justice are, as has been demonstrated, profoundly integrated into the historical innovations in the West. The application of the innovations has occurred in a specific manner, resulting in compromises that vary from place to place. The Nordic experiences therefore underline that the practical modes of socioenvironmental governance easily turn into further strengthening of the values of the Western regime. This is the case especially when the main direction is toward cultures of expertise, confirmed at the cost of local-global co-learning.

In a Finnish context, Ville Lähde, a researcher-activist in the Finnish socioenvironmental justice movement, has argued for further *yhteiskunnallistaminen*, which can be roughly translated as "societalization", of the movement. He summarizes that:

> *Mutta pitkän aikavälin liike ei voi nojata siihen, että joko yhteiskunnan toimintaa ymmärtämättömät asiantuntijaekologit tai "ideologinen papisto" kanavoi luonnon käskyjä massoille. Parhaimmillaan ympäristöliike voisi tarjota perinteiselle politiikalle haasteen. Ympäristöongelmat osoittavat, miten illusorinen on kuvitelma elämästä äänettömän luonnonnäyttämön keskellä. Ihmisyhteiskuntien elämä on lukemattomin tavoin kytkeytynyt elävään ympäristöön, jonka tarjoamat haasteet, vastukset ja mahdollisuudet osallistuvat elämän reunaehtojen luomiseen. Yksinkertaista teknologista ratkaisua näiden ehtojen sanelemiseen ei ole.*[67]

> In the longer run the movement cannot lean on "ideological clergy" and expert ecologists who are ignorant of societal dynamics but serve, however, as translators of nature's orders to the lay people. At its best, the environmental movement can offer a challenge to traditional politics. Environmental problems show how illusory it is to see human life as though surrounded by passive nature. Human communities are tied in numerous ways to the living environment affording the setting of challenges, troubles and options. No simple technological solution to modify these conditions exists. (Translated from Finnish by the author)

Lähde summarizes well the gap between the ecological constructions of expert cultures and the practical co-associations of culture-natures varying in time and space. This tension has been repeatedly met and challenged by Nordic geographers. The third chapter therefore gathers the main lines of thought of Nordic geographers paying attention to socioenvironmental matters. The chapter ends with an explication of the methodological choices of the case studies of the Greenbelt.

Notes

1. Ernst Friedrich, "Wesen und geographische Verbreitung der Raubwirtshaft," *Dr. A. Petermann's Mitteilungen* 50 (1904), 68.
2. Jussi Raumolin, "Reflections on the Destructive Economy on the Globe," in *Valtavirran Varrelta. Essays in Honour of Kyösti Pulliainen on his 50th Birthday* (Joensuu: Joensuu University Press, 1987), 113-114; Henry E. Lowood, "The Calculating Forester: Quantification, Cameral Science, and the Emergence of Scientific Forestry Management in Germany," in *The Quantifying Spirit in the 18th Century*, eds. Tore Frängsmyr, J. L. Heslbron and Robin E. Rider (Uppsala: Uppsala Studies in History of Science, no. 7, 1990), 315-42.
3. Karl-Erik Michelsen, *History of Forest Research in Finland I* (Helsinki: The Finnish Forest Research Institute, 1995).
4. The Danish-Norwegian Union was broken in 1814 and Norway was connected to Sweden by an agreement between Denmark and Sweden. The Swedish-Norwegian Union ended in 1905 and Norway got her independence.
5. Sverker Sörlin and Anders Öckerman, "Forskning om svensk skogshistoria—ett idéhistoriskt perspektiv," in *Skogshistorisk forskning i Europa och Nordamerika*, ed. Ronny Pettersson (Stockholm: Kungliga Skogs- och lantbruksakademien, 1999), 29-31.
6. Anders Öckerman, "Culture versus Nature in the History of Swedish Forestry: A Case for Pluralism," in *Sustainability the Challenge. People, Power and the Environment*, eds. L. Anders Sandberg and Sverker Sörlin (Montréal: Black Rose Books, 1998), 73-74; Ebba Lisberg Jensen, *Som man ropar i skogen: modernitet, makt och mångfald i kampen om Njakafjäll och i den svenska skogsbruksdebatten 1970–2000* (Lund: Lund Studies in Human Ecology no. 3, 2002), 84-85.
7. Nils Adolf Erik Nordenskjöld, "Festskriften Per Brahes minne," *Geografiska Föreningens Tidskrift* 3 (1891), 267-69. See also Tom Mels, "Nature, Home, and Scenery: The

Official Spatialities of Swedish National Parks," *Environment and Planning D: Society and Space* 20 (2000), 135-154.

8. Ari Aukusti Lehtinen, "Northern Natures. A Study of the Forest Question Emerging within the Timber-line Conflict in Finland," *Fennia* 196, no. 1 (1991), 79-80.

9. Judith Tsouvalis, *A Critical Geography of Britain's State Forests* (Oxford: Oxford University Press, 2000), 10.

10. Tsouvalis, *A Critical Geography of Britain's State Forests*; Gregory Barton, "Empire Forestry and the Origins of Environmentalism," *Journal of Historical Geography* 27, no. 4 (2001), 529-52; David Demeritt, "Scientific Forest Conservation and Statistical Picturing of Nature's Limits in the Progressive-era United States," *Environment and Planning D: Society and Space* 19, no. 4 (2001), 431-60.

11. Barton, "Empire Forestry and the Origins of Environmentalism," 529.

12. Lowood, "The Calculating Forester;" Michelsen, *History of Forest Research in Finland I*, 31-55; Barton, "Empire Forestry and the Origins of Environmentalism," 542; Demeritt, "Scientific Forest Conservation and Statistical Picturing of Nature's Limits in the Progressive-era United States," 440-41.

13. Kenneth Robert Olwig, *Hedens natur. On natursyn og naturanvendelse gennem tiderne* (Copenhagen: Teknisk Forlag, 1984); Arnold Alanen, Berit Kaae and Salvör Jónsdóttir, *Nordic Environment. Historical and Contemporary Perspectives* (Madison: University of Wisconsin, Department of Scandinavian Studies, 1995); Mels, "Nature, Home, and Scenery;" Ari Aukusti Lehtinen, "Mnemonic North: Multilayered Geographies of the Barents Region," in *Encountering the North. Cultural Geography, International Relations and Northern Landscape*, eds. Frank Möller and Samu Pehkonen (Aldershot: Ashgate, 2003), 31-32; Teijo Rytteri, "Ensimmäisten kansallispuistojen perustaminen poliittisena kysymyksenä," *Terra* 117, no. 1 (2005), 3-16.

14. Sverker Sörlin, *Framtidslandet. Debatten om Norrland och naturresurserna under det industriella genombrottet* (Stockholm: Carlssons, 1988); Eli Moen, *The Decline of Pulp and Paper Industry in Norway, 1950–1980: A Study of A Closed System in an Open Economy* (Oslo: University of Oslo, Department of History, 1997); Sarah Lloyd, *The Emergent Forest Landscape in Sweden: A Case Study of Relationships between Socio-economic and Ecological Space in Jokkmokk* (Uppsala: Swedish University of Agricultural Sciences, Department of Rural Development Studies, no. 13, 2001).

15. Tarmo Koskinen, "Metsäsektori sosiaalisena ja sosiologisena kysymyksenä Suomessa," in *Työ, talous ja suomalainen yhteiskunta*, ed. Tarmo Koskinen and Kari Lilja (Vaasa: Proceedings of the University of Vaasa, no. 92, 1983), 36-73; Jussi Raumolin, *Metsäsektorin vaikutus Suomen taloudelliseen ja yhteiskunnalliseen kehitykseen* (Oulu: University of Oulu, The Research Institute of Northern Finland, 1984); Jarmo Kortelainen, "The River as an Actor-network and River Systems," *Geoforum* 30 (1999), 235-47; Jarmo Kortelainen, "Forest Industry on the Map of Finland," *Fennia* 180, nos. 1-2 (2002), 227-35.

16. Reino Kalliola, "Luonnonsuojelusta ja sen tehtävistä," *Suomen Luonto* 1 (1941), 15-20; Alanen, Kaae and Jónsdóttir, *Nordic Environment*, 28; Mels, "Nature, Home, and Scenery," 139.

17. Matti Leikola, "Metsien hoidon aatehistoriaa," *Silva Fennica* 21, no. 4 (1987); Lloyd, *The Emergent Forest Landscape in Sweden*, 8-10.

18. Jussi Raumolin, "Global Scene, Natural Resources and Development Problems in the Periphery Country Finland: Some Reflections on Ilmari Hustich's Worldview," *Fennia*

159, no. 1 (1981), 15-23; Eeva Hellström and Aarne Reunala, *Forestry Conflicts from the 1950s to 1983* (Joensuu: European Forest Institute, 1995), 33-39. See a collection of papers from the Princeton Symposium in 1955: William L. Thomas, ed., *Man's Role in Changing the face of the Earth* (Chicago: The University of Chicago Press, 1956).
19. Christer Petersson, *Finsk ingenjörskunst och svensk imperiebyggande. En jämförande studie av finsk och svensk skogsndustri* (Stockholm: SNS Förlag, 1996), 107-09; Alanen, Kaae and Jónsdóttir, *Nordic Environment*, 22-24.
20. Antti Vahtera, *Ydinenergian uhkapeli* (Helsinki: Wsoy, 1986), 196-98.
21. Alanen, Kaae and Jónsdóttir, *Nordic Environment*, 22-24; Charly Hultén, "Yes-and-No. A Winning Strategy to Preserve Sweden's Nuclear Industry?," *WISE News Communique*, no. 545, http://folkkampanjen.se/ch20010323.html (16 Jan. 2005).
22. Jørgen Milwertz, ed., *Nordic Visions, Alternative Future* (Helsingør: Nordic Alternative Campaign and IPC Print&Press, 1986); Ari Aukusti Lehtinen, *Regionalismin ja ekokehityksen yhteys aluepoliittisessa murroksessa* (Helsinki: Publications of the Association of Planning Geography, no. 28, 1987); Helena Nynäs, Ekokommuner som motkultur i Norge (Oslo: Universitetet i Oslo, Institutt for Kultur och Samfunnsfag, Hovedoppgave i samfunnsgeografi/Master's thesis in Human Geography, 1992, mimeo).
23. Olli Tammilehto, *Ekofilosofia, vaihtoehtoliike ja ydinvoima* (Helsinki: Ympäristökeskus, 1982), 87-122.
24. Environmental Protection Agency was established in Sweden in 1967, with broad administrative and societal responsibilities. The Swedish Ministry of the Environment, founded in 1986, was reorganized and broadened into the Ministry of Sustainable Development in 2005. The Ministries of the Environment were launched in the rest of the Nordic countries in the following years: Denmark 1971, Norway 1972, Finland 1983, Iceland 1990. Green political parties were established in the 1980s: Miljöpartiet de Gröna/Sweden 1981, De Grønne/Denmark 1983, Green League/Finland 1988. The Finnish Parliament has had green representatives since 1983. In Norway and Icend, socioenvironmental issues are included in the programs of other parties. See Tammilehto, *Ekofilosofia, vaih toehtoliike ja ydinvoima*; Karin Jørgensen, Inge Hedegaard and Henrik Halkier, eds., *Miljøpolitik i Danmark: Den Grønne Bølge* (Copenhagen: NOAH, 1989).
25. Pentti Sierilä, "Energy Strategies of the Forest Industries," in *The Green Kingdom. Finland's Forest Cluster*, eds. Aarne Reunala, Ilpo Tikkanen and Esko Åsvik (Otava and Metsämiesten Säätiö: Helsinki, 1999), 160-65; Ari Aukusti Lehtinen, "Johdanto: ympäristö, yhteisö ja oikeudenmukaisuus," in *Oikeudenmukaisuus ja ympäristö*, eds. Ari Aukusti Lehtinen and Pertti Rannikko (Helsinki: Gaudeamus, 2003), 9-10.
26. Ari Aukusti Lehtinen, "Globalization and the Finnish Forest Sector. On the Internationalization of Forest-industrial Operations," *Fennia* 180, no. 1 (2002), 237-50.
27. Hannu Hernesniemi, Markku Lammi and Pekka Ylä-Anttila, *Kansallinen kilpailukyky ja teollinen tulevaisuus* (Helsinki: Elinkeinoelämän tutkimuslaitos/ETLA, 1995); Matti Pohjola, *Tehoton pääoma. Uusi näkökulma taloutemme ongelmiin* (Helsinki: Wsoy, 1996).
28. L. Anders Sandberg, ed., *Trouble in the Woods* (Fredericton: Acadiensis Press, 1992), 2-3.
29. Jussi Raumolin, "Recent Trends in the Development of the Forest Sector in Finland and Eastern Canada," *Zeitschrift der Gesellschaft für Kanada-Studien* 11 (1986); 89-114. Michelsen, *History of Forest Research in Finland I.*
30. Sörlin, *Framtidslandet*; Lars Östlund, *Exploitation and Structural Changes in the North Swedish Boreal Forest 1800–1992* (Uppsala: Swedish University of Agricultural

Sciences, Dissertation in Forest Vegetation Ecology, no. 4, 1993); Gabriel Bladh, *Finnskogens landskap och människor under fyra sekler* (Karlstad: Högskolan i Karlstad, Forskningsrapport no. 11, 1995); Lloyd, *The Emergent Forest Landscape in Sweden.*

31. Bjørnar Sæther, "Environmental Improvements in the Norwegian Pulp and Paper Industry—From Place and Government to Space and Market," *Norsk Geografisk Tidsskrift* 52 (1998), 181-94; Bjørnar Sæther, *Regulering og innovasjon: Miljøarbeid i norsk treforedlingsindustri 1974–1998* (Oslo: Universitetet i Oslo, Institutt for Sosiologi og Samfunnsgeografi, Dr. Dissertation, 1999).

32. *Avain Suomen metsäteollisuuteen* (Helsinki: Metsäteollisuus, 1996); Jaakko Kiander, "Työttömyyden puolittamisesta," *Kansantaloudellinen aikakauskirja* 93, no. 4 (1997), 571-73; Pertti Rannikko, "Forest Work as a Cause of Settlement and Depopulation in the Remote Parts of Finland," in *The Green Kingdom. Finland's Forest Cluster*, eds. Aarne Reunala, Ilpo Tikkanen and Esko Åsvik (Otava and Metsämiesten Säätiö: Helsinki, 1999), 222-26.

33. Bladh, *Finnskogens landskap och människor under fyra sekler.*

34. Lloyd, *The Emergent Forest Landscape in Sweden.*

35. Lloyd, *The Emergent Forest Landscape in Sweden,* 34.

36. Sörlin, *Framtidslandet*; Peter Friis and Rasmus Ole Rasmussen, *The Development of Greenland's Main Industry the Fishing Industry* (Roskilde: Roskilde University Center, North Atlantic Regional Studies, no. 6, 1989); Lehtinen, "Northern Natures"; Bladh, *Finnskogens landskap och människor under fyra sekler*; Jørgen-Ole Bærenholdt, *Innovation and Adaptability of the Murmansk Region Fishery Kolkhozes* (Roskilde: Roskilde University Center, Publications from the Department of Geography and International Development Studies, no. 106, 1995).

37. Päivi Oinas, "On the Socio-spatial Embeddedness of Business Firms," *Erdkunde* 51 (1997), 23-32; Päivi Oinas, *The Embedded Firm?* (Helsinki: Helsinki School of Economics and Business Administration, no. A 143, 1998); Sæther, *Regulering og innovasjon*; Ari Aukusti Lehtinen, Jakob Donner-Amnell and Bjørnar Sæther, eds. *Politics of Forests. Northern Forest-industrial Regimes in the Age of Globalization* (Aldershot: Ashgate, 2004), 275.

38. Alf Hornborg, "Mi´kmak Environmentalism: Local Incentives and Global Projections," in *Sustainability the Challenge. People, Power and the Environment*, eds. L. Anders Sandberg and Sverker Sörlin (Montréal: Black Rose Books, 1998), 202-211; Sari Kuvaja, Marko Ulvila and Thomas Wallgren, eds., *Suomi ja maailman metsät* (Helsinki: Kehitysyhteistyön Palvelukeskus, Maan Ystävät ja Vihreä Sivistysliitto, 1998).

39. *Pro Silvis. Metsien puolesta* (Helsinki: Metsämiesten Säätiö, 1995).

40. L. Anders Sandberg, ed., *Trouble in the Woods* (Fredericton: Acadiensis Press, 1992), 2-3.

41. Heikki Eskelinen and Mika Kautonen, "In the Shadow of the Dominant Cluster—The Case of Furniture Industry in Finland," in *Regional Specialization and Local Environment—Learning and Competitiveness*, ed. Heikki Eskelinen (Copenhagen: NordREFO 3, 1997), 177.

42. Aarne Reunala, Ilpo Tikkanen and Esko Åsvik, eds., *The Green Kingdom. Finland's Forest Cluster* (Helsinki: Otava and Metsämiesten Säätiö, 1999).

43. *Forest Industries Finland* <http://forestindustries.fi/tilastot> (15 Jan. 2001).

44. Perttu Vartiainen and Janne Antikainen, *Kaupunkiverkkotutkimus 1998* (Helsinki: Kaupunkipolitiikan yhteistyöryhmä, 1998); Timo Kopomaa, *The Rise of the Mobile-phone Society* (Helsinki: Gaudeamus, 2000). For example in Joensuu, a town of approximately

58,000 inhabitants in eastern Finland, the continuing high profile of municipal investments in the local Science Park has received broad and unanimous support. Critical voices have been rare but not completely absent: "Of the 18 Science Parks founded in Finland only a few will finally survive, and the most recently witnessed economic crises and lay-offs in IT enterprises should be taken as a warning, not as a signal to further expansion," said Pentti Keskitalo ("Tiedepuisto laajenee vauhdilla," *Karjalan Heili* 28 March 2001, 4, translated from Finnish by the author), a member of the Town Council of Joensuu when the Council accepted major new financing for the second phase of the enlargement in the Science Park. The Science Park of Joensuu, which completed the first phase of expansion during winter 2000–2001, is a result of intense cooperation between the town of Joensuu and the University of Joensuu, headed during this period by rector Perttu Vartiainen, Professor of Human Geography with a background in *samhällsgeografi*.

45. Pohjola, *Tehoton pääoma*.

46. Lehtinen, "Globalization and the Finnish Forest Sector."

47. Sæther, *Regulering og innovasjon*; Lehtinen, "Globalization and the Finnish Forest Sector;" Teijo Rytteri, *Metsäteollisuusyrityksen luonto. Tutkimus Enso-Gutzeitin ympäristö- ja yhteiskuntavastuusta* (Joensuu: University of Joensuu, Department of Geography Publications, no. 10, 2002).

48. Hernesniemi, Lammi and Ylä-Anttila, *Kansallinen kilpailukyky ja teollinen tulevaisuus*.

49. Douglas J. Porteous. "Topocide: The Annihilation of Place," in *Qualitative Methods in Human Geography*, eds. John Eyles and David M. Smith (London: Routledge, 1988), 75-93.

50. Tommi Hoikkala, "Traditiosta vapaan valinnan illuusio," in *Elämänpolitiikka*, eds. J.P. Roos and Tommi Hoikkala (Helsinki: Gaudeamus, 1998), 162-164.

51. Manuel Castells and Pekka Himanen, *Suomen tietoyhteiskuntamalli* (Helsinki: Wsoy and Sitra, 2001).

52. Bladh, *Finnskogens landskap och människor under fyra sekler*, 351; Anders Lundberg, *Lindøy. Historia om folket som budde der og landskapet dei forma* (Aksdal: Nord-Rogaland och Sunnhordland Friluftsråd, 2002); Hannes Palang, Helen Sooväli, Marc Antrop and Gunhild Setten, eds., *European Rural Landscapes: Persistence and Change in a Globalizing Environment* (Dordrecht: Klüwer, 2004).

53. Harri Andersson, *Rakennettu ympäristö kaupunkirakentamisen modernina projektina* (Turku: Turun yliopiston täydennyskoulutuskeskus, 1993); Jaana Nevalainen, *Tilapelin tiedonpolitiikat kamppailu kaupunkikeskustan muutoksesta* (Joensuu: University of Joensuu, Publications in Social Sciences, no. 67, 2004).

54. Gunhild Setten, *Bonden og landskapet. Historier om natursyn, praksis og moral i det jærske landskapet* (Trondheim: Norges teknisk-naturvitenskapelige universitet, Geografisk institutt, Dr. dissertation, 2002).

55. Marketta Kyttä, "Aidattu lapsuus," *Alue ja Ympäristö* 25, no. 2 (1996), 24-33. Anders Löfgren, "Choreographies of Life: Youth, Place and Migration," in *Voices from the North. New Trends in Nordic Human Geography*, eds. Jan Öhman and Kirsten Simonsen (Aldershot: Ashgate, 2003), 191-208.

56. Petri Hottola, *The Intercultural Body. Western Women, Culture Confusion and Control of Space in the South Asian Travel Scene* (Joensuu: University of Joensuu, Department of Geography Publications, no. 7, 1999); Hille Koskela, *Fear, Control and Space* (Publicationes Instituti Geographici Universitatis Helsingiensis, no. A 137, 1999; Nina Gunnerud Berg and Gunnel Forsberg, "Rural Geography and Feminist Geography: Dis-

courses on Rurality and Gender in Britain and Scandinavia," in *Voices from the North. New Trends in Nordic Human Geography*, eds. Jan Öhman and Kirsten Simonsen (Aldershot: Ashgate, 2003), 173-93.
57. Hille Koskela, "Urban Space in Plural: Elastic, Tamed, Suppressed," in *A Companion to Feminist Geography*, ed. Lise Nelson and Joni Seager (London: Blackwell, 2005), 257-70.
58. Eeva Berglund, "Facts, Beliefs and Biases: Perspectives on Forest Conservation in Finland," *Journal of Environmental Planning and Management* 44, no. 6, (2001), 833-49; Ari Aukusti Lehtinen, "Vastuu- ja oikeudenmukaisuuskysymykset globalisoituvassa metsäyhteistyössä", in *Leipäpuusta arvopaperia*, eds. Ari Aukusti Lehtinen and Pertti Rannikko (Helsinki: Metsälehti Kustannus, 2004), 266-68.
59. Ville Hallikainen, *The Finnish Wilderness Experience* (Rovaniemi: Finnish Forest Research Insititute, Research Papers, no. 711, 1998), 203-08.
60. Leena Vilkka, "Lapin erämaat ympäristöfilosofin silmin," in *Erämaapolitiikka*, ed. Jarkko Saarinen (Rovaniemi: Finnish Forest Research Institute, Research Papers, no. 827, 2002), 69.
61. Lehtinen, Donner-Amnell and Sæther, *Politics of Forests*.
62. Teijo Rytteri, *Metsäteollisuusyrityksen luonto*.
63. Roger Andersson and Irene Molina, "Racialization and Migration in Urban Segregation Processes," in *Voices from the North. New Trends in Nordic Human Geography*, eds. Jan Öhman and Kirsten Simonsen (Aldershot: Ashgate, 2003), 261-82.
64. Jouni Häkli, "Cultures of Demarcation: Territory and National Identity in Finland," in *Nested Identities. Nationalism, Territory, and Scale*, ed. Guntram H. Herb and David H. Kaplan (Lanham: Rowman and Littelfield, 1999), 123-49; Anne-Mari Keskisalo, "Puhu homo suomee! Suomalais- ja maahanmuuttajanuoret kansainvälisessä luokassa," in *Valkoisen vallan lähettiläät. Rasismin arki ja arjen rasismi*, ed. Vesa Puuronen (Tampere: Vastapaino, 2001), 173-207.
65. Lehtinen, "Johdanto: ympäristö, yhteisö, ja oikeudenmukaisuus," 30.
66. Juha Kotilainen, "Between the Global and the Local in Environmental Politics," *Nordisk Samhällsgeografisk Tidskrift*, no. 23 (1996), 61-68.
67. Ville Lähde, "Ympäristöliike ja uudet allianssit," *Muutoksen Kevät*, no. 28 (2003), 9.

3.

Samhällsgeografi and the Politics of Nature

The cultural turns in human geography[1] broadly challenged the widely applied critical realism of earlier approaches in the 1980s and 1990s. Textual orienteering, maps of the mind, narrative and linguistic emphases, and sensitivity to the everyday—all more or less inspired by different variations of social constructionism—forced the critical geography of structures and structurations to face the strength of heterogeneity and polyvalency in research practices. Soon, there was no way back to foundational overviews and solid stances. The powerful subject of geography was questioned. Some geographers identified themselves as nomads with mobile study positions and they increasingly focused their interests on sociospatial flows and fluidities. The cultural turns had also a profound impact on the culture-natures of human geography, and the environmental question was widely included in the reorientation.[2] The renewal was, however, in no way a simple metamorphosis with unisonous applause from all the corners of human geography.

Nordic human geographers soon reacted to and participated in the cultural turns, albeit with striking internal variance. Some adopted quickly the new codifications while others warmed slowly. Many remained skeptical. In general, the gradual reformulation of Nordic *samhälls- och kulturgeografi*[3] took place. The apparently slow and rigid dynamics of the Nordic renewal resulted in the rise of critical voices among the younger geographers,[4] but it also secured a firm basis for developing hybrid conceptions and stances that could help to grasp the interconnections between the (old) societal and (new) cultural concerns. These interconnections, as will be shown below, appealed strongly to geographers who had an interest in environmental issues or, more generally, in interrelations of culture-nature.

The search for hybrid re-conceptualization roots back to Bruno Latour's critique of modern scientific practices. "[We] need to get rid of all the categories like those of power, knowledge, profit or capital, because they divide up a cloth that we want seamless in order to study it as we choose," argues Latour[5], an influential technology and knowledge researcher from France, and points out a need for radical reorganization of our way of identifying subjectivity in connection with the environing world, including its organic content and material foundations. The modern worldview has, according to him, been entangled in abstractions that in fact refer to portions of collective associations and relations that cannot be cut into pieces without losing their intrinsic dynamism and heterogeneity. Therefore, we remain conceptually ignorant of the interrelations of which we as individuals and cultures are indelibly constituted.

Geographically speaking, the modern mind has remained silent on the actual "land and lifescapes" we inhabit corporeally and through myriads of practical co-productions of culture-nature. The "categories," including those listed above by Latour, are not abandoned in this volume but instead situated in their specific spatiocultural settings. The differences between landscape, *landskap* and *maisema* are considered crucial for example when aiming at understanding the "deep spaces"[6] of culture-nature in the Nordic context. This reflects the (post)constructionistic dependency underlined here: the concepts we use refer to earlier respective statements within a particular discursive continuum and this is something we cannot avoid or purify ourselves from. We can only endeavor to increase awareness of these dependencies.[7] Some hybrid formulations—such as culture-nature and local-global—are systematically used in this volume in order to remind us of the practical coexistence and vestedness of the poles to which these dual conceptions refer. The hybrid stance is hence taken here as an inspiring way of noticing and underlining the actual interconnections between the artificially distanced spheres of land and life. This way of looking at the world is familiar to Nordic *samhällsgeografi*, as will be shown later in this chapter, and Latour is by no means alone in pointing at the crucial dependencies between the things divided by the key categories of modernization.[8]

It is argued in this volume that, both due to and in spite of the cultural turns, human geographies have gradually and increasingly become inspired by the layered existence of spatiocultural and socioenvironmental hybrids, and this holds true especially in the Nordic countries. Nordic geographers were able to occasionally construct a fruitful comparative setting, a Nordic interpretation based on both Continental European and anglophonic debates.[9] We can talk in a similar manner about several waves of the environmental turn within Nordic human geography, featuring such key concepts as territorial structure (*territorialstruktur*), landscape (*landschaft, landskap, maisema*), terrestrial nature, nature compressions (*natursammenhænge*), northern natures, recreational natures and culture-natures; including also thorough comments on such popular (late) modern practices of governance as ecological modernisation, risk management and biopolitics.[10]

Socioenvironmental Turn in Geography

In the Nordic context, the longest traditions of the culture-nature debate within (poststructural) human geography can be found in Denmark, where inspiring programs have been initiated in the field of landscape studies and as part of the research program on lifemodes.[11] In Norway, historical geography of landscapes is well developed in Trondheim,[12] whereas in Oslo the culture-nature formulations range from environmental feminism to environmentalism within economic *samfunnsgeografi*, inspired for example by cultural interdependencies of non-traded origin.[13] The long history of human geographical research on culture-nature in Sweden is well known and it is especially due to the outlines in historical landscape research and in analyses of modernization and resource use as well as in lifestyle studies.[14] Some scholars from closely related disciplines have also made important geographical contributions.[15]

The Finnish human geographical studies of culture-nature have also a long history, rooted in the classical works of J.G. Granö, Väinö Tanner and Ilmari Hustich.[16] These initial approaches were later read in the light of explicit socio-cultural theory by younger colleagues[17] and they were also connected to the rise of environmentalism in Finnish social sciences.[18] The gradual establishment of Finnish geography as a discipline with a social scientific status[19] resulted soon in several new openings in culture-nature research with explicitly poststructural orientations. The most energetic formulation took shape in connection with the studies of the various spheres of urban natures, which was soon accompanied by a constructionist re-reading of rural and marginal natures, for example in the context of organic farming. The globalization of environmentalism was also reflected in the studies of environmental consciousness and ethics, accompanied by multiethnic and gender-sensitive analyses of postcolonialism and interculturalization. Thematic explorations of the culture-nature hybrids were published at the turn of the century.[20] Finnish geographers received also support for their theoretical elaboration from scholars of closely related disciplines, for example from environmental anthropology, ecology and environmental policy and environmental sociology.[21]

The Nordic human geography of culture-nature became increasingly integrated with the Anglophonic schools in the 1990s but even then it kept its specific Nordic intonation, colored by contacts to the Continental European streams of thought. The socioenvironmental renewal in Nordic geography, influenced by the cultural turns in environmental approaches, was in general connected to the politicization of natures. This movement was integrally linked to the contested networking of sociospatial identifications and community activities stretching from individual (embodied) and local practices up to international contests within the brand markets (certificates of sustainability). The culture-nature practices were critically evaluated as questions of domination and empowerment, both within the spheres of intimate and intersubjective discourses as well as in relation to the industrial-technological change within the local-global continuum. These questions have also repeatedly been re-worked through the more general debate on the changing role of the material processes of nature in the discourses on the environment. The last-mentioned question is perhaps the most fundamental and long-lived of the challenges within Nordic *samhällsgeografi.*

The Nordic view on culture-nature is indelibly connected to the continuing rearticulation of power relations emerging within environmental discourses and written in the physical-symbolic landscapes under human agency. The emphasis of power rests on the historical sensitivity toward shared decision-making and representativeness in the Nordic societies and communal life. Collective responsibility among and between the families of the villages during the era of hunting economies (*erätalous*) and the ancient customary public access (*allemansrätten*) to lands and forests beyond the centers of settlement have become rooted in the modern Nordic practices of culture-nature, only to surface when threatened by pressures of modernization.[22] The questions of freedom, equality and justice are therefore integral elements of the Nordic identification, and they also guide the basic formulation of geography. Nordic *samhällsgeografi* can in fact be seen as a program launched against regional and environmental inequalities as well as class and gender-based discriminations faced during the post World War II period of speeded modernization.[23]

These concerns of socioenvironmental discrimination can be understood as expressions of a specific sensitivity to various forms of biopolitical repression and empowerment, when following the Continental European discourses of nature and power, whereas the Anglo-American interpretation would underline the connections to socioenvironmental justice issues. The biopolitical view sheds light on the conditions of culture-nature control, articulated through such concepts as governmentality and environmentality, but it reaches its full explanatory power when focused on the most nuanced versions of (self-)control infiltrated in and through everyday life, both bodily and in environmental terms.[24] On the other hand, the sensitivity to (in)justice is derived from the growing awareness of the alarmingly unfair distribution of environmental "goods and bads."[25] In Nordic geography, this interfacing has resulted in approaches where the new challenges of local and individual governance are seen as rooted in translocalization launched both by the new economy of shareholder interests and by the global management programs of environmental organizations. Here, the Nordic forest-based networking of power regimes covers both the local-global and culture-nature dimensions and can therefore be used as an illustrative example of the practical societal challenges of Nordic *samhällsgeografi*.

The biopolitical view referred to here is based on the understanding of power as a web of dependencies between countless actors and positions in a continuously evolving setting of fluid relations. Power has thus thoroughly permeated our societal practices and it emerges both in macro and micro levels of our sociospatial being. It is an immanent and unavoidable element of social coexistence, taking shape via continuous processes of re-negotiations.[26] Power (*makt*) becomes activated both through submission (*vanmakt*) and counter-reactions (*motmakt*). This triangularity forms multilayered regimes with networks of reciprocal ties and endless series of inclusions and exclusions. Biopower emerges in those situations where both our bodily existence and our intimate sociospatial relations become eroded according to the dominating interests (of systematization and control), more or less reproduced in our daily decisions by our willing selves or through our respective reactions and proactions. The biopolitics of forests surface for example in the negotiations of the contested origins of the timber behind the newspapers we consume on a daily basis. Biopolitical studies highlight the modes and variations of local-global "paper landscapes" in the era of intensive forest-industrial reorganization. The question is about uneven distribution of information related to decision-making power, including positional variation in the ability to encode and decode the signals of forest-based knowledge materialized in paper processing and consumption.[27]

The comparative elaboration of biopolitical and justice approaches is especially linked to the gradual strengthening of the socioenvironmental sensitivity of *samhällsgeografi*, influenced both by Continental European and Anglo-American debates on geography and power. From the beginning, the question of justice was included in the process in the form of criticism against the unevennes of economic development.[28] Later, this orientation was criticized as exclusively emphasizing economic aspects and it faced a need for more nuanced and multilayered articulation of power relations.[29] The biopolitical vocabulary became gradually integrated into this reorientation—as a line of thought—but it also seemed to distance Nordic human geographers from societal involvements and activities. The cultural turns in general, while contrasted with the painful traps of recession of the 1990s in the environing world, were also seen as signs of a return to conservative geographies and resulting in an aestheticization of societal relations of domination.[30]

In the Finnish context, psychohistorian Juha Siltala, while rooting his argument in the social criticism of the Frankfurt School,[31] criticized in detail the fashionable turn of social scientists towards deconstructions, discourse analyses and biopolitical choreography. According to him, the discourse orientation became a methodological fetish that closed the connection to individual authenticity under the concrete conditions of societal change, therefore constraining our ability to renew ourselves as researchers in dialogue with the subjects in study focus. Siltala also argued that the discursive approach limits our understanding of the human and social existence behind the symbolic representations, surfacing for example in the form of disconnections, overreactions and other discontinuities in the spheres of communication.[32]

The biopolitical analysis is crucially dependent on the creativity of the scholars applying it: the limits we face are primarily the limits of our own. The biopolitically inspired cultural turn in human geography has undoubtedly faced difficulties in noticing the multilayered needs and motives of individuals anchored in the multilayered dynamics of societal projections, and this has become evident in connection with the more unarticulated spheres of human existence. It has a tendency to distance professional geographers from the lay geographies of the everyday.[33] The biopolitical orientation thus tends to weaken the social constitution of the critical voices of geography.

The stance taken in this volume is, however, (i) broadly utilizing the sensitivity of the biopolitical view within the field of articulated power but it is carefully (ii) situated in a dialogue between the "politics of academia" and the "poetics of activism," and (iii) linked to an aim to get closer to the community-based variations of coping with oppression and violations of the sense of justice. This interpretation is derived from the traditions of *samhällsgeografi*. The specific methodological combination developed here, nevertheless, enables a critical self-reflection on the contemporary solutions of culture-natures in the Nordic branches of human geography. The critical remarks are finally summarized in the conclusive part of this volume.

To specify, this study leans methodologically on the Nordic traditions of *samhällsgeografi* by interpreting them in the broader framework of politicization of nature, which refers both to general conceptual and paradigmatic renewal in disciplinary approaches as well as to sociocultural changes conditioning the academic circles. The interpretation is inspired both by the political ecology literature highlighting the justice concerns in resource exploitation and environmentalism and by the (post)constructionist approaches broadly under the umbrella of biopolitics. This framework is further developed in this chapter in the context of forest-industrial reorganization. The question is formulated in connection with the Nordic forest provinces that have their own traditions of community-based decision-making—and tensions impelled through ages by demands of modernization.

As became evident in chapter two, the traditional local senses of self-sufficiency and justice have become eroded by the modern industrial and environmentalistic practices and further modified by the more translocal models of decision-making. The earlier solutions for local representativeness and social responsibility have in other words faced the subsequent demands of intensifying resource extraction and nature conservation, both based on the high status of landownership and, consequently, developed into complex hybrids with traces from all the eras of the past. Derived from these assumptions, the current uneven positioning of forest communities, both local and translocal, is discussed below and related to the ongoing globalization of the Nordic forest industry.

Throughout the centuries of forest-based modernization, the local and regional forest communities have been modified by the export actors of forest trade. The market interests, emerging beyond the conditions of negotiated decision-making, have gradually become part of the local lifemodes. Some have benefited from the new challenges, some others have suffered. Today, in the era of forest-industrial globalization, the setting is still much the same. However, the more translocal the companies have grown the less dependent they have become on specific localities, or provinces, as their partners. While making new contracts, the companies can therefore more easily ignore those local interests that deviate from their strategies. The question is about loyalty to two confronting formulations of interests and, moreover, about tensions between two forums of identification, the local and translocal (forest) communities. This is the argument of this chapter and the grounds for further elaboration on the entire volume: during the current local-global transformation, our community basis is under intensive redefinition and this has an impact on our understanding of socioenvironmental governance, sustainability and sense of justice.

Biopolitics and Environmental Justice

The environmental debate seriously questioned the expansive societal modification of nature in the 1990s and the renewed debate covered also worries about intensifying modification of culture via the changes in nature. The animal liberation movement was especially active in highlighting the ethical problems in animal testing, livestock husbandry and outdoor hunting, and from here we can find the most informative articulations of nature-cultures as co-productive processes and collective associations. The contested reconfiguration of the positions of the various coalitions of culture-nature is by no means an exclusive characteristic of the animal liberation debate. On the contrary, it seems to take shape as one of the organizing principles of the environmental debate.[34]

Examples of this type of new contestation are numerous and easily recognized. The widely applied biodiversity programs in environmental monitoring are tools for underlining the injustices in the exploitation of natural resources but they also function as universal(izing) matrices and claims for various community-based practices of culture-nature. The concept of biodiversity has "progressed from a scientific community of North American conservation biologists to North Karelian lumberjacks," states Juha Kotilainen,[35] a geographer from Finland, and criticizes its discursive dominance in an eastern Finnish context. The spread of concern for biodiversity is a good example of the biopolitical configuration of power. The question is primarily about the increasing domination of the (late) modern technological trajectories with socioenvironmentally erosive and discriminatory outcomes. The apparent conflict between nature conservation and exploitation—dividing nature and culture into oppositional entities—turns here into a more nuanced, interdiscursive and fragmented battle over particular hegemonic positions. The question is about the contingent emergence of organizing power or, more precisely, about the macrogeometrics of globally uneven development, which becomes articulated as time-space specific modifications of the environment, identifiable only within and through the microgeometrics of the everyday.[36]

Criticism of the new manifestations of biopower has recently surfaced rather dramatically in the form of large-scale civic demonstrations in different parts of the world against the politics of the World Trade Organization and International Monetary Fund. The wave of actions started in Seattle on November 30th in 1999, and the critical demonstrations became thereafter an integral part of global corporate and intergovernmental meetings for many years.[37] The demonstrations have brought the environmental risks and injustices of the current economic-technological globalization into public awareness. The media success of the actions also forced the criticized ones to raise their voice against the activists, claiming that the new wave of demonstrations is based on a hierarchic networking that takes shape according to the impulses of the few centers of globalization critique. Some ideological leaders of the global movement such as Walden Bello, Susan George and Lori Wallach were mentioned.[38] The new movement was thus criticized for using methods of biopower similar to those used by the main forces of globalization.

Environmental justice is a familiar concept and well-known viewpoint to researchers. Especially geographers have studied it carefully, both theoretically and as an empirical research challenge.[39] The questions of discrimination and justice in environmental research have mainly concentrated on the ethical basis and the social responsibility dimensions of societal practices. The mechanisms of uneven socioenvironmental development have been examined, including ecosystems with their defenders and transformers, individual consumers and consumer groups, both non- and (inter)governmental bodies of regulation, as well as transnational companies with their suppliers and clients.[40] The clear boundary between ecological and societal concerns has vanished in research practices.

According to Wolfgang Sachs,[41] an environmental researcher and activist from Germany, the crisis of justice and the crisis of nature stand in an inverse relationship to each other. Any attempt to ease the crisis of justice threatens to aggravate the crisis of nature, and vice versa: any attempt to ease the crisis of nature threatens to aggravate the crisis of justice. The changes in nature turn into changes in society turn into changes in nature. Nature and society became indivisible.

This unification has bred new questions and, also, new ways of formulating the old ones. First, the extension of nature, as a central constituent of the Western worldview,[42] is once again under intensive redefinition. The motor of the current change is connected to the articulations of biodiversity concerns and animal rights. Poor living conditions of livestock affect the animals and concern their defenders but they have also emerged as questions of health for the consumers and, therefore, translated into new entrepreneurial risks. Bovine Spongiform Encephalopathy (BSE) or, in popular language, the mad cow disease, is a dramatic example of the boomerang phenomenon within the interrelations of nature and culture, guiding consumers to demand safer food production and transitions towards organic farming.[43]

Second, during the era of dramatic global time-space compressions, the interconnections between the self (e.g. as a Western consumer) and the other (e.g. as child labor in Southeast Asia) have surfaced as questions of moral reflection; continuous local-global scaling is part of our daily lifeworld while shopping in the nearby grocery. The certificates of sustainability, demanded by the critical consumers and focused both on the products and the processes behind them, are presently under contested definition. The reading of these certificates has consequently become a necessity for a careful consumer. Both the price tags and green labels are today essential while making purchases. The lengthening of product chains has also emphasized the socioenvironmental costs of transporting. Regional preferences in production and consumption patterns—for example local food projects—are therefore introduced as part of the sustainability criteria.[44]

Third, the companies participating in the global economic contest have faced new risks based on the fluidity of their operational contexts. The credibility problems caused by "wrong moves" or bad image easily get reflected both in the final product markets and within the stock markets in the form of worsening options. This type of new vulnerability has become an integral part of the competing markets, and many of the most successful companies have become much more sensitive to external signals and changing value horizons.[45]

The geographically and biopolitically interesting debate on environmental justice is focused on how the use of nature is intertwined with power. This tradition concentrates on social and ecological impacts of environmental changes by examining the mechanisms that cause inequality and injustice in the routines of everyday life. Environmental racism has been for example brought up in the debate when documented that environmentally harmful land use has a tendency to accumulate in the areas inhabited by people from ethnic minorities.[46] Topocide, on the other hand, refers to the dramatic weakening of local conditions of living caused by the development projects accepted and run by municipal authorities.[47] Unequal progression of social and ecological vulnerability has been analyzed in a similar manner, following certain patterns of risk production that we often take for granted and consider natural.[48] Perhaps the most common dimension of the predicament of environmental justice has appeared along the debate on sustainable development: the worries about future generations are indeed a sign of sensitivity to the trajectories of biopower, now across the generations.

In regard to the forest-based development processes in Northern Europe, fundamental questions of environmental discrimination readily emerge as issues related to the position of the northern periphery, including both nature and human communities, in the deepening integration of Europe. The impact of the global forest trade already has remarkably, often throughout, modified local and regional conditions. The questions of environmental discrimination cover a variety of social effects arising also from the programs of nature conservation. Local cultural values in the northern peripheries quite often seem to be undervalued, or even ignored, when appearing seemingly against translocal conservation plans.[49]

The question of representativeness, including age, gender and other social dimensions, is central both in the formation of local voices and governmental policy plans, as well as within transnational corporate strategies.[50] Participation is constantly contested within and between the actors and across all the spatial scales within the local-global continuum. The identification of the critical moments of inclusion and exclusion is therefore a complicated research challenge, loaded with risks emerging from the side of the subject groups as well as from within the institutional academic world. Susan L. Cutter,[51] a geographer from South Carolina, has called attention to the difficulty of verifying environmental discrimination. While debating the correlation between the definition of research topics and the results achieved, she elaborates on the problem of geographical scaling: environmental changes with locally worrying consequences might completely disappear while framing the question within a broader sociospatial scale.

The question of perspectives is of key importance when studying biopower. The credibility of the research is easily questioned among the broader audience if proved that the results do vary according to perspective or the level of abstraction. Researchers with a different background can also easily nullify the work of their colleagues by showing remarkably deviating results. The interconnections between the researcher and her or his subject groups are also often sensitive.[52] Local experiences of injustice can be modified—exaggerated or underrated—to meet the explicit or implicit research premise by varying the basic focus or framing. For a professional academic, covering these modifications with technical choices or ways of representation is easy. Therefore, as seems evident, research always and inevitably becomes interlinked with the mechanisms that strengthen or weaken the practices of discrimination.

The problem of perspective can, at least partially, be overcome by comparative research settings, and by careful reflections upon the consequences of sociospatial scaling. It is especially important to learn to recognize the context-specific conditions whence and within the sensitivity to certain forms of domination grow. Giovanna Di Chiro,[53] an environmental justice researcher from Massachusetts, discusses the critical role of communities in (re)producing the notions of nature and the sense of justice. In her own words, "Environmental justice groups, while strongly criticizing mainstream conceptions of nature, also produce a distinct theoretical and material connection between human/nature, human/environment relations through notions of 'community'." Community is for her the idea, place, and the relations and practices that generate what these activists consider more socially just and ecologically sound socioenvironmental configurations.

The community, in the form of a locality or network, thus lays both the value basis and practical frames that condition the formation of environmental preferences and sense of justice. The community produces the system of identification by which the ideas and practices of culture-nature are formulated. This system can only be understandable and meaningful from the "inside," while seen as co-developed from within the ideas, values and experiences shared by the members of the community.[54] This demand for authenticity, based on socially negotiated experiences and interpretations of sociospatial order—that is, conceived and lived spaces—can emerge as an insuperable barrier for the researcher but it can, nevertheless, function also as basic research motivation and a challenge.

Communities, Domination and Sense of Justice

The need to identify the community-based variations in environmental preferences is by no means a new question in geographical research. The community-based dynamics behind the development of the sense of (environmental) domination and justice can, however, help us as researchers to become more sensitive to the uneven distribution of risks, including fears of them, faced in the daily lives of communities. The questions thus are: How do major environmental changes, and the culturally varying responses to these changes, take shape in different contexts? How are the changes articulated and justified? What are the outcomes of these changes? These research questions contain at least three complementary formulations that are presented here in reference to Nordic forest communities.

First, the traditional formulation of the culture-nature relationship was initially a local process in the Nordic forest provinces. Local communities are still today important mediums for the development of the sense of justice. Nordic geographers have introduced a variety of community and identity approaches, for example in connection with historical *landskap* research and as part of the programs of village studies,[55] and this work has widely contributed to the understanding of the historical spaces that are both socially inherited and societally produced. These research traditions inform us for example about the background of the provincial criticism of the EU integration and against expanding nature conservation. Local expressions often seem to become labeled as provincial and outdated exaggerations in the dominating media even though the problem, at least partly, rises from the experience of humiliation based on marginalization (from the central information flows) and deep, heritage-like experiences of injustice.[56] Environmental policy measures are confronted in the forest provinces in the context of the local sense of justice which is more or less internally shared, and this often tends to differ from the external translocal principles of justice derived from the more universal standards.

For the people in the provinces, biodiversity programs can appear strange means for promoting nature conservation, while the "lived diversity of land" is based on inherited patterns of land use and topographic identifications, including the immediate experiences of seasonal changes—whereupon the viability of human existence is finally constructed. The multiple senses of snow[57] hardly belong to the vocabularies of biodiversity programs and might perhaps more easily be connected to notions of earthly sensitivity and geodiversity relations. In a similar manner, to give a tangible and acute example, people in the backwoods villages in eastern Finland find it difficult to cope with the EU limitations on hunting bears that terrorize the forest farms and villages.[58]

Even though the local cultures of community decision-making in the Nordic forest peripheries have never been turned into oppressive patrimonial practices, uneven social positioning has been an unavoidable and common feature in Northern Europe.[59] The Nordic regional voices have traditionally taken shape through certain representative practices, by the *landskap* meetings (or *ting* gatherings), but not without distress between pressures of conformity and sociocultural diversification. The local power relationships have in time gone through intensive transformations toward broader representativeness but, also, toward external dependencies. The intensifying export orientation during the centuries of forest-industrial modernization tangibly transformed the specific structuring of landownership, economic positions, gender settings and intergenerational relations.[60] The development projections "from the outside," including cultural variations in adaptation, have in general differentiated the local social groupings and increased local heterogeneity and powerlessness against the external interests. The locality is in this respect perhaps a weaker actor today than ever before.

Second, the culture-nature relationship is also (re)produced within the translocal or nonlocal network communities that we participate during our daily practices. Today, it is argued, these posttraditional community relations even exceed the local community effects as conditioning factors of our lifeworlds.[61] Within this translocal world, the basic formulation of environmental values takes place indirectly, without personal experience of the immediate strength of the environing nature (first nature). Nature becomes modified to second nature that becomes meaningful to us for example in the form of questions about pollution control and trade.[62] Within the Nordic countries, and in connection with forest politics, the most influential of these translocal network communities are the big forest companies with their resource areas, suppliers and clients, as well as the (inter)governmental and nongovernmental organizations for environmental regulation.

The current global contest of the Nordic companies puts much pressure on the researchers to conduct studies on the socioenvironmental consequences of this change, both within the Nordic forest peripheries and within the new target countries of the companies. Careful monitoring of these changes is crucially important for the peripheral communities but it has also become a necessity for the leading local-global actors. The question is about vulnerability. Today, companies with global strategies need to be sensitive to the voices of suppliers, consumers and shareholders. A more respectful attitude toward environmental pressure groups has also become a necessity. Bad image easily turns into credibility problems and worsening economic options. The translocal communities of environmentalists need in a similar manner to be aware of the risks of becoming labeled as green imperialists or busy professionals for whom the planet earth is primarily a management object.[63]

Third, the community-based culture-nature relationship emerges as a question of academic engagement.[64] The research motives often find legitimacy by aiming at bringing up facts and viewpoints that are only partially visible in the everyday lifeworld. Research on human communities, for example, is in general supposed to add something analytical, interpretative or summary-like to the articulations and actual views produced by the subject actors of the case studies. Research might even become emancipative while opening new views, for example latent options and risks, on the questions under investigation. The societal relevance of research depends on its capability to cope with the concrete socioenvironmental factors constraining and conditioning the action spaces of the subject groups. The repeatedly faced question here is: How much are the research motives shaped by the scientific communities surrounding the study projects and how well does the researcher identify her or himself as part of the communities in study focus? Different identifications and prioritizations result in different rankings of the most important research issues. The preliminary research design has thus a decisive impact on the acuteness of the questions studied.

While focusing on biopolitics and environmental discrimination, the primary aim of this volume is to highlight those socioenvironmental processes and projections that remarkably transform the most marginal(ized) of the lands and people of Northern Europe. This task directs our attention to those historical mechanisms of exclusion and inclusion that have been, and still are, dominating the practices and experiences of our lived spaces in the Nordic forest peripheries, including, if possible, the voiceless groups of the North. The empirical work is, however, equipped (and framed) by the tools offered by the communities of geographers that have worked with similar issues. In the proceeding pages, this three-partite community approach is developed within the context of socioenvironmental reorganization, modifying and being modified by both local and translocal communities of the Greenbelt.

Tools of Greenbelt Research: Just Geography

The earlier parts of this chapter have tried to demonstrate the usefulness of the biopolitically informed justice approach in human geography focused on environmental and forest questions. It was argued that the specific Nordic interpretation in human geography, which underlines the basic (hybrid) co-dependence of societal and cultural as well as non-human and human features of the ongoing local-global change, has responded to and further developed the Anglo-American and Continental European debates of environmental discrimination and empowerment.

The proceeding pages specify the practical methodological choices of the Greenbelt travelogue, derived from the general framework explicated above and applied in the individual cases and socioenvironmental settings studied. The Greenbelt of the Finnish-Russian border is introduced at the end of the chapter. The methodological explication begins with a short outline of the multilayered organization of the research framework and thereafter the method is specified stage by stage, in connection with the sociohistorical (postcolonial), ethnocultural (multitude) and biopolitical (politics of nature) framing of the Greenbelt.

Layers and Scales of Greenbelt Geography

When analyzing the historical emergence of the Greenbelt as part of the local-global and socioenvironmental configurations of the European North, it becomes evident that the most fundamental framing element is related to the geohistorical formation of the border landscapes. Postglacial succession explains much of the overall ecological character of the Belt, but the concrete outcome is far from homogeneous and zonal. The variation in vegetation types broadly follows the latitudinal conditions but is practically reorganized according to other geohistorical factors, including the human impact. From a global zonal perspective, the Greenbelt is strikingly young and species-poor if compared, for example, with the ecosystems of the more southern latitudes. Despite that, the sub-regions of the Belt vary dramatically in the north-south axis. Extreme seasonal changes in temperature also characterize the Belt. Warm summers are followed by icy winters and this has had a decisive impact on the tree species selection. Tree growth is slow, and the maturation of stands takes at least 80 years in the southern part of the Belt, whereas treeless tundra dominates at the northern end.

The eleven millennia of (i) the postglacial past are thus thoroughly present in the Greenbelt, as are the younger layers of socioenvironmental change. The layers of (ii) early human settlements surface today in the northern part of the Belt as questions about ethnic aboriginality and indigenous landownership, whereas (iii) the modern past has become manifested in the form of increasing state control and intensified exploitation of natural resources.

The layered identification of the past in the present is central for the analysis of the diverse socioenvironmental formulations of the Greenbelt politics. The biodiversity of the conifer-dominated Belt is hardly comparable to the one of tropical rainforests but it is, instead, based on wide seasonal and geomorphologic landscape changes. Topographic details, ancient trees and old-growth backwoods as well as the numerous rivers, lakes and peatlands exist as archives of the natural-cultural past, both in scientific and lay terms. The progression of the timber frontier has offered new sources of livelihood for the Belt communities, both indigenous and colonial, but it has also eroded the older traditions, especially those of the Sámi people and reindeer herders. The everyday land and lifescapes of the Belt have in this way become hot spots of forest conservation, underlining biodiversity losses and disappearing wilderness values.

The emergence of the hot spots serves as a sign of the growing emphasis on the interrelatedness of the geohistorical, ethno-cultural and industrial layers of the lifeworlds of the Belt. The Belt forests can be grouped as biodiversity reserves or carbon sinks but they can also be defended as home lands for the Sámi and other local inhabitants. They also appear as economic forests for loggers and mill communities, and as tree plantations or, in extreme cases, examples of idle capital in the eyes of professional investors. In order to be justified today, any one of these images, however, has to be placed in the broader networking of forest-related interests. The northern conifer realm of the Belt is comprised of complex combinations of the historical and current socioenvironmental projections, and they become concrete within the intersections of contested endeavors. It is especially here, at the level of the particular, that we can work out the contested rankings of the overlapping projections.

The above indicates that the local-global formation of the Greenbelt is identified here with the help of geohistorical scaling, concretely surfacing as part of the multilayered co-governing of such issues as socio-environmental heritage, indigenous and local land rights, and resource control. The empirical analysis of (i) local development paths serve as an example of sociospatial variations in relation to (ii) country-specific solutions, both Finnish and Russian, which in turn are described as historical contexts within and whereupon (iii) the processes of globalization have developed as new phases of socioenvironmental activity. These scales and phases are, however, seen as integrally characterized by strong interdependencies between and across these dominating spatiotemporal scales and marked by rapidly evolving discursive contents.

Tracing the Postcolonial Changes: Spatial Zooming

The postcolonial approach in the case studies takes the shape of social criticism of the dominating state-centered and federal transformations of the frontier conditions between Russia and Finland (European Union). This becomes evident already in the preliminary spatial zooming: the Greenbelt is an anomaly in between two jurisdictionally and culturally different territorial organizations. The dividing line runs through the Belt and the boundary awareness composes the communities, both local and translocal.

Researching an anomaly demands hybrid instruments that can identify and register the low signals of the marginalized groups from the shadows of the dominating discourses. The case studies in this volume therefore take the shape of episodic and multiperspective analyses of the local-global development paths of the Belt communities and processes. The approach guides toward identifying intersections of Belt initiatives and projections, varying case by case. The case studies together produce a polyvocal picture of the Greenbelt politics. The voices of forest owners, nature conservationists, local and state authorities, entrepreneurs and companies, lay people, cultural workers and artists as well as minority folks are documented and interpreted in connection with their daily practices. The portraits of the border communities finally function as steps in the prismatic documentation of the Belt dynamics, stretched in between signs of domination, oppression, *vanmakt* (submission), ambiguity, difference, unevenness and senses of (in)justice. The episodes of the excursion serve as proof of the development potentials not corresponding with the unifying geopolitical macrohistories of the border.

The case studies aim at explicating how marginality and submission are produced as byproducts of the cross-border co-governance and how the macro-scale divisions of labor turn into strange mixtures of confrontation and cooperation at the border. North Karelia in Finland and the Republic of Karelia in Russia share the historical interface experiences but they have grown into indelible elements of two different geopolitical realms. The common history thus primarily divides. The Sámi in Upper Lapland have, on the other hand, been officially recognized as the only indigenous people within the EU, but the Finnish government has been unable to solve the question of ethnic land rights. Behind the land solution there exists a broader issue of compensation in the face of the injustices of the colonial past.

Both North Karelia and Upper Lapland have for centuries served as a mirror to the southern cultures of expansion and domination, and this past has today grown into a deep (post)colonial dependency. The Belt peripheries with their wilderness parks have become the frontiers where the urbanized world seeks for refreshment and silence. The marginal lands function as central therapeutic resources for the contemporary nomads of the centers.[65] The hybrid constitution of the Belt—central resources in frontier locations—will be illustrated in detail in the following case analyses. The episodic pictures grow into interpretations of power relations across the political and cultural borders and within the border communities, both local and translocal. The spatial zooming of the Greenbelt is accompanied by analyses of ethnic and intergenerational tensions, the emphasis varying according to the respective local-global framing. Multilingual issues are emphasized throughout the case studies as examples of the flexibility of the local communities under the turmoil of geopolitical changes.

The case studies cover both the geopolitical macrogeometrics and microgeometrics of the Belt. The former scope (global-local view) is reached by analyzing the main trends of forest-industrial reorganization in Finland and Russia (chapters 7 and 12), whereas the rest of the chapters identify the Greenbelt merely as a local construction (local-global view). The latter perspective helps us to identify the critical views and alternatives to the dominating translocal trends. It guides the examination of the various reactions of local communities in defending their identity, origin and sources of livelihood under the pressure of homogenization.

Studying Multilingualism: Paratactic Translations

The practical co-mingling of the micro and macrogeometrics of the Greenbelt politics requires interdiscursive and postconstructionist re-reading of the Belt proposals and decisions, including the diverse local-global reactions to them. The Greenbelt initiatives have mostly been introduced from a distance, far away from the local communities of the border. The Belt is thus a macrogeometric construction launched from the centers of Northern Europe. Consequently, from within the local communities at the border, the Belt exists both as a threat (a limit to local activities) and an option (new source of livelihood and identity). The setting underlines the fluid relations between those benefiting from the Belt decisions and those suffering from them. The decisions tend to rank individuals and communities according to their location and flexibility in the communicative networks. The Belt is an international border and an ecological corridor and these facts profoundly shape the everyday lifeworld of the border. The Greenbelt is thus a question of identity politics: the relationship between us and them, and who benefit and suffer, is continuously in contest—and therefore the fate of those in between is easily ignored.

Language skills and communicative practices are natural and necessary elements for human identity construction and community-building.[66] The border conditions of the Belt are a particular case in this respect as several territorial lingual regimes overlap the local lifeworlds. Finnish, Karelian, Russian, Sámi and Scandinavian languages and dialects meet at the border communities and the main cultural divide runs in between Finno-Ugric and Indo-European languages (Fig. 3.1). The former is spoken by the more local and indigenous groups of Northern Scandinavia and Northwest Russia, such as the Sámi, the Finns, the Karelians, the Komi, the Mansi and the Samoyeds.[67] The main dividing line becomes manifested not only in daily difficulties in coping with strange words but also in coping with strange worlds. In addition to hardships in practical communication, the overcoming of the lingual borders means always a reflection upon the distance between two radically differing systems of signification; Finno-Ugric and Indo-European. This means the worlds not only look different across the lingual border but they in fact are different.

The most local and indigenous of the ethnic communities of the Belt have for geopolitical and historical reasons found it necessary to learn several neighboring languages, and it is for example not rare to meet in Upper Lapland true polyglots able to communicate through the whole spectrum of local-global languages, ranging from several Sámi languages (out of the total of nine) to their Scandinavian and Finnish counterparts and sometimes covering also Russian. English is also currently a necessity for many, and it is due to the needs of tourism entrepreneurship. Rather paradoxically, again, the polyglot communities from

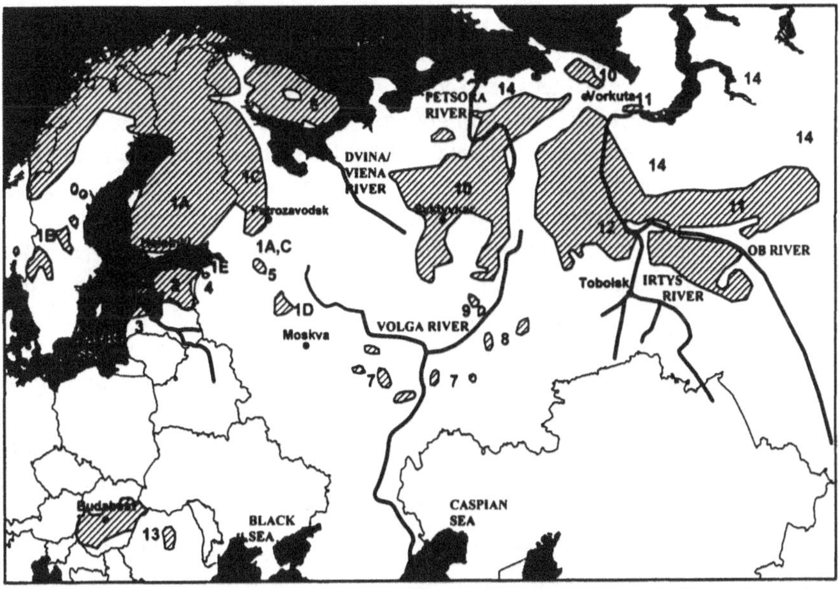

Fig. 3.1. Finno-Ugric peoples in Northern Europe. The shaded areas indicate the territories settled by a Finno-Ugric population speaking some of the Uralic languages. The total number of Uralic speakers is approximately 24 million, consisting mostly of Hungarians (15 million), Finns (5 million) and Estonians (1 million). The rest of the Uralic languages are endangered minority languages with a serious risk of disappearing. The numbers on the map refer to the following lingual groups (with the estimated number of speakers): 1A: Finns (5 million), 1B. Forest Finns in Sweden (*skogsfinnar*, since the 16th century, currently assimilated in the majority culture, 1C. Karelians (63,000), 1D. Tver Karelians (15,000 with an ethnic background, spoken only in a few villages), 1E. Ingrians (300), 2. Estonians (1 million), 3. Livonians (<20), 4. Vod (<20), 5. Veps (6,000), 6. Sámi (32,000), 7. Mordvinians (800,000), 8. Mari (Cheremissians, 500,000), 9. Udmurtians (Votyaks, 500,000), 10. Komi (Zyrians and Permyaks, 400,000), 11. Khanty (Ostyaks, 14,000), 12. Mansi (Voguls, 3,000), 13. Hungarians (15 million), 14. Samoyeds (Nenets, Nganasan, Enets and Selkup groups, 29,000).[68]

the extreme geopolitical margins look at the surrounding worlds from a multilingual "top position;" they are able to compare the surrounding power regimes and cultural cosmologies from various complementary angles (see chapter 13).

The multilingual configuration of the Belt is, however, not something fixed or unchanging. The polyglot skills are continuously challenged by the same geopolitical and national ambitions of which they were initially forged. The historical dynamics of the Belt is concrete in the variations of local and generational dialects as well as in multiethnic mixtures. The geopolitical changes in regime formations have also resulted in violent transformations and compromises in the border communities in the form of forced and voluntary evacuations and resettlements. The regime changes have consequently had a deep impact on the practices of domination, both in terms of governance and in the formulation of expertise. The tension between authorized and lay forms of communication has remained in the practical core of the Belt politics; the historical mechanisms of this tension are examined throughout the case studies. Particular attention is cast on the expert languages of the conservationists and protagonists of the Greenbelt.

This volume argues that the local-global conditions of the Greenbelt cannot be understood satisfactorily without paying attention to the multilingual dynamics of the Belt communities as anomalies or hybrids that are co-produced, and constantly also co-challenged, by the historical changes in the surrounding regimes of authority and expertise. Paratactic translations and interlingual compromises are taken in the case studies as signs and symbols through which to identify the politico-ideological content of the Belt. The act of naming (of things/processes) is thus seen here as a political move, and it incites proactions and reactions, or approvals and denials. Naming refers both to proposing and actuating an order. Depending on the perspective, for example, nature conservationists are named both as defenders and robbers of the North, and similar labels are used to characterize the industrial developers. The labels invite others to join this or that side but they also suggest changes or confirmations in the dominant socioenvironmental order.

The case studies apply and develop an approach that focuses first on the political proposals and orders aiming at producing a dominating socioenvironmental order. Political proposals and orders are identified here as purified representations guarded and controlled by those communities that launch and develop them. The practical coalescence of these purified representations is thereafter examined in the sphere of societal practices, by studying the continuous contamination, compromises and re-purification of the guarded representations. This spiraling analysis finally reveals, case by case, the conditions and rules of the endless co-forging of the Greenbelt order. The argument goes that only by identifying the purified presentations, and the communities that cultivate and control them, can we find socioenvironmental sense in the actual interdiscursive copresence of multilingual communication across cultural borders. The multitude, that is: the spectrum of critical reactions to the dominating order of the Belt,[69] can only be identified by paying attention to the cultivation and control mechanisms that keep the purification of conceptions, and the communities they bound together, in function, despite the contaminations constantly threatening them in the sphere of biopolitical practices.

The case studies focus on different sides of the purification versus contamination and together they produce a detailed analysis of the Greenbelt politics.

Three processes of discursive dominance are examined. First, the case studies document the arguments put forward by nature conservationists. The Greenbelt is primarily a political construction that aims at protecting the last remaining old-growth forests at the border zone. This motive is indelibly linked to the long tradition of park conservation that roots from the idea of indigenous nature to be protected from human modification. All the case studies examine from various angles the formulation of the arguments for protecting the original natural areas of the Greenbelt and the way the other stakeholders of the Belt have responded to these proposals.

Second, the border circumstances are seen here as offering a comparative setting where two radically different models of forest utilization have been developed. Both the Russian and the Finnish forest professionals have developed their own effective forest model that has gained a guarded position within their respective jurisdictions. The diverging development of the two forest orders stands as proof of the existence of the contest among the control mechanisms guarding the models against from critical contamination. The Russian model, rooting from the Soviet era, divides forests into three different classes that then gain various statuses, ranging from conservation to clear-cutting (without reforestation), whereas the Finnish, or Nordic, model emphasizes reforestation with standardized management routines. The idea of purified nature emerges in both cases through a prior method of classifying and utilizing forests. Purification finally results in exemplary forest stands that fulfill the official requirements. The case studies offer detailed pictures of forest management variations starting from comparations of state forestry in Finland (North Karelia and Upper Lapland, chapters 6 and 11) and state forestry in Russia (Viena and Pjaozersk, chapters 8 and 9), and further extending to variations of the attitudes from the side of private forestry in Finland (North Karelia and Kuusamo, chapters 6 and 10).

Third, the case studies also document those notions of pure nature that serve as means of contestation in local-global place-marketing. Unpolluted nature of the North has for long been used as a tourist attraction, and the long history of marketing campaigns has resulted in strange co-constructions of imaginary sceneries that have been widely promoted also by the locals. The purified presentations have in a way successfully questioned with the contamination of the daily hardships of the North.[70] The case studies on North Karelia, Kuusamo, Upper Lapland and the Barents Region uncover the representations of a clean North and contrast them with the practical socioenvironmental conditions of the Greenbelt. The Greenbelt is thus examined as a mask that hides the actual transformation of the socioenvironmental conditions,[71] forcing the Belt communities to adjust to the changes in the dominating practices as natural and unavoidable (see chapter 5). The case studies document for example the innovations that have been introduced and taken as inevitable outcomes of physical or societal dynamics in the local-global surroundings. The case studies scrutinize those pure explanations that support the dominant socioenvironmental order.

Coping with Biopolitical Co-governance

The case studies finally bring to the surface the biopolitical dimension of the Belt transformation. The contested projections of the Greenbelt are now seen as means for governing demographic development by transforming (the conditions of) the everyday land and lifescapes of the Belt communities. Both the changes in the physical surroundings of the communities and the changes in attitudes toward these changes are documented, and particular attention is paid to the practical coping strategies of the Belt communities themselves. The research question in general is: How deeply and thoroughly are the Belt innovations and projections (from a distance) settled down in the minds and thoughts of the border people and communities? The success of the projections is assessed by the degree of willingness and awareness with which the local communities have become integrated into the macrogeometrics of the Belt transformation. The research question can thus be expressed this way: How well have the communities, both local and translocal, been informed and how actively and selectively have they searched for information on the motives and consequences of the proposals they have received? All the case studies share the assumption that the self-organization of the Belt communities proceeds by selecting and prioritizing certain innovations and by simultaneously denying others (that seem to deviate from the reflected preferences). The mechanisms of selection and denial are most explicitly developed in the case of Kuusamo Forest Common (chapter 10), focusing on the symptoms of provincialism.

Three different modes of change in the practices of selection are in general followed in the case studies, namely spatio-technical, aesthetic-qualitative and metaphoric changes.[72] The analysis of (i) spatio-technical improvement starts with a critical view on the operational changes introduced and adopted as tools for strengthening the local-global participation in the renewal of socioenvironmental governance. In Kuusamo, for example, the timber frontier turned into a Greenbelt in a rather short period of time, through confrontations, and the change was possible due to quick local adaptation of new techniques of bioprospecting, offered by the Finnish government. Nature at the border could now be saved by selling it,[73] and the episode had a direct impact on the later formulations concerning the trade with the values of nature (*luonnonarvokauppa* in Finnish). The reorientation in Kuusamo was a symptom of a broader paradigmatic change in socioenvironmentalism, and the case study describes the crucial role of the pioneers who first learned the way how to benefit from the practical changes in their operational settings. The local-global pioneers are seen here as those actors that make the innovations concrete by reshaping and thus re-directing them, to be then applied by others.

The broadening of the means of bioprospecting is indelibly connected to the general strengthening of trade and marketing options in socioenvironmentalism. The (ii) rise of aesthetic and qualitative values in the production chains has highlighted ecological values as promoters of place and identity and as certificates of sustainability. Nature is today one of the central branding elements of tourism and trade in Northern Europe[74] and the Greenbelt is one of these new brands in the North. Some border locations have in this development turned into hot spots of greening in tourism entrepreneurship and among the consumers of Belt products. The ethical and ecological "footprints" of the paper consumed in the urban concentrations of Europe have for example become targets of contested steering and this has had a profound impact on the patterns of production, trade and consumption in the forest industry. In the context of the European Union, the interests of the indigenous Sámi groups and the fate of *Urwälder* are particular threshold questions that increasingly modify the operational space of the forest industry in the North. Each of the proceeding chapters documents the multilayered comingling of material and discursive values in Greenbelt politics from complementary angles. Particular attention is paid to the changes caused by the aesthetization and culturalization of trade conditions, which concretely means qualitative examination of the role of institutional co-dependencies, cultural identities and social power of the Belt actors and processes.[75]

Finally, the (iii) metaphoric changes of the Greenbelt are identified in the Belt studies by documenting the signs of re-articulation of community identities linked to deeper layers of cultural mapping of the North. The Belt is for example a key metaphor of this research and it helps us to value the border forests as an ecological corridor. This is, of course, ecologically and politically problematic, keeping in mind the fragmented character of the border forests realistically worth conservation. The Belt initiative has reanimated several of the historical signposts of cultural orienteering at the border, mobilized for ideological and political purposes in the cross-border contacts. It is argued in this volume that the cultural dynamics of the Belt, and border, can only be understood by recognizing the key constituents of "othering" in community-building, ranging from expressions for the risks of nature to a variety of fear elements cast over those others, beyond the border dividing us and the rest.

The metaphoric excursion through the Belt forests starts with an introductory narration of the bear, or *karhu*, in Finnish geopolitical and socioenvironmental orienteering. The bear has been through centuries a central liminal figure, clothed by a variety of euphemisms, in Finnish and Finno-Ugric cultural identifications and bearings. It is loaded with a mixture of respect and fear. The almost human guardian of the northern forests is for many also a merciless beast of the wildernesses. In this volume, the bear is seen as a partial "explanation" to locally popular attitudes against Belt conservation. The Belt is feared to become a territory of the beast, a home area for a terrorist from nature learning to live close to human settlement and regularly visiting the border villages. The Belt also reminds the Finns of the close relationship to their eastern neighbor, the Bear of Russia (chapter 4).

The Greenbelt excursion is thereafter continued by a textual analysis of the dominating characterizations of Finnish mires as marginal, but also central, landscapes of fear (chapter 5). Mires represent those elements of northern land and lifescapes that symbolize the passive and non-communicative features of communities and individuals. The Scandinavian *vanmakt* is an expression for a submissive character but in Finnish, perhaps tellingly, no clear equivalent is to be found.

The metaphoric role of Siberia in the border politics of Russia is further studied in the context of Viena Karelia and Pjaozersk. Chapters 8 and 9 summarize the local consequences of the administrative ranking of civil servants in Russia according to the distance from the capital city. The Siberia nearest to Moscow has within this framework been identified as the marginal settlements of the Karelian Republic, close to the border of Finland. The chapters also deal with the Russian attitudes toward the West, emerging for example in the distinctions between domestic and foreign firms operating in the Belt business world.

The metaphoric Belt excursion is thereafter completed by picturing the North as the most intimate companion in the everyday geographies of the local communities. The North is now seen as a destiny. It is both a limiting and enabling factor, and a source of inspiration, but it also carries the notion of the Edge, the gate to the other side of earthly existence. The Northwind is in this view the voice to be listened to and respected. It carries in many pre-Christian belief traditions the messages from the late ancestors but it also brings bad weather. You need to learn to identify the early warning of the rising Northwind to survive in the wilderness. The metaphoric excursion is finally completed by analyzing the presence of the South among the Sámi in Upper Lapland. This study explicates the political repertoire through which the southern interest has become justified in the Sámi homeland.

The comparisons of spatial metaphors bound to the Belt can also be seen as the grounding methodological solution for the entire volume. The question is about continuities: the continuity of the Greenbelt is threatened by industrial activities considered as guarantees of the continuity of the border settlements, and the collision of interests takes place by mobilizing and applying the deep-rooted continuums of identity construction, namely the discursive tools of symbolic communities. The analysis of the Belt is, in other words, practically stretched along the continuities between the political margins and centers, among relatives and strangers, across non-human and human realms, and within local and global endeavors.

A Local-global Greenbelt

The Greenbelt is a political projection launched in the early 1990s by nature conservationists and the Ministries of the Environment in Finland and Russian Karelia. As a result of this kind of semi-official setting, and due to the socioeconomic reorganization in Russia, the Belt cooperation was initially motivated by worries about the fate of the border forests in the Republic of Karelia.[76] Karelia has been since then the main target, and challenge, for the Belt proponents, even though the border forests of Murmansk and Leningrad Oblasts and eastern Finland have also become integrated into the process. Thus the Greenbelt of Karelia gradually grew into the Fennoscandian Greenbelt.[77] This re-naming is, however, loaded by geopolitical connotations rooting back to the scientific mapping of the natural extension of Finland in the East during the World War II years.[78] In the background there is a long history of border disputes between Sweden-Finland and Russia-Soviet Union (Fig. 3.2). The main hot spots of the Belt are located on the Russian side of the border and the first public introductions of the Belt took place in January 1994 in a joint meeting between Russian Karelian and Finnish environmental authorities.[79] The launch was cooperative, and should have been taken as a clear signal to limit any forms of Fennoscandinavianism in the Belt politics. The case studies on Viena and Pjaozersk examine in detail the "goods and bads" of Western pressure in the border politics of Russia.

The Belt connects, according to the conservationists, the continental Russian taiga to the more oceanic boreal forests of Fennoscandia. The fragmented islands of protected forests on the Finnish and Norwegian side[80] of the border are fueled by species migration from the "genetic mainland" in the east.[81] The Belt, extending over a thousand kilometers from the Gulf of Finland up to the Barents Sea, also bridges several vegetation zones within the north-south axis. The conservationists value this as an important biogeographical characteristic, forming a natural corridor for the species to adjust to the ongoing global climatic changes.

The Belt is in general valued as a zone that has never been exploited by large-scale forestry. This is due to the fact that the border forests have throughout the historical times remained in the margins of settlement pressure in Northern Europe. The "iron curtain" of the Cold War also secured the zone from logging operations and some of the westernmost villages in the Soviet Union were moreover emptied or, in Russian terminology, liquidated. These evacuations lessened the already minimal human pressure on the surrounding nature. The natural(ized) history of the Russian side of the Belt has left the species and ecosystems, such as old-growth forests and peatlands, on their own, only to be later found and identified as remnants largely disappeared from the well-managed forests of Fennoscandia.

The Greenbelt is concretely made of several nature conservation areas, or proposed areas, interconnected by forests that constitute the narrow military zone

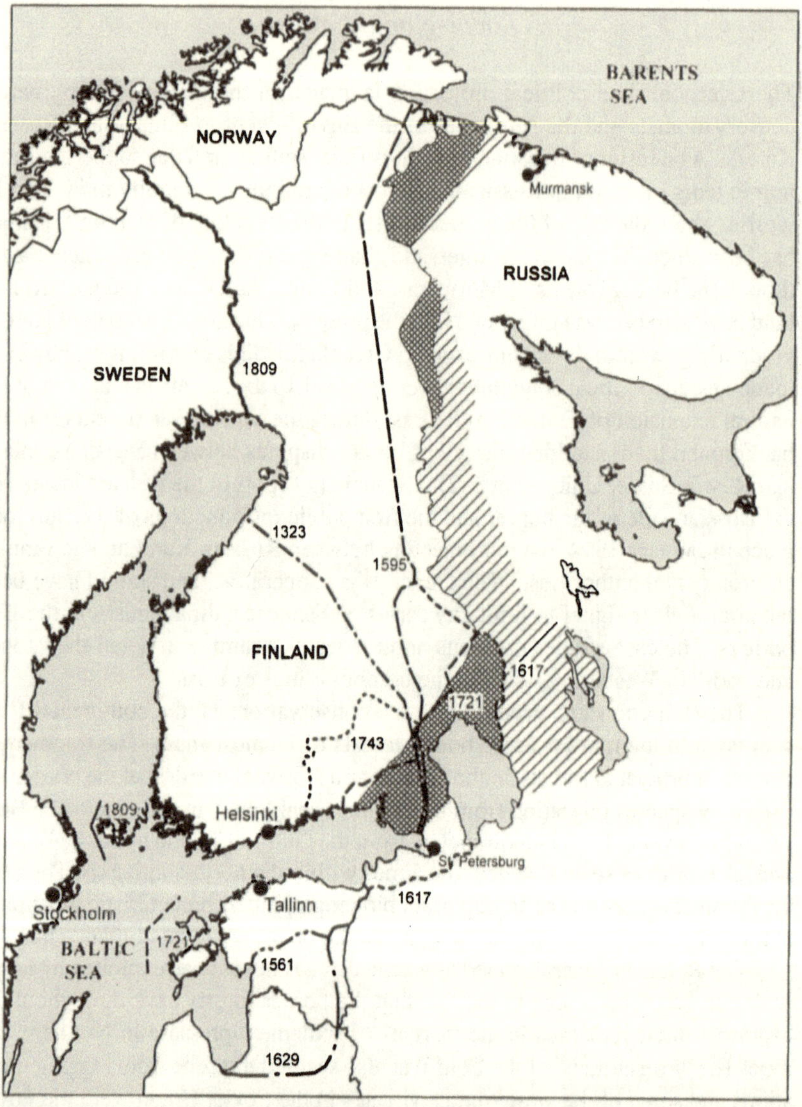

Fig. 3.2. The historical interface between Sweden-Finland and Russia. Swedish expansion eastward started in the late 16th century and resulted during the 17th in complete governing of the northern shores of the Baltic Sea. Russian counter-expansion westward took place in the 18th century, integrating both Estonia (1721) and Finland (1809) under the Russian rule. Contemporary state borders form the background of the map. The Finnish areas ceded to the Soviet Union in 1944 are marked with dark shade whereas the lighter shade refers to the areas occupied by Finnish troops in 1941–1944. Estonia was an independent republic in 1918–1939 and since 1991 again.[82]

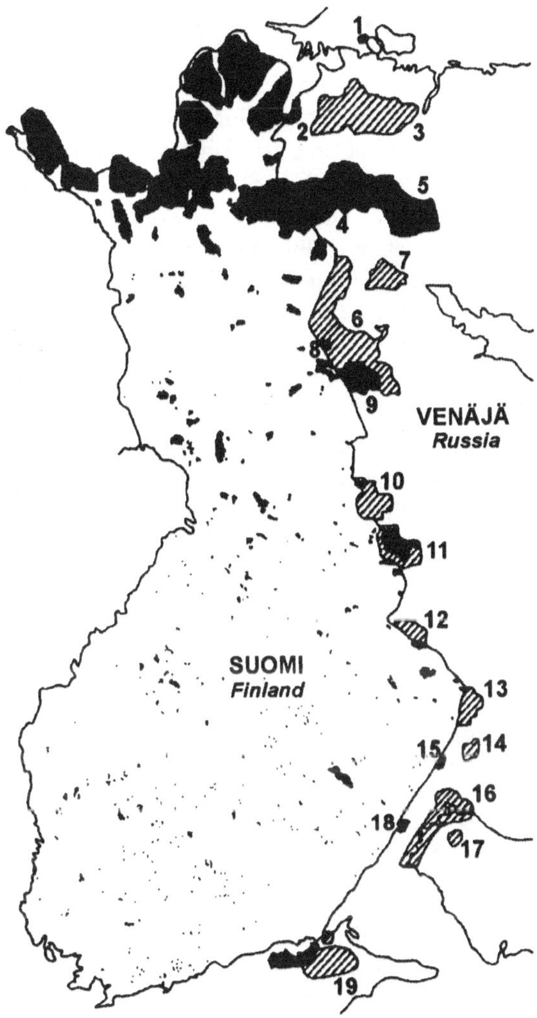

Fig. 3.3. The Greenbelt of the Finnish-Russian border. The dark shaded area refers to strict nature conservation, such as nature parks (*zapovednikii* or *zap.*) and national parks (*kansallispuistot* or *kp.*), while the gray color refers to looser conservation, namely wilderness regions and game reserves (*zakasnikii* or *zak.*). The areas marked with lines indicate the parts of the Belt under planning. 1. Ainovski Islands (zap.), 2. Pasvik (*kp.*), 3. Alla-Akkajärvi (*zak.*), 4. Laplandsky Les (*zap.*), 5. Laplandsky Zap. 6. Tenniejoki-Kutsa (*zak.*), 7. Kanda (*zak.*), 8. Näätätunturi (*zak.*), 9. Paanajärvi (*kp.*), 10. Kalevala (*kp.*), 11. Kostomukshsku Zap., 12. Tuulijärvi (*kp.*), 13. Koitajoki (*kp.*), 14. Tolvajärvi (*kp.*), 15. Rillinkisuo (*zak.*), 16. Ladoga Archipelago (*kp.*), 17. Valamo (monastery island), 18. Iso-Iijärvi (*zak.*), 19. the Gulf of Finland (*kp.*).[83]

between the states. The Belt extends beyond the immediate border forests both eastward and westward, and it finally functions as a Russian-Fennoscandian link to the global Greenbelt of the conifer-dominated taiga.[84]

Locally, at the border zone between Finland and Russia, the most debated hot spots of nature conservation have been concentrated around a few cases that in Russia are (listed from the North): Laplandskii Les, Paanajärvi, Kalevala and Kostomuksha parks, Koitajoki and Tuulijärvi areas, the northern shores of Lake Ladoga and the Karelian Isthmus (Fig. 3.3). The most debated episodes on the Finnish side have been focused on the wilderness forests in Kessi, Kuusamo, Kainuu and North Karelia (Fig. 4.2). The following case studies cover several of these hot spots. The aim of this volume is, however, not to concentrate only on nature or forest conservation but also to locate the conservation issues into the broader local-global setting of sosioenvironmental challenges in Northern Europe and at the conifer-dominated North. The selected hot spots are analyzed within this framework and several wider societal issues of Finno-Ugric, Russian and Western European origin are also examined.

Notes

1. The first of the two cultural turns in geography was characterized in general by a remark that cultural phenomena are thoroughly spatial. Cultural-spatial practices are within this view central in understanding how the socially produced becomes natural. The second turn forced geographers to reconsider the subjective interpretations and embodied practices of the everyday. Both turns were crucial in the further specification of the interrelations between the local and the global in geographical thinking. See Henri Lefebvre, *The Production of Space* (Oxford: Blackwell, 1991), the original in French: *La production de l'espace* (Paris: Anthropos, 1986); Benno Werlen, *Society, Action and Space. An Alternative Human Geography* (London: Routledge, 2003); Samu Pehkonen, "Kaivoksen geografia. Ympäristö ja nostalgiset yhteisökuvaukset," in *Maantiede, tila, luontopolitiikka. Johdatus yhteiskunnalliseen ympäristötutkimukseen*, ed. Ari Aukusti Lehtinen (Joensuu: Joensuu University Press, 2005), 161-91.

2. Denis Gosgrove, *Social Formation and Symbolic Landscape* (London: Croom Helm, 1984); Kenneth Robert Olwig, *Nature's Ideological Landscape* (London: George Allen & Unwin, 1984); Neil Smith, *Uneven Development* (Oxford: Basil Blackwell, 1984); John Rennie Short, *Imagined Country. Environment, Culture and Society* (London: Routledge, 1991); Anne Buttimer, ed., "A Special Issue on Cultural Variations in Concepts of Nature," *Geojournal*, no. 2 (1992), 99-172; David Harvey, *Justice, Nature and the Geography of Difference* (Oxford: Blackwell, 1996).

3. *Samhällsgeografi*, literally societal geography (*samhällsgeografi* in Swedish, *samfunnsgeografi* in Norwegian, *samfundsgeografi* in Danish, *yhteiskuntamaantiede* in Finnish), refers here to Nordic critical human geography launched during the 1970s in connection with the radical leftist orientation among the students and younger university teachers.

The Nordic contacts have been further developed in the Symposiums for Critical Human Geography, and by publishing the journal *Nordisk Samhällsgeografisk Tidsksrift.* On the other hand, *kulturgeografi* covers a broader spectrum of approaches within Nordic geography, initially constituted as the part of geography that studies the human impact on the landscape—distinguished from physical geography, or *naturgeografi,* largely concentrating on the (paleo)ecological or geomorphological origin and structure of the landscape.

4. Ari Aukusti Lehtinen, "Oren geografi och dess samhällspraxis," *Nordisk Samhällsgeografisk Tidskrift,* no. 12 (1990), 73-74; Helena Nynäs, "Hur är det möjligt att ha monopol på kritik?," *Nordisk Samhällsgeografisk Tidskrift,* no. 12 (1990), 72-73; Inger Birkeland, "Nature and the 'Cultural Turn' in Human Geography," *Norsk Geografisk Tidsskrift,* no. 52 (1998), 229-40.

5. Bruno Latour, *Science in Action* (Cambridge, Ma.: Harvard University Press, 1987), 223.

6. Smith, *Uneven Development*; Derek Gregory, *Geographical Imaginations* (Oxford: Blackwell, 1994), 5; Jouni Häkli, "Discourse in the Production of Political Space: Decolonizing the Symbolism of Provinces in Finland," *Political Geography* 17 (1997), 340; Petri Hottola, *The Intercultural Body* (Joensuu: University of Joensuu, Department of Geography Publications, no. 7, 1999), 4-5.

7. Michael Lynch, *Scientific Practice and Ordinary Action. Ethnomethodology and Social Studies of Science* (Cambridge: Cambridge University Press, 1993), 107-13; Juha Kotilainen, Globaali luonto tarua vai totta? (Joensuu: University of Joensuu, Department of Geography, 1997), 95, Phil.Lic. Dissertation, mimeo.

8. Donna Haraway, *Simians, Cyborgs, and Women* (London: Free Association Books, 1991); Anne Buttimer, *Geography and the Human Spirit* (Baltimore: The Johns Hopkins University Press, 1993); Eeva K. Berglund, *Knowing Nature, Knowing Science. An Ethnography of Local Environmental Activism* (Cambridge: White Horse Press, 1997); Yi-fu Tuan, *Escapism* (Baltimore: The Johns Hopkins University Press, 1998); Lawrence D. Berg, "Cultural Politics and the Local(e)," *Nordisk Samhällsgeografisk Tidskrift,* no. 28 (1999), 3-22.

9. See some early formulations of critical human geography in the Nordic countries: Kenneth Robert Olwig (1980), "Historical Geography and the Society/Nature 'Problematic': The Perspective of J.F. Schouw, G.P. Marsh and E. Reclús," *Journal of Historical Geography* 6 (1980), 29-45; John Jensen and Kirsten Simonsen, "The Local State, Planning and Social Movements," *Acta Sociologica* 24, no. 4 (1981), 279-91; Anssi Paasi, "Den regionala identiteten och det samhälleliga medvetandet," *Nordisk Samhällsgeografisk Tidskrift,* no. 1 (1984), 47-53; Perttu Vartiainen, *Maantieteen konstituoitumisesta ihmistieteenä* (Joensuu: University of Joensuu, Publications of Social Sciences, no. 3, 1984); Bjørn Terje Asheim, *The History of Geographical Thought in Scandinavia* (Oslo: University of Oslo, Department of Geography, Meddelser fra Geografisk Institutt, Ny Kulturgeografisk Serie, no. 15, 1985); Gunnar Olsson, "Om planeringens paradoxer," *Nordisk Samhällsgeografisk Tidskrift,* no. 2 (1985), 3-9; Perttu Vartiainen, "Om 'det geografiska' i samhällsteorin," *Nordisk Samhällgeografisk Tidskrift,* no. 3 (1986), 3-16; Perttu Vartiainen, "Kritisk samhällsgeografi i Västtyskland—om Eisels och Becks kontext och produktion," in *Den senindustriella utvecklingen och den regionala problematiken i Norden,* eds. Perttu Vartiainen, Bo Forsström and Seija Virkkala (Helsinki: Publikationer av Föreningen för Planeringsgeografi, no. 24), 13-22; Perttu Vartiainen, "The Strategy of

Territorial Integration in Regional Development: Defining Territoriality," *Geoforum* 18 (1987), 117-26; Kirsten Simonsen, "Postmodernisme og kritisk geografi," *Nordisk Samhällsgeografisk Tidskrift*, no. 8 (1988), 7-13; Kirsten Simonsen, "Postmodernisme og kvindegeografi." *Nordisk Samhällsgeografisk Tidskrift*, no. 13 (1991), 44-52; Ann-Cathrine Åquist, "Om patriarkatteorin—en o-modern betraktelse," *Nordisk Samhällsgeografisk Tidskrift*, no. 10 (1989), 37-48; Jørgen Ole Bærenholdt, Kirsten Simonsen, Ole Beier Sørensen and Peter Vogelius, "Lifemodes and Social Practice," *Nordisk Samhällsgeografisk Tidskrift*, no. 11 (1990), 72-86; Pauli Tapani Karjalainen and Perttu Vartiainen, "Dwelling in Geography: Joensuu," *Nordisk Samhällsgeografisk Tidskrift*, no. 11 (1990), 98-105. See also a Danish view on Nordic human geography in-between social theory and cultural studies and at the interstices of Anglo-American and Continental European intellectual movements in Kirsten Simonsen, "On Being 'In-between': Social and Cultural Geography in Denmark," *Social and Cultural Geography* 4, no. 2 (2003), 255-68.

10. See for example Bue Nielsen, "Naturens betydning for territorialstrukturens udvikling," *Fagligt Forum—Kulturgeografiske Hæfter*, no. 9 (1976), 68-78; Mogens Buch-Hansen and Bue Nielsen, "Marxist Geography and the Concept of Territorial Structure," *Antipode* 9 (1977), 35-44; Perttu Vartiainen, "Maantieteilijän 'luonnosta' ja ns. luonnonmaantieteestä," *Terra* 91, no. 4 (1979), 240-48; Björn Axelsson, Sune Berger and Jon Hogdal, *Vikmanshyttan: Lära för framtida bruk. En bok om studiearbete, frigörelser och Stora Kopparberg* (Arlöv: Prisma, 1982); Olwig, *Nature's Ideological Landscape*; Jørgen Ole Bærenholdt, "Livsformer og natursammenhaenge i kritisk geografi," *Nordisk Samhällsgeografisk Tidskrift*, no. 9 (1989), 15-25; Frank Hansen, "Nature in Geography," *Nordisk Samhällsgeografisk Tidskrift*, no. 11 (1990), 87-97; Michael Jones, "The Elusive Reality of Landscape," *Norsk Geografisk Tidsskrift* 45, 229-44; Perttu Vartiainen and Heikki Vesajoki, "Ekologisen maantieteen haasteista," in *Saimaalta Kolille. Karjalan tutkimuslaitos 1971-1991*, eds. Pekka Hakamies, Väinö Jääskeläinen and Ilkka Savijärvi (Joensuu: University of Joensuu, Karelian Institute, 1991), 169-95; Helena Nynäs, Ekokommuner som motkultur i Norge. Uppfattningar om naturen och lokalsamhället (Oslo: University of Oslo, Department of Human Geography, 1994), Master's thesis, mimeo; Jürgen Ossenbrügge, *Umweltsrisiko und Raumentwicklung* (Berlin: Springer-Verlag, 1993); Gabriel Bladh, *Finnskogens landskap och människor under fyra sekler* (Karlstad: University of Karlstad, Reseach Reports, no. 11, 1995); Kenneth Robert Olwig, "Recovering the Substantive Nature of Landscape," *Annals of the Association of American Geographers* 86, no. 4 (1996), 630-53; Rolf Lidskog, "Teknologiska katastrofer i det senmoderna samhället," *Nordisk Samhällsgeografisk Tidskrift*, no. 27 (1998), 29-50; Jarmo Kortelainen, "The River as an Actor-network and River Systems, " *Geoforum*, no. 30 (1999), 235-247; Kirsten Simonsen, "The Body as Battlefield," *Transactions of the Institute of British Geographers, New Series* 25, no.1 (2000), 7-9; Mia Vepsäläinen, "Environmental Image of the Industrial Town—Image Asprirations of Town Authorities and Industrial Companies in Varkaus during the 20th Century," *Nordisk Sammhällsgeografisk Tidskrift* 30 (2000), 75-92; Tom Mels, "Nature, Home, and Scenery: The Official Spatialities of Swedish National Parks," *Environment and Planning D: Society and Space* 20 (2002), 135-54: Kenneth Robert Olwig, *Landscape, Nature and the Body Politic* (Madison, Wi.: The University of Wisconsin Press, 2002).

11. Olwig, *Nature's Ideological Landscape*; Olwig, "Recovering the Substantial Idea of Landscape"; Olwig, *Landscape, Nature and the Body Politic;* Tina Hansen and Keld Buciek, "Landskabet som samfundsmæssig forestilling," *Nordisk Samhällsgeografisk Tidskrift, no* 31 (2000), 59-76; Bærenholdt, "Livsformer og natursammenhænge i kritisk geografi;" Jørgen Ole Bærenholdt, *Bygdeliv* (Roskilde: Roskilde University Center, Department of Geography, Social Analysis and Computer Sciences, Research Report, no. 78, 1991).
12. Jones, "The Elusive Reality of Landscape;" Gunhild Setten, *Bonden og landskapet. Historier om natursyn, praksis og moral i det jærske landskapet* (Trondheim: University of Trondheim/NTNU, Department of Geography, 2002).
13. Inger Birkeland, "The Feminine Hotel and the Man-made Cultural Landscape," *Nordisk Samhällsgeografisk Tidskrift,* no. 19 (1994), 64-74; Bjørnar Sæther, "Environmental Improvements in the Norwegian Pulp and Paper Industry. From Place and Government to Space and Market," *Norsk Geografisk Tidsskrift,* no. 52 (1998), 181-94; Inger Birkeland, "The Mytho-poetic in Northern Travel," in *Leisure/Tourism Geographies. Practices and Geographical Knowledge*, ed. David Crouch (London: Routledge, 1999), 17-33; Bjørnar Sæther, *Regulering og innovasjon: miljoarbeid i norsk treforedlingsindustri 1974–1998* (Oslo: University of Oslo, Doctoral Dissertation in the Department of Sociology and Human Geography, 1999).
14. Torsten Hägerstrand, "The Two Vistas," *Geografiska Annaler* 86 B (2004), 315-23; Peter de Souza, *Territorial Production Complexes in the Soviet Union—with Special Focus on Siberia* (Gothenburg: University of Gothenburg, Department of Geography Publications, no. B 80, 1989); Jan Lundqvist, "Trade and Regulations of Pesticide Usage. Some Observations Regarding the Third World Situation," in *The Environment and Free Trade*, eds. Anders Hjort af Ornäs and Jan Lundqvist (Uppsala: University of Uppsala, Research Programme on Environmental Policy and Society/EPOS, 1994), 85-94; Klas Sandell, "Outdoor Recreation—Re-creation or Recreation?" *Nordisk Samhällsgeografisk Tidskrift,* no. 14, 35-46; Anne Buttimer, Stefan Anderberg, Tom Andersson, Klas Sandell and Sverker Sörlin, "Woodland polyphony," in *Society and the Environment: A Swedish Research Perspective*, ed., Uno Svedin and Britt Hägerhäll Aniansson (Dordrecht: Kluwer, 1992), 177-98; Erik Westholm, *Mark, människor och moderna skiftesreformer i Dalarna* (Uppsala: University of Uppsala, Geografiska Regionstudier, no. 25, 1992); Per Olof Hallin, "Miljökris och gröna handlingstilar," *Nordisk Samhällsgeografisk Tidskrift,* no. 17 (1993), 14-22; Bladh, *Finnskogens landskap och människor under fyra sekler*; Michael Sjöberg, "Writing the Edge: Revisiting the Margins of Spatial Restructuring," *Nordisk Samhällsgeografisk Tidskrift,* no. 20 (1995), 75-87; Anders L. Sandberg and Sverker Sörlin, eds., *Sustainability the Challenge. People, Power and the Environment* (Montréal: Black Rose Books, 1998); Sofus Christiansen, Peter Hagget and Perttu Vartiainen, *Swedish Research in Human Geography* (Uppsala: Swedish Council for Research in the Humanities and Social Sciences, 1999); Berit K. Svanqvist, "Naturumänge ur ett individperspektiv," *Nordisk Samhällsgeografisk Tidskrift,* no. 31 (2000), 37-57; Mels, "Nature, Home, and Scenery."
15. Sverker Sörlin, *Framtidslandet. Debatten om Norrland och naturrersurserna under det industriella genombrottet* (Stockholm: Carlsson, 1988); Anders Hjort af Ornäs and Sverre Lodgaard, eds., *The Environment and International Security* (Uppsala: Uppsala University, Research Programme on Environmental Policy and Society/EPOS, 1992); Sverker Sörlin, "The Articulation of Territory: Landscape and the Constitution of Region-

al and National Identity," *Norsk Geografisk Tidsskrift*, no. 53 (1999), 103-12; Anders Hjort af Ornäs, ed., *Approaching Nature from Local Communities. Security Perceived and Achieved* (Linköping: University of Linköping, Environmental Policy and Society/ EPOS, 1996); TiiRiitta Granfelt, ed., *Managing the Globalized Environment* (London: Intermediate Technology Publications, 1999).

16. Väinö Tanner (1881–1948), J.G. Granö (1882–1956) and Ilmari Hustich (1911–1982) carried out influential anthropogeographical studies that in their own way questioned the position of Finnish geography exclusively among the natural sciences. Tanner (see e.g. Väinö Tanner, "Antropogeografiska studier inom Petsamo-området I. Skoltlapparna," *Fennia*, 49, 1929, 1-518) was interested in the indigenous ethnocultural naming of places and land forms as a method for deeper understanding of symbolic and aesthetic landscapes, whereas Granö (*Pure Geography*, Baltimore: The Johns Hopkins University Press, 1997; published initially in 1929 in Germany under the title *Reine Geographie* and in 1930 in Finnish as *Puhdas maantiede*) looked for the perceptional categories of landscapes through the spectrum of all the five senses. Hustich (the editor of "A Special Issue on Man's Influence on Nature in Finland," *Fennia* 85, 1960) in turn studied the regularities and particularities of culture-nature as part of the societal dynamics. See further debate on the early history of human geography in Finland: Anssi Paasi, "Subjektiivisen elementin merkityksestä J.G. Granön maantieteellisessä ajattelussa," *Terra* 94, no. 2 (1982), 140-56; Ilmo Massa, "Problem of the Development of the North between the Wars: Some Reflections of Väinö Tanner's Human Geography," *Fennia* 162, no. 2 (1984), 201-215; Ari Aukusti Lehtinen, "Northern Natures. A Study of the Forest Question Emerging within the Timber-line Conflict in Finland," *Fennia* 169, no. 1 (1991), 58-77; Paulo Susiluoto, "Two Skolt Geographies of Petsamo during the 1920s and 1930s," in *Encountering the North*, eds. Frank Möller and Samu Pehkonen (Aldershot: Ashgate, 2003), 75-102. According to Paulo Susiluoto, Väinö Tanner can be regarded as the first of the Finnish geographers in the genre of human geography, see Paulo Susiluoto, "Suomen ajan ihmismaantiedettä Petsamosta," in *Väinö Tanner. Ihmismaantieteellisiä tutkimuksia Petsamon seudulta*, ed. Paulo Susiluoto (Helsinki: Suomalaisen Kirjallisuuden Seura/Finnish Literature Society, 2000), 9-31.

17. Vartiainen, "Maantieteilijän 'luonnosta' ja ns. luonnonmaantieteestä;" Vartiainen, *Maantieteen konstituoitumisesta ihmistieteenä*; Anssi Paasi, "Subjektiivisen elementin merkityksestä J.G. Granön maantieteellisessä ajattelussa;" Anssi Paasi, "The Institutionalization of Regions. Theory and Comparative Case Studies," *Fennia* 164 (1986), 105-46; Pauli Tapani Karjalainen, *Geodiversity as a Lived World. On the Geography of Existence*, (Joensuu: University of Joensuu, Publications in Social Sciences, no. 7, 1986).

18. Jussi Raumolin, "Global Scene, Natural Resources and Development Problems in the Periphery Country Finland: Some Reflections on Ilmari Hustich's World View," *Fennia* 159, no. 1 (1981), 15-23; Ilmo Massa, "Problem of the Development of the North between the Wars;" Ari Aukusti Lehtinen, *Regionalismin ja ekokehityksen yhteys aluepoliittisessa murroksessa. Esimerkkinä Mikkelin ekolääni* (Helsinki: Publications of the Association for Planning Geography, no. 28 (1987); Lehtinen, "Northern Natures."

19. Perttu Vartiainen, "(Kritisk) Samhällsgeografi i Finland?," *Nordisk Samhällsgeografisk Tidskrift*, no. 7 (1988), 25-33.

20. Hottola, *The Intercultural Body,* 188-222; Samu Pehkonen, *"Tänne, muttei pidemmälle!" Alta-kamppailu ja Pohjois-Norjan monikulttuurinen maisema* (Tampere: Tampere Peace Research Institute, Research Reports, no. 88, 1999); Ari Aukusti Lehtinen, "Modernization and the Concept of Nature: On the Reproduction of Environmental Stereotypes," in *Encountering the Past in Nature*, eds. Timo Myllyntaus and Mikko Saikku (Athens: Ohio University Press, 1999), 29-48; Frank Möller and Samu Pehkonen, eds., *Encountering the North. Cultural Geography, International Relations and the Northern Landscape* (Aldershot: Ashgate, 2003); Juha Kotilainen, "Between the Global and the Local in Environmental Politics," *Nordisk Samhällsgeografisk Tidskrift,* no. 23 (1996), 61-68; Mikko Kumpulainen, *Maan ja talouden välissä. Viisi kertomusta suomalaisen luontosuhteen muutoksesta* (Joensuu: University of Joensuu, Department of Geography Publications, no. 5, 1999); Teijo Rytteri, "Metsäteollisuuden yhteiskunnallinen vastuu," *Alue ja ympäristö* 29, no. 1 (2000), 5-17; Minna Tanskanen, *Näkyvän takana. Tutkimus metsäojitetun suomaiseman kulttuurisuudesta* (Joensuu: University of Joensuu, Department of Geography Publications, no. 8, 2000); Tiina Silvasti and Tuija Mononen, "Ruoka liikkeessä," *Yhteiskuntapolitiikka* 66, no. 1 (2001), 43-51; Kortelainen, "The River as an Actor-network and River Systems;" Ari Aukusti Lehtinen, "Mires as Mirrors. Peatlands—Hybrid Landscapes of the North," *Fennia* 178, no. 1 (2000), 125-137; Marko Karvinen, "The Interpretation of Sea in Urban Planning in Helsinki," *Nordisk Samhällsgeografisk Tidskrift,* no. 20 (1995), 131-39; Jaana Nevalainen; "Ikuisesta kesästä talvikaupunkiin—vuodenajat suomalaisessa kaupunkiympäristössä," *Alue ja Ympäristö* 24, no. 2 (1995), 6-14; Jouni Häkli, "Culture and Politics of Nature in the City," *Capitalism, Nature, Socialism* 7, no. 2 (1996), 125-38; Jarmo Kortelainen, ed., *Vihertyvä kaupunkiseutu. Suunnittelun ja hallinnan ekomoderni käänne* (Jyväskylä: SoPhi, 2000); Vepsäläinen, "Environmental Image of the Industrial Town;" Anne Virtanen, *Tilasta paikkaan, estetiikasta ekologiaan. Maantieteellisiä tulkintoja eletystä kaupungista* (Turku: Annales Universitatis Turkuensis, no. C 155, 2000): Ari Aukusti Lehtinen, ed., *Maantiede, tila, luontopolitiikka. Johdatus yhteiskunnalliseen ympäristötutkimukseen* (Joensuu: Joensuu University Press, 2005).

21. Yrjö Haila and Richard Levins, *Humanity and Nature* (London: Pluto Press, 1992); Yrjö Haila and Lassi Heininen, "Ecology: A New Discipline for Disciplining?," *Social Text* 42 (1995), 153-171; Eeva K. Berglund, *Lost in the Woods? Competing Knowledges in Finland's Forest Debates* (Berkeley: University of California, College of Natural Resources, Discussion Papers, 1997); Eeva K. Berglund, *Knowing Nature, Knowing Science. An Ethnography of Local Environmental Activism* (Cambridge: White Horse Press, 1997); Pertti Rannikko, "From Functional to Symbolic Local Community: A Case Study of a Forest Village in Eastern Finland," *Research in Community Sociology* 7, 223-46; Pertti Rannikko, "Combining Social and Ecological Sustainablity in the Nordic Forest Periphery," *Sociologia Ruralis* 39, no. 3 (1999), 394-410; Pertti Rannikko, "Forest Work as the Cause of Settlement and Depopulation in the Remote Parts of Finland," in *The Green Kingdom. Finland's Forest Cluster*, eds. Aarne Reunala and Ilpo Tikkanen (Helsinki: Metsämiesten Säätiö, 1999), 222-26.

22. Sven-Erik Åström, *Natur och byte. Ekologiska synpunkter på Finlands ekonomiska historia* (Ekenäs: Söderströms, 1978); Kenneth Robert Olwig, "Eurooppalaisen kansakunnan pohjoinen luonne," in *Vapauden lähde. Pohjolan merkitys Euroopalle*, ed. Svenolof

Karlsson (Helsinki: Valtion Painatuskeskus/Vapk, 1992), 158-82; Bladh, *Finnskogens landskap och människor under fyra sekler.*
23. Bjørn Terje Asheim, "Social Geography—Welfare State Ideology or Critical Social Science?," *Geoforum* 10, no. 1 (1979), 5-18; Vartiainen, "Maantieteilijän 'luonnosta' ja ns. luonnonmaantieteestä;" Kirsten Simonsen, Henrik Toft Jensen and Frank Hansen, *Lokalsamfund og sociale bevægelser* (Roskilde: Roskilde University Center, Kritisk Samfundsgeografi II, 1982).
24. Kirsten Simonsen, "What Kind of Space in What Kind of Social Theory?," *Progress in Human Geography* 20, no. 4 (1996), 494-512; Simonsen, "The Body as Battlefield," *Transactions of the Institute of the British Geographers, New Series* 25, no. 1 (2000), 7-9; Sakari Hänninen and Jouko Karjalainen, eds., *Biovallan kysymyksiä* (Helsinki: Gaudeamus, 1997); Michel Foucault, *Seksuaalisuuden historia* (Helsinki: Gaudeamus, 1998), originally published under the title *Histoire de la sexualité* I-III (Paris: Gallimard, 1976-1984); Sakari Hänninen, ed., *Displacement of Politics* (Jyväskylä: SoPhi, 1998); Yrjö Haila, "Ekologiasta politiikkaan: kurinpitoa vai solidaarisuutta?," *Tiede ja Edistys* 25, no. 2 (2000), 81-96; Rauno Sairinen, *Regulatory Reform of Finnish Environmental Policy* (Helsinki: Helsinki University of Technology, Centre for Urban and Regional Studies Publications, no. A 27, 2000); Ari Aukusti Lehtinen, *Maantiede, tila, luontopolitiikka* (Joensuu: Joensuu University Press), 24-32.
25. Susan Cutter, "Race, Class and Environmental Justice," *Progress in Human Geography* 19, no. 1 (1996), 111-122; Harvey, *Justice, Nature and the Geography of Difference*; Anders L. Sandberg and Sverker Sörlin, eds. *Sustainability the Challenge. People, Power and the Environment* (Montréal: Black Rose Books, 1998); Ari Aukusti Lehtinen, "Ympäristönkäytön oikeudenmukaisuus—haaste maantieteelliselle tutkimukselle," *Terra* 111, no. 4 (1999), 209-12.
26. Paul Rabinow, "Kaupunkitilan säätely," in *Kaupunki, tila, valta*, eds. Michel Foucault and Paul Rabinow (Tampere: Tampere University of Technology, Department of Community Planning Publications, no. 16, 1989); Foucault, *Sexuaalisuuden historia*, 70-71.
27. Thomas Mathiesen, *Makt och motmakt* (Gothenburg: Korpen, 1982); Pehkonen, *"Tänne, muttei pidemmälle!"*; Sarah Lloyd, *The Emergent Forest Landscape in Sweden: A Case Study of Relationships between Socio-economic and Ecological Space in Jokkmokk* (Uppsala: Swedish University of Agricultural Sciences, Department of Rural Development Studies, Master's Thesis, no. 13, 2001); Jarmo Kortelainen, "Forest Regimes as Heterogeneous Networks: Polarization of the Russian Forest Industry," in *Politics of Forests. Northern Forest-industrial Regimes in the Age of Globalization*, eds. Ari Aukusti Lehtinen, Jakob Donner-Amnell and Bjørnar Sæther (Aldershot: Ashgate, 2004), 107-32,
28. Steen Folke, "First Thoughts on the Geography of Imperialism," *Antipode* 5, no. 3 (1973), 16-20; David Harvey, *Social Justice and the City* (London: Edward Arnold, 1973); Mogens Buch-Hansen, Hans Folke, Steen Folke, Jette Gottlieb, Frank Hansen, Anna Marie Hellmers, Poul Kroijer and Bue Nielsen, *Om geografi* (Copenhagen: Hans Reitzel, 1976).
29. Kenneth Robert Olwig, "The Childhood 'Deconstruction' of Nature and the Construction of 'Natural' Housing Environments for Children," *Scandinavian Housing and Planning Research* no. 3 (1986), 129-43; Kirsten Simonsen, "Postmodernisme og kritisk geografi," *Nordisk Samhällsgeografisk Tidskrift*, no. 8 (1988), 7-13; Bærenholdt, "Livsformer og natursammenhaenge i kritisk geografi;" Ari Aukusti Lehtinen, "Lokalsamhället och skogsgränskonflikten," *Nordisk Samhällsgeografisk Tidskrift*, no. 1 (1990), 40-51.

30. Ari Aukusti Lehtinen, "Kulttuuristuminen yhteiskuntatutkimuksessa: ihmisläheisyyttä vai todellisuuspakoa?," in *Maantieteen maisemissa*, ed. Pauli Tapani Karjalainen (Joensuu: University of Joensuu, Human Geography and Planning, Occasional Papers, no. 25, 1993), 73-82; Jouni Häkli, "Territoriality and the Rise of Modern State," *Fennia* 172, no. 1 (1994), 1-82; Jouni Häkli, "Discourse in the Production of Political Space," *Political Geography* 17 (1997), 331-63; Kotilainen, "Between the Global and the Local in Environmental Politics;" Jørgen Ole Bærenholdt, "Regioner er politiske rum—også for geografer," *Nordisk Samhällsgeografisk Tidskrift*, no. 26 (1998), 3-21; Hottola, *The Intercultural Body*, 179-221.

31. Herbert Marcuse, *Eros and Civilization* (Boston: Beacon Press, 1966); Max Horkheimer and Theodor W. Adorno, *Upplysningens dialektik* (Gothenburg: Röda Bokförlaget, 1981). The original: *Dialektik der Aufklärung* (New York: Social Studies Association, 1944).

32. Juha Siltala, *Valkoisen äidin pojat* (Helsinki: Otava, 1999), 9-28. See also the debate by Nordic human geographers: Häkli, "Discourse in the Production of Political Space," 340-341; Birkeland, "Mytho-poetic in Northern travel."

33. Kaisa Pennanen, *Ihminen ja maa. Eric Dardellin maantieteestä* (Joensuu: University of Joensuu, Department of Geography Publications, no. 2, 1997). Pennanen's book includes insightful translations and interpretations of the main themes of Eric Dardell's *L'homme et la terre. Nature de la réalité géographique* (Paris: C.T.H.S., 1952).

34. Kortelainen, "Forest Regimes as Heterogeneous Networks;" Yrjö Haila and Chuck Dyke, eds. *How Nature Speaks: The Dynamics of the Human Ecological Condition* (Durham: Duke University Press, 2005).

35. Kotilainen, "Between the Global and the Local in Environmental Politics," 67.

36. Sandberg and Sörlin, *Sustainability the Challenge*; Markku Koivusalo, "Biopolitical Displacement and the Antinomies of Biopolitical Reason," in *Displacement of Politics*, eds. Sakari Hänninen and Jussi Vähämäki (Jyväskylä: SoPhi, 2000), 116-59; The biopolitical view applied here should not be confused with the conceptualization of biopolitics as a synonym for green or environmental politics, see for example David Goodman, "Agro-food Studies in the 'Age of Ecology': Nature, Corporeality, Bio-politics," *Sociologia Ruralis* 39, no. 1 (1999), 17-38. See also an insightful view on the micro- and macrogeometrics of globalization, Doreen Massey, "Geographies of Responsibility," *Geografiska Annaler* B 86, no. 1 (2004), 5-17.

37. Maria Fannin, Sarah Fort, Jeanine Marley, Joe Miller and Sarah Wright, "The Battle in Seattle: A Response from Local Geographers in the Midst of the WTO Ministerial Meetings," *Antipode* 32, no. 3 (2000), 215-21; Ville Lähde, "Viisi vuotta Muutoksen Kevättä," *Muutoksen Kevät* 20 (2001), 4.

38. Mari Manninen, "Kansalaisliikkeiden mielipidevalta on hyvin pienellä ydinjoukolla," *Helsingin Sanomat*, 1 April (2000), C1.

39. Cutter, "Race, Class and Environmental Justice;" Ari Aukusti Lehtinen and Pertti Rannikko, *Oikeudenmukaisuus ja ympäristö* (Helsinki: Gaudeamus, 2003).

40. Alf Hornborg, "Mi'kmak Environmentalism: Local Incentives and Global Projections," in *Sustainability the Challenge. People, Power and the Environment*, eds. Anders L. Sandberg and Sverker Sörlin (Montréal: Black Rose Books, 1998), 202-11; Kortelainen, "The river as an Actor-network and River Systems;" Raimo Lovio, "Yritykset, alueet ja ympäristöt—luonnolliset ja luodut ympäristökilpailutekijät," *Alue ja Ympäristö* 28, no. 1 (1999), 44-53; Sæther, *Regulering og innovasjon.*

41. Wolfgang Sachs, "Sustainable Development and the Crisis of Nature: On the Political Anatomy of an Oxymoron," in *Living with Nature*, eds. Frank Fischer and Maarten A. Hajer (Oxford: Oxford University Press, 1999), 28.
42. Raymond Williams, *Key words* (Glasgow: Fontana, 1979).
43. Anne Buttimer, "Circuits of Calories: Flows of Food and Energy in Germany, Ireland, the Netherlands and Sweden 1960–1990. *European Review* 4, no. 3 (1996), 193-214; Barbara Adam, *Timescapes of Modernity* (Routledge, London, 1998), 163-92.
44. Anne Buttimer, "Landscape and Life: Appropriate Scales for Sustainable Development," *Irish Geography* 31, no. 1 (1998), 1-33; Tiina Silvasti and Tuija Mononen, "Ruoka liikkeessä," *Yhteiskuntapolitiikka* 66, no. 1 (2001), 43-51.
45. Sæther, *Regulering og innovasjon*; Teijo Rytteri, *Metsäteollisuusyrityksen luonto. Tutkimus Enso-Gutzeitin ympäristö- ja yhteiskuntavastuusta* (Joensuu: University of Joensuu, Department of Geography Publications 10, 2000); Ari Aukusti Lehtinen, "Globalisation and the Finnish Forest Industry: On the Internationalization of Forest-industrial Operations," *Fennia* 179, no. 1-2 (2002), 237-50.
46. Laura Pulido, "A Critical Review of the Methodology of Environmental Racism Research," *Antipode* 28, no. 2 (1996), 122-42.
47. Douglas J. Porteous, "Topocide: The Annihilation of Place," in *Qualitative Methods in Human Geography*, eds. John Eyles and David M. Smith (London: Routledge, 1988), 75-93.
48. Piers Blaikie, Terry Cannon, Ian Davis and Ben Wisner, *At risk. Natural Hazards, People's Vulnerability, and Disasters* (London: Routledge, 1994).
49. Heikki Eskelinen and Mika Kautonen, "In the Shadow of the Dominant Cluster—The Case of Furniture Industry in Finland," in *Regional Specialisation and Local Environment—Learning and Competitiveness*, ed. Heikki Eskelinen (Copenhagen: NordREFO, 1997), 171-92; Pertti Rannikko, "Combining Social and Ecological Sustainablity in the Nordic Forest Periphery," *Sociologia Ruralis* 39, no. 3, (1999), 394-410.
50. Bladh, *Finnskogens landskap och människor under fyra sekler*; Hottola, *The Intercultural Body*; Hille Koskela, *Fear, Control & Space* (Helsinki: Publicationes Instituti Geographici Universitatis Helsingiensis, no. A 137, 1999); Inger Birkeland, *Stories from the North. Travel as Place-making in the Context of Modern Holiday Travel to North Cape, Norway* (Oslo: University of Oslo, Department of Sociology and Human Geography, Report, no. 2, 2002); Hille Koskela, "Urban Space in Plural: Elastic, Tamed, Suppressed," in *A Companion to Feminist Geography*, eds. Lise Nelson and Joni Seager (Oxford: Blackwell, 2005), 257-70.
51. Cutter, "Race, Class and Environmental Justice."
52. Samu Pehkonen, "Kaivoksen geografia. Ympäristö ja nostalgiset yhteisökuvaukset," in *Maantiede, tila, luontopolitiikka. Johdatus yhteiskunnalliseen ympäristötutkimukseen*, ed. Ari Aukusti Lehtinen (Helsinki: Gaudeamus, 2005), 161-91.
53. Giovanna Di Chiro, "Nature as Community," in *Uncommon ground*, ed. William Cronon (New York: Norton, 1996), 310. See also Giovanna Di Chiro, "Performing a 'Global Sense of Place': Women's Actions for Environmental Justice," in *A Companion to Feminist Geography*, eds. Lise Nelson and Joni Seager (Oxford: Blackwell, 2005), 496-515.
54. Kent C. Ryden, *Mapping the Invisible Landscape* (Iowa City: University of Iowa Press, 1993); Thomas Beckley, "Pluralism by Default: Community Power in a Paper Mill

Town," *Forest Science* 42, no. 1 (1995), 35-45; Anna-Lisa Lindén, "Values of Nature in Every-day Life," in *Sustainability the Challenge. People, Power and the Environment*, eds. Anders L. Sandberg and Sverker Sörlin (Montréal: Black Rose Books, 1998), 34-41; Sarah Lloyd, *The Emergent Forest Landscape in Sweden*.

55. Sörlin, *Framtidslandet*; Jones, "The Elusive Reality of Landscape;" Bladh, *Finnskogens landskap och människor under fyra sekler*; Petri Raivo, *Maiseman kulttuurinen transformaatio* (Oulu: Nordia Geographical Publications 25, no. 1, 1996); Olwig, "The Substantive Idea of Landscape;" Lauri Hautamäki, *Kylätoiminnan opas* (Jyväskylä: Gummerus, 1979); Sauli Rouhinen, "A New Social Movement in Search of New Foundations for the Development of the Countryside: The Finnish Action-oriented Village Study 76 and 1300 Village Committees," *Acta Sociologica* 24, no, 4 (1981), 265-78; Jukka Oksa and Pertti Rannikko, *Kylä yhteiskunnassa* (Joensuu: University of Joensuu, Publications of the Karelian Institute, no. 11, 1985); Seppo Knuuttila, Ilkka Liikanen, Pertti Rannikko, Hannu Itkonen, Merja Koistinen, Jukka Oksa and Sinikka Vakimo, *Kyläläiset, kansalaiset* (Joensuu: University of Joensuu, Publications of the Karelian Institute, no. 114, 1996).

56. Rannikko, "Combining Social and Ecological Sustainablity in the Nordic Forest Periphery".

57. Peter Hœg, *Frøken Smillas førnemmelse for sne* (Copenhagen: Munksgaard, 1992).

58. Karjalainen, *Geodiversity as a Lived World*; Pennanen, *Ihminen ja maa*.

59. Axelsson, Berger and Hogdal, *Vikmanshyttan*; Seppo Knuuttila, "Kansanomainen yhteisö ja avunanto," *Mielenterveys*, no. 1 (1980), 7-11; Seppo Knuuttila, "Kansanomaisen maailmankuvan ihanteita", in *Sukupolvien perintö 2. Talonpoikaiskulttuurin kasvu*, eds. Toivo Hakamäki, Heikki Kirkinen and Arno Rautavaara (Helsinki: Suomalaisen Kirjallisuuden Seura/Finnish Literature Society, 1985), 347-65; Seppo Knuuttila, *Kansanhuumorin mieli* (Helsinki: Suomalaisen Kirjallisuuden Seura/Finnish Literature Society, 1992).

60. Bladh, *Finnskogens landskap och människor under fyra sekler.*

61. Anthony Giddens, "Elämää traditionaalisessa yhteiskunnassa," in *Nykyajan jäljillä*, eds. Ulrich Beck, Anthony Giddens and Scott Lash (Tampere: Vastapaino, 1995), 83-152; See, however, a critical remark on post-traditionalism: Tommi Hoikkala, "Traditiosta vapaan valinnan illuusio," in *Elämänpolitikka*, eds. J. P. Roos and Tommi Hoikkala (Helsinki: Gaudeamus, 1998), 152-68.

62. Barbara Adam, *Timescapes of Modernity* (London: Routledge, 1998), 29-39; Jouni Häkli, "Culture and Politics of Nature in the City," *Capitalism, Nature, Socialism* 7, no. 2 (1996), 125-38.

63. Wolfgang Sachs, "Sustainable Development and the Crisis of Nature: On the Political Anatomy of an Oxymoron," in *Living with Nature*, ed. Frank Fischer and Maarten A. Hajer (Oxford: Oxford University Press, 1999), 23-41; Yrjö Haila, "The North as/and the Other: Ecology, Domination, Solidarity," in *Living with nature*, eds. Frank Fischer and Maarten A. Hajer (Oxford: Oxford University Press, 1999), 42-57.

64. Paul Routledge, "The Third Space of Critical Engagement," *Antipode* 28, no. 4 (1996), 399-419; Ian Maxey, "Beyond Boundaries? Activism, Academia, Reflexivity and Research," *Area* 31, no. 3 (1999), 199-208.

65. Ville Hallikainen, *The Finnish Wilderness Experience* (Rovaniemi: Finnish Forest Research Institute, Research Papers, no. 711, 1998), 198-218; Juha Ridanpää, "Postcolonialism in a Polar Region?," *Nordea* 27, no. 1 (1998), 75.

66. Stuart Hall, *Identiteetti* (Tampere: Vastapaino, 1999).
67. Fernand Braudel, *A History of Civilizations* (London: Penguin Books, 1993), 529-31; Kaisa Häkkinen, *Nykysuomen etymologinen sanakirja* (Helsinki: Wsoy, 2004), 6-16.
68. Pirkko Suihkonen, "The Uralic Languages," *Fennia* 180, nos. 1-2 (2002), 165-76: Häkkinen, *Nykysuomen etymologinen sanakirja;* Kalevi Wiik, *Suomalaisten juuret* (Jyväskylä: Atena, 2004).
69. Multitude refers here in general to civic struggles, both local and global, against centralized and authoritarian constructions of norms and sanctions. Multitude surfaces for example in the form of globalization critique toward the tightening governance of transnational corporations and agencies (see note 10 in chapter 1 in this volume) Michael Hardt and Antonio Negri connect in *Empire* (Cambridge, Ma.: Harvard University Press, 2000, xv-xvi) the Multitude to the geography of alternatives emerging from within the creative forces of democratization and emancipation. The particular application of the Multitude in this volume, however, covers primarily the local and marginal voices in the border peripheries of Northern Europe. This Multitude has no necessary contacts to the Multitude of global civic movements, underlined by Hardt and Negri but, instead, occasionally takes a position against the fluid networks of globalization activists.
70. Riikka Sorsa, "Paluu luontoon? Erämaapuistot matkakohteina ja luontosuhteen muokkaajina," in *Maantiede, tila, luontopolitiikka. Johdatus yhteiskunnalliseen ympäristötutkimukseen*, ed. Ari Aukusti Lehtinen (Joensuu: Joensuu University Press, 2005), 109-33; Kati Pitkänen, "Kesä Suomessa. Semioottinen tulkinta 2000-luvun järvimatkailumaisemasta," in *Maantiede, tila, luontopolitiikka. Johdatus yhteiskunnalliseen ympäristötutkimukseen*, ed. Ari Aukusti Lehtinen (Joensuu: Joensuu University Press, 2005), 135-60.
71. Don Mitchell, "Writing the Western: New Western History's Encounter with Landscape," *Ecumene* 5, no. 1 (1998), 21-?; Don Mitchell, *Cultural Geography. A Critical Introduction* (Oxford: Blackwell, 2000), 89-144.
72. Nigel Thrift, "Still Life in Nearly Present Time: The Object of Nature," *Body and Society* 6, no. 3, (2000), 34-57; Ari Aukusti Lehtinen, "Ympäristötutkimus kulttuurimaantieteessä," in *Maantiede, tila, luontopolitiikka. Johdatus yhteiskunnalliseen ympäristötutkimukseen*, ed. Ari Aukusti Lehtinen (Joensuu: Joensuu University Press, 2005), 11-34.
73. Kathleen McAfee, "Selling Nature to Save It?," *Society and Space* 17 (1999), 133-54; Noel Castree, "Bioprospecting: From Theory to Practice (and Back Again)," *Transactions of the Institute of British Geographers, New Series* 28 (2003), 35-55.
74. Pitkänen, "Kesä Suomessa. Semioottinen tulkinta 2000-luvun järvimatkailumaisemasta."
75. About the practical challenges of "doing" cultural economic geography, see Henry Wai-chung Yeung, "Practicing New Economic Geographies: A Methodological Examination," *Annals of the Association of American Geographers* 93, no. 2 (2003), 442-62.
76. Jarmo Pyykkö, "The Green Belt of Karelia at Risk," *Taiga News*, no. 10 (1994), 6-7.
77. Virpi Sahi, "Metsäinventoinnit käynnissä vihreällä vyöhykkeellä," *Metsätiedote,* no. 3 (Helsinki: World Wide Fund Finland, 1997), 3; Virpi Sahi, "Vihreän vyöhykkeen suojelua Venäjällä ja Suomessa," *Metsätiedote,* no. 1 (Helsinki: World Wide Fund Finland, 1999), 2.
78. Anssi Paasi, "The Rise and the Fall of Finnish Geopolitics," *Political Geography Quarterly* 9, no. 1 (January 1990), 53-65.
79. Jaakko Pihlaja, "Suomen ja Venäjän Karjalan rajalle ehdolla vihreä vyöhyke," *Helsingin Sanomat,* 13 January 1994, 13.

80. The western part of the river valley of Pasvik at the northern end of the Greenbelt is under Norwegian jurisdiction. The Övre Pasvik National Park in Norway, at the crossroads of Finnish, Norwegian and Russian borders, was linked to the wilderness debate in Upper Lapland in Finland in the late 1980s by those who argued for the conservation of the backwoods of Kessi on the Finnish side of the border; see Ari Aukusti Lehtinen, "Northern Natures," *Fennia* 169, no. 1 (1991), 110-42. See also chapter 11 in this volume.
81. Pyykkö, "The Green Belt of Karelia at Risk," 6.
82. Matti Klinge, *A Brief History of Finland* (Helsinki: Otava, 1981), 173-75; Paasi, "The Rise and the Fall of Finnish Geopolitics," 58; Wiik, *Suomalaisten juuret*, 351.
83. Olli-Pekka Tikkanen, "Karjalan vihreä vyöhyke," *Alue ja Ympäristö* 26, no. 1 (1997), 60-67; Ari Aukusti Lehtinen, "Globalization and the Finnish Forest Sector: On the Internationalization of Forest-industrial Operations," *Fennia* 180, no. 1-2 (2002), 237-50.
84. There are several Greenbelts, or Green Belts, in the world, the most famous being in Kenya, where it refers to the Green Belt Movement which has planted tens of millions of trees to limit the processes of desertification and erosion. Wangari Maathai, the initiator of the Movement, was granted the Nobel Peace Prize in Norway in 2004. On the other hand, the global circumboreal zone of conifer-dominated forests in the northern hemisphere can also be characterized as the Greenbelt of the North; see Ari Aukusti Lehtinen, Jakob Donner-Amnell and Bjørnar Sæther, eds., *Politics of Forests. Northern Forest-industrial Regimes in the Age of Globalization* (Aldershot: Ashgate, 2004), 19-20.

Part II. A Greenbelt Travelogue

4.

Layered Landscapes: Taming of the Land in the Finnish Northwoods

Late Wednesday evening, 17 June 1998, a highly dramatic event took place in Ruokolahti, a rural municipality in southeastern Finland. A man was killed by a wild bear, only two kilometers from his home. The bear with her one-year-old offspring had accidentally come across the unlucky man, an experienced outdoor hiker who was out for his usual evening jog. The marks on the trail told the searchers later that he, after having noticed the bear, had hurriedly turned around—only to be caught by her in a few seconds. The body was found later, in the early morning, close to the trail. The bear and her cub were located and shot by the police and frontier guards.

Before the drama, no recorded killing of a human being by a bear was known in the 20th century Finland. During the midsummer weeks and throughout the rainy summer of 1998, the whole of Finland discussed the danger imposed by the gradually growing number of bears learning to live close to settled areas. The widely-shared conclusion was that anyone who wants to go out in the forests to pick berries or mushrooms, or only to wander around in nature, has to keep in mind the risen risk of facing a bear. The number of wild bears had doubled in a decade and exceeded one thousand, which was much due to successful control of hunting. No more than about 100 bears were known in Finland in the early 1970s and the average had been even below that throughout the century. Only a few of the present bears have, however, turned into unnaturally fearless individuals letting the humans observe them.[1]

Bears and the debates on them have since the mid-1990s emerged in Finland regularly, every summer. A similar discussion took place for example in 1997, when a lonely female bear was observed in southwestern Finland wandering slowly, during two months, the distance of 200 kilometers from the capital city region to the town of Rauma on the western coast. Before her being shot by the police, the "city bear" had terrified the guests of a garden party in Vantaa, killed a lamb in Kirkkonummi and feasted upon honey in an apiary in Masku.

The debates fueled by these confrontations and the growing number of observations of bears in general have gradually strengthened the criticism of nature conservation in Finland. Bears are symbols of the wild nature of the conifer-dominated taiga[2] and their increased number in Finland are naturally connected to the recent extension of conservation of the old-growth forests in eastern and northern parts of the country. The bear also reminds the Finns, as most of the people of the taiga, of the days of the past when their ancestors lived under the constant pressure of the hostile backwoods nature, threatening their very existence as individuals and as a civilization.[3]

Recreational hunters have now, due to the incidents and the subsequent media attention, good reason to apply for more licenses to kill bears during the hunting season and whenever finding them close to human settlement. Enthusiasm is high in this respect and the moral support of the lay people is strong, regardless of the statistics expressing the actual dangers to human life in Finland. Several hundred Finns are, in comparison, killed in traffic accidents every year, for example 400-650 road deaths annually in the 1990s, but no strong voice has emerged against the growing number of cars. Moreover, even though traffic accidents with the semi-wild moose result in approximately ten human lives lost in Finland each year, no agreement on reducing the elk population has been reached.[4]

The background reasons for this concern with bears are examined in this chapter, first by discussing the historical-cultural mechanisms producing the present debate on wild nature and, second, by specifying the variations of wilderness appreciation and utilization in contemporary Finnish forests. An etymological and comparative conclusion is thereafter made by evaluating the specific cultural features of Finnish forest landscape in a Northern European context. The excursion into Finnish wilderness forests begins with an excerpt from a classic novel on Finnish backwoods struggles, the final scene from Ilmari Kianto's *Punainen viiva* (*The Red Line*).

The Lore of the Backwoods

Topi isäntä itse se oli, joka lehmäänsä paimentaen oli hakkaillut veräjäpuita metsän reunassa ja havahtunut vasta siihen, että aita oudosti rymähti ja Jysky haukkuen pakeni pihaan. Silmänräpäyksessä Topi silloin oli älynnyt tapahtuman ja nytpä hän kirves ojona ryntäsi karhua vastaan.
"Voi perrr...!"
Hirmuinen vihanpuuska oli miehen vallannut, ja hätä teki hänestä sankarin. Juuri kun peto saaliineen oli kapuamassa yli aidan, silloin kirveen isku osui sen rintaan. Mutta puolensa piti peto. Silmänräpäyksessä se irrotti kyntensä lehmästä ja hyökkäsi miehen päälle.
Ei ehtinyt Topi toista kertaa kirvestään kohottaa. Verta purskuten hän kaatua jymähti aidan taakse, ja kirves kirposi loitos kädestä. Toisella puolen aitaa virui kuolonkoriseva Ämmikki sorkat pystyssä.
Hätähuuto ja hälinä oli kuulunut ylös mökkiin: siunaillen, pahaa aavistaen, sydänalaansa painellen riensi sieltä Riika emäntä alas pellon kuvetta...
Silloin oli jo vertatihkuva karhu pakenemassa metsään. Koira ei sitä seurata uskaltanut, vaan ulvoi ja vapisi, häntä koipien välissä, saunan takana.
"Topi hoi, Topi...!"
Mutta ei Topi enää vastannut. Hän makasi hievahtamatta pälvellä, ja hänen kaulansa poikki valui veri—punaisena viivana.
Mökin pärepaikkaisen akkunaruudun takaa näkyivät tyttölapsen kalpeat, kauhistuneet kasvot.[5]

It was Topi himself, whilst tending his cow and cutting wood for gate posts at the edge of the forest, who had first been startled by the fence mysteriously crashing and Jysky, barking, fleeing back to the farmyard. In a flick of an eye, Topi had taken in the scene and charged at the bear with his axe raised.
"What the helll...!"
Terrible anger washed over him, and the emergency brought the hero forth. Just as the beast was climbing over the fence with its prey, the axe whacked it in the chest. But the beast defended itself. In an instant it released its claws from the cow and hurled itself over the man.
No time for Topi to raise his axe for the second time. Spurting blood, he fell behind the fence with a thump, and the axe flew from his hand. On the other side of the fence, Ämmikki in the throes of death lay with her hooves in the air.
The commotion and cry of anguish had been heard up at the cottage: Riika ran down along the side of the field, agonizing, fearing the worst, clutching at her heart...
The bleeding bear was by then vanishing into the forest. Jysky dared not follow but howled and trembled, tail between legs, behind the sauna.
"Topi, hoy, Topii...!"
But Topi did not answer. Unmoving, he lay where the snow had melted, and across his neck ran blood—in a red line.
Behind the shingle-mended windowpane could be seen the pale, terrified face of a girlchild. (Translated from Finnish by Sisko Porter)

Ilmari Kianto, the celebrated author of the deep backwoods of eastern Finland, draws in *Punainen viiva* a thrilling picture of the early 20th century frontier life in the Nordic East. Kianto paints for us a landscape of the "northern hungerland" striving for survival in the margins of civilization. For the generations after him, the book has functioned as a memory source, or a collective logbook of the experiences based on the permanent threats from the external world; both from the wildernesses enveloping the small islands of human settlement and, also, from the vast eastern continent neighboring the Finnish frontier culture. The bear of Kianto comes from the eastern wilderness, that is: from beyond the familiar Finnish world, and it symbolizes the hostile nature characteristic of forest life in the North. Without doubt, it also contained a hidden reference to the threatening expansive acts of the contemporary Russian panslavists, as symbolized by the Bear of Russia.[6]

The novel, finished as a manuscript in 1909, recalls the first experiences of democratic parliamentary elections in Finland in March 1907. A radical political reform had only recently been carried out, and it gave the unenfranchized classes the right to vote. Women were also included in the extended suffrage. A rather radical unicameral system of representation was adopted, where the whole parliament, not only the lower chamber, was to be elected by democratic elections. The reforms were remarkable, keeping in mind the geopolitical setting of Finland during the days when Finland was part of the Russian Empire, with a fragile status as an autonomous Grand Duchy.

Punainen viiva illustrates well the early beliefs of nature in Finland, rooted in traditions of forest life, but it also introduces the geopolitical and economic motives that had gradually been made concrete in the form of forest-based modernization and welfare. The book shapes the frames of the Finnish model; the specific way of coping with the North, and the way of building a welfare society on the historical demarcation zone between the East and the West.

The North completely surrounds human life in Kianto's hungerland. The severe winter is strongly present in the lifeworld of the northerners. The snow extends her fingers through the window panes. The kitchen shelves run short of rye flour already during early spring, only to be supplemented by pine bast. Topi Romppainen and his family struggle desperately toward another growing season. The severe climate of the North, together with the wild beast from the East, finally concludes the play. The fatalism of the marginal North stands in stark contrast to the early democratic practices boldly played at the municipal center during those days.

Kianto's message is clear. Life in the backwoods means hard and tireless work, immense efforts against the enemy with its superior force. Only by defending against the environing threats and only by taming the surrounding wilderness would human life and civilization be guaranteed. The experience of constant insecurity beyond the known world was countered by expansive modification of the lands within reach. The success in farm work during the short growing season was crucial, and the long winter could only be overcome by hunting. The old custom of killing bears in their winter nests was an important means of survival in the northern backwoods, especially toward the spring when daily nourishment was often critical. The hunter Martti Kitunen (1747–1833) has been the hero of the forest lore, with his record of 198 adult bears killed, joined by countless numbers of their cubs (Fig. 4.1).

Living in and off the forests meant organized hunting by the villages, extractive slash and burn cultivation and tar production and, later, modern industrial forestry. The Finnish success story, or the tale of those who were lucky enough to succeed, is based on the initial challenge of taming the forest, hence turning wilderness into a source of livelihood. The challenge has been supported by the authorities throughout centuries. Already in 1550 King Gustav I Vasa of Sweden[8] wrote about the necessity of colonizing the eastern backwoods: "The wilderness in Finland must be cleared and settled in order to augment the revenue due the Crown of Sweden." This aim was, of course, motivated by geopolitical interests of consolidating the frontier conditions of the East. Only later, during the 19th century, did the support of colonization turn into official fear of forest devastation by the peasants. Then, however, the concern was focused on exploitation of the woodlands close to the settled areas, not in the backwoods. The primeval backwoods, mostly untouched by human beings, have thus broadly functioned as a security issue both for families and the authorities and, in economic terms, they were to grow into a question of not fully utilized property.[9] The gradual loss of the old-growth forests has in other words been the outcome, and price, of the emergence and independence of Finland.

Forest Models and the Layers of Landscape

As argued above, the historical formation of Finland is thoroughly bound to the question of the success of living in and off the northern forests. Every generation has been forced to face this challenge, a realm of necessities caused by conditions in the northern backwoods. The Finnish forest landscape carries therefore plenty of signs of historical solutions of forest utilization, and it thus reflects in many ways the Finnish attitudes toward forest, land, and nature in general. This historical forest model is indelibly bound to human creativity aiming toward expanding control over the natural environment.[10]

The early forest model was developed as the driving force for the farmers settling down and clearing forests. Forest devastation was the only means of earning one's living in the backwoods. There was no alternative: the taming of the land was a question of life and death for the early invaders. Nature was a cause of both awe and threat for the pioneers. This had, of course, grown from the bitter experiences of the unforeseen and fierce nature. Severe climate was a constant threat, wild beasts were regular visitors to the grazing cattle, and frosty nights during the growing seasons resulted in dramatic years of famine. The uncleared forest, whence all the setbacks beyond human control originated, was a perpetual challenge for the peasants in the northern hungerland.[10]

The land reform, or the Great Land Enclosure (*Isojako*), during 1750–1950 gradually reorganized the traditional economy based on the clearing of forests for arable land. The common lands of the villages were divided and shared among the farms. Those who received large forest areas soon became the fortunate suppliers of industrial timber. The peasant way of coping with the land, originating from traditional agricultural practices, was expanded to cover the utilization of the privatized forests. The limits of intensive land use were cast far beyond the hunting grounds, and finally close to the extreme wilderness forests belonging to the Crown.[11]

A need for state-led forest management became soon apparent in the Grand Duchy of Finland. This was a direct response to the growing official concern about the devastation of the private forests by the peasants. The German model of intensive forest management was also introduced to state forests. The German guidelines faced criticism in Finland but slowly became accepted as they were understood to support the idea of expanding control and utilization of nature. Efficient forest management soon covered the whole country, occasionally reaching the most distant old-growth forests in the backwoods.[12]

Finland became integrated into international pulp and paper markets in the 20th century, and this put much pressure on domestic forest management and utilization. The conceptual tools for official forest management, both in private and state forests, became grounded on official national forest inventories and standardized methods of plantation forestry. The actual outcome was a compromise between the German influence, state interests and the traditional peasant practices. Forests became largely treated as agricultural land with the exception of a decades-long maturation of the yield. The national forest policy was built on an idea of full utilization, or maximized sustained-yield, which refers to an ideal situation where the annual level of cuttings extends to the level of the wood increment. No part of the annual gross increment of wood is in this view deliberately allowed to be lost to nature in the form of rotting timber.[13]

The criticism of the conservation of the last remaining old-growth forests at the timber frontier grew also from within the sustained-yield thinking. The economic effects of the conservation plans were estimated from the point of view of full utilization. The annual growth rates of wood in the planned conservation areas served as the key to the economic calculations. Nature conservation in the form of particular parks was regarded as a source of direct and indirect losses in the national economy. It was therefore easy to underline the negative results of this type of conservation, and exclude the positive options attached to it in the markets of sustainability.

The contemporary Finnish forest landscape thus broadly reflects the historical innovations and compromises in the contest for expanding control over the unmanaged and untamed nature. Rotting resources of the wilderness are repeatedly seen as threatening the welfare of the country. In this view, the deep and "overaged" forests symbolize backward conditions and economic decline which need to be eliminated by more efficient management measures—even at the risk of losing markets among the environmentally aware consumers in Western Europe.

Marginal Lands at the Center: Shade Forests

The above-said indicates that the expansion of control over forests is the "red line" of the Finnish past. The scenic formation of Finnish forests is a result of intensifying domination of the nature within reach, developed through generations and gradually becoming more and more motorized in character. It is therefore difficult to find a place in today's Finland without a strong visual message of apparent human domination. The debate over the last remaining old-growth forests becomes in this framework a contest over the control, and fate, of the last indigenous wildernesses forming a scenic connection or memory chain from the early human history to the present.

The remnants of the indigenous forests serve as memoirs of the historical landscapes where naturalness symbolizes wildness and external unpredictability, life at risk. The same forests also remind many Finns of the days of the past from which they wish to completely distance themselves. Earlier life in the backwoods is something to be forgotten, or at least to be reduced to a historical curiosity. On the other hand, the value of the old *erämaa* forests is connected to their qualitative uniqueness. Nowhere else has ecological and cultural continuity been preserved to the same degree as within these marginal areas that have never been subjected to intensive utilization. The interrelatedness of the ecological and cultural aspects is the reason why the perception of these areas as untouched wilderness has in general caused much trouble in Finnish forest policy. The indigenous in nature is a matter repeatedly inciting critical counter-reactions, and this is especially the case among those who value the extensive use of *erämaa* natures as an immemorial right.[14]

The debate in the 1990s about the extension of the old-growth forests clearly illustrated the difficulties in defining the indigenous in nature. A popular view among the forest professionals classified all forests with dominant trees reaching the average age of 120 years as old-growth forests. This definition includes all (over)aged forests with falling rates of annual wood increment and with delayed final cuttings. It is therefore correct to show that the coverage of old-growth forests, thus the share of aged forests, has more than doubled from the 1920s in the southern part of Finland. This means a rise from 0.7 percent up to 1.6 percent of the total area of forest land.[15] The qualitative difference between an aged economic forest and an authentic old-growth forest is, however, significant. The share of the latter covers only a few percent of the total area of aged forests. From a forest conservational perspective, it is in other words correct to say that the aged economic forests are ecologically poor because of the breaks in species continuity caused by the cuttings in the past and by subsequent forest management. From a biodiversity perspective, the economic forests of the 1920s were also much more valuable than the aged economic forests of today where the key biotopes have disappeared.[16]

Indigenous forests can in present-day Finland only be found in the margins of northeastern Finland, that is in Forest Lapland, Kainuu and North Karelia. These shade forests (*katvemetsät* in Finnish) have been saved from the historical effects of slash-and-burn cultivation, tar production and industrial forestry due to their extreme peripheral location. The areal extension of these shade forests is, above all, an ecological matter, or a biodiversity concern, but it is also a cultural challenge, a question about the admittance of the Finnish past, both in the form of individual experiences and collective identity constructions.

Despite the overall success of the standardizing sustained-yield model in Finnish forestry, the ecological and cultural organization of forest landscapes vary greatly in different parts of the country. The regional histories are different and the regional landscapes and identities vary accordingly. One of the dividing lines runs along the Suomenselkä, the back of Finland, which is the main bifurcation area for the natural waterways of the southeastern lake area and the northwestern "land of eleven rivers." A remarkable belt of old-growth forests exists within this dividing zone (Fig. 4.1).

The present landscape of the Finnish lake area is in broad terms a product of forest-industrial development utilizing the main drainage system and water courses. The territorial structure is originally based on the floating of logs, on the mobilization of the energy potentials of the rapids and on the market options at the seashore, and this history of land use still conditions landscape formation and the internal configuration of regional economic and political problems. The southern part of the lake area in the late 20th century coped with radical changes in the forest industry mostly caused by organizational merging, redevelopment and the automatization of the industrial units. Intensified public pollution control has also framed the modernization of the production processes. The northern part, as a regional resource periphery, has on the other hand suffered from low industrial refining, as well as from socioenvironmental limits to wood utilization, such as forest conservation and green image problems.

The northern part of the Finnish lake area carries the traces of slash-and-burn cultivation and industrial forestry. The forestry-based regional landscape turned, during the politicization of environmental concerns in the 1960s, into a battleground for logging corporations and forest conservationists. The economic recession of the early 1990s was brought to a head in the resource peripheries, and this made it easy for the logging interests to blame expanding forest conservation for the growing unemployment. The falling regional economic options in a way favored a more aggressive criticism toward conservation policy, which was regarded as oversized, turning forests into outdoor museums and, moreover, places for bears and wolves to increase in number. The insecurity caused by the perception of the external threat to the provincial economy, that is, environmentalism from the South, provided the basis for full-scale criticism of any conservation initiative.

The forest landscape north of the Maanselkä ridge, namely Northern Ostrobothnia, Kainuu and Kuusamo, is largely transformed by the historical effects of tar production and industrial forestry. The town of Oulu on the northern shore of the Gulf of Bothnia has for centuries functioned as a trade center for the developing regional economy. The details of the landscape connected to tar production are gradually disappearing, due to ecological succession and the expansion of the industrial timber frontier. The scenic remnants of tar production are, however, still important cultural contacts to the past, in the form of outdoor parks and museums where cultural-natural evolution is limited and as gradually vanishing memories of the layers of land-use history.

This historical setting fueled the arguments of the conflict on the old-growth forests in the 1990s, which especially focused on the last remaining shade forests behind the "tar woods". The debate was broadly organized around two contrasting visions of the backwoods: the view of the great logging frontier was challenged by a vision of an ecological Greenbelt along the Finnish-Russian border.

It had become common in the backwoods provinces to blame the environmentalists for the worsening local economic conditions. This state of affairs has been further fueled by the publicity about the regular visits of wild beasts of the wilderness, and thus about constant state of alertness under the pressure of uncontrolled nature. Criticism of proposed expansion of nature conservation became, however, reorganized after the Finnish membership in the European Union in 1995. The environmental strategies of the EU have aimed both at the unification of national conservation criteria (under the banner of the Natura 2000 Programme) and at setting limits to hunting practices. The bear is considered within the EU a species needing specific protection and this in turn has limited the number of licenses for killing bears. The backwoods experience is, therefore, quite understandably, in principal opposition to the EU regulation.

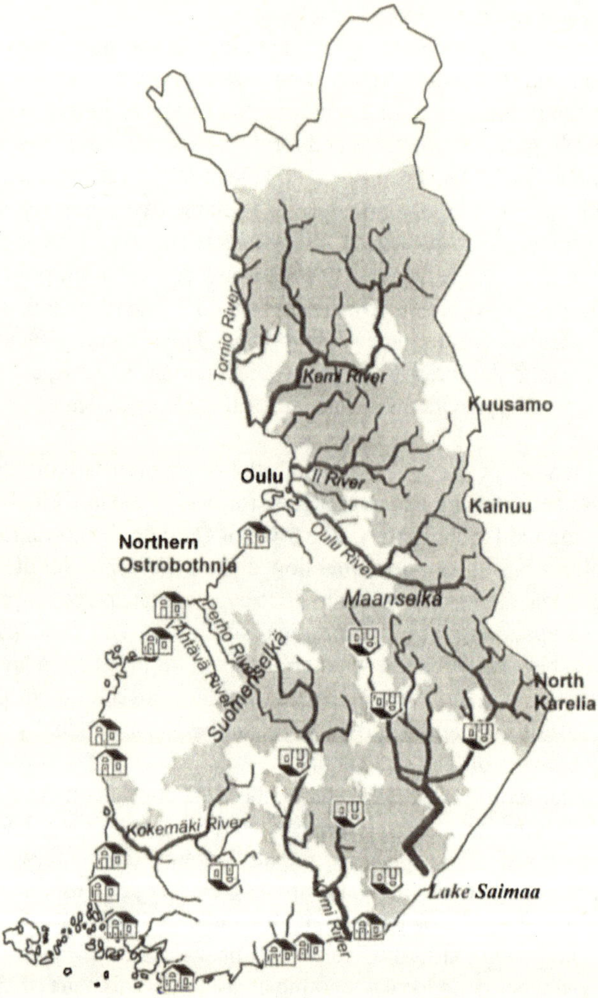

Fig. 4.1. The formation of forest landscapes in Finland. The regional differentiation of Finland is greatly modified by forest exploitation, transport of logs and wood processing. Export orientation resulted in a regional division of labor where the backwoods served as resource peripheries for the forest industry located in the lower courses of the rivers. Floating was the initial mode of log transportation. The shaded area in the map refers to those parts of Finnish countryside where forestry work exceeded 20 percent (of the gross time of paid work) in 1950, and the thickness of the river symbol shows the volume of timber floating along the river and lake systems, ranging from 15,000 to 3 million cubic meters in 1951–55. The buildings on the map symbolize the locations of the main "wooden towns" in Finland, and the buildings upside down refer to those towns where the old wooden quarters have been demolished since the 1960s.[17]

Local and Translocal Landscapes

The model of industrial forest management in Finland is an outcome of the historical merging of German innovations, motives to strengthen state governance and private forestry methods rooting from the old peasant routines. The intensity and efficiency of this hybrid was developed into full-scale exploitation during the era of forest plantation economy, launched in the 1950s. As a result, both the economic forests and marginal shade forests were drawn under intensive regulative control. Forest inventories were the practical tool for this project, initially prioritizing the timber growth aspects but later also developed to cover the main forest ecological features. The *erämaa* wilderness was finally transformed into a landscape that was thoroughly tamed. It became cultivated land, where the relationship between the annual wood increment and cutting, calculated in cubic meters, was considered sustainable when the former exceeded the latter. In some cases it became conservation land, where the ecological ranking of the species under extinction risk guided toward right forms of park governance.

The conserved forests covered approximately 2–9 percent of the total area of forest land in Finland in the 1990s[18] and each extension of conservation was perceived as a threat to social welfare expectations in the forest provinces. The indigenous values of nature have in general been considered within the Finnish model as elements not yet fully utilized, and thus in need to be transformed into economic resources. The progress of the timber frontier has accordingly had a profound impact on the species of the forests. The economic forests under different stages of standardized regeneration have for example become unsuitable habitats for the wild bear, the earlier guardian and ruler of the deep forests. Behind the emergence of "city bears" is the fact that the deep forests have become poorer and poorer habitats for these wilderness dwellers, pushing them closer to settled lands for feeding.

The northern forest landscape in Finland is primarily a resource base subjected to intensive exploitation, a means to economic growth. It is, however, also a frame for Finnish self-reflection and identity construction: a link to the past. It functions sometimes as an old black-and-white photograph in a family album, showing the ancestors of the past, with hollowed cheeks and deeply grooved faces. The past is kept in the modernizing Finland safely in the album (as a curiosity), for the purpose of remembering, but otherwise it is considered something primitive and poor, something from which to keep distance.

The uncontrollable and the unpredictable in the Finnish nature is in this setting considered a threat and a risk from the past, whereas the expansive manipulation of nature is thought of as an option for a better future. However, due to profound geopolitical changes in the environing world, both in Europe and globally, the feasibility of the old Finnish model has been repeatedly put under question. Doubts have arisen of its usefulness and competitiveness in today's local-global world. How to cope with the international worries of sustainability and the related criticism attached to the legitimacy of the expansive transformation of nature? How to assess the impacts of the rapidly developing image issues on Finnish forestry and forest industry? What are the consequences of the rise of socioenvironmental values and shareholder interests in the forest provinces? Concretely, how to respond to the growing international conservation interests that aim at transforming the Finnish backwoods into a European Greenbelt? Both Kianto's hungerland and the bear have undeniably become hot spots for international environmentalism and, therefore, their future largely depends on the development of these networks of translocalization.

The bear has through ages emerged in Finnish home yards as a visitor from the deep backwoods. It has also come from the East, and from the South (in the form of nature conservation). As part of these attacks from the outside, the bear has become an indelible part of Finnishness, especially in the forest provinces. It is a hybrid remnant from the past, but it is also a key element in projecting the socioenvironmental risks on the outside and constructing culturally defensive arguments. The Finnish "home yard" is well defended and it is therefore badly equipped to meet the era of radical translocal time-space compressions.

The hungry bear of Kianto, awakening from her long winter sleep to take those bloody actions, represents the whole genesis of threats from the outside, burdening the smallholders of the northern hungerland. The environing risks appear as question of life and death. The geopolitical location of Finland in the North is accordingly adopted as a popular explanation for all the setbacks of the past and present. The self-image of the Finns is reproduced in a dual process: by underlining the apparent external dependencies that have resulted in bad years and, simultaneously, by practically turning the immediate factors at hand into objects of replaced domination. Only by facing the difficulties in a collective manner (*talkoo* work in Finnish), single-mindedly, can success be gained. This interpretation has repeatedly led to authoritative solutions.[19]

The country's fate in the late 20th century was to be anchored in the success of forest-based modernization, which emphasized the role of the forest-industrial cluster as "the stem of the Finnish economy."[20] Finland was thought to live in and off the forests as always, and by conditions set by the prioritized sectors of paper export. The pressures for economic diversification grew, however, big enough to burst out in the form of information technology in the 1990s. Paper production with its capital-intensive machinery was challenged by the expansion of new technology based on the paperless modes of communication.

Punainen viiva reflects experiences of parallel social efforts aiming at breaking the deterministic and authoritarian construction of Finnishness. The red line grows in the dramatic epilogue on the throat of the poor Topi Romppainen but, earlier during the same spring, the red line was drawn on a ballot paper, voting for the social reforms mentioned at the outset. *Punainen viiva* is a symbol of political awakening, a sign of willingness to free the country from the fate of determinism. While the historical self-image was based on naturalization and externalization of the reasons for bad years, the emerging political activism dealt also with internal causations and trusted in self-made reforms. The modern independent Finland was in fact forged by those social movements that believed in their own efforts to change the poor life conditions.[21]

The break and the promise were revolutionary. The remark that the problems are partially self-made and can be solved accordingly was to become an alternative to the "religion" of fate. The external enemies and neoromantic self-portraits, which were products of national awakening, were gradually replaced by articulations of social inequality and injustice as an outcome of our own actions. Both of those explanations—the deterministic and self-reflexive ones—have remained as key features of political life in Finland, and they appear as part of the confrontations and competitions in today's environmental and (geo)political challenges.

The official and popular westward orientation of contemporary Finland is a telling example of this competition. Urban Finland has become smoothly integrated into the international community, while the rest of the country has absorbed one more layer of suspicion in her landscape. Parallels between the evacuation of the frontier populations during the wars of 1939–1944 and the current migration from the rural areas because of unemployment and nature conservation have been drawn in eastern Finland (see chapter 6). The reactions against any kind of environmental concern were, once again, expressions of projections of compensative replacement to the causalities of the bad years of the 1990s. However, only by an extremely selective interpretation of the most recent past can the expansion of nature conservation be understood as a reason for the chronically high level of unemployment (varying between 20–30 percent in the 1990s) in the eastern provinces. The EU's Natura 2000 nevertheless became a swear-word for many in the forest provinces of the northern hungerland.

The disagreement concerning the key criteria for sustainability within forestry and wood-based production has in this framework been fueled by a projected need to identify the external cause for the eroding economic wellbeing in the forest provinces. The introduction of eco-certificates, as well as the evaluation of the life cycles of the forest-based products, could have been taken as an opportunity for enlarging the export markets, for example in a form of proactive eco-modernization. This opportunity was, instead, regarded as an external threat impelled by forest conservationists and environmentalist consumers in Western Europe. As a result, image campaigns designed to promote Finland as an ecologically-aware paper producer have been easily shot down by critics, with the consequent eroding of the credibility of the green products and image of the northern backwoods.

The Finnish forest landscape, shaped by the economic policy integrating Finland as a resource periphery into international markets and characterized by deep regional economic decline of the early 1990s, stood in clear opposition to the image landscape of the green campaigns, where social sustainability and biodiversity are represented as key elements of the green welfare of the European North.

The Nordic East as a Landscape

The concept of landscape is used here as a bridging tool for two deep-rooted dualisms of modern world-viewing, namely that of nature and society on the one hand, and that of materiality and experience on the other. Landscape refers to the basic embeddedness of natural and cultural elements in our terrestrial environment. Landscape is a social artifact based on the materiality of nature. Landscape refers in other words to those terrestrial processes conduced by human efforts and resulting in continuing transformation of land, i.e. landscaping. Therefore, for humanity, there is nothing in nature that would not be marked by culture. The same is also conversely true: there is nothing in culture that is not built upon nature.[22]

As an artifact, landscape is a human creation, it is a result of social production and human imagination. Landscape is both terrestrial and experiential, it is made of physical materiality but, simultaneously, becoming part of our lifeworld as a mental mindscape, a way of seeing and perceiving the environing world. There is no way out of this embeddedness. Landscape helps us to become free from dualisms.[23] It is for example easy to think within this framework that while talking about forests the Finns talk about themselves.

In contemporary Finland, as elsewhere under Western influence, the conceptual definition of culture as being external to nature has been a historical necessity. The initial national emergence and self-reliance was based on this distantiation. Nature was the primary reason for the bad years and it functioned as an excuse for setbacks, the *force majeure* beyond human control. The causal links of the famine years and recessions had to be externalized and here the natural realm functioned as a useful explanation. The external(ized) threats were, partly purposefully, projected in extreme natural conditions. On the other hand, nature had also become a symbol of the past life at natural risk and it has been used as a negation to much-welcomed processes of modernization. Nature, as the primitive past, was to be left behind in modernization. The dualism was constructed as a compensation, or a message of relief, for the deep awareness of the indelible dependence on nature.

Landscape is here used as a tool for identifying the practical links between humanity and nature. It helps to see environmental phenomena as meaningful terrestrial and symbolic entities. It is a way of seeing and producing space or place-bound orientations. Landscapes are continually evolving as cultural code systems helping us to notice, select, interpret and renew our world(view)s as meaningful spatial categories. Landscaping is accordingly a process emerging when an environmentally loaded impression or expression takes place. It refers to a process where our mind produces ties to regional identity formation or "gathers" place-related details from the messages we face in our daily lives. Landscaping is a process where spatial connections and contexts are constructed. Landscape is thus the environmental dimension in the (re)production of cultural identities. It is the spatial basis for social commemoration and, therefore, a tool for drawing territorial lines and borders between us and them. Landscape is finally an ever-developing product of competing projections of domination.[24]

Landscape refers now both to (i) an aesthetic appreciation of the terrestrial forms of land and life, and (ii) the practices of territorial integration and control. Landscape emphasizes the importance of both visual and scenic attributes in human place orientation and, perhaps even more fundamentally, the terrestrial roots of regional identity formation and territorial division of lands. Kenneth Olwig has argued that the historical concepts of *Landschaft* and *landskap* have in Northern Europe referred to shared terrestrial and territorial values belonging to the local traditional communities and regional administrative complexes. *Landschaft* is in this respect a territorial unit with shared values, customs and collectively accepted practices of justice. In his own words: "The link between customary law, the institutions embodying that law, and the people enfranchised to participate in the making and administration of law is of fundamental importance to the root meaning of Land in *Landschaft.*"[25]

The dual character of Scandinavian *landskap* and German *Landschaft* has emerged in a particular way within the Finnish context. The aesthetic *landskap* has found its Finnish synonym in *maisema*, whereas the administrative *landskap* refers to *maakunta*. Both words are derivations of a Finnish root concept *maa*, applicable in several spatial contexts extending from soil stratification to land areas and worldviews, and from countries and countrysides to global dynamics and earthly cosmologies. The translation of *landskap* as *maakunta* has been marginalized in Finnish administrative practices and it is well developed only on the island of Åland (Ahvenanmaa) in the Baltic Sea. Ahvenanmaa has an autonomous status as an administrative *landskap* and linguistically it belongs to Scandinavia. *Maakunta* refers in present-day Finland to provinces or counties, derived both from the early settlement and administrative history of the historical provinces and from the more recent functional spatial system of economic provinces.[26]

Maisema, as a synonym of landscape, is generally connected to visual and aesthetic viewing but it also refers to regional morphological categories and spatial scales in geographical research as well as in descriptive and encyclopedic literature.[27] The Finnish *maisema* is, however, socioenvironmentally tied to regional identification of local particularities and provincial interests. The provincial landscapes of Finland were originally constructed in the late 19th century by Zacharias Topelius in his famous *Vårt land*[28] which became, especially after the translation into Finnish in 1876, the geography book in schools and homes for generations. Topelius emphasized the scenic values of cultivated landscape where harmony between nature and culture existed. Local events and histories were told in the spirit of enlightenment to teach the Finnish folk to learn from the past.

The landscapes were tools of education for Topelius. They were ideal events and sceneries with which to construct the territorial extension of Finnishness. The message was widely read and adopted in Finland. The message was not only linked to territorial construction of Finland but also to the way of making that construction. Landscape was a framework to be used for identity formation. The Finnish landscapes have since those days carried the double emphasis of visual aesthetics and territorial identity formation. Landscape is for the Finns a central medium with which to evaluate, orientate and compete in the environing world. The link from the Topelian landscapes to present-day campaigns of place marketing, designed by the exporters of Finnishness and Finnish products, is in this respect clear.

The historical interpretation of the role of Finnish landscapes brings to the forefront three key elements of landscape formation. First, Finnish landscape seems to serve as a spatial framework by which the familiar and the well-known within the environing world are identified as a "home yard" or territory under domestic control. Second, landscape is also a collective means for excluding the elements of the environment that deviate from learned codes. It is a tool for (re)producing the difference between the well-known and the not-so-well-known. Landscape divides us and them and it helps us to make and maintain the distinction between the familiar and the unpredictable. The scenes and events thus become landscapes in a continuous process of socioenvironmental exclusion and inclusion. The central content of landscape is therefore permanently under intensive competition and commodification. The image campaigns with impressive commercial landscapes are often export-oriented, but they also function as tools for collective identity formation.[29] The familiar is reproduced in connection to the external(ized) world via export marketing.

Third, Finnish landscapes can be identified on varying levels of abstraction, from short-lived "export landscapes" down to archetypal basic landscapes of self-identification and cultural differentiation. The complementary motifs of dependence and self-reliance have in general served as "red lines" of identity-building throughout the history of settlement and state formation in Finland.[30] This has regularly surfaced in the debates on Finland's geopolitical position within the belt of conifer-dominated northwoods and between the East and the West. The basic spatial orientation of Finnishness has been shaped by the awareness of the intimacy of easterness and backwoodness in the Finnish landscape. The East and the Forest are historical necessities, past dimensions constantly faced and, therefore, needing spatial and temporal antipodes: westernization and modernization. The Finnish bear has, however, not yet become extinct, it has just moved closer to the cultural cores of the West.

Notes

1. Erkki Pulliainen, *Petoja ja ihmisiä* (Helsinki: Tammi, 1984); Timo Helle, "Karhu pysyköön korpiemme kontiona," *Suomen Luonto* 57, no. 8 (1998), 23.
2. Juha Pentikäinen, "Metsä suomalaisten maailmankuvassa," in *Metsä ja metsänviljaa*, eds. Pekka Laaksonen and Sirkka-Liisa Mettomäki (Helsinki: Suomalaisen Kirjallisuuden Seura/Finnish Literature Society, 1994), 7-23.
3. Pulliainen, *Petoja ja ihmisiä.*
4. *The Report on Death Cases in Traffic Accidents in 1995* (Helsinki: Liikennevakuutuskeskus/Center for Traffic Insurances, 1996).
5. Ilmari Kianto, *Punainen viiva* (Helsinki: Otava, 1946), 210-11. The quotation is published by permission of the Kianto copyright holder, Kiannon Turjanlinna Oy (Raija-Liisa Kianto).
6. Eino Jutikkala and Kauko Pirinen, *A History of Finland* (Helsinki: Weilin&Göös, 1984), 211.
7. Jutikkala and Pirinen, *A History of Finland*, 60-61.
8. Ilmari Hustich, *Suomi tänään* (Helsinki: Tammi, 1965); Matti Leikola, "Metsien hoidon aatehistoriaa" (Summary: "Leading Ideas in Finnish Silviculture"), *Silva Fennica* 21, no. 4 (1987): 332-41.
9. Ari Aukusti Lehtinen, "Modernization and the Concept of Nature. On the Reproduction of Environmental Stereotypes," in *Encountering the Past in Nature*, eds. Timo Myllyntaus and Mikko Saikku (Athens: Ohio University Press, 2001), 29-48.
10. Leea Virtanen, "Suomen kansa on aina vihannut metsiään," in *Metsä ja metsänviljaa*, ed. Pekka Laaksonen and Sirkka-Liisa Mettomäki (Helsinki: Suomalaisen Kirjallisuuden Seura/Finnish Literature Society, 1994), 134-40.
11. Martti Linkola, "Metsä kulttuurimaisemana" (Summary: "The Forest as a Cultural Landscape"), *Silva Fennica* 21, no. 4 (1987), 362-73.
12. Leikola, "Metsien hoidon aatehistoriaa."
13. Viljo Holopainen, "The Forest Policy of Independent Finland," in *The Forest Industry in Independent Finland*, eds. Juha Laurila, Eino Mäkinen and Heikki Vuorimaa (Helsinki: The Central Association of Finnish Woodworking Industries, 1968), 76-103; *Metsä 2000. The Main Report of the Forest 2000 Program* (Helsinki: Talousneuvosto/The Board of Economics, 1985); Hannu Hautala, Lasse Lehtinen and Lassi Rautiainen, *My Forest* (Helsinki: Edita, 2002), 122.
14. Pertti Veijola, *Suomen metsänrajametsien käyttö ja suojelu* (Rovaniemi: Metsäntut-

kimuslaitoksen tiedonantoja, no. 692, 1998).

15. Matti Kärkkäinen, "Missä vanhojen metsien uhanalaiset lajit piileskelivät 1930-luvulla?," *Karjalainen*, 23 January 1995, 13.

16. Heikki Simola, "Land-use History Explains the Value of the North Karelian Biosphere Reserve in Preserving Old-growth Forests," in *Karelian Biosphere Reserve Studies*, eds. Timo J. Hokkanen and E. Ieshko (Joensuu: University of Joensuu, Biosphere Studies, 1995), 15-20.

17. Harri Anderson, *Rakennettu ympäristö—kaupunkirakentamisen modernina projektina* (Turku: University of Turku, Publications of the Center for Continuing Education/ Täydennyskoulutuskeskuksen julkaisuja, no. A 10, 1993); Jarmo Kortelainen, "Forest Industry in the Map of Finland," *Fennia* 180, nos. 1-2 (2002), 227-35.

18. Variations in the proportions of the land area under conserved forests in the 1990s were due to different methods of calculation and, of course, depended on the ideological standpoint. The official estimate extended conserved forests up to nine percent of the total forest area, but this share included much of the stunted lands of marshes and high latitude forests beyond the limits of economically feasible cuttings. The nine percent share also included forests under nature-imitating loggings with options of exploitation. According to the Nature League of Finland, only 420,000 hectares (2.1 percent of forest land area) were protected in the early 1990s on the grounds of the Conservation Acts and over 95 percent of forest land was in commercial use. Both the official and Nature League's statistics were estimates before the acceptance of the Natura 2000 Programme by the European Union. Natura 2000 is a process that aims at harmonizing the measures of nature conservation in the EU by applying particular nature directives. The main motive is to clear the status of the already-existing nature conservation areas. The establishment of the Natura network in Finland was completed in January 2005 when the European Commission accepted the Finnish proposal, which covered 4.9 million hectares (14 percent) of Finland's surface area. However, several open questions in the extension of the Natura network still exist, due to complaints by landowners and the pressure from the EU to expand conservation. Sources: Juho Pennanen, "0,27% Protected!," in *Finland and Forest—A Success Story?*," ed. Harri Karjalainen (Helsinki: World Wide Fund for Nature Finland, The Finnish Association for Nature Conservation, Greenpeace, The Finnish Wilderness Movement, The Nature League and The Finnish Forest Action Group, 1993), 13-15; *Criteria and Indicators for Sustainable Forest Management in Finland* (Helsinki: Ministry of Agriculture and Forestry, 1997); Ilkka Heikkinen, "Luonnonsuojelu lähemmäs kansalaisia," *Helsingin Sanomat*, 26 August 1998, 2; Pyry Lapintie, "EU:n komissio hyväksyi Suomen Natura-alueet," *Helsingin Sanomat*, 15 January 2005, A9.

19. Ari Aukusti Lehtinen, "Northern Natures," *Fennia* 169, no. 1, (1991), 144; Juha Siltala, "Yksilöllisyyden historialliset ja psykologiset ehdot," in *Yksilö modernin murroksessa*, eds. Antti Hautamäki, Eerik Lagerspetz, Juha Sihvola, Juha Siltala and Jarmo Tarkki (Helsinki: Gaudeamus, 1996), 117-204.

20. *Pro Silvis. Metsien puolesta. Metsäpoliittisen keskustelun tueksi* (Helsinki: Metsämiesten Säätiö, 1995). Forest and development researcher Jussi Raumolin has used the concept of forest fundamentalism to illustrate the popular thinking among forest professionals that Finland can only gain a successful path with her forest industry, see for example Jussi Raumolin, "Myyttinen metsä-Suomi," *Metsälehti*, no. 23 (1987), 69.

21. Risto Alapuro, *State and Revolution in Finland* (Berkeley: University of California Press, 1988).
22. Yrjö Haila, "In Search of the Wilderness," in *Ikijää—Permafrost*, eds. Yrjö Haila and Marketta Seppälä (Pori: Pori Art Museum, 1995), 168; Kenneth Robert Olwig, "Recovering the Substantive Nature of Landscape," *Annals of the Association of American Geographers* 86, no. 4 (1996): 630-53.
23. Michael Jones, "The Elusive Reality of Landscape. Concepts and Approaches in Landscape Research," in *Norsk Geografisk Tidsskrift* 45 (1991), 229-44.
24. Jacquelin Burgess, "The Production and Consumption of Environmental Meanings in the Mass Media: A Research Agenda for the 1990s," in *Transactions of the Institute of British Geographers, New Series* 15 (1990), 139-61; Don Mitchell, "Writing the Western: New Western History's Encounter with Landscape," *Ecumene* 5, no. 1 (1998), 7-29; Don Mitchell, "The Lure of the Local: Landscape Studies at the End of a Troubled Century," *Progress in Human Geography* 25, no. 2 (2001), 269-82.
25. Olwig, "Recovering the Substantive Nature of Landscape," 633.
26. Anssi Paasi, *Suomen väliportaan aluejärjestelmän kehitys ja hahmottuminen suomalaisten aluetietoisuudessa* (Helsinki: University of Helsinki, Publications of the Association of Planning Geography, no. 14 (1984), 9-23; Kenneth Robert Olwig, "Sexual Cosmology: Nation and Landscape at the Conceptual Interstices of Nature and Culture, or: What does Landscape Really mean?," in *Landscape: Politics and Perspectives*, ed. Barbara Bender (Oxford: Berg, 1993), 307-43; Olavi Granö, *Tieteellisen maisemakäsityksen muodostuminen ja tulo Suomeen* (Turku: University of Turku, Department of Geography Publications, no. 154, 1996).
27. Tarja Keisteri, "The Study of Changes in Cultural Landscapes," *Fennia* 168, no. 1 (1990), 31-115; Pentti Alalammi, *Maisemat, asuinympäristöt. Suomen Kartasto 350* (Helsinki: National Board of Survey and Geographical Society of Finland, 1993); J.G. Granö, *Pure Geography* (Baltimore: The Johns Hopkins University Press, 1997). Published initially in 1929 in German under the title *Reine Geographie* and in 1930 in Finnish as *Puhdas maantiede*.
28. Sacharias Topelius, *Maamme kirja* (Helsinki: Werner Söderström, 1981).
29. Kati Pitkänen, "Kesä Suomessa," in *Maantiede, tila, luontopolitiikka*, ed. Ari Aukusti Lehtinen (Joensuu: Joensuu University Press, 2005), 135-60.
30. Risto Alapuro, *Suomen älymystö Venäjän varjossa* (Helsinki: Tammi, 1997), 192-200.

5.

Politics of the Margin: Contested Mirescapes

Finnish mires are studied in this chapter as cultural landscapes reflecting and framing Finnishness and its attributes. Empirical material is collected from the generations of textbooks of Finland's geography, from where the descriptions of mires—that is, mirescapes—are gathered and related to their respective societal contexts. First, mirescapes are interpreted as documents of cultural projections of Finnish enlightenment, loaded both by advice of wise use of natural resources and by warnings about the risks embedded in harsh northern nature.

Second, mirescapes are taken as signs of changing attitudes of Finns about themselves, forming a dialogue between the expressions of self-confidence (trust in land) on the one hand, and indications of dissatisfaction and fatalism embodied in the North (fate of the land) on the other hand. Third, mirescapes are considered as tools of demarcation: they function as frontier landscapes symbolizing the line between us and them. Finland is fenland, and this makes a difference.

The mirescapes of the textbooks, constructed according to professional scientific knowledge, are evaluated in the framework of hybrid landscape approach by asking the question: What is represented and, in particular, what is left underrepresented in the descriptions of mires? Persistence of certain professional and scientific mirescapes is discussed and linked to the more general question of intertextual repetition across the academic generations. The role of nature descriptions as explanations of historical events is also examined.

Mires as Mirrors

The northern landscape of the backwoods reaches its culmination at the most distant corners of the conifer-dominated forest belt, where the taiga changes into tundra. It matures at the border of the settled world. The deep North is the edge of ecumene. The northern landscape is a product of seasonal cycles: it grows inward during the periods of low winter light, opens outdoors under the bright sun of the springs months and reaches its full intensity during the nightless summers with the burst of passionate mosquitos. The far North is, in addition, loaded with strong visible signs of human presence: nature and culture become one within these vast landscapes of logged backwoods and drained mires. The North is expansive by nature and by culture.

Finnish mires are part of the far North, and they also form a key element of Finnish marginality, both in physical and symbolic terms. Two-thirds of the Finnish peatlands, originally covering one-third of the country, have been transformed by draining. This change was originally justified by the needs of agriculture and later by the interests of the forest industry and peat-burning activities. On the other hand, eight percent of peatlands have been conserved, mostly during the last decades of the 20th century,[1] but no harmonious balance has yet been achieved between the land uses.

A widely accepted local opinion in different parts of rural Finland regards conservation as the main threat to livelihoods whereas nature conservationists consider draining as destroying the wetland biodiversity. The confronting attitudes were sharpened in the 1990s in the debate on the energy status of peat. Nature conservationists regarded mires as archives of fossil past and thus gaining a status of fossil fuel in energy politics. This was against the idea of industrial developers defining peat as biofuel, renewing in a similar manner as the rest of the regenerating elements of nature.[2] The position—for or against the draining of the remaining natural mires—depended on the energy status of peat adopted and thus on the basic value attached to peatlands.

This is the Finnish mirescape: nature turning to culture, marginal becoming central and, moreover, wastelands located at the core of heated disputes. This configuration is due to the cultural fact that Finnish mires are, overlappingly, the edge and the source of existence. They are the neighboring zone of uncertainty, a well-known but still strange hybrid between the firm ground and open waters. Mires are both a threat and a challenge.

Facing a quagmire, that is, a hybrid beyond the categories of the known, can grow into a deep and intimate experience. Jorma Luhta[3], the widely known photographer of Finnish mires, has sought for decades for the most abandoned places of the North, the real outcasts of Finland. His motive reveals something characteristic about the Finnish landscape. The desolated fringes emerge as emotional references. Mirescapes serve both as a means for cultural reflection and as ecological paradises stimulating all the six senses. The mires thus appear as mirrors.

Mires contain the past and represent the present. They are both a history book and a map. The physical existence of mires, constituting of deep sediments underground, underlines the layered and only partly conscious past coexisting with our reflected being. The peripheral location beyond the forests is also a reminder of the marginal stance. Mires connect Finland into the northern margins and they demonstrate the cultural and economic consequences derived from that position. It is, however, possible to live in and off the peatlands, to survive in the most remote wildernesses.

"Wolf does not get lost on marshes", says an old Finnish proverb and emphasizes both the peculiar strangeness and unique originality connected to northern lifemodes. Originality is a way of locating oneself and, undoubtedly, also a source of pride. Those surviving in fenland find, in a traditional sense, the wolf in themselves, which means they are familiar with the skills needed to make one's living within the northern wildernesses. To identify with the wolf brings about a certain kind of self-respect based on an awareness of one's sensitivity and "know-how" in the taiga. The wolf identity is an archaic confirmation of the North.

The layers of mires have a specific role as the memory bank of the North. The Holocene history is concretely sedimented in the bogs. This view of the past guides the northerners toward regarding themselves as latecomers and visitors, basing their livelihoods on the resources developed during the eleven millenniums of northern nature's postglacial regime. The lands, waters and mires have evolved according to their own logic, finally becoming more and more affected by human endeavors. The bogs, therefore, help us to regard humanity as a geohistorical agent that modifies future conditions far beyond its limited time horizons. This hybrid stance forces us to face the question about our ability to become aware of the various timescapes enveloping our earthly existence. How well are we equipped to reflect upon the consequences of human endeavors in different timescales?

This is the question to be dealt with in this chapter. The analysis is focused on different ways of seeing the mires—as important but often undervalued dimensions of Finnish landscapes and identities. The aim is to discover the dominant cultural categories of mires underlined in the books of Finland's geography read at different levels of schooling and draw some conclusive remarks on the societal context of the mirescapes.

The descriptions found in the textbooks are seen as evidence of those attitudes by which the Finns have constructed their own specific position as part of the conifer-dominated North. It is argued that the mirescapes of the textbooks illustrate, maintain and develop the beliefs attached to the country's geopolitical location, risks projected onto the harsh natural conditions and, in general, elements of national fate determinism. In the end, the mires become concrete as the fringes and frames of existence, frontier landscapes against which cultural consolidation has taken place.

Landscaping the Mires: Three Questions

The landscape approach applied here is grounded on the understanding of the hybrid nature of the basic concept: landscape is the geographical means for connecting the two basic dualisms of modern world-viewing, namely the one of nature vs. society and the other of materiality vs. experience.[4] This hybrid (i) offers us an alternative to break the earlier colonial models built upon the binary oppositions of the known and the alien, or us and them, and it thus helps us to take into consideration the historical and constantly changing conditions of inclusion and exclusion.[5] The new landscape approach consequently (ii) highlights the reciprocal dependencies between centrifugal and centripetal practices. The most peripheralized and excluded cultural dimensions seem to turn often, after more thorough examination, into key constituents of our identity formation. The fringe areas become in other words the heartlands through which we construct ourselves as individuals and cultures.[6] Landscape has accordingly become (understood as) a means of (iii) representing and modifying cultural heritage and, even, a tool for reorganizing arenas of social commemoration and cultural remembering.[7]

This three-partite landscape approach guides us into the following specific questions on the social construction of mirescapes in the textbooks on Finlands's geography. The first question directs our attention to the historical constructions of mirescapes as symbolic messages and cultural projections trying to make sense of the dominant geographical dependencies and their concrete outcomes. Nature, in the form of landscape, serves as an arena where the cultural debate proceeds. The process is fragmentary and occasional, i.e. context dependent, but not without certain general characteristics: naturalization, in the form of nature-based explanation, translates the societal setbacks into hardships emerging from the nature "out there," whereas culturalization transforms the elements of nature into socially appropriate and meaningful units. Nature is seen both as an explanation and a reflection of culture.[8] Finnish mires, perhaps the most unclear and hybrid ecosystem complex in Finnish nature, currently grouped into more than one hundred different ecological subcategories,[9] have served as an excellent medium for these projections. Mirescapes are consequently considered in this chapter as documents of cultural projections of the dominant modes of Finnish enlightenment during the 20th century. This emphasis is not meant to underline the corresponding strength of the descriptions of mires to their physical-material counterparts.

The second question focuses on those elements of mirescapes that seem to serve as a means for the (re)production of a marginal stance—both in identity politics and also within the broader societal division of labor. The peripheries often seem to be discursively mired in their provincial position, sometimes even locked in their roles as marginal actors. The process is, however, a complicated one and far from deterministic. The marginal stance is developed according to the attitudes and deeds of those living in the margins and the way new external dependencies are introduced "from above" (see chapter 10). Breaking down the vicious circles is thus possible, for example during periods of intensive redefinition of societal interdependencies. Peripheries have often served as containers of traditions[10] and they have occasionally become reinvented as cultural or ecological heritage areas for broader audiences. The margins can even emerge as hot spots of political battles in the metropolises, as has been repeatedly witnessed in modern nature and culture conservation.

Mires can be seen both as the fringe elements of Finnish landscape and as framing tools for cultural identification. Mires, left and preserved in the extreme limits, contain attractions and options based on their primeval existence. Sole awareness of the safe existence of wild lands and old-growth forests was a valid argument in the wilderness debate in Finland (1986–1991) for the conservation of the extreme nature of the North. Searching for and imagining the wild lands untouched by human feet can thus become a basic motive for sublime and, even, subliminal experiences. Those zones of the North that have not yet been visibly modified by human touch can in other words function as central sources of social commemoration and identity building, places of re-membering. Both the indigenous northerners and immigrants, as well as the visitors, have throughout the ages reproduced their connection to (wild) nature and, hence, made it a part of their culture. The extreme margin has in this way become established, and is continuously reproduced, as part of the human world and its centers.[11]

Jorma Luhta[12] explains his striving toward the most extreme and desolate mires in this way: "My ambitions were directed towards the open mires of Lapland, the lands most deserted of all before the invention of the rubber boot". Here, I dare to summarize, we can find something central and, also, paradoxical in the Finnish mirescape. The most barren of all lands turns into focus. The marginal grows into focus. Now, the desolate wetland is the land of hidden values; it is a place of individual standstill, a moment of self-realization.

The third question directs attention to those elements of mirescapes that function as important archives for memorizing, both (paleo)ecologically and metaphorically. The mirescapes remind us of the particularity of the North: the great geonarratives of postglacial spreading of mires, often repeated in the textbooks, posit the present into deeper layers of time-space that are dominated by the competing forces of nature. In the timescape of thousands of years, lakes, forests and mires were the actors of the scene; and the natural landscape was under continuous competitive formation. The peatland is the element in nature that hides the millennial past in its sediments. In the mires the Finns can read the natural past and, in addition, figure out their own position as part of the Northern realm. This ability to read the mires stands as the critical means to cultural distinction. The mirescapes found in the geography textbooks are therefore taken here as evidence of sociospatial commemoration and cultural re-membering: descriptions of mires stand as determinants of identification and tools of demarcation between us and them.

Expansive Bogs

Luonnontieto I (*Nature Knowledge I*), published in 1956, discusses how the ancient forests of Finland have been replaced by expansive mires: "Sphagnum moss continuously spreads into its surroundings. In this way, the mires gradually grow and penetrate woodlands and even climb up the slopes and hills."[13] In a similar manner, *Oma maamme* (*Our Land*) from the year 1960 paints in front of us a mirescape that is expansive and threatening. The chapter on mires, titled "Mire—the enemy of forests", explains how the northern woodland, due to natural geohistorical evolution, gradually turns to wetland and how the mosses slowly swallow even the most noble of the old-growth forests. *Oma maamme* colorfully describes how the humble mosses can beat the noble trees and devour smaller forest ponds: "Sphagnum moss proceeds and transforms itself into peat and finally completely fills the water basin. The process can also continue in the nearby forests."[14]

Nyky-Suomi (*Modern Finland*) explained some years later that the high degree of bog formation in Finland is due to the climate and specific features of the soil structure and topography. "The bogs are earlier lakes, rivers and forests, or as results of land rise at the coastal areas," says *Nyky-Suomi*, and continues that "[p]aludification can take place with such a speed that the forest turns into a dry dead stand."[15] In a perspective of thousands of years, this landscape dynamic, called paludification, favors spruce and pine swamps and aims toward open mires. Often the process is slow and gradual but, in certain topographic and soil conditions, for example in the case of a sudden rise in the groundwater level, the transformation can occur surprisingly fast. Evidence of these processes is deposited in the deep layers of the bogs.

The post Ice Age drama of the millenniums is described in these examples as part of the basic competition between the key elements included in Finnish landscape. Mires emerge in this context as a natural threat, challenging also the basic identity construction and economic development of Finland. Finland lives off the forests and by the lakes, and now the books reveal that they are at risk of becoming wetlands. Mires and mosses are considered as expansive risk factors eroding the sources of northern livelihoods.

The threatening landscape of expanding mosses was a regular view in the textbooks up until the 1960s.[16] The original agricultural motives for draining mires were gradually challenged by forest management interests, and the initial shift took place by accident. The results of the first experiments of drainage after the famine of the 1860s in Finland[17] showed that the increment of timber growth was remarkable on the drained areas originally dried for the purposes of acquiring new and appropriate land for farming. This observation was important for Finnish forest industry as it increased the confidence in national independence based on forest-industrial modernization.

Industrial forest management, which favored forest plantation, became the dominant mode of forest use during the 1950s and was at its most intensive during the subsequent decades. Draining of the mires was an integral part of the new forestry. The mirescapes of the geography books and those in the maps of professional foresters seemed to be starkly oppositional. An ideological link between the two, however, existed. The fear of expanding mosses motivated and justified the actual disappearance of natural mires. The post Ice Age problem got its solution in a few decades, and with the help of modern ditching machinery. It would be easy to assess afterwards that the geography books in a way prepared the Finns for the drainage project by repeating the millennial geohistorical perspective as the only significant perspective in natural history. The question is, of course, more complicated.

The drainage project was considered necessary for Finland in the 1950s, as the country was recovering from the losses and reparations of World War II. It seemed there was no alternative.[18] This argument fueled the project and kept the ditching tractors busy up until the early 1980s. The tractors and peat ploughs became integral elements of mire landscapes throughout the long daylight hours of the summer seasons. The traditional use of mires for local gathering economies (berry picking, hunting) was forced to give way but, outside the small circles of nature conservationists, no strong voice against the draining took place. The message of the geography books was in this respect well received. Finland built its modern identity and economy as a forest-based national unit. Some inventories of the attitudes of those who actually did the job have only recently been collected and it seems that doubts were rather common, especially when the ditchers reached the open mires with no tree growth awaiting them anyway. Well-paid contract work was, however, welcomed by smallholders in the backwoods and critical voices were kept low.[19]

The first of the Finnish geographers to express doubts about the ever-increasing draining was Ilmari Hustich. In his book *Suomi tänään* (*Finland To-*

day), published in 1965, Hustich was worried about the disappearance of mires and the possible changes in the ecosystems. "Instead of becoming absorbed into the soil, waters do run faster into the sea which is due to forest loggings and the draining of peatlands," wrote Hustich[20] and opened the critical discussion about the ecological and social losses caused by the drainage project.

The expanding mirescapes of the geography books in any case reveal some key features of Finnishness, rooted in archaic beliefs but also accepted as a useful explanation for the setbacks and hardships faced in agrarian Finland and during the long run of modernization. In the growing seasons, the night frost was a regular visitor to lowland fields and it was widely regarded as the main reason for the famine years. The frost, it was believed, emerged from the mires and could only be overcome by cultivating them and thus expanding agricultural practices to the lands most at risk from frost.

Invisible Mires

Mires are not only seen in Finnish geographical textbooks as active and expansive risks dwelling in nature but, also, as risks due to their mere existence. Mires emerge as challenges not to be left in their passivity. They become valued according to their usefulness as transformed landscapes, non-mires. "The peatlands are of inestimable importance for the country's agriculture and forestry, not to mention industry", wrote Väinö Voionmaa[21] in his *Suomen talousmaantieto* (*Economic Geography of Finland*) and underlined the role of the Finnish Association of Peat Cultivation, founded in 1896. In *Maantieto* (*Geography*), published by Väinö Auer and K. Merikoski in 1939, the transformation of mires into a more utilizable form was similarly seen a necessary task: "Over 35 percent of Finland consists of peatlands which, in their expansiveness, threaten the valuable forests of Finland, if not drained and dried. By doing so we will get fast-growing woodlands and fertile fields."[22]

Mires became gradually integrated into industrial forestry programs. The increment of annual timber growth achieved by draining was estimated to reach the level of 30 million cubic meters in the 1960s, which equaled approximately a 70 percent increase for the then assessed gross growth of timber in Finnish forests.[23] The Forest 2000 programs continued later the industrial trajectories based on the speeding up of the annual growth, and the top estimate even reached the level of 85 million cubic meters in the early 1990s. The rise in environmental awareness and the growing controversies in forestry methods made, however, the harvesting of the raised yield unrealistic.[24]

Mires were areas of potential use in the forest programs. They were often indirectly identified in the official forest statistics, for example in the form of forest hectares drained. The mires were repeatedly classified as part of the larger category of stunted lands or wastelands. Mire draining was often categorized as forest draining. Mires as such were mostly invisible in the official forest-industrial vocabulary.[25]

A new interest was attached to mires during the energy crisis of the 1970s, and this was also reflected in the geography books. Mires became potential sources of domestic fuel. The energy value of peat was already mentioned in some of the textbooks of the 1930s[26] but it was not until the 1970s that the message got a stronger emphasis. Seppo Sikkinen states in *Suomen maantiede* (*Geography of Finland*) that there exists in Finnish nature about 20 billion cubic meters of peat, which equals 2000 million tons of oil.[27] Peat, calculated in oil equivalents, became in the 1970s an issue in Finnish regional policy and an additional domestic resource for the energy industry. However, the viability of peat as fuel was, and still is, much dependent on the shifting trends of oil prices, and this has made the local projects rather vulnerable. The draining of a mire is the beginning of a long industrial process that largely modifies the surrounding ecosystems and communities. Socioenvironmental costs grew gradually and this meant severe local environmental debates within the peat-burning localities.[28] When criticized, the peat-burning industry has defended its strategies with arguments defining peat as a resource that regenerates itself and can thus be utilized in a manner similar to forests.[29]

Mires have traditionally been seen in the eyes of the forest industry and beat-burning companies as stunted lands only needing to be transformed into valuable resources. In their view, mires are empty and valueless places as though awaiting human manipulation. The wetlands of stunted pines need to be ploughed into economic forests and the surface peat layers should similarly be converted into energy units. The passively existing mire is a marginal land to be re-created by human efforts.

In the heart of Finnish mirescape there clearly exists an area of low productivity. Mires are the lands of lost and decaying options. Leo Aario expressed this well in 1966 in his *Suomen maantiede* (*Geography of Finland*), while describing the mirelands of Northern Ostrobothnia: "This region is among the most boggy ones in the whole country. The open treeless mires cover over half of the land area and, moreover, a remarkable portion of woodlands can be regarded as boggy wastelands."[30]

The negative value of Finnish mirescapes also surfaces in the form of exclusions in Finnish geography. *Maamme kirja* (*The Book on Our Land*),[31] which was the most popular geography book in schools and homes for generations, forgets the mires as an element of Finnish landscapes. The 34 famous *Paintings of Enlightenment* (*Valistuksen taulut*), published by the Association of Primary School Teachers of Finland during the years 1903–32, had only one painting with a partial focus on a mire.

The invisibility of mires is not only a feature of school geography. Remarkable exclusions can also be found in the main body of regional and landscape descriptions of Finland. The 53 folios of the fifth edition of the *Atlas of Finland*, published during 1976–1993, had no folios dedicated to mires, and the folios on topographic forms and forestry only occasionally refer to them. The celebrated collection of Finnish paintings and poems, under the title *Suomalaisen maiseman neljä vuodenaikaa* (*The Four Seasons of Finnish Landscape*), does not contain any pages on mires.[32]

The non-existence of representations of mires supports the argument that they are the hidden or even the embarrassing dimension of Finnishness. Mires are perhaps the most abandoned land of the North. Culturally excluded mires, physically covering one-third of the Finnish landscape, might be therefore regarded as the "blind spot" of the country, the zone of uncertainty repeatedly denied.

Tamed Lands

Reino Kalliola discusses the problems caused by the intensive draining of mires in the already mentioned *Suomen maantiede* (*Geography of Finland*) from 1977. He writes[33] that "the task of draining is now practically completed and only one-fourth of the mires, mostly located in Lapland, remain in their original state." Kalliola begins his article with a detailed description of the varying vegetation categories of mires and continues with morphological and hydrological specifications. The emerging new mirescape was an integral element of the general scientific turn in nature research, which also influenced the work of geographers during the second half of the 20th century.[34] The earlier emphasis on the expansion and morphogenesis was complemented by a detailed analysis of the taxonomic types of mires and their actual combinations in nature.

The new mirescapes, conceptualized as ecosystemic categories and complexes, were understandood by the professionals but caused confusion among the lay people. Sometimes the new scientific names even conflicted with the traditional identifications of mires based on regional dialectics and specific local customs and memories. For example, the academic geographical *keidassuo* (raised bog) was, and still is, incompatible to the lay geographical understanding of *keidassuo* (a bog with puddles) in some parts of western Finland and, in addition, the open aapamires of northern Finland confusingly often mean different things for the lay people and ecologists.[35]

The scientific form of geographical mirescapes was well represented in the 6th edition of the *Atlas of Finland*, where Heikki Seppä introduces an updated and comprehensive summary of the research results. Seppä first introduces the postglacial morphogenesis and its varying time-spaces: "In the beginning the mires progressed rather quickly. The spreading could reach the speed of several hundreds of meters per century, but was gradually slowed down according to topographic limits."[36] The speed of spreading was, as Seppä emphasizes, much influenced by external climatic variations and internal dynamics of peat accumulation. Climatic drying in general retarded growth. A major part of the article concentrates on the classifications of mire types, which are basically divided into ideal types according to vegetation and habitat factors, only to be reconnected to form varying combinations of the ideal types, exceeding one hundred in number. Seppä also identifies the most important surface elements of mires, carrying such poetic Finnish names as *kuljut* (hollows), *kermit* (hummocks), *jänteet* (hummock ridges) and *rimmet* (flarks). The utilization of peatlands is briefly discussed and related to mire conservation and more recent restoration programs. Ecological changes caused by the forest industry and peat-burning activities are also mentioned.

The scientific construction of mirescapes is multidimensional and complicated and, of course, sensitive to the physical reality "out there" in nature. By strengthening the informational basis of the mires it became possible to learn to know them throughout. The expansive or unpleasantly stagnant mires of the older generations received new contour lines that brought them closer to human control. Mires were tamed and they became safe representations of Finnish nature. The earlier quagmires thus became doubly eliminated: as a result of scientific mapping and industrial draining.

During this double transformation, the cultural dimensions of Finnish mirescapes were mostly ignored or, if discussed at all, integrated into economic assessments. This happened simultaneously within the academic and economic practices. The new mirescapes of the textbooks were to be grounded on scientific facts, whereas the earlier mirescapes included broad generalizations and even dramatic descriptions with strong symbolic messages. The scientific turn purified the old cultural biases by constructing new determinants of bog description. The updating of cultural viewpoints was frozen. The sophistication potential of the earlier aesthetic sensitivity was accordingly lost. No serious attention was paid to regional cultural variations of mirescapes, which was undoubtedly a reflection of the major trends within the practices of academic geography. The consequences of these exclusions became multiplied in the context of schooling and education. The new, more urbanized generations met the scientific representations of mires in the textbooks of geography and biology[37]—and experienced these new mirescapes as their first and perhaps only contact with mires. Finally, however, the outdated cultural mirescapes emerged in the media, introduced now by artists, aestheticians and cultural geographers.[38] The cultural dimensions of mires were identified in cooperation with geographers and scholars in *humaniora*.

Jorma Luhta[39] writes how deeply he dreaded the positive ideals of land clearings of the old geography books and how he could not easily free himself from nightmares of the ditches on the destroyed mires. The aesthetic emphasis of Jorma Luhta serves as a telling contrast to the artificial geometry of the modern mirescapes, and the scientific inventories behind them. It is easy to see from within the aesthetic view that the hybrid challenge for cultural geographers clearly is to (re)open the connection between professional and lay geographies, between analysis and interpretation, between science and humanities. The "empty pages" of the textbooks need to be filled with cultural mirescapes—written, for example, by cultural geographers of nature.

Conclusion: Timescapes of Mires

The mires in the textbooks of Finland's geography were up until the 1960s depicted either as natural factors which eroded the national resource base or as risks due to their mere passive existence. Both motives directed interests toward further mapping and utilization of mires. The fear of losing the options by not transforming enough "wastelands" into "cashlands" was a product of Finnish enlightenment. Mires left alone resembled the phlegmatism against which the whole northern version of modernization was directed. Finland was to become more than a province mired in the margins.

The early academic construction of expansive mires was a short synopsis of the slow co-evolution of nature during the postglacial era. Eleven thousand years in a few sentences. Gradual paludification was only a normal phenomenon in the cool climate of the North, especially during the periods of high humidity. While briefly describing the slow postglacial development, and simultaneously set against the promises of industrial draining, the scalar perspective was, however, changed from geohistorical to cultural-historical. Paludification was seen as a problem during the decades when mires were almost completely turned into drained lands.

The postglacial geohistorical perspective underlined the expansive character of mires and in its own way justified the maximal effort given to draining. Confusion within the time scales is apparent. A similar confusion exists in the more recent debate on the energy value of peat, as was mentioned earlier. The peat industry, while considering peat to be a resource similar to forests, undervalues the fossil dimension of mires. Fossilization refers to time scales far beyond the modern scope by covering the long history of peat formation and by emphasizing the atmospheric effects of sudden intensive peat burning. The fossil perspective is sensitive to differing spans of time-space horizons, or timescapes, and takes care of the consequences of "jumping" from one time scale to another.

The Finnish "mire case" clearly underlines the geographical need to analyze and popularize the causes and consequences of socioenvironmental scaling. The case also demonstrates how geomorphologic matters of the postglacial past are tangibly linked to the late modern politics of re-scaling.

Despite the fact that ice ages are coming and going within the longer geohistorical perspective, cultural and ecological values are threatened during the nearest decades. Certain ecosystems of mires are disappearing, the biodiversity of northern wetlands is weakening and the amount of carbon dioxide in the atmosphere is growing. The drained mires have made the waters downstream eutrophic and they have possibly become emissive sources of carbon dioxide.[40] These questions worry us now, but in the longer run we might become surrounded by continental ice sheets and endless marshlands thereafter.

Notes

1. Kaisu Aapala, Raimo Heikkilä and Tapio Lindholm, "Suoluonnon monimuotoisuuden turvaaminen," in *Suomen suot*, ed. Harri Vasander (Helsinki: Suoseura, 1998), 45-57.
2. Raimo Sopo, "Turve—fossiilinen vai biopolttoaine?," *Helsingin Sanomat*, 6 May 1998, A19; Raimo Sopo and Aimo Aalto, "Turveteollisuus Suomessa," in *Suomen suot*, ed. Harri Vasander (Helsinki: Suoseura, 1998), 84-87.
3. Jorma Luhta, *Tansseja aavalla* (Oulu: Pohjoinen, 1994).
4. Yrjö Haila, The North as/and 'the Other'," in *Strangers in the Arctic*, ed. Marketta Seppälä (Pori: Pori Art Museum, 1996), 112-19; Kenneth Robert Olwig, "Recovering the Substantive Nature of Landscape," *Annals of the Association of American Geographers* 86, no. 4 (1996), 630-53.
5. David Sibley, "Outsiders in Society and Space," in *Inventing Places*, eds. Kay Anderson and Fay Gale (Melbourne: Longman, 1992), 107-21; Samu Pehkonen, *"Tänne, muttei pidemmälle!" Alta-kamppailu ja Pohjois-Norjan monikulttuurinen maisema* (Tampere: Tampere Peace Research Institute/Tapri, Rauhan- ja konfliktintutkimuskeskuksen tutkimuksia, no. 88, 1999).
6. Rob Shields, *Places on the Margin* (London: Routledge, 1991); Simon Schama, *Landscape and Memory* (London: Fontana Press, 1995), 75-135.
7. Paul Connerton, *How Societies Remember* (Cambridge: Cambridge University Press, 1989).
8. Neil Smith, *Uneven Development* (Oxford: Basil Blackwell, 1984); Yrjö Haila, "Onko adaptaatio evoluution johtava teema?," *Luonnon Tutkija* 96 (1992), 61-65.
9. Heikki Seppä, "Mires of Finland," *Fennia* 180, no. 1-2 (2002), 43-60.
10. Hannes Sihvo, *Karjalan kuva* (Helsinki: Suomalaisen Kirjallisuuden Seura/Finnish Literature Society, Helsinki, 1973); Elias Lönnrot, *Matkat 1828–1844* (Espoo: Weiling & Göös, 1980).
11. Ari Aukusti Lehtinen, "Northern Natures," *Fennia* 169, nos. 1, (1991), 110-29.
12. Luhta, *Tansseja aavalla*, 62; the quotation is translated by the author.

13. Toimi Kangasniemi, Matti Koskenniemi, Lyyli Miettinen and Oiva Saari, *Luonnontieto I* (Porvoo: WSOY, 1956), 78; translated by the author, as are all the quotations from the textbooks.
14. Vilho Myrsky and Arvo Ulvinen, *Oma maamme* (Porvoo: Werner Söderström, 1960), 51.
15. Helmer Smeds and Paul Fogelberg, *Nyky-Suomi kuvin ja kartoin* (Porvoo: Werner Söderström, 1967), 46-48.
16. Väinö Voionmaa, *Suomen talousmaantieto* (Porvoo: Werner Söderström, 1922); Väinö Auer and K. Merikoski, *Maantieto.* (Helsinki: Otava/Valistus, 1939, second edition in 1951); Iivari Leiviskä, *Suomen maantieto* (Porvoo: Werner Söderström, 1947); Leo Aario, *Suomen maantiede* (Helsinki: Otava, 1966).
17. Crop failures and famines occurred repeatedly in Finland in the late 19th century, occasionally having catastrophic impacts on the rural poor. Approximately 10-12 percent of Finnish people died of hunger or related diseases during the most severe periods of famine in the late 1860s. Climatic strain has served in the official histories as the main cause and explanation for these hunger disasters, as "farming is always a risky business at these northern latitudes," Matti Klinge, *A Brief History of Finland* (Helsinki: Otava, 2000), 100. The then general atmosphere of industrial-liberalism largely ignored the need for agricultural reforms (in a period with a rapid population growth in rural areas), and this undoubtedly had an impact on the birth of the disaster, see Ari Aukusti Lehtinen, "Pohjoinen: uhan ja hallinnan maisema," *Terra* 110, no. 1 (1998), 44-45. The natural explanation has served through decades as a unifying factor behind the collective construction of Finnishness, whereas the latter explanation, focusing on the unjust production of social vulnerability, has functioned as a tool for politicizing the practical socioenvironmental choices.
18. Urho Kekkonen, *Onko maallamme malttia vaurastua?* (Helsinki: Otava, 1952).
19. Minna Tanskanen, *Näkyvän takana. Tutkimus metsäojitetun suomaiseman kulttuurisuudesta* (Joensuu: University of Joensuu, Department of Geography Publications, no. 8, 2000).
20. Ilmari Hustich, *Suomi tänään* (Helsinki: Tammi, 1965), 16.
21. Voionmaa, *Suomen talousmaantieto*, 99.
22. Auer and Merikoski, *Maantieto*, 310.
23. Viljo Holopainen, *60-luvun metsäpolitiikka* (Porvoo: WSOY, 1967), 31.
24. *Metsä 2000. The Main Report of the Forest 2000 Programme* (Helsinki: Talousneuvosto/The Board of Economics, 1985); *Indicators for Sustainable Forestry in Finland* (Helsinki: Ministry of Agriculture and Forestry, 1992); *Pro Silvis. Metsien puolesta. Metsäpoliittisen keskustelun tueksi* (Helsinki: Metsämiesten Säätiö, 1995).
25. Martti Aarne, Matti Uusitalo and Helena Herrala-Ylinen, eds., *Metsätilastollinen vuosikirja 1989* (Helsinki: Metsäntutkimuslaitos, 1990).
26. Auer and Merikoski, *Maantieto*, 49
27. Seppo Sikkinen, "Teollisuus," in *Suomen maantiede*, ed. Kalevi Rikkinen (Keuruu: Otava, 1977), 87.
28. Tanskanen and Palviainen, "Rahkamättäitä, ojia vai turvekenttiä?"
29. Sopo, "Turve—fossiilinen vai biopolttoaine?;" Sopo and Aalto, "Turveteollisuus Suomessa."
30. Aario, *Suomen maantiede*, 260.
31. Sakari Topelius, *Maamme kirja* (Porvoo: WSOY, 1981).

32. Yrjö Kaijärvi and Leo Tiainen, *Suomalainen maisema runoudessa ja maalaustaiteessa* (Helsinki: Tammi, 1946); Eija Kämäräinen, *Suomalaisen maiseman 4 vuodenaikaa* (Porvoo: WSOY, 1990).
33. Reino Kalliola, "Eliömaantiede," in *Suomen maantiede*, ed. Kalevi Rikkinen (Keuruu: Otava, 1977), 46.
34. Hannele Rikkinen, *Maantiede koulussa* (Helsinki: Helsinki University Press, 1989), 16-19; Yrjö Haila and Richard Levins, *Humanity and Nature* (London: Pluto Press, 1992), 1-13; Perttu Vartiainen, "Geografi som lärdomsämne i Finland," in *Traditioner i Nordisk kulturgeografi*, ed. Jan Öhman (Uppsala: Nordisk Samhällsgeografisk Tidskrift, 1994), 63-69; Jouni Häkli, *Meta hodos. Johdatus ihmismaantieteeseen* (Tampere: Vastapaino, 1999), 45-62.
35. Luhta, *Tansseja aavalla*, 158; see also Eino Leino, *Elämäni kuvakirja* (Keuruu: Otava, 1996, originally published in 1925), 187-98, for an insightful comparison between school geography and lay geographies of nature.
36. Seppä, "Mires of Finland," 44.
37. Matti Leinonen, Teuvo Nyberg and Olavi Vestelin, *Koulun biologia. Metsä ja suot* (Keuruu: Otava, 1994); Matti Leinonen, Teuvo Nyberg, Pirkko Kenno and Olavi Vestelin, *Koulun maantieto. Suomi* (Keuruu: Otava, 1996).
38. Kirsi Hakala, ed., *Suo on kaunis* (Helsinki: Maahenki, 1999); Arto Seppälä, ed., *Suon syvä syli* (Helsinki: Maahenki ja Suoseura, 1999); Tanskanen, *Näkyvän takana*.
39. Luhta, *Tansseja aavalla*.
40. Jukka Alm, *CO2 and CH4 Fluxes and Carbon Balance in the Athmospheric Interaction of Boreal Peatlands* (Joensuu: University of Joensuu, Publications in Sciences, no. 44, 1997).

6.

Raubwirtshaft in the North? Branding the Northern Forests

Together with several leading authors in the UK, the "mother" of Harry Potter, J.K. Rowling, announced in October 2003 that her forthcoming books should solely be published on nature-friendly paper, based either on recycled fiber or from forestry not utilizing old-growth forests. The famous author argued with several of her British colleagues for the preservation of forests, and the message was widely directed to the leading forest companies of the world. The British forest worry emphasized in particular that in Finland and Canada loggings largely still threaten old-growth forests.[1]

The message was received in Finland with contradicting reactions and with large publicity. Forest companies UPM (UPM-Kymmene) and M-real (Metsä-Serla) quickly provided a letter to Rowling that assured the sustainability of forestry behind their paper processing. The paper of Harry Potter books was guaranteed to come from other than old-growth forests. The representative of Rowling replied promptly that there was no need for further clarification in respect to Finland and Sweden: the forestry practices of these countries satisfied the author.[2]

The public debate in Finland, however, boomed for a while. The speculation on the initial sources of "false information" of the UK authors surfaced and environmental organizations, especially Greenpeace, were those most suspected. One Finnish newspaper, *Iltasanomat*, even launched a patriotic poll for the readers whether the Finns should boycott Harry Potter.[3] Finnish forest professionals also participated in the debate and for example Kirsi-Marja Korhonen, the district director of the Finnish State Forest Service in western Lapland, considered the British attack unfair. According to her, all the old-growth forests are not worth conserving and in Upper Lapland, which was the main target of the UK campaign, 40 percent of the forests have already gained a conservation status. Korhonen also criticized Rowling's willingness to defend reindeer herders against loggings in the old-growth forests. She thought that Greenpeace had taken advantage of the authors by offering them false and one-sided information: "The authors do not have the opportunity to assess what is really going on", argued Korhonen and continued that one central problem is "the emotional talk on the old trees threatened by loggings."[4]

Arto Paasilinna, a well-known Finnish author, used much stronger words against the British colleagues and Greenpeace. He commented that Finnish forestry is "at the top of the world" and "it conserves nature better than any other system, for example in Central Europe." Paasilinna did not value the environmentalists high who according to him are only looking for sensations: "Greenpeace staff are good-for-nothing people, only after adventurous life." He was primarily worried about loggers and blamed the environmentalists and the British authors for the rising risk of unemployment in the forest provinces.[5]

This type of environmental dialogue has a decades-long history in Finnish forest politics. Already in the 1980s and early 1990s, during the initial phases of current internationalization of Finnish forest-industrial operations (see chapter 12), environmental worries of the same kind came into international publicity and also then they were followed by strong patriotic opposition. *Wie in Brasilien* (*Die Zeit,* 14 April 1989) and *Plünderer im Norden* (*Der Spiegel,* 15 November 1993), declared the headlines of the articles in German journals dealing with Finnish forestry. Finnish forestry practices were considered as harmful to the forest ecology as the clear-cuttings of the rain forests in Brazil.

The immediate reactions in Finland emphasized the dirty tricks of the environmentalists who were then regarded as mainly Finnish. The environmentalists distributing this critical material were cited as conspirators and traitors of the country.[6] The rise of international environmental concern about Finnish forests, however, forced the national forest sector to strengthen its efforts in image competition. Active branding of the sector started in the early 1990s.

Fears of a reduced market share led the Finnish forest sector to organize in autumn 1992 an international campaign to polish the tarnished ecological image of the national industry. The Finnish Forest Association launched the *PlusForest* campaign aimed at ridding the paper markets of the "threat of emotion." The thrust of the campaign was directed toward Western and Central Europe and described the healthy forests and sustainable forestry behind Finnish paper products. The needs of free public access to outdoor nature, multiple use and natural biodiversity were also proclaimed to be guaranteed in Finnish economic forests.[7]

Image campaigns took on more and more importance in Finnish forest politics during the 1990s, and this was the case especially among the largest companies. The practical reason for this was the increased media attention and the intensified consumer interest on the product cycles and their ecological and social "footprints." Consumer attitudes at the international scale are the factor strongly affecting the market share of the industry that exports about 90 percent of the paper produced in the country. The competition over image has inevitably become an essential part of European forest politics. The forest debate has accordingly expanded from the meetings of the forest and environmental professionals to the daily life of lay citizens, worrying for example about the sustainability of the process behind their morning newspaper. The debate is increasingly shaped by symbolic moves in the popular media.

This development has brought with it a widening bifurcation of forest discourses. Corporate responsibility reports, published by the key companies, undoubtedly mirror the ongoing changes within the organizations, and strengthen their credibility in the eyes of the larger public, but the reports also tend to shade the actual trends taking place in the forest-industrial practices.[8] Reflections upon falling employment caused by corporate redevelopment or signs of trade cartels are, for obvious reasons, nonexisting on the pages of responsibility reports. They turn into publicity only by those journalists who have contacts with critical researchers or inspectors of antitrust laws. Similar signs of decoupling (of images and actual profiles) can also be noticed among the environmentalists and forest conservationists. Media successes have become celebrated as "environmental victories" and this achievement is not tarnished by analyses of the worrying trends in industrial development. The media tricks of the conservationists have also been sharply criticized by the industry and the rural people earning their living in and off the forests.

This chapter discusses the brands, images, prejudices and stereotypes afoot in the forest debate. The empirical study focuses on the environmental debate concerning the forests in Ilomantsi, North Karelia, in eastern Finland.[9] First, the mechanisms and processes through which the debate proceeds are illustrated. This section includes an interpretation of the most recent reorganization of the power relations between rural residents and forest owners, forest conservationists and the industry. Second, some central rural perceptions of conservationists reproduced within the forest debate are examined. Third, a critical evaluation of the logic of forest conservation is presented. The conclusive part of the chapter is concerned about the sociocultural ignorance of nature conservationists, which seems to push local rural residents, as defenders of their home forests, in environmental opposition. The empirical analysis is focused on the first years of international reorganization of environmental debate in rural Finland. "Environmental fronts" were reshaped then and this has largely affected the formation of later debates, for example within Natura 2000 planning and when formulating forest certification models.[10]

Environmental Co-networking

The 1990s witnessed significant changes in the Finnish forest debate. The power relations between and within the central interest groups underwent a thorough reformulation. This was due to the deep economic recession Finland underwent in the early 1990s. Radical reforms within most fields of public financing were considered necessary and reductions in nature conservation costs also became actual. This initiation was largely welcomed in the forest provinces of Finland where nature conservation was ranked as one of the prime reasons for the economic crisis and widespread unemployment. The broader political reorganization was also related to the internationalization of the forest industry, which had increased uncertainty and vulnerability in Finnish forest-based development. Entrepreneurial strategies had freed themselves markedly from the national framework and therefore the old state-centered arguments and groupings became outdated.

The role of forest conservation groups also changed in the 1990s. Cooperative contacts were established between conservationists and industrial actors. The main corporations were forced to pay more attention to environmental issues and this gradually eased the entrenched confrontations between industrial exploitation and conservation. Many of those concerned about environmental issues became professionals of ecological matters in governmental bodies or within the industry. The new environmental expertise could in this way construct a new authority across the old environmental fronts, a kind of green regime and framework through which environmental challenges could increasingly be managed.[11]

Forest companies thus became proactive in green issues and in some cases the companies and environmental organizations co-forged solutions satisfying also the consumers of paper. This link is based on the trade mechanism that includes forest certification and green branding, and it is negotiated without any necessary coordinative help from local, national or intergovernmental bodies of administration. The felling moratorium at the Finnish-Russian border was a good example of this type of actor-networking (see chapter 9). In the current globalization, both the main environmental organizations and forest companies operate across several spatial scales, from local to global, and this provides them with particular spatial mobility—if compared with local interest groups, such as forest dwellers, rural residents and local landowners that base their arguments on experiences of changes in their daily living conditions. This setting also explains many of the local attitudes against translocal actors, rising from a humiliation rooting in the experience of not having an equal voice in decisive goal formulation.

How has this power reorganization affected the relationship between local rural actors on the one hand and forest conservationists and environmental organizations on the other? How have the role and behavior of the conservationists changed in the new actor-networking and along with internationalization and professionalization? What about the environmental thoughts of rural lay citizens in general? Have they any voice in today's local-global environmental co-management? These questions are dealt with below by focusing on the debate on the old-growth forests in Ilomantsi in eastern Finland.

The Fight over the Old-growth Forests

One of the initial episodes of the internationalization of forest-based decision-making was related to the future of the pristine old-growth forests in Finland. The backwoods, or *Urwälder*, where no large-scale logging had taken place during the last hundred years or more, became an issue among the consumers in Central Europe. In addition, protection of biodiversity became a leading concern in conservation discussion, and 40 percent of the Finnish species of flora and fauna facing extinction were estimated to live in forests. The old-growth forests were understood as home areas for species of high risk. The ecological inventories of the remaining pristine forests, therefore, became the main project in Finnish forest conservation in the 1990s.

Those arguing for biodiversity wondered about the ongoing expansion of industrial forestry into the last frontiers of the old-growth forests—at the same time when forest professionals stressed the sustainability of Finnish forest management. The estimations of the national annual wood increment had shown that it markedly exceeded (periodically up to 40 percent) the annual cuttings and this could easily be understood as a fact protecting the old-growth forests. The old-growth defenders repeatedly emphasized that raw-material potential from the economic forests that cover about 90 percent of Finnish forest land should be considered large enough to meet the industrial demand.

Some historical and sensible reasons for the expansion of industrial forestry into the old-growth forests can, however, be identified. The most important of these roots in the old German tradition of sustainability applied in Finnish forestry.[12] Sustainability has been for decades measured mathematically, in cubic meters, from the estimated wood increment and drain. When the latter exceeds the former, it is called sustained-yield forestry. Overproduction in the official forestry language refers to rotting timber left to circulate in the forest ecosystems and not mobilized for industrial processing. The fear of losing this raw material to the forest ecosystems has been the primary worry for the official forestry strategists. The fear has been expressed in the forest programs from the 1980s and 1990s, including the latest National Forest Plan, as a desire for full utilization.[13]

The yield from the young planted economic forests, which currently produce the main share of the annual wood increment, is due to their scanty wood biomass not easily utilized. This fact increases the pressure to exploit the old-growth forests. The exploitation has functioned as a means of realizing the demand based on the abstract figures from the matrices of sustained-yield forestry. The result, i.e. the rising wood increment, of the costly intensification of forest management during the last decades is deliberately not seen as a loss to nature.

One central reason for the persistence of Finnish forest conflicts lies in the fact that the official forest policy has been built on the ideal of full utilization of the annual wood increment. This goal is based on the supposition that it is possible to run an overall nationally coordinated forest strategy regardless of the differences and challenges caused by regional and sociocultural variations inside the country. The supposition flies in the face of experiences from the recent decades and it also undermines the social and societal obstacles to maximal utilization.

The idea of sustainability based on calculations in cubic meters furthermore highlights a common limitation rather central in the modern Western ideology of nature. It is not rare to find arguments in forest policy following the notion of nature as something from where absolute facts can be directly derived. These facts are often seen as forming a firm and unconditional basis for resource exploitation and environmental policy. Official sustainability in forestry means that an indicator that reflects some aspects of the biotic potential of forests is considered to contain an unquestioned value in forest policy. The selection of the indicator and the mode of calculations are seen as neutral actions not affected by cultural or societal ambitions.

The above criticism of official measurements in forestry can and should also be extended to cover similar calculations in forest conservation, for example in nature inventories, measures of biodiversity, red lists of species facing extinction, etc. As formulated in the introductory part of this volume, the starting point here is the remark that a direct application of the results of these inventories neglects the cultural and social dimensions of our interrelationships with nature. It serves as an example of natural science-dominated explanatory power extended to the fields of human action and value-formation. This neglect has become of lasting importance in forest conservation, especially in issues concerning the old-growth forests. The following description of an episode in this debate serves as an illustration of local formation of environmental opposition and communicative difficulties between the interest groups involved.

Hattuvaara: Forest Microhistory at the Greenbelt

"Not one more square meter for conservation," was the conclusion of a meeting held in Hattuvaara in Ilomantsi in autumn 1992 by the representatives of the easternmost municipalities in Finland. The message, clear and rather unanimous, was directed against the new national proposal for protecting the last state-owned old-growth forests in the southern half of the country. The proposal was considered to be undemocratically drafted and fundamentally in violation of the Finnish Constitution. The fact that the national proposal affected only state-owned lands, and not privately-owned, did not apparently disturb the collective attitude. The locals were represented as united in their opposition to the conservationists from the South.[14]

The meeting in Hattuvaara estimated that the national program for conserving the old-growth forests would cost, if enacted, four billion Finnish Marks, equaling close to 700 million euros in today's currency. This sum was derived from the amount and value of timber lost in the conserved forests, if left uncut. In the case of Hattuvaara, it was stated that the program would mean loss of work for ten permanent loggers and an evacuation of the village. The word evacuation is rather emotionally loaded in Finland, calling up memories of the Winter War and the Continuation War of the early 1940s and the common enemy who threatened from the East at that time.

The village of Hattuvaara in eastern Finland had remained long on the front pages of the newspapers. In 1980, the villagers demonstrated against the airplane-assisted chemical extermination of the deciduous ground vegetation of their home forests. The continuance of local gathering practices (picking mushrooms and wild berries) was a shared motive for the villagers and conservationists. Actions of this type, which soon spread to different parts of Finland, finally resulted in the cancellation of the sprayings from the air.[15]

In 1985, the village functioned as the main arena for protests against the Forest Karelia plan initiated by Enso (Enso Gutzeit, Stora Enso), a forest company that holds the dominant position in wood processing in the province of North Karelia. The central aim of the Forest Karelia plan was to transfer over 100,000 hectares of state forest to Enso Gutzeit which would then guarantee the continuance and further development of Enso's pulp production in North Karelia. The demonstrators against the land transfer were afraid of large-scale company forestry that would dramatically affect forest work and local gathering practices.[16]

In the early 1990s, the strong reactions against the conservation of the old-growth forests highlighted the role of Hattuvaara, the small eastern village of 230 inhabitants, as a symbol of Finnish forest tensions. Hattuvaara can be seen as a "short summary" of Finnish forestry history. Interestingly enough, the battle lines between stakeholders were completely changed during the late 1980s and early 1990s. The message from the village was previously directed against the questionable forest management methods and against the "number one" in the North Karelian economy, Enso Gutzeit, but later the main enemy become nature conservation from the South.

How had this turn become possible? What had happened in Finnish society to make nature conservation the main threat in the backwoods? Had nature conservation methods—the means of argumentation and action—changed to such an extent that the rural criticism from Hattuvaara was understandable? The answers to these questions can be found by examining the perceptions of nature conservation commonly held in the backwoods villages and thereafter by returning to the societal reliability of contemporary nature conservationists. The empirical material comes from the actual debate carried on in the media and from the interviews[17] made in Ilomantsi in autumn 1993.

Neo-Karelian Folklore

On the basis of the interviews, it is easy to see the main problem in the heated situation: little valid information had been available to either the laymen or the local politicians. On the other hand, very little had apparently been done in Ilomantsi to broaden the informational background. The Committee Report[18] containing the proposal for old-growth conservation had not even been seen by most of those interviewed. Attitudes had therefore been largely founded on occasional hearsay and debates in local and provincial newspapers. This lack of accurate information had resulted in rumors persistently circling and developing within the local forest debate.

The interviewees were as a rule convinced that the old-growth forests that would gain the legal conservation status would become areas where no human visitation is allowed. The status of the old-growths was thus considered equal to that of the strict nature reserves that have been primarily founded for scientific purposes. This argument was also put forward at the meeting of the Ilomantsi Municipal Council in April 1992, when the decision to "defend the municipality from full conservation" was made.[19] The Committee Report, however, notes that the degree of conservation of demarcated old-growth forests only seeks to protect against human actions that would be harmful to the biophysical conditions of the area at large.[20] This being the case, all gathering activities are to be allowed in the demarcated old-growth forests.

The view that new conservation forests will be founded only for some particular endangered species of flora or fauna was commonly shared among the local people. Opinions against the necessity of protecting strange tiny beetles, instead of loggers, were repeatedly expressed. The understanding of forest ecology was in general rather focused: The old-growth forests, full of rotting wood, were considered to be places for the reproduction of those beetles and mushrooms that are extremely harmful to the economic forests surrounding them.

The local opinion about the forest ecology was thus quite opposite to that expressed in the Committee Report by the nature specialists. An intensive inventory of the values of nature formed the basis for the official old-growth proposal. The Report considered the virgin forests as reserves for the future—both in ecological and economic terms. It stated that the last remaining wildernesses in Northern Europe could become particular attractions for tourism and also an image-building factor for the Finnish forest industry.

During the interviews, estimations of the percentage of forests to be protected in Ilomantsi by the Committee proposal confusingly fluctuated between 2 and 20. The official documents of the Ilomantsi Municipal Council[21] even mention such conservation measures that would cover 30,000 hectares and thus represent 10 percent of the land area of the municipality. The estimation included everything conserved by legislation or by some other administrative agreements. A uniqueness of Ilomantsi is that large areas of treeless peatland have been conserved. However, as was stated by conservationists, if we talk logically about forest conservation, the legislated conservation area covered 2.6 percent of the forest area of Ilomantsi, and this area would be doubled if the official proposal were to be enacted. The final total would then reach approximately 3000 hectares.[22]

In the light of the fluctuating numbers, the most commonly used argument of the interviewees against forest conservation was based on its effects on employment. They believed that loggers would disappear as a result of exaggerated conservation, and this attitude was often expressed very colorfully:

> The village lives and dies with the loggers.
> The loggers will become museum curiosities.
> Our land will become a deserted wilderness, visited only by nature conservationists and frontier guards.
> Southerners with long hair and beards will replace the natives of Ilomantsi.

In the easternmost municipalities, the end cuttings of the forests had become rare due to the disappearance of old-growth forests that today form a sparse network of small relics between the even-aged and monotonous economic forests. Due to the fragmentation and scarcity of pristine forests, the relationship between local residents and foresters on the one hand and conservationists on the other had become strained. It was broadly accepted that the conservation of these last "islands" of old-growth would rather directly affect the employment of the loggers.

The total of the hectares "threatened" by conservation is, however, so small that it could not seriously be seen as any challenge to employment in the local forestry sector. The introduction of motorized logging tractors was already continuously lessening the employment of more manually-employed forest workers.[23] Despite the fact that the interviewees were well aware of these trends in motorization and automatization, their willingness to criticize the redevelopment strategies of the Finnish State Forest Service and Enso Gutzeit was strikingly limited. The official redevelopment was mainly considered to be a necessary accommodation during the economic recession and a means of dealing with the escalating international competition.

The view of the nature conservation from the South as the common enemy seemed to create cohesion between the local residents. It was apparent that the southerners and newcomers confronting the majority attitude had become the inspiration of a new Karelian folklore. Borderland dwellers seemed to amuse one another during the neighborhood visits with exaggerated images of the invaders as day-dreamers and utopians, beetle men with iron chains to tie themselves to forest tractors and, above all, stealthy propagandists from the South.

The new folklorization concerning the protectors of the virgin forests reached a climax already in spring 1992 when municipal leaders in Ilomantsi announced that a group of "nature activists" were silently preparing a major conservation program covering large areas of the municipality.[24] Thereafter it was understood in Ilomantsi that:

> The ecological inventory of the old-growth forests is the work of conspirators. Whoever started the whole thing was apparently without any kind of useful work.

The conservationists received also some sympathy and the sympathizers considered it necessary to protect the beautiful scenery, natural biodiversity and valuable nature areas to be left for the future generations. Sometimes this view was, however, expressed in an ironic form:

> Of course, young people should learn to know what real peatland looks like.

The idea of conserving forests because of some tiny endangered fauna was regularly seen as bizarre:

> Why do they come here to conserve an area because of a worm that is one millimeter long and has six spots on its back, instead of the normal four? How on earth did they even come to find these poor creatures? Over there, behind our barn, there are eight-spot worms living in manure, why don't they protect them?
> No household needs to be evacuated because of a woodpecker.
> It is in the long beards of the southerners that the strangest of the small creatures live.

A common attitude in Ilomantsi was that there were already enough conservation areas and no new ones were needed. The observed exaggerations in nature conservation were clearly labeled as the inanities of people ignorant of the living conditions in the forest provinces:

> The forests of Ilomantsi are more protected than the people living here.
> The forests have been here forever, what's the hurry to conserve them now?
> The forests will not disappear by cutting them down.
> They come here, those young men from the cities with long hair and pony tails, and tell us what to do, even though they have no practical connection to this world.
> Those long hairs from the urban upper class criticize us for making our living here.
> They only lie in their tents while the loggers work. And then they hang around here with their beer cans and polluting old Ladas—only disturbing the nesting wild birds.

The district state forester, Tarmo Uusitalo, became a central instigator of the new folklore. In spring 1993, immediately after his early retirement, he declared in an interview that the hunger of the conservationists has no limits and their aim is to take every hectare out of forestry. The welfare of this country is, he argued, based on wood, and by processing wood the country will also become free from the economic recession. The old forester was also critical of the increased sensitivity of the forest industry toward its green image. According to him, the industry passed the problem onto the forest administrators by supporting the conservation of the old-growth forests: "They thought they could free themselves from the wolves but it does not work that way."[25]

In November 1993, Uusitalo further unleashed his undiluted anger toward nature conservationists in a large reportage in the *Karjalainen*, the main provincial newspaper in North Karelia. The retired state forester saw the conservationists as a threat to global development: "Conservationists have become greedy for power, and they want to govern the whole world. The conservation ideology in Finland is similar to extreme nationalism and communism, and it also resembles all those fundamentalist religious movements."[26] The main provincial newspaper gave a good deal of space to the state forester's anger.

It was apparent that local attitudes against nature conservation were produced and strengthened on the basis of a strange mixture of a deep-rooted senses of injustice and sporadic rumors about the acts of the conservationists. A large amount of biased information had emerged during the old-growth debate. The responsibility of spreading valid and easily accessible information naturally lay in the hands of the Old Growth Committee and its background organization, the Ministry of the Environment. Ministerial links to Ilomantsi were strikingly weak. This state of affairs was partially caused by the unwillingness of the local civil servants to cooperate with the nature conservationists.

The Limits of Ecological Mind

The change in local attitudes in relation to nature conservation reflects the broader contours of local-global development but it also mirrors the changes in the general argumentation of conservationists. The conservation debate had been strongly redirected in the 1980s toward the indigenous values of nature. Nature in itself was increasingly seen in need of conservation.[27] The spirited discussion about biodiversity as an intrinsic value of nature was a good example of this reorientation. The argumentation for saving the endangered species was then, as it still is, largely conditioned by urban values: nature is considered more as an outdoor park to be occasionally visited than a concrete everyday condition for human life. Such an external attitude to nature is viewed as incomprehensible in the forest villages—where the environing nature often emerges in the form of everyday challenges of livelihood and where nature becomes meaningful only when integrated into daily social practices.

The viewpoint emerging from the everyday lifeworld of the forest provinces is often manifested in the form of stark expressions of self-confidence based on the understanding of the indigenous lifemode. It is emphasized that this is the way we have lived here for centuries, and this is the way we are going to make it also in the future. No comments by outsiders are welcomed. The locals also think they know how to conserve nature and it is often stressed that this in fact is the reason why the "green people" are here now; aiming at conserving the nature we have been living in and off for centuries.[28]

Behind these expressions from the inside of the rural lifeworld, it is not difficult to find signs of broader societal dependencies. The inserts of the interviews lean on the history of logging and welfare bound to wood processing, but they also refer to the war-time evacuations, life conditions at the border area and frontier guards. The local events and their interpretations seem to carry a wide spectrum of traces of broader societal changes. In the eastern forest provinces of Finland, the societal dependencies are strongly tied to the continuous reproduction of the values of Western modernization, especially those connected to industrialization and the sociospatial division of labor following it.[29] The introduction of new values have in practice gradually modified the local routines even though they are often, if selectively, considered practices inherited from the local past. The practical changes and the reflected expressions of the changes serve as an example of local decoupling, a mechanism that seems to be used to maintain local self-confidence, the cohesion of the local community.[30]

The collective view of the locals can therefore be regarded as an abstraction on two levels. First, local opinion is by historical necessity a result and a tool of the broader societal reorganization. It is tied to countless overlapping politico-economic and cultural projections from the "the outside". Second, local opinion is often a programmatic vision expressed by those in leading positions, and with specific personal co-dependencies with the outside. Locality is seldom, if ever, a homogeneous subject. An illusion of shared interests is, however, often used as a ground for political legitimacy.[31]

On the other hand, the ecological framework of forest conservation, encircled around rare species of flora and fauna, tends to ignore the questions of human survival and local social viability. Forest ecology, not the regional variations of forest cultures, motivates the conservationists. The Ministry of the Environment has been repeatedly assessed as being poorly motivated and equipped to cope with the general public and those primarily affected by its projects. The first two decades (1983–2003) of the Ministry's history were a period of deepening conflicts with rural people and their lobby groups.[32]

Finland is still a country where peasant values have a strong effect on politics and this fact has been largely neglected by the official strategists of nature conservation. Rural criticism against nature conservation is part of the politico-historical conflict between the urban values defended by the Social Democrats and the Conservatives and rural-industrial values defended by the Finnish Center Party. From the backwoods point of view, the Ministry of the Environment is seen as having initially been established to serve the urban ideology and therefore its role is automatically contrary to the interests of rural residents. As a result of these deep-rooted political confrontations, and due to weaknesses in public relations, it has been easy for the rural lobbyists to construct caricatures of nature conservation. According to this view, the conservationists come from the South and are willing to turn our home forests into nature parks where human beings are not allowed.

This image is a simple political tool, but it follows the general characteristics of conservationists. The arguments for nature conservation are exclusively based on abstract ecological facts about the state of the environment with no clear adjustment made for the cultural lifemodes affected by the new conservation programs.[33] For a nature conservationist, nature functions everywhere according to the same natural laws. There is no room for doubts about the capability of the modern natural sciences to fully explain the events of nature. No credence is given to the possibility that the objectified nature of the natural sciences might only be one interpretation of nature—a particular Western metanarrative about nature's structures and processes, currently occupying the dominant position. This dominance allows no flexibility toward social sensitivity in our interrelations with nature. It allows no room for culture-specific ideas and practices of nature. Nature is then solely universal, not context-dependent or local-global. This gap can be seen in the eastern Finnish context as one of the main obstacles to a more comprehensive nature conservation policy with broader societal support.

Accordingly, the field-work practices of forest conservationists tend to increase rural suspiciousness. The forest inventories have excluded the locals as key informants of their home forests and therefore they have been left alone to develop their own interpretations and attitudes. The locals have perhaps been only afterwards able to read from the media about new findings of rare and strange species in the nearby forests. Along with ignoring the local knowledge on nature, the local motives for conserving some parts of their home forests are left to erode. In some cases, radical forest conservationists who lean their strategies on successful media campaigns and actions have also become easy targets for categorical condemnation. The rural stereotype of a conservationist thus does not emerge from nothing. It much reflects the social ambitions and conditions of the locals but it also corresponds with the overall actions of nature conservation.

The tension between rural people and conservationists is deeply rooted in the cultural and political disagreements but fuelled and sharpened, and thus forged, by the strategic weaknesses of conservationists. The "ecological eye" of the conservationists ignores too many of the values important for the people living in the forest provinces. A way out of this setting preconditions a profound rethinking of the motives and targets of nature conservation: a shift from ecological reasoning to socioenvironmental thinking is needed. The final part of this chapter examines one of the socioenvironmental challenges that have thoroughly modified the context of forest conservation in Finland, namely forest taxation. The renewal of taxation has not yet become an issue among the nature conservationists.

At the Core of Socioenvironmentalism: Forest Taxation

One of the key mechanisms of Finnish forest politics, and central modifiers of rural dependency, has been the forest taxation system that has undergone a substantial change during the late 1990s and the early 21st century. In 1993, forest taxation changed radically. Timber sales have since then formed the underlying criteria for taxation, not the regional criteria tied to estimated wood increment, as was the case earlier. The transitional period was prolonged to 13 years, giving each forest owner the right to choose the date of the personal shift to the new system.

The old practice of taxation had its roots in the 1920s but the taxation system was profoundly modified after World War II in favor of industrial and export activities. The steady flow of raw material to pulp and paper plants was to be ensured by guiding the forest owners to make regular annual cuttings. Finland had to be rebuilt after the wartime damage and reparations, and wood processing was considered to be the locomotive of Finland's economy. For forest owners, area-based taxation offered no feasible alternatives to industrial forest management. The taxes had to be paid every year and it was therefore expensive to leave larger areas uncut.

The new taxation based on timber sales provides, in principle, alternatives to industrial forestry. The long transitional period resulted, however, in a growing supply of wood from private forests. As was expected, most forest owners were willing to free themselves from the annual taxes by selling their mature forests as soon as possible and moving thereafter over to the new tax system. As a result, the 1990s witnessed an oversupply of wood in relation to the demand of end products of wood processing abroad. The position of forest owners in sales negotiations consequently worsened and the price of timber fell. Towards the end of the transition period, the deadline for tax-free selling of timber has moreover pushed forest owners to maximize timber outflow from their woods, and this has resulted in a decline of the old-growth forests with particular ecological and recreational values.

The changes in forest taxation have revealed many of the undercurrents in Finnish forest politics. Forest owners, of whom less than half are bound to the agricultural lifemode today, are gradually losing their practical connection to forest-based living and influence in central decision-making. The forests owners represent a wide array of interests groups but in general, along with broader societal changes, the motive of valuing forests as capital has become popular. Forests have increasingly turned into investment targets paying secure dividends to the shareholders.[34]

The gradual environmental co-learning of the conservationists and rural forest owners has also resulted in new, if still rather weak and preliminary, models of forest conservation by further capitalizing the values of nature in ways that would not harm it. This trend is traceable for example in negotiations on establishing new nature conservation areas on private lands. Landowners have learnt how to utilize the options of nature conservation (see chapter 10) and, in southern Finland, new tools for voluntary forest conservation have been tested as part of the Metso program.[35]

The private forests that have been established as conservation areas, periodically or permanently, give remarkable financial returns to the landowner. The new Metso model is aimed at breaking the sharp historical dualism between conservation and exploitation and at least in principle it offers the landowner an alternative to nature conservation by selling values of nature. It provides a mechanism for those forest owners critical of the dominating trends in Finnish forest management who happen to own forests with significant ecological values. It also offers a tool for speculation as periodical conservation, covering often ten years, can also be seen as only a delay in logging plans. The Metso model is, however, an important tool when seeking for alternative courses in nature conservation.[36] For many of the environmental co-actors, selling and saving nature are no longer necessarily conflicting with each other.

Notes

1. Tuomas Manninen, "Enso ja UPM kilpailevat Potterin paperista," *Ilta-Sanomat*, 22 October 2003, 12; Uki Kiviranta, "Potter-kirjailija eksyi suomalaismetsään," *Apu*, 11 October 2003, 13.
2. Pasi Kivioja, "Potter-kirjailija hyväksyy suomalaisen paperin," *Iltasanomat*, 28 October 2003, 2.
3. Tuomas Manninen, "Joulupukki ei riittänyt, entä metsäteollisuus?" *Ilta-Sanomat* 22 October 2003, 2.
4. Kiviranta, "Potter-kirjailija eksyi suomalaismetsään," 13.
5. Kiviranta, "Potter-kirjailija eksyi suomalaismetsään," 12-13. The quotation is translated from Finnish by the author.
6. Lehtinen, Ari Aukusti, "Tales form the Northern Backwoods: Fairy Tales and Conspirators in Finnish Forest Politics," in *Approaching Nature from Local Communities. Security perceived and achieved*, ed. Anders Hjort-af-Ornäs (Linköping: Linköping University, Research Programme on Environmental Policy and Society/EPOS, 1996), 37.
7. Lehtinen, "Tales from the Northern Backwoods, 37-39.
8. Ari Aukusti Lehtinen and Pertti Rannikko, eds., *Leipäpuusta arvopaperia. Vastuun ja oikeudenmukaisuuden haasteet metsäpolitiikassa* (Helsinki: Metsälehti Kustannus, 2004), 19-21.
9. Ilomantsi is a municipality (6800 residents in 2002, 3172 square kilometers) in the province of North Karelia in eastern Finland. Ilomantsi is made up of small villages, forests, lakes and peatlands and it has about 100 kilometers of common border with Russia. Pogosta is the main center and both Lutheran and Orthodox churches are active in the municipality.
10. Ismo Björn, "Life in the Borderlands: The Takeover of Nature and Its Social Organization in North Karelia," in *Encountering the Past in Nature*, eds. Timo Myllyntaus and Mikko Saikku (Athens: Ohio University Press, 2000), 49-73; Hannes Mäntyranta, *Forest Certification* (Helsinki: Metsälehti Kustannus, 2002).
11. Wolfgang Sachs, "Sustainable Development and the Crisis of Nature: On the Political Anatomy of an Oxymoron," in *Living With Nature*, eds. Frank Fischer and Maarten A. Hajer (Oxford: Oxford University Press, 1999), 23-41; David Demeritt, "The Construction of Global Warming and the Politics of Science," *Annals of the Association of American Geographers* 91, no. 2 (2001), 307-37; Ari Aukusti Lehtinen and Pertti Rannikko, eds., *Oikeudenmukaisuus ja ympäristö* (Helsinki: Gaudeamus, 2003) 235-37.
12. Historically, the concept of sustained-yield forestry has been bound to (i) the idea of keeping the gross-extension of forest cover unchanged through replacement of the cuttings, either by natural or artificial means; to (ii) the maintenance of unchanged cut and; to (iii) the maintenance of the growing stock unchanged. Later the principle of sustainability was completed by (iv) the idea of progressiveness, which emphasizes active forest management that results in gradually increasing yield. The total drain, which includes the natural drain and the drain caused by loggings, is then kept below the level of wood increment in the longer run. These conceptions of sustainability and progressiveness within forestry highlight the relation between physical (absolute) wood increment and loggings within a given region. When the balance is positive, increment thus exceeds the total drain, the forestry is characterized as sustainable and progressive. However, the reduction

of the biotic potentials of forests into wood increment underestimates the silvicultural traditions and alternatives, i.e. the broader spectrum of forest utilization on a multiple-use basis, on conditions of modern wood refining and marketing interests (industrial and export-oriented forest management). The idea of sustainability grounded on estimates of absolute wood increment is invalid when taking into consideration the actual societal hindrances of forest management and loggings, taking shape as part of the innovations within agroforestry, expanding urban forest ownership and recreational appreciations. See a detailed explication of the problems of the sustained-yield paradigm: Jussi Raumolin, "Recent Trends in the Development of the Forest Sector in Finland and Eastern Canada," *Zeitschrift der Gesellsschaft fur Kanada -Studien* 11 (1986), 89-114.
13. *Metsä 2000. Pääraportti* (Helsinki: Talousneuvosto, 1985); *Metsä 2000. Tarkistustoimikunnan mietintö. Komiteanmietintöjä, no. 5* (Helsinki: Valtion Painatuskeskus, 1992); Jouni Suoheimo, "Kansallinen metsäohjelma kansainvälisenä mallina," *Helsingin Sanomat*, 14 August 2003, 2.
14. Ari Aukusti Lehtinen, "Satumetsiä ja metsäsatuja" in *Metsä ja metsänviljaa*, eds. Pekka Laaksonen and Sirkka-Liisa Mettomäki (Helsinki: Suomalaisen Kirjallisuuden Seura, 1994), 151.
15. Riitta Launis, ed., *Metsä Huutaa* (Helsinki: WSOY, 1984).
16. Only seventeen years later Enso Gutzeit, under the banner of Stora Enso, started preparations to externalize its forests. A subsidiary company, Tornator, was established to govern and (partially) sell the company forests. This was mainly due to signals from the stock markets considering forest as "idle capital" straining the shareholders' interests in Stora Enso. See Jukka Oksa, "Metsä-Karelia ja kansanliikkeet," *Yhteiskuntasuunnittelu* 23, no. 3, (1985), 15-23; Stora Enso, "Asset Restructuring Programme," <http://www.storaenso.com/2002> (15 Jan. 2002).
17. The interviews were made in Ilomantsi in August 1993. Those interviewed were both ordinary people from Ilomantsi and decision-makers or other key persons in the municipality. Forty-five students of geography at the University of Joensuu carried out the interviews and close to two hundred thematic interviews were completed and documented. The inserts are chosen from the large material by selecting only the most illustrative and representative comments. The translations are made by the author.
18. *Vanhojen metsien suojelu valtion mailla Etelä-Suomessa.* Komiteanmietintöjä, no. 70 (Helsinki: Ympäristöministeriö, 1992).
19. *Kannanotto hakkuista valtion mailla sekä Ilomantsin hoitoalueen ja sen työpaikkojen säilyttäminen.* Ilomantsin kunnanhallituksen pöytäkirja, no. 184 (Ilomantsi: Ilomantsin kunta, 1992).
20. *Vanhojen metsien suojelu valtion mailla Etelä-Suomessa.*
21. *Kannanotto hakkuista valtion mailla sekä Ilomantsin hoitoalueen ja sen työpaikkojen säilyttäminen.*
22. Veli-Matti Sorvari, "Ilomantsin hoitoalueen metsistä on lakisääteisesti suojeltu vain 2,6%,"
Karjalainen, 21 November 1992, 14; *Vanhojen metsien suojelu valtion mailla Etelä-Suomessa.*
23. Pertti Rannikko, "Forest Work as the Cause of Settlement and Depopulation in the Remote Parts of Finland," in *The Green Kingdom. Finland's Forest Cluster*, eds. Aarne Reunala, Ilpo Tikkanen and Esko Åsvik (Helsinki: Otava and Metsämiesten Säätiö, 1999), 222-26.

24. *Kannanotto hakkuista valtion mailla sekä Ilomantsin hoitoalueen ja sen työpaikkojen säilyttäminen.*
25. Petri Pöntinen, Pienten lukujen Hattuvaara (Tampere: University of Tampere, Institute of Communication Studies, 1993). An unpublished seminar paper (mimeo).
26. Reijo Erttola, "Miksi virkistys, suojelu ja metsätalous ei voi kulkea käsi kädessä?" *Karjalainen*, 8 November 1993, 4.
27. Pertti Rannikko, "Ympäristökamppailujen aallot," in *Kolilta Vuotokselle. Ympäristökamppailujen uusi aalto*, eds. Ari Aukusti Lehtinen and Pertti Rannikko (Helsinki: Gaudeamus), 11-28.
28. Ari Aukusti Lehtinen, "Northern Natures," *Fennia* 169, no.1 (1991), 132-5; Jarno Valkonen, *Lapin luontopolitiikka* (Tampere: Tampereen yliopisto, sosiologian ja sosiaalipsylokologian laitos, 2003), 201-10.
29. Ismo Björn, "Life in the Borderlands: The Takeover of Nature and Its Social Organization in North Karelia;" Ari Aukusti Lehtinen, "Modernization and the Concept of Nature: On the Reproduction of Environmental Stereotypes," in *Encountering the Past in Nature*, eds. Timo Myllyntaus and Mikko Saikku (Athens: Ohio University Press, 2000), 29-48.
30. Nigel Thrift, "Still Life in Nearly Present Time: The Object of Nature," *Body and Society* 6, nos. 3-4 (2000), 34-57.
31. Tim Ingold, *The Scolt Lapps Today* (Cambridge: Cambridge University Press, 1976); Sanna Aaltonen, "Jerisjärven ympäristökonflikti Rauhalan kyläläisten tulkitsemana," in *Kolilta Vuotokselle. Ympäristökamppailujen uusi aalto*, eds. Ari Aukusti Lehtinen and Pertti Rannikko (Helsinki: Gaudeamus, 1994), 72-91; Tim Beckley, "Pluralism by Default: Community Power in a Paper Mill Town," *Forest Science* 42, no. 1 (1996), 35-45.
32. Ismo Björn, "Oikeutta vai kansainvälistä ympäristöoikeutta?" in *Oikeudenmukaisuus ja ympäristö*, eds. Ari Aukusti Lehtinen and Pertti Rannikko (Helsinki Gaudeamus, 2003), 181-94; Annukka Oksanen, *Paikallisuuden ja kansainvälisyyden kohtaaminen luonnonsuojelussa. Tapaustutkimuksena Natura 2000 -ympäristökonflikti Lounais-Suomessa* (Turku: Turun yliopiston julkaisuja, no. C192, 2003).
33. Osmo Sarin and Kimmo Kumpulainen, eds., *Vanhaa metsää etsimässä* (Vantaa: Metsähallitus, 1998).
34. Ari Jokinen, "Temporalities and Routines in the Control of Private Forestry in Finland," in *Social Sustainability of Forestry in Northern Europe: Research and Education*, ed. Marjatta Hytönen (Copenhagen: Nordic Council of Ministers, 2001), 341-58.
35. Ari Jokinen, "Metsänomistajien osallisuus ja puunkasvun politiikka," in *Leipäpuusta arvopaperia. Vastuun ja oikeudenmukaisuuden haasteet metsäpolitiikassa*, eds. Ari Aukusti Lehtinen and Pertti Rannikko (Helsinki: Metsälehti Kustannus, 2004), 145-72.
36. See parallel remarks: Anja Nygren, "Environment as Discourse: Searching for Sustainable Development in Costa Rica," *Environmental Values* 7 (1998), 201-22; Noel Castree, "Bioprospecting: From Theory to Practice (and Back Again)," *Transactions of the Institute of British Geographers, New Series* 28 (2003), 35-55.

7.

Coping with the Local-Global Border: Westerning the Forest Sector in Russia

When President Vladimir Putin signed the decree to reorganize the Federal Forest Service and the State Committee for Nature Protection (Goskomekologya) on 17 May 2000, a major administrative change in environmental policy took place in Russia. The relatively autonomous status of both institutes was lost as they were integrated into the Ministry of Natural Resources. The Ministry's primary task has been resource mobilization, especially oil and gas production and mining, and now its responsibility has been expanded to include the fields of forestry and nature conservation.[1]

The decision ignited debates in the federal and local parliaments as well as throughout the administration. In addition, the European Union and the World Bank asked for an explanation in order to gain reassurance to continue their environmental and forestry projects in Russia. The Russian partner of the joint projects had disappeared, or at least had become reorganized, and confusion existed about the future form of cooperation. In addition, environmental non-governmental organizations soon collected 2.5 million signatures in Russia, demanding a referendum on the governance of the Russian environment. This included questions on the role and location of the Federal Forest Service, as well as a need for an independent environmental monitoring unit in Russia.[2]

The debates on the administrative reorganization mirror the deep problems of forestry and timber exploitation in Russia. During the 1990s, Russia had turned into an important exporter of roundwood. In 1999, about nine percent of the world's roundwood trade was supplied by Russia, which was equivalent to 41 million cubic meters. Western Europe has increasingly purchased timber from

Northwest Russia, whereas wood resources in the Russian East have attracted Japan, China and South Korea. These countries accounted for over 13 percent of Russia's total timber export in 1999. Of the individual countries, Finland receives a major share of the outflow of Russian timber, reaching 11.2 million cubic meters in 1999. Japan is the second most important client with seven million cubic meters in 1999.[3]

The above numbers indicate that both the western and eastern shores of the Russian taiga are currently under intensive forest-industrial change. Domestic industrial wood processing, especially pulp and paper production, is increasingly overrun by foreign companies offering higher prices for timber. In some places, local plants are short of raw material when the suppliers look across the borders. This is the case especially in the European part of Russia, and the forest industry in Siberia is aware of the problem. The Baikal region and the Russian Far East have become connected with the timber demand of the Pacific Rim. China is becoming a growing consumer of Siberian timber due to the shortage of its own raw material. The serious floods in the main Chinese rivers, partially caused by the widespread deforestation of the upstream woodlands, have resulted in strict regulation of the domestic wood supply.

This chapter gives an overview on the main forest-industrial areas in Russia; namely (i) the northwestern regions in the European part of the country, and (ii) the Russian East, consisting of two separate units: Baikal–Upper Yenisey region and the Far East at the Pacific coast. The differing industrial paths of these regions are described on a multi-scale basis, paying attention to differences in regional, federal and international interactions. Finally, some general remarks on the characteristics of the forest-industrial regime in Russia are formulated.

The Regional Forest-industrial Past

Forest-industrial development within the Russian taiga was initially concentrated on the European side of the taiga belt. In the late 19th century, the industrial triangle Sokol, Kondrovo and St. Petersburg constituted the core region for wood processing. An abundance of wood resources close to the centers of consumption underlined the market orientation in forest-industrial strategies.

The Soviet regime inherited the industrial structure of small pulp and paper mills around the main centers of the northwestern region. The decades following the October Revolution witnessed a remarkable turn toward virgin resources more distant from the centers of the country. New plants were located in national and provincial towns within the northern and eastern backwoods. This reorientation during the interwar years produced a more decentralized industrial structure, which also reflected the premises of nationality policy. The new development projects were, however, still concentrated exclusively west of the Ural Mountains. As a result, Soviet wood processing was established around five regions outside the old core: the Kondopoga and Segeza plants in Karelia, the Arkangelsk and Solombala mills in Arkhangelsk, the Marisk and Balakhna mills in Mari, the Krasnovishersk and Kamsk mills in Perm, and some minor ones in the Caucasus (Fig. 7.1).

The intensive industrialization was interrupted by the World War II, which ruined a substantial share of the wood-processing capacity. However, the annexation of the Baltic States, the Kaliningrad Region (Königsberg), Finnish Karelia and southern Sakhalin (from Japan) considerably increased the production basis. The postwar years up to the 1960s were characterized by the reconstruction of the damaged industrial structure and no spatial or production expansion took place.[4]

Figure 7.1 Main pulp and paper units in the Russian taiga[5]

The first steps of integrating the forest resources of the taiga east of the Ural Mountains into the Soviet forest-industrial development were taken during the 1960s. The upper reaches of the Yenisei and Angara rivers, as well as the shores of Lake Baikal, were chosen as new locations for pulp and paper processing. In addition, a new plant was founded by the Amur River in the Far East. The expansion eastward soon faced severe economic difficulties due to long distances and high transport costs. This resulted in critical re-evaluations of the transcontinental strategies. Therefore, during the 1970s, growing awareness of the marketing realities and cost structuring led to a slowing down of the eastern expansion. Diversification of the raw-material base, especially expansion of production based on recycled paper, also gained much support.[6]

In the Soviet Union, the pulp and paper industry accounted for close to seven percent of the total industrial production of the early 1980s. However, the gross national and territorial figures do not say much about the societal cohesion of the forest-industrial agglomerations in Russia. Within the above-mentioned industrial regions (territorial production complexes/TPCs), the role of the forest sector was much more important, being one of the pioneer sectors. In the Soviet economy, it was natural that the mill provided not only the housing for workers but also the daily care of children and the delivery of everyday commodities. In addition, the extreme working and living conditions within the TPCs were compensated by higher salaries and bonuses. The livelihood was thus formally secured, albeit in extremely poor conditions. The financial security was, however, usually counteracted by the absence of job opportunities for female spouses. Five years in one of the TPCs could result in a rise in living conditions upon return to the home region: one could then afford a home and a car, and pursue a new career and a better life.[7]

The Soviet model of the forest industry also introduced a specific feature of forest prison camps as suppliers of timber for the pulp and paper mills in the northwestern and Baikal–Upper Yenisey regions. The North Koreans also had two camps in the Russian Far East where the forest workers lived under prison-like circumstances. Moscow finally terminated the agreement with the North Koreans in 1993. The Ministry of International Affairs, which managed the forest prison camp system, was in fact the third largest of the loggers in the former Soviet Union, with the annual cut being 20 million cubic meters in 1990. According to Aleksei Grigoriev,[8] a Russian forest conservationist, approximately 200,000 Russian prisoners lived and worked in these camps in the early 1990s. The post-Soviet regime converted the camp system into a network of private enterprises with privileges to export timber.[9]

The Soviet model produced an extremely vague regional structure for forest-industrial production, as timber localities were merely islands that were isolated from the rest of the local settlement. The prison camps had their own reasons for isolation but also the rest of the logging and wood-processing communities functioned as islands. They were characterized by high transience and a biased age structure of young families that had no intention of staying permanently. The production units were places to stay as long as it was necessary or could be tolerated. No firm ties to the environing settlements were created. This being the case, no deep relations with the local and indigenous peoples were established. In other words, there was no basis for local collective initiatives to balance the Moscow-centered division of labor and to construct alternatives emanating "from below". The forest-industrial agglomerations constituted the hinterland of the Soviet Union.

The Heritage of the Patrimonial State

Throughout history, the Russian Empire has been forced to face the impulses from the European "peninsula". Asiatic and European cultures have met and merged in the land of the Slavs and, most frequently, on conditions shaped in the West. The Russian aristocracy has repeatedly tried to strengthen its domestic position and ties to Europe by westernizing the country, a project that has always faced resistance from the patriarchal peasant societies of the East.

The Russian patrimonial state was founded on the idea of land ownership as a natural extension of political authority. The country was quite commonly understood to be a huge estate owned by the Tsar. No clear distinction between the official and the private or the state and civil society has yet been drawn. The ruler is the state and the state is the owner.[10]

During the early 1900s, the Tsar's regime was severely challenged by the liberal-capitalistic expansion. A competitive logic for the state (as the owner and ruler) was introduced to peasant societies, which in turn rather paradoxically strengthened the local patriarchal structures. Western liberal modernization reached the traditional societies in the form of new rural cooperatives and alliances. However, the October Revolution brought an end to the peasant initiatives and soon led to mega-scale industrialization. As a response, the peasant societies were divided—often in a rather tragic manner—as the dividing line ran between the generations.

The older generation turned inward and leaned silently on the traditional values (peasant archaization), whereas the new generation took the lead and adjusted the local patriarchal structures to the conditions of state and party patriarchy. The traditional elements of the regions and villages were destroyed and replaced by the statues and symbols of the rule in Moscow. The local churches and graveyards acquired new functions that were, indeed, disgraceful in the eyes of the older generations. Simultaneously, local economic life was transformed, often by force, into collectives and monoculture. The actual transformation was carried out village by village by the sons, while the old gradually lost interest in the "outer life." Finally, the modernization of the archaic rural villages succeeded and the peasants were drawn into the industrial era.[11]

Gradually, the Bolshevik regime produced a new strong state, which was led by the Communist Party and safeguarded by a powerful military-industrial organization. The Party became an all-embracing and centripetal institution in charge of the administrative and economic affairs of the state. The centripetal system was maintained and deepened by a network of personal contacts based on the principle of reciprocity (*nomenklatura*). A single call to or from the right person was enough to remove the obstacles to the Soviet modernization.[12]

The politico-economic collapse of the 1980s in the Soviet Union was, in many respects, a direct cause of unilinear and centrally controlled industrialization of the Stalin, Khrushchev and Brezhnev regimes. Extremely deep and widespread spatial division of labor had led to industrial monocultures with severe social and ecological problems. This occurred mostly within the mining centers but also around localities with wood-processing units. In fact, the warnings concerning the pollution of Lake Baikal had a central role in breaking the deadly silence around the ecologically alarming Soviet development. Lake Baikal, as the largest freshwater reservoir on earth, is partially threatened by the wood-processing industry surrounding it. In addition, the suffering forests around urban settlements and the increasing problems with human health within wood-processing centers such as Arkhangelsk and Segezha functioned as impulses for broad and fundamental criticism of the Soviet model. The counter-reactions were channeled first via literary radicals and soon after by environmental activists.[13]

As part of the ongoing forest-industrial reorganization in Russia, the huge timber resources of the taiga have been made accessible to foreign enterprises. This opening has brought with it new societal confrontations. Problems have arisen from the fact that all civic and entrepreneurial contacts across the border have been started from nothing. International trading and joint ventures on a decentralized and private basis are practices new to Russia. Therefore, the uneven and insecure relationships within the newly-started economic cooperation have created many drawbacks and much distrust. On the one hand, the multinational companies have substantial power over the local Russian administrators and entrepreneurs who are hampered by a chronic lack of foreign currency. On the other hand, the joint ventures have often been grounded on loose agreements resulting in an insecure atmosphere surrounding the cooperation.

Of course, the question concerns the difficulties in building contacts between historically isolated political cultures: Russia and its eastern and western neighbors. Pacific Asia is different from the European Union, but both regional economic units have been identified as optional economic leaders of future globalization.[14]

As was shown in the brief historical introduction, two mega-scale forest-industrial regions can be distinguished in the Russian taiga: the European part (northwestern region) and the Russian East, often divided into Baikal–Angara–Yenisei area and the Pacific coast forests (the Russian Far East). Severe societal and environmental tensions have surfaced within both of these industrial macro-regions. These tensions are described on the proceeding pages, which then function as a general frame for a more detailed concentration on the comparative formulation of the Russian "forest paths."

Post-Soviet Westernization of the Northwestern Region

The economic drawbacks of the forest-industrial projects during the 1970s in the Russian East resulted in wide redevelopment plans within the European part of the Soviet Union. The late 1970s witnessed a turn toward processing based on recycled paper close to the main centers of consumption. New investment plans within the existing plant capacity in the northern part of the coniferous belt west of the Ural Mountains were also published. Only a few pulp and paper projects were, however, accomplished during the 1980s due to the socioeconomic tensions that were emerging at that time.

As a result of the centrally planned projects in the Soviet Union, the forest-industrial structure in the northwestern region was divided into three zones of differing character. The old core (Leningrad–Sokol–Kondrovo) dating from the Tsarist era consisted of outdated and severely polluting sulphite-based mills, whereas the northern territories (Karelia, Arkhangelsk, Komi, Kotlas, Kamsk) were characterized by mechanical pulp processing and newsprint production by mills founded during the interwar expansion. The most recent zone of plants based on recycled paper was situated farther south in Belorussia, Ukraine and Moldavia.

The collapse of the Soviet regime opened a completely new basis for forest-industrial development in the northwestern territories. On the one hand, the old plants were considered to be environmental risks, with the most dangerous ones being closed. On the other hand, international cooperation and joint ventures were welcomed to help in renewing the whole forest-industrial infrastructure. This latter aspect, in particular, has been welcomed as a challenge and opportunity for the Finnish forest industry and consultancy. Most of the Finnish pulp and paper enterprises initiated joint projects in the Karelian backwoods in order to diversify the raw material flow to their factories in Finland. Enso Gutzeit was the most prominent of the new transborder actors and it established already in 1989 a Karelian-Finnish enterprise, Ladenso, to import timber from the forest north of Lake Ladoga over to the Uimaharju pulp mill in Eno, located on the Finnish side of the border.[15]

Jaakko Pöyry International, a forest consulting company, conducted an assessment and development planning project (the so-called Master Plan) in 1990–92 for the entire forest sector of the northwestern taiga. The plan was initially ordered by the Soviet Gosplan in Moscow, and it covered the coniferous taiga belt west of the Ural Mountains. Pöyry's Master Plan extended over the regions of Leningrad, Karelia, Arkhangelsk, Komi, Perm, Vologda and Novgorod and contained proposals for intensifying forestry practices, as well as suggestions for renewing and enlarging the wood-processing capacity. Annual cuttings were planned to be doubled from the then 110 million cubic meters and the general infrastructure was to be designed in a Western manner; the modernization of forest work, the construction of logging roads, communication networks and new pulp and paper plants were central to the plan.[16]

The contract was a historical one, because it was the first time that Gosplan, a central economic planning organization in Moscow, relied on a foreign enterprise in planning the future development of the forest industry. It was also the first time that an integrated planning strategy was drawn up in the Soviet Union, covering all aspects of forestry, wood processing and marketing.[17]

The Master Plan could also be considered historical for several other reasons, related to the culture of decision-making and planning that it was promoting. First of all, the negotiations were run bilaterally, and without any publicity, between the consulting company and Gosplan in Moscow. This form of low-profile planning was, and is, extremely tempting in a country where all the forests are practically under central state control. The Master Plan for Northwest Russia concentrated on acute technical and logistical issues and this meant ignoring local communal participation. It was also claimed that Western enterprise and the Master Plan procedures were used as tools within the internal forest policy for continuing the old administrative practices dictated from Moscow.[18]

Second, the Master Plan cooperation was noteworthy in its forest-ecological concerns. Ecological matters were primarily considered by the Plan as an obstacle to overcome, derived from the idea of the vastness and endlessness of the Russian space. Infinite resources, casting no limits to the progression of the timber frontier, turned into a logistical hindrance.[19] Ecology became synonymous with long distances, and with mud and loam problems during the wet seasons. Ecology was also understood as a technical and numerical question, expressed in calculations about the volume of annual timber growth and loggings: cubic meters were the primary indicators of the sustainability of the planned loggings.[20] In the Master Plan, there were thus no signs of forest-industrial renewal based on the utilization of options of socioenvironmental modernization as factors to strengthen the local-global justification of production and marketing. The primary aim of the Master Plan cooperation was, according to Matti Kärkkäinen, the consultant centrally in charge of the Plan, "to encourage the Russian managers to think in a more business-oriented way."[21]

Western consulting is, in many respects, of key importance in redeveloping the Russian forest industry. In the present situation, Western cooperation seems the only possible solution to the problem of heavy pollution emissions from the old plants, i.e. toward ecological modernization. Joint ventures have become integral elements of the Russian forest industry.

In 2002, ten years after the completion of the Master Plan, ten major plants were responsible for more than two-thirds of the pulp and paper production in Russia and the most international of them were located in Northwest Russia. The

Svetogorsk pulp and paper mill, owned by the US-based International Paper Ltd., is Russia's leading supplier of office-quality paper. In addition, Swedish SCA owns the tissue paper unit in Svetogorsk, supplying one-fifth of the demand in the Russian market.[22]

The pulp mill in Arkhangelsk produces 700,000 tons of pulp per year, accounting for 12 percent of the Russian production, and it also has an important unit for board production. The company was almost bankrupt in 1996 and survived only by profound reorganization in ownership and management. Russian, Austrian and German investors took over the plant and committed to intensive modernization. The pulp mill is export-oriented, having its main foreign customers in Europe.[23]

Syktyvkar Forest Enterprise in the Komi Republic is a large paper mill with broad international ownership, ranging from European (Austria) and South African to American (United States). Mondi Paper (South Africa) gained a strong hold of the plant by buying the majority of the shares in 2001. The ongoing cycle of investments aims at product upgrading and has been financially supported by two US-based banks, namely the Bank of America and ExIm Bank.[24]

The rest of the large pulp and paper plants in Northwest Russia are currently in the hands of Russian owners and look for new investments in a rather different financial setting. Lack of capital greatly constrains the renewal process. The ongoing speeded-up concentration of domestic ownership gradually, however, seems to be leading into increased economic flexibility, including investments in new production capacity and socioenvironmental modernization. Ilim Pulp Enterprise, headquartered in St. Petersburg, is currently the major domestic owner of the forest-product industry in Northwest Russia. The company owns such key producers as the Kotlas pulp and paper mill and St. Petersburg Cartonboard Mill and Printing Plant. Titan Group, partially in foreign ownership, controls a major forest-industrial cluster in the northern part of the region. The pulp and paper mills in Kondopoga and Segezha, jointly owned by the mill workers and the state, form a significant local cluster of paper production in the Republic of Karelia. Segezha is the leading producer of sack paper in Russia.[25]

Each of the above-mentioned plants has an important role as the backbone of its respective local economy. They all serve as major employers in their areas, offering jobs for several thousands of residents in the nearby towns. The Kotlas mill had close to 10,000 employees in 2001 and the Kondopoga mill was the employer of 6900 workers in the same year.[26] These numbers indicate that the mill towns are, as a rule, extremely vulnerable to changes in the production setting, e.g. taking the form of technological automatization or financial profit maximization.

Forest-industrial Reorganization in the Russian East

The forest industry east of the Ural mountains encircles two large-scale territorial agglomerations with completely differing industrial settings. Baikal–Upper Yenisey region is an industrial center established in the 1960s as the first step of the transcontinentalization of the Soviet forest industry. The Far East region has not yet attracted any large-scale wood-processing industry but instead has become defined as a promising logging frontier for the neighboring countries of the Pacific Rim.

During the 1960s and 1970s, the major part of Soviet forest-industrial investments was focused on Eastern Siberia, mainly on Baikal–Upper Yenisey region. Easy access to virgin resources and cheap hydroelectric power were the reasons for this shift eastward. The building of the Baikalsk, Krasnoyarsk, Bratsk and Ust-Ilimsk pulp and paper mills and the expansion of the Lesosibirsk industrial center as well as the construction of hydroelectric power plants have modified the landscapes of the Upper Yenisey and Angara almost completely. The coniferous evergreen forests around the industrial centers have been turned to wasteland and plantations. The Baikalsk mill, producing special dissolving pulp, requires great volumes of pure water for the production processes and was therefore located at the southern end of Lake Baikal. The Selenginsk mill, producing pulp and board, was located by the lower reaches of the Selenga River. The Selenga discharges into Lake Baikal and the pollution of the lake is directly linked to the volumes of waste water from the plant. The unique flora and fauna of the lake, including the famous nerpa (freshwater seal), are therefore under continuous local-global monitoring.[27]

The logging of the lower Angara pine forest has served as an arena for a long-lasting environmental conflict. The river valley has been transformed during the last 40 years by several large dams and water reservoirs, air pollution, and felling of the old-growth pine forest that is 250-300 years old. This industrialization, proceeding rapidly down the Angara valley, has been criticized by both the local and ecological action groups. The local environmental debate was especially intensive in the early 1990s and it became part of the erosion of the Soviet Union.[28]

The Angara Rescue Committee was already established in July 1989, and it was soon broadened to include the forest question within the Upper Yenisey. The action group was accordingly renamed the Angara–Yenisey Rescue Movement at the Lesosibirsk meeting in December 1991. Negotiations with the Krasnoyarsk Territory Council were initiated and this resulted in some positive agreements, such as improvements in official recommendations for forestry. An Ecological Safety Program for the Angara basin was also prepared in cooperation with the Krasnoyarsk Scientific Center.[29]

As all of the region's mills, the Baikalsk pulp and paper mill is old-fashioned and in need of modernization. Lake Baikal belongs to the list of World Heritage Sites and it has a profound ecological and symbolic value in the wider local-global agenda. The state of the lake is therefore of importance for the forest industry. Despite the already existing emission treatment facility, the plant still severely loads the water system, especially with dioxin. The large number of workers (close to 3000 in 2000) serves as a good argument for renewing and continuing the operations of the plant. However, modernization in the forest industry as a rule leads toward increased capital intensity and diminished need for labor. Therefore the decisions made will in any case be painful to the local mill community. A move to a non-chlorine bleaching process in order to eliminate the dioxin problem would be the first step toward securing the future of the mill, and this alone demands investments and loans from abroad.[30]

In 1998–2000, Jaakko Pöyry Consulting conducted an EU-funded evaluation of the Baikalsk and Selenginsk pulp mills, which resulted in recommendations to renew the production processes and logistics of the mills. The costs of wood transport were suggested to be lowered by expanding the loggings at the shores of Lake Baikal and also in the old-growth forests by the Trans-Siberian Railway between the cities of Krasnoyarsk and Irkutsk.[31]

The mills at Lake Baikal have increasingly been supplied by timber from the more eastern forests at the Chinese border, but the recent activation of Chinese timber purchasers has modified the supply and demand structures. The regional authorities of the Chita Forest Service have for example leased large forest areas to private domestic logging companies that in turn have allowed the Chinese companies to manage the operations. It seems that most the remaining pristine forests of Southeast Siberia are being cut for the foreign demand and this means new pressure to those inland forests that have for some reason stayed beyond logging practices. Baikal–Upper Yenisey region is located at the center of these bifurcating interests, whereas the resources of the Russian Far East are dominantly integrated into the international lumber trade within the Pacific Rim.[32]

The forest industry in Baikal–Upper Yenisey region is currently searching for new paper purchasers after the loss of markets in the Soviet Middle East and looking westward to Europe. The pulp and paper mills in Bratsk and Ust-Ilimsk are today owned by Ilim Pulp, which also controls the largest of the Russian pulp and paper units in Koriazhma (Kotlas) in Northwest Russia.[33] Ilim Pulp is headquartered in St. Petersburg, which practically "draws" the mills in Baikal–Upper Yenisey region closer to the European markets. The European connection is also emphasized in the website of the company, even though a major share of the company's export production in Baikal–Upper Yenisey region is sold to China.[34] The ownership of the main plants of Ilim Pulp—Kotlas, Bratsk, Ust-Ilimsk—has been under intensive contestation during recent years, and the confrontations have repeatedly resulted in aggressive and arbitrary actions by the oligarchs of the domestic economic elite. The fierce competition is due to the fact that Ilim Pulp not only owns the three largest pulp and paper mills in Russia but it is also the leading exporter of Russian pulp and paper, having good logistical contacts abroad, especially in Eastern Europe, the Middle East and China. Ilim Pulp also controls 42 logging companies in Russia.[35] Yulia Latynina, a Russian journalist, illustratively summarizes her analysis of the present dramatic state of affairs around Ilim Pulp in this way: "The main means of economic exchange in this country is war" which takes place between "vertically integrated fiefdoms."[36]

The Baikalsk pulp and paper mill is an old one and in need of intensive redevelopment, eagerly supported by its 3000 mill workers. However, the locally-globally sensitive question of Lake Baikal has made the new investors cautious of the risks of involvement. A plan to switch to non-chlorine manufacturing, including aims at diminishing the emissions of dioxin, waste water and the burning of coal, has therefore been sketched, paid for by the US Agency for International Development.[37]

The North Koreans have had logging camps in the Khabarovsky and northern Amurskaya regions in the Russian Far East since the 1960s. The bilateral cooperation initiated in the Brezhnev era was realized by labor-intensive methods, and the workforce and machinery were completely under North Korean control. The bilateral contract from the Soviet era was criticized for giving no economic benefits to local communities. The logging based on this old contract continued, however, at least until the end of 1993.[38]

The 1990s witnessed an activation of foreign forest companies in the Russian Far East. South Korean Hyunday, US enterprises Weyerhaeuser and Pioneer Group as well as Rimbunan Hijau from Malaysia have each in turn tried to act as mediators in between the timber resources in the Russian Far East and the Pacific markets. In addition, the leskhozes, which are the local forestry units of the Federal Forest Service, have oriented toward lumber export.[39] Lumber flows across the border thus take place by the domestic leskhozes and by leases to foreign companies (concession loggings).

Leskhozes have a dual function in forestry, serving as regulative units monitoring the state of the forests and running the logging operations. The lumber trade and logging licenses are a means of financing the functioning of the leskhozes. The logging role of the leskhozes seems to be strengthening under the coordination of the Ministry of Natural Resources, at the cost of forest protection. The erosion of forest protection is due to economic necessities and administrative reorganization. The lack of regulative governance has also resulted in an increase in illegal loggings. Forged logging licenses, wood certificates and export papers are widely in use and this is connected to corruption within the leskhozes and at the border checkpoints. The estimates of the share of illegal logging of the total vary between 10 and 50 percent.[40]

Hyundai, famous for its car production, was fast in initiating cooperation in timber mobilization in Primorsky Kray. The early move reflected the interest of South Korea to strengthen its regional economic role in the Russian Far East and hence correct the "bias" rooting from the geopolitical grouping favoring the Russia–North Korea connections inherited from the Cold War era.[41] Hyundai started loggings close to the village of Svetlana on the Pacific coast in 1989 and soon thereafter expanded west toward the upper watershed of the Bikin River. The company received in 1992 permission from the Primorsky administration and the Forest Service of Primorsky Kray to log in the Upper Bikin, even though the region is vital to the indigenous Udege people and is also considered to be one of the last remaining habitats of the Siberian Tiger. Both the State Committee for Nature Protection (Goskomekologya) and the Primorsky Regional Committee for Ecology and Nature Use, along with the local Pozharsky Rajon that has jurisdiction over the watershed of the Bikin, recommended that these lands be protected and that the rights of the local and indigenous groups had to be recognized.[42]

The construction of the logging road continued and the confrontation escalated into an open conflict in the late summer of 1992 when a group of Udege people and their local companions stopped the progression of Hyundai by threatening to shoot out the tires of the trucks. Hyundai finally had to withdraw from the Bikin in fear of launching a wider international debate which would have eroded the image of the company.[43] This also meant the end of the expansive period in timber harvesting for Huyndai in the Russian Far East. The Udege, who had become famous as the tribe in Akira Kurosawa's *Dersu Uzala*, could thus postpone the disappearance of their home lands and traditional ways of life for a while.

The US enterprise Weyerhaeuser had also ambitious plans in the early 1990s to set up a logging project in the forest area north of the Bikin River. As a result of several years of negotiations with the Russian partners, Weyerhaeuser signed a deal with Koppinskii Lespromkhoz to cut trees in the area of the Koppi and Botch Rivers and launched costly campaigns to convince the local people, politicians and even scientists of their environmentally responsible forestry methods. Weyerhaeuser aimed to use clear-cutting, followed by seedling-planting. As a harvesting method, clear-cutting carries with it many ecological risks due to the fragile soils of the region.[44] Weyerhaeuser also gave funding to the local Far Eastern Scientific Research Institute for Forest Management but finally abandoned the venture in the Russian Far East in 1994.[45] Of the US companies, Georgia-Pacific, Boise Cascade and Pioneer Group have also shown their interest in the timber resources of the Russian Far East but no broader launch has yet taken place. Pioneer Group, however, made a contract in 1997 for logging up to 260,000 cubic meters of timber per year in Khabarovsky Kray.[46]

Further in 1997, Rimbunan Hijau (RH) bought logging rights for 49 years in Upper Sukpai, a subdistrict of Lazo in Khabarovsky Kray, for an annual cut reaching the level of 500,000 cubic meters. Sukpai is a town initially founded for the purposes of Soviet forestry and, after the economically bad years of the 1990s, it is gaining a new economic stimulus due to the landing of RH. The Sukpai contract ties RH to invest in a road construction project east of the Sea of Japan through the Samarga River watershed, which is again one of the disputed pristine forest areas in the Russian Far East. The company has also bought up concessions for two other forest regions in the Russian Far East, namely the Solnechsky and Ulchsky areas which are located farther north. The actions of RH in the Russian Far East have alarmed the international environmental movement due to RH's reputation in using socially and ecologically destructive logging practices, as witnessed in Malaysia and Papua New Guinea. Rimbunan Hijau, owned by the Sarawakian timber and media tycoon Tiong Hiew King, operates primarily in Southeast Asia, mainly in Malaysia but also in Hong Kong, Papua New Guinea, Cambodia, the Solomon Islands and Vanuatu.[47]

It is estimated that approximately half of the timber cut in the Russian Far East is exported to Japan, China and South Korea, of which Japan is the leading importer with 68 percent of the share (in 1998). The exported wood is mostly used for housing construction as the Siberian larch is currently replacing tropical wood as a preferred choice for wooden architecture, especially the plywood industry in Japan. South Korea imports about 90 percent of its timber consumption, mostly from New Zealand and Chile but the share of Russian logs is continuously growing. China looks increasingly across the Russian border to cover her own timber demand but also to intensify production of wooden constructs to Japanese markets. Russian wood thus finds its way over to Japan via Chinese merchants as well.[48]

Co-managing the Greenbelt across the Taiga: A Summary

It has already become clear that no single outline of the Russian forest industry can be identified. Despite the repeatedly emerging ambitious plans to make the country a centrally administered one, the taiga and the boreal wood processing have grown into a complex spatial network that deviates from any unifying characterization. Due to historical reasons, the spatial configuration can be grouped into regions as layers of territorial production encircled around St. Petersburg and Moscow. Then, however, both the internal variations and the differences in internationalization within each of the forest-industrial complexes become overlooked or even ignored, as if seen panoptically from within one totalizing framework.

The rapid reorganization of ownership is also currently interconnecting the spatially isolated units of wood-processing, as is for example the case with the plants under the control of Ilim Pulp. Sister plants with an orderly division of labor from the Soviet era have suddenly found themselves in opposing camps due to intensified contestation between the supply and demand sectors. The territorial production complexes have thus become *more regionalized*, while reshaped differently according to wood demand across international borders, and *de-territorialized* at the same time, due to the fluid restructuring of company ownership.

In this chapter, however, my conclusive remarks aim at collecting the general features of the Russian forest-industrial sector, both at the federal level and in respect to the fluidity of reorganization within and between the two major territorial production complexes. The sketched view then aids in locating the detailed local case analyses from the Russian side of the Greenbelt (chapters 8 and 9 in particular) in a broader transcontinental context.

(i) The unifying elements of the Russian forest sector are composed of two tensional fields of governance. First, the central administration is repeatedly facing the challenge of distances. Central control and coordination of local activities in different parts of the country have been only partially successful, emerging within the legal agenda and deriving their factual background from the official federal statistics. Officially, industrial logging intensity fell below 100 million cubic meters per year during the 1990s, which is only about one quarter of the top level during the Soviet times and far below the level of annual allowable cutting, with estimates varying between 500 and 900 million cubic meters.[49] The numbers, however, ignore the loggings that take place illegally (and out of reach of taxation), adding perhaps even 50–100 percent more to the official calculations.[50] Central coordination in Moscow has to rely on the gross numbers implicating the unused options at the federal level. The average numbers tell little about the regional overharvesting in the forests surrounding the territorial centers of the forest sector, and function even less as an informational basis for solving politico-economic weaknesses or ethnoenvironmental problems. This state of affairs is perhaps an expression of the specific spatial paradox of Russia, initially derived from the vastness of the country, i.e. from the plenitude of Russian space. The spatiality of Russia becomes comprehensible only if grouped and identified as comprised of territorial hierarchies and divisions, that is: by reducing the variation in the spatial existence. Spatial diversity is no longer a resource but turns into a nuisance.[51]

(ii) The more recent tightening of the central coordination of forest management and environmental protection measures under the umbrella of the Ministry of Natural Resources has caused increasing interest among environmentalists. Some local-global environmental problems, e.g. Lake Baikal and the Amur Tiger, have stayed long in the agenda of nature conservation whereas the constant expansion of the logging road network across the pristine taiga has only recently become a major challenge to the protectors of both ecological and human communities. Tense observations of regional overcuttings have turned into fears of losing certain rare biotopes. Fears of eroding water and permafrost balances have been expressed, highlighting the risks of local ecological crises, e.g. desertification and floods as in China. Generally slow progress of nature protection has also been observed, especially in connection to the Greenbelt planning at the Finnish–Russian border.[52] Such solutions as nature conservation on a private international basis have been introduced[53] as well as the alternative of integrating wood processing into international certification systems—as reactions to the emerging local-global socioenvironmental tension.[54]

(iii) The trends in lumber trade and process ownership have divided the forest industry into two camps, namely domestic actors short of capital and timber supply, and international ventures embedded in risks of insecure logistics. The gradually increasing presence of foreign capital has favored certain leskhozes and wood-processing units whereas the rest of the forest sector is stuck in the old infrastructure trajectories and path dependencies. The domestic logging culture as well as the wood-processing machinery are in need of socioenvironmental modernization, which requires investors. The necessity of keeping the forest machinery going has underlined the short-term solutions for enlarging the exports of timber and for running mills without modernization. This has left the forest-industrial complexes in a peripheral role within the integrating international division of labor.

(iv) The output of refined wood products, e.g. wood-based panels and pulp and paper, fell during the 1990s to between 40 and 25 percent of the installed production capacity, which was run at maximum level as recently as 1989. One-fifth of Russian paper and board production, almost two million metric tons, was exported in 1989 and nearly three-quarters of that amount went to the non-Russian republics of the Soviet Union in East-central Europe, especially Ukraine. Decline in exports was rapid during the early 1990s, being down nearly 50 percent in 1993, which reflected the fall in exports to the republics of the former Soviet Union.[55] The rapid disintegration of the earlier tight division of labor within the Soviet Union caused deep imbalances in regional forest-industrial economics only to be overcome by searching for new targets for the export products. The neighbors in Western Europe and the Pacific Rim became important target areas for exporting pulp and paper but they have, instead, shown their selective interest in lumber imports with a view to have the lumber processed in their own factories. The asymmetries of the export profiles are the most serious challenges for the Russian forest industry, both in the East and in the West.

The international reorientation in Russia during the 1990s was rapid and included several parallel characteristics. Wood exports to the earlier southern republics of the Soviet Union fell dramatically and instead grew markedly toward its Western and Eastern neighbors, with Finland and Japan as the main purchasers. Pulp and paper companies had difficulties in selling their products abroad and the role of Western Europe grew in importance. The forest industry became more reliant on Western European export markets for its economic continuity, and new international mixed structures of ownership emerged. Despite its large forest resources, the Russian East has failed to grow into an attractive area for international investors in the forest industry and has therefore turned into an exporter of roundwood. The demand for mechanical wood products—sawn timber, plywood and panels—is high at the Pacific Rim but no local reorientation to cover this market niche has yet been launched.

(v) The vast conifer-dominated forests of Russia have become a means for gathering private profit for the owners of the companies. The forest areas and the old industrial centers have lost the post-Soviet option for gaining control over their resources. The areas and the companies are ranked differently within the networks of wood processing. Some areas e.g. in the Baikal and Amur watersheds have remained unattractive due to environmental and ethnic risks connected to the continued logging and wood processing. Most of the companies, especially those from the West, have learned to become cautious of the image risks connected to the ethnoenvironmentally alarming trends taking place here and there. Withdrawals after years of negotiations and groundwork serve as bad experiences but only minor ones if compared with the benefits of following a business culture that is credible in the eyes of the main consumers of the end products.

The vacuums left by the companies worrying about their international image and credibility have been filled by those companies, e.g. Rimbunan Hijau, that rely on socioenvironmentally aggressive strategies. Withdrawals are thus often losses for the areas under forest-industrial planning. This argument is not merely based on the loss of local economic impulses but more on the remark that actors investing in more or less sustainable practices are rare but crucial while working with the ethnoenvironmentally sensitive areas at the logging frontier or redeveloping the old mill communities and machinery.

(vi) Consequently, the regions of Russia most dependent on the forest industry have found it difficult to cope with the historical-cultural prejudices cast on foreign actors: the new stimulus from abroad is both needed and feared at the same time. The newcomers are often seen as potential occupants only interested in securing their own profit and this has surfaced both in economic and environmental cooperation.[56] Undoubtedly, local fears are not something born solely from inside but also from the actions of the newcomers. James Clay Moltz, while studying the post-Soviet setting in the Russian Far East, underlines the problem of provincial protectionism inundated with claims to the effect of foreign invaders attempting to take over the region. According to Moltz, a researcher of geopolitical tensions from California, the claims have served as a mask distracting local attention from the exclusive privatization of the local economic sphere. Strongly nationalistic foreign relations have thus been fueled in the media to justify the activities of the provincial elite. Consequently, as a byproduct of this policy, the province has become isolated from the development potentials linked to Pacific cooperation.[57] Seen from abroad, and from within the local-global framework of this book, protective provincialism is one of the main obstacles to deepening cooperation. The fears and prejudices need, however, fuel also from the outside in order to be adopted by the "insiders." The joint projects in the forest industry are full of episodes encouraging mutual reflective learning, as has been witnessed in this article. Cooperation is demanding also for the "outsiders," and particular knowledge and sensitivity to the target cultures are crucial, as is critical awareness of the cultural biases of one's own. The need for mutual reflection covers all the partners—environmental activists included.

(vii) The complex relations between the forest provinces, multinational companies and ethnoenvironmental networks have highlighted the political potential of local-global agendas. Networks of indigenous peoples and nature conservation groups have been established across the Russian taiga. The initiatives for this kind of international cooperation have, however, revealed the weaknesses of civil society in the face of multinational corporations. The withdrawal of the "good companies" is only one dimension of the problem. Some conservationists have learned to focus their attention to the main actors of the scene, and there especially to the multinational companies. Today, the home pages of the most prominent socioenvironmental groups are good sources for those interested in economic actors. The home pages also reveal that less attention is paid by the environmentalists to cultural tensions within the actor-networks fluidly clustering (and dispersing) as part of the evolution of individual hot spots.

The environmental discussions are focused on ecological losses—such as threats to biodiversity, Lake Baikal, the Amur Tiger—and the main politico-economic causalities behind these losses. Only marginal interest is cast on the daily environments of the ordinary people in the middle of the economic downturn. Not much concern is yet focused on the unemployed seeking for daily survival or, perhaps, returning—willingly or by necessity—to self-sufficiency in the backwoods. Co-defending both the local life modes and the daily environments of the taiga is the kind of hybrid challenge that still awaits to be recognized and emphasized by environmentalists. The local-global environmental politics of the taiga are still exclusively based on specific expertise and factual authorization (from above). This tends to annihilate the multilayered articulation of the practical problems of people aiming to earn their living from and within the land and lifescapes of the taiga.[58]

The technical discourses have tended to narrow and polarize the formulation of the taiga question: now we have dialogues between experts and counter-experts. The daily sphere of living has entered the scene in the form of indigenous people and their concerns on the fate of their home lands. The broadening of the debate is ethically important as the most oppressed ones have in this way been identified as having a voice in the issue. The selective inclusion has, however, at the same time carried with it two implicit categorizations. On the one hand, indigenous cultures have been considered in the same terms as the elements of the taiga nature under threat. The indigenous peoples have thus repeatedly been defined as the "Other" to be conserved in a manner similar to nature conservation. On the other hand, a dividing line has been drawn between the indigenous peoples and the rest of the human settlements with no specific status of aboriginality. This has brought with it much blindness toward societal diversity. It has also meant an inability to cope with the sociopolitical processes producing social inequality and resource extraction, including the horizontal (regional) and vertical (multi-scale) variations in facing and experiencing these power asymmetries.

The cooperation in industrial paper processing faces the same challenges of inclusion and exclusion. Technological and ecological modernization of the pulp and paper mills in Russia are indeed tasks for engineers or ecologists but, as has become clear from the previous pages, it is definitely as much a matter of community change. These transformations should therefore not be realized without broader concerns for social responsibility. The modernizers of the major mills, each of which currently employs several thousands of workers, have to face the drama of everyday life in the surrounding communities. The most modern of the mills (of similar size), when equipped with the latest innovations of automatization, need only a few hundred employees. The Kondopoga mill is for example today a "life-line" to 6900 workers living in the mill town of about 45,000 inhabitants. Severe cuts through the modernization of the plant would definitely constitute a catastrophe for the whole mill community. Those who ask for efficiency and profit maximization based on faster and cleaner machines are from a local community view thus categorized as "potential occupants ensuring their own profit." It seems evident that the only way out of the confrontations and groupings between us and them can be cleared by careful study of the social circumstances of the communities in which we are networked. Would this be called socioenvironmental modernization?

Notes

1. Oleg Yanitsky, "Risk Society and Environmental Policy in Russia," in *The Struggle for Russian Environmental Policy*, eds, Ilmo Massa and Veli-Pekka Tynkkynen (Helsinki: Kikimora Publications, 2001), pp. 27-48; Antonina Kuliasova and Ivan Kuliasov, "Reorganisation of Environmental Administration," in *Environmental Transformations in the Russian Forest Industry: Key Actors and Local Developments*, eds. Jarmo Kortelainen and Juha Kotilainen (Joensuu: University of Joensuu, Publications of Karelian Institute, no. 136 , 2002), 72-82.
2. Mikhail Karpachevsky, "What Future for the Taiga?," *Taiga News*, no. 32 (2000), 1; Elisa Peter, "Living with the Taiga," *Taiga News*, no. 33 (2000), 1.
3. Mark van Dorp, Martina Kriesch and James Hewitt, "Timber Trade Trends," *Taiga News*, no. 34 (2001), 4.
4. Jarmo Eronen, *Location Strategy and Patterns. An Empirical Investigation of the Soviet Pulp and Paper Industry* (Helsinki: The Helsinki School of Economics, no. A42, 1984); Jarmo Eronen, *Cluster Analysis and Russian Forest Industry Complex* (Helsinki: The Research Institute of the Finnish Economy/ETLA, Discussion Papers, no. 682, 1999).
5. Jarmo Kortelainen, "Forest Regimes as Heterogeneous Networks: Polarization of the Russian Forest Industry," in *Politics of Forests*, eds. Ari Aukusti Lehtinen, Jakob Donner-Amnell and Bjørnar Sæther (Aldershot: Ashgate, 2004), 109.
6. Eronen, *Location Strategy and Patterns*, 47-61
7. Peter de Souza, *Territorial Production Complexes in the Soviet Union—With Special Focus on Siberia* (Gothenburg: University of Gothenburg, Department of Geography Publications, no. B80, 1989); Matti Kärkkäinen, "Master Plan for the Soviet Forest Industries—A Challenging Task to Jaakko Pöyry," *Jaakko Pöyry Co Magazine* (1990), 20-21; Andrew R. Bond, "A Panel on Siberia. Economic and Territorial Issues," *Soviet Geography* 22, no. 6 (1991), 363-432.
8. Aleksei Grigoriev, "Mapping the Shrinking Taiga," *Taiga News*, no. 9 (1994), 6-8.
9. Aleksei Grigoriev and Roger Olsson, "Forced Labour Logging Russia's Forests," *Taiga News*, no. 6 (1993), 4; Roger Olsson, *The Taiga—A Treasure, or Timber and Trash?* (Jokkmokk: Taiga Rescue Network, 1993); Grigoriev, "Mapping the Shrinking Taiga."
10. Mark Lupher, "Power Restructuring in China and the Soviet Union," *Theory and Society* 21, no. 5 (1992), 665-701; Paul Fryer, "Heaven, Hell, or...Something in between?," in *Beyond the Limits. The Concept of Space in Russian History and Culture*, ed. Jeremy Smith (Helsinki: Studia Historica, 1999), 95-106.
11. Ari Aukusti Lehtinen, *The Fall of the Forest Villages: Ecological and Cultural Conflicts in the Russian Taiga* (Uppsala: University of Uppsala, Research Programme on Environmental Policy and Society/ EPOS, Research Report, no. 1, 1993); Judith Pallot and Dominique Moran, "Surviving the Margins in Post-Soviet Russia: Forestry Villages in Northern Perm Oblast," *Post-Soviet Geography and Economics* 41, no. 5 (2000), 341-64.
12. Viktor Sergeyev and Nikolai Biryukov, *Russia's Road to Democracy. Parliament, Communism and Traditional Culture* (Vermont: Edward Elgar, 1993).
13. Andrei Saharov, *Muistelmat*, (Helsinki, Wsoy, 1991).
14. Chris Brook, "The Drive to Global Regions?," in *A Global World?*, eds. James Anderson, Chris Brook and Allan Cochrane (Oxford: Oxford University Press, 1995), 113-66.

15. Ari Aukusti Lehtinen, "Northern Natures," *Fennia* 169, no. 1 (1991), 99.
16. Kärkkäinen, "Master Plan for the Soviet Forest Industries—A Challenging Task to Jaakko Pöyry;" Ari Aukusti Lehtinen, "Questions on Environment and Democracy within Northern Boreal Forestry: The Finnish Forest Conflict Becoming an International Issue," in *The Environment and International Security*, eds. Anders Hjort-af-Ornäs and Sverre Lodgaard (Uppsala: University of Uppsala, Research Programme on Environment and International Security/EPOS, 1992), 67-78.
17. Kärkkäinen, "Master Plan for the Soviet Forest Industries—A Challenging Task to Jaakko Pöyry," 20.
18. Aleksei Grigoriev, "Hot Spots in Russian Forests," *Taiga News*, no. 2 (1992), 2; Grigoriev, "Mapping the Shrinking Taiga."
19. Fryer, "Heaven, Hell, or...Something in Between?"
20. Kärkkäinen, "Master Plan for the Soviet Forest Industries—A Challenging Task to Jaakko Pöyry;" Lehtinen, "Questions on Environment and Democracy within Northern Boreal Forestry: The Finnish Forest Conflict Becoming an International Issue;" Ari Aukusti Lehtinen, "Tales from the Northern Backwoods—Modernisation and Colonialism in the Eurasiatic Taiga," *Nordisk Samhällsgeografisk Tidskrift*, no. 18 (1994), 11-21.
21. Kärkkäinen, "Master Plan for the Soviet Forest Industries—A Challenging Task to Jaakko Pöyry," 21.
22. Juha Kotilainen, "Shifting between the East and the West, Switching Between the Scales: Forest-industrial Regimes in Northwest Russian Borderlands," in *Politics of Forests*, eds. Ari Aukusti Lehtinen, Jakob Donner-Amnell and Bjørnar Sæther (Aldershot: Ashgate, 2004), 133-56.
23. Jan Willem van Gelder, "Foreign Investments in Russia's Pulp and Paper Industry," *Taiga News*, no. 37 (2002), 8-9.
24. van Gelder, "Foreign Investments in Russia's Pulp and Paper Industry;" Hannu Hernesniemi, "The Green Gold of Russia," *The Finnish Economy and Society*, no. 1 (2002), 59-65.
25. Eronen, *Cluster Analysis and Russian Forest Industry Complex*; Hernesniemi, "The Green Gold of Russia;" Jarmo Kortelainen, "Forest Regimes as Heterogeneous Networks: Polarization of the Russian Forest Industry," in *Politics of Forests*, eds. Ari Aukusti Lehtinen, Jakob Donner-Amnell and Bjørnar Sæther (Aldershot: Ashgate, 2004), 107-32.
26. Hernesniemi, "The Green Gold of Russia," 63.
27. Divish Petrof, "Siberian Forests under Threat," *The Ecologist* 22, no. 6 (1992), 267-70; Socio-ecological Specifications. (1992), Socio-ecological Specifications of the Lower Angara Area (Angara-Yenisey Rescue Movement, 1992), mimeo; "The Battle for Baikal: Before it's too Late!" *The-Wave-On-The-Net* (Baikal Environmental Wave, 2002) <http://www.baikalwave.eu.org/battle.html)> (4 April 2002).
28. Grigoriev, "Hot Spots in Russian Forests."
29. Socio-ecological Specifications of the Lower Angara Area.
30. van Gelder, "Foreign Investments in Russia's Pulp and Paper Industry."
31. Elisa Peter, "On Jaakko's Tracks," *Taiga News*, no. 37 (2001), 5.
32. Inger Zinovieva, "From Chita to China," *Taiga News*, no. 34 (2001), 8.
33. Jørn Holm-Hansen, ed., *Environment as an Issue in a Russian Town* (Oslo: Norwegian Institute for Urban and Regional Research/NIBR, Report no. 11, 2002).

34. Ilim Pulp Enterprise home page. <http://www.russianpapermills.com> (4 Feb. 2002).
35. "Ilim Pulp Continues to Fight Hostile Takeover Attempt," *Paper Industry News*. <http://www.paperage.com/news/08_20_2002ilim.html> (10 Feb. 2002).
36. Yulia Latynina, "Forestry Industry: Ripe for Carving up," *Moscow Times*, 17 July 2002. <http://www.cdi.org/russia/johnson/6357-7.cfm> (10 Feb. 2002).
37. van Gelder, "Foreign Investments in Russia's Pulp and Paper Industry."
38. Grigoriev, "Mapping the Shrinking Taiga."
39. Josh Newell, Anatoly Lebedev, David Gordon and Mary Rees, *Plundering Russia's Far Eastern Taiga* (Vladivostok: Bureau for Regional Oriental Campaigns, Tokyo: Friends of the Earth in Japan and Oakland: Pacific Environmental and Resources Center, 2000).
40. Newell, Lebedev, Gordon and Rees, *Plundering Russia's Far Eastern Taiga*; Mary Rees, "Illegal Loggings and Trade Endanger Russian Forests," *Taiga News*, no. 32 (2000), 8; Arjan Alkema, "Who's Responsible?," *Taiga News*, no. 34 (2001), 6.
41. James Clay Moltz, "Core and Periphery in the Evolving Russian Economy: Integration or Isolation of the Far East?," *Post-Soviet Geography and Economics* 37, no. 3 (1996), 175-94.
42. David Gordon, "Joint Logging Ventures in the Russian Far East," *Taiga News*, no. 2 (1992), 3; David Gordon, "Hyundai Has Go-ahead to Log Native Forests in Russian Far East," *Taiga News*, no. 3 (1992), 6.
43. Kalle Koponen, "Udehikansa taistelee taigan puolesta," *Helsingin Sanomat*, 2 October 1996, C3.
44. Gordon, "Joint Logging Ventures in the Russian Far East."
45. Home page of Weyerhaeuser <http://www.endgame.org/global-weyer.html> (4 April 2002).
46. Josh Newell, "Plundering Russia's Far Eastern Taiga," *Taiga News*, no. 29 (1999), 12-13.
47. Kar Yen Leong, "Rimbunan Hijau Logging in Russia Sparks Eco-fears," *Forest Conservation News Today* (2001) <http://forests.org/recent/2001/ruhilogg.html> (4 April 2002).
48. Newell, "Plundering Russia's Far Eastern Taiga."
49. Charles A. Backman, "The Russian Forest Sector: Prospects for Trade with Former Soviet Republics," *Post-Soviet Geography and Economics* 37, no. 1 (1996), 20-21; Charles A. Backman, "Russia," in *Forest Policy. International Case Studies*, eds. Bill Wilson, G.C. van Kooten, Ilan Vertinsky and Louise Arthur (New York: CABI Publishing, 1998), 233-54; Charles A. Backman, "The Siberian Forest Sector: Challenges and Prospects," *Post-Soviet Geography and Economics* 40, no. 6 (1999), 454.
50. Otso Ovaskainen, Minna Pappila and Jyri Pötry, *The Finnish Forest Industry in Russia* (Helsinki: The Finnish Nature League, 1999), 18; Mary Rees, "Illegal Loggings and Trade Endanger Russian Forests," *Taiga News, no.* 32 (2000), p. 8; Alkema, "Who's Responsible?"
51. Fryer, "Heaven, Hell, or...Something in Between?"
52. Ovaskainen, Pappila, Pötry, *The Finnish Forest Industry in Russia.*
53. Philip R. Pryde, "The Privatization of Nature Conservation in Russia", *Post-Soviet Geography and Economics* 40, no. 5 (1999), 383-93.
54. Nadezhda Srakhova, "Forest Fair Trade. How a Russian Community Benefits from Fair Trade?," *Taiga News*, no. 35 (2001), 9.
55. Charles A. Backman, "The Russian Forest Sector: Prospects for Trade with Former Soviet Republic," *Post-Soviet Geography and Economics* 37, no. 1 (1996), 33.

56. Pryde, "The Privatization of Nature Conservation in Russia."
57. Moltz, "Core and Periphery in the Evolving Russian Economy: Integration or Isolation of the Far East?," 183-6.
58. Pallot and Moran, "Surviving the Margins in Post-Soviet Russia: Forestry Villages in Northern Perm Oblast;" Kuliasova and Kuliasov, "Reorganisation of Environmental Administration:" Maria Tysiachniouk and Jonathan Reisman, "Co-managing the Taiga: Russian Forests and the Challenge of International Environmentalism," in *Politics of Forests*, eds. Ari Aukusti Lehtinen, Jakob Donner-Amnell and Bjørnar Sæther (Aldershot: Ashgate, 2004), 157-75.

8.

Siberia in the Neighborhood: *Lesopromishlennij Kompleks* in Viena Karelia

> Kostamus on murros. Kekkonen vaihtui Koivistoon, Brezhnev lyhyin väliajoin vaihtuviin hajoavan neuvostotasavallan presidentteihin. [*Kostamus*] on suurin koskaan toteutettu suomalainen siirtotyömaa keskellä Vienan Karjalan neitseellistä kalevalaista maisemaa. Kainuun työllistämiseksi rakennettu kaupunki tuhosi tai pelasti Viena Karjalan näkökulmasta riippuen.[1]

> Kostamus is a turning point. Kekkonen was followed by Koivisto, Brezhnev turned into short-lived leaderships in the eroding Soviet Union. [Kostamus] was the largest work camp ever built by the Finns, founded in the middle of the pristine landscapes of Kalevala in Viena Karelia. Depending on the perspective, the project that offered employment to Finns in Kainuu saved or destroyed Viena. (Translated from Finnish by the author)

The villages and forests of Viena Karelia have stayed in the core of cross-border debate from the early years of Soviet disintegration. Culture conservationists on both sides of the state border initiated the debate by identifying and emphasizing the high heritage value of the traditional Karelian villages that had survived the Communist Regime. The pristine old-growth forests around the villages soon became a hot spot of nature conservation. Viena became a conservation issue where ecological and cultural views clashed and coalesced. The remnants of the traditional local architecture, language and belief systems were valued as an authentic connection to the pre-Soviet mode of living when an intimate relationship between the people and forests existed.

In terms of nature conservation, the Vienansalo wilderness emerged the most disputed of the forests in Viena Karelia. The forest area, which is also known in conservation plans as Kalevala National Park, is located in between the village of Vuokkiniemi and the state border. Vienansalo received a reprieve during the years of the logging moratorium (see chapter 9) but the conservation status of the wilderness area has remained unclear. The government of Karelia, however, published a plan in 2002 that contained a proposal for the Kalevala National Park of 12,000 hectares. The suggestion was a significant reduction to the initial wish of the conservationists who aimed at founding a park of 100,000 hectares of forests in the core of Vienansalo.[2]

The contemporary form of cross-border cooperation of culture and nature conservationists of Viena begun in the 1980s by occasional contacts between individual enthusiasts from Viena, Kuhmo (on the Finnish side) and Petrozavodsk. The inspiration for cultural cooperation owes much to the publications of the main literary production of Nikolaj Jaakkola and Ortjo Stepanov in Finnish in Petrozavodsk in the late 1970s.[3] These regional novels describe in detail the local histories of the Viena villages before and during the forced collectivization of the Soviet time. On the other hand, transborder nature conservation dates back to the late 1980s when the preparations for founding the Friendship Area of Nature Conservation were officially started. The project covers the Nature Park of Kostomuksha (Kostomukshsky Zapovednik, Kostamus Nature Park) south of the proposed Kalevala National Park and Ystävyyden puisto (the Park of Friendship) at the Finnish side of the border, consisting of five smaller units of nature conservation.[4]

The simultaneous commencement of culture and nature conservation was a direct outcome of the historical changes in the Soviet Union. As was argued in the introductory insert above, the Brezhnev Era was gradually vanishing and the large mining-industrial complex of Kostomuksha fed the local conservation debate. Kostomuksha had grown during the 1990s into an urban concentration of more than 30,000 inhabitants of whom about 8000 were employed by the mining combine. The city, founded in the late 1970s in the middle of Viena Karelian forests, had grown into a dramatic contrast to the historical forest villages. It also functioned as a warning to the conservationists: industrial modernization of this type threatens the surrounding ecosystems by emissions and it also risks the continuance of folk traditions.

The gradual erosion of the Brezhnevian control resulted in profound changes in the institutional setting of cross-border operations. The fate of the Viena villages and forests was the main cultural and ecological question at the border zone, but the changes resulted in shared initiatives that were established across several spatial scales, from local to federal and beyond. The emergence of foreign partners from the West further modified the multiscale character of the cooperation. Enso Gutzeit, a Finnish forest company, was the first to transform the forest-industrial challenges of the border into practical cooperation. The company aimed at solving the limits in domestic wood supply by extending its logging operations eastward. The plan was made concrete by founding in 1989 a joint venture, Ladenso, with the Soviet partner in Petrozavodsk, Karellesprom. This initiative was broadly considered in Finland as a sign or at least a promise of a new industrial era: a historical turn from bilateral to open trade across the border.

The following years have, however, witnessed severe setbacks that have gradually eroded the positive options. The persistent social and economic problems are repeatedly seen in Karelia as caused by difficulties in forest-based production. The forest industry, oriented toward wood export, was in the 1990s responsible for about the half of the budget returns to the Republic, and close to 80 percent of wood export was then driven to Finland, equaling 13 million cubic meters, mainly birch.[5] The official views in Karelia blame the tightened international environmental concerns in forestry as the main reason for the socioeconomic problems, whereas environmental actors emphasize both the inefficiency of the forest sector and the unjust division of the forest income. The environmentalists also underline both the low price of wood and the lack of local refining as reasons for the socioeconomic difficulties.[6]

The joint projects have thus in practice proven unsuccessful in generating sound societal development in Karelia. The promising new era has turned into backlashes and growing insecurity. What are the concrete problems like and how are they practically related to broader societal dynamics? What is the historical constitution of the dilemma? These questions are discussed in this chapter, first by analyzing the historical socioenvironmental trends within the Republic of Karelia and thereafter concentrating on the villages of Viena.

Historical Burden

Karelia has functioned throughout known history as an interface zone and battlefield for political ambitions from the East and the West. The geopolitical tensions between Novgorod and Stockholm, confrontations concerning the Orthodox and Lutheran Protestant missions as well as the demarcation of Pan-Slavism in relation to the historical territorial formation of the Swedish Empire and "Greater Finland" have all left deep traces on the Karelian nature and culture.

In 1920, soon after the October Revolution, the Workers Commune of Karelia was founded, based on a hierarchic administration under the rule of the Communist Party. Three years later, Karelia was granted the status of an Autonomic Socialistic Soviet Republic (ASSR), which gave Soviet-Karelia the three elements of Soviet administration: parliament, supreme soviet and government. The republic was renamed immediately after World War II the Karelian-Finnish Socialistic Soviet Republic (KFSSR), which reflected the spatial expansion of the republic westward, over the regions Finland had lost as a result of the war. The renaming meant a remarkable rise in the administrative hierarchy of the Soviet system. The republic was, however, returned to ASSR status in 1956, as part of the *Sovnarkhoz* reform, by the new president Khrushchev. The years of Brezhnev's rule (1964–1982) kept the republic in a marginal position by strengthening its role as a wood-processing periphery for the Soviet development. The Republic of Karelia declared sovereignty in 1990 as an outcome of the years of *perestroika.*

The industrialization of Soviet Karelia took place in the form of large-scale modernization of forestry and wood processing. The result was a regional division of labor where Karelia was finally responsible for close to one-third of the Soviet newsprint production and half of the Soviet paper-bag production.[7] Most of the decisions crucial for the republic's development were made within the system of Soviet administration, such as the Ministry of Forestry, Karellesprom (Karelian Forest Integrate) and leskhozes (regional Forestry Commissions), all of which were hierarchically integrated in the forest policy designed in Moscow. The leskhozes controlled local forestry and gave permits for loggings. These administrative structures still form the organizational framework for the operations in the forest sector, even though demands to strengthen the hierarchical power of the Federation by abolishing the "level" of leskhozes has gained more and more support in Moscow.

The regional infrastructure of Karelia was also thoroughly reorganized during the Soviet years. The rural settlement system became dominantly industrial and the exclusive favoring of wood processing left the agricultural development potential rather unused. Migration to urban centers and the construction of a modern network of forestry villages became reflected in the form of abandonment of the traditional rural life in the backwoods. The old agricultural life mode with private farmers was replaced by central villages established around the state estates. Most of the old rural villages and the cultivation of the small agricultural fields disappeared.[8]

Modernization according to the Soviet model resulted in Karelia in serious environmental problems within the main industrial agglomerations. Several of the industrial units were considered to pose a serious risk for the surroundings. The emissions of the mills of Kondopoga, Segeza, Pitkyaranta, Lyaskelya and Kostomuksha gained much international attention soon after the collapse of the Soviet system. The production complex in Segeza, which produces aluminum, paper bags and sawn goods, was ranked as the most polluted locality in Karelia. The risks to human health, which had become acute through airborne and water pollution, are acute for the entire Republic, as over 80 percent of Karelia's close to 800,000 inhabitants live today in the industrial agglomerations founded after the October Revolution.[9]

Viena Karelians and Finnish Karelianism

A growing Finnish interest toward Karelian culture could be noticed throughout the 19th century. This enthusiasm was connected to the geopolitical changes that had raised Finland's status from a backward province of Sweden to an autonomous part of Russia. The war between Russia and Sweden in the early 1800s resulted in a solution wherein Finland's 500-year-long history under the Swedish Crown was broken and a new one constructed eastward, in the form of a Grand Duchy of Russia. The peace agreement in 1809 gave rise to a new autonomous nation between St. Petersburg and Stockholm.

The sudden "emergence" of a respectively independent cultural area led to a search for a Finnish national identity. A construction of the collective picture of the common basis of Finnish culture was put forward in the spirit of nationalism blossoming in Europe at that time. The backwoods of Karelia played a central role in Finnish national identity-building. The folk poems, still commemorated and even sung in both daily routines and festivities in Viena Karelia, made up the basis of *Kalevala*, the book which was to become the national epic of Finland. Half of the poems in the first edition of *Kalevala* (1835) and close to a quarter of the poems of the second edition (1849) were collected from the forest villages of Viena.

Elias Lönnrot (1802–1884) was the Karelianist who understood the value of the folk poems, and he had the idea of reconstructing them into the form of a complete narrative with heroes in arts and metaphysics. In addition to his widespread travels across the northern forests, he made several visits to the rune singers of Viena and filled his notebooks with songs from the bygone times.

The activists of early Karelianism in the first half of the 19th century concentrated on collecting folk poems to construct the basis for a Finnish identity originating in the northern wildernesses. The later Karelianism, inspired by the publication and popularity of the second edition of *Kalevala*, further widened the means of spreading the message: neoromanticist paintings (Akseli Gallen-Kallela), realist photography (I.K. Inha), sentimental music (Jean Sibelius) and geopolitical writings (Ilmari Kianto) together composed the picture of Finland originating in the Karelian backwoods. The later Karelianism culminated during the last two decades of the 19th century, which were the years when Pan-Slavic Russification took a stronger hold on Finland.

The work done by the Karelianists had strengthened the self-consciousness of the Finns to such an extent that by the turn of the century the Pan-Slavists faced a "single-minded nation" standing against the February Manifesto of Nicholas II in 1899.[10] Wide political demonstrations and cooperative initiatives during the first years of the new century paved the way toward economic sufficiency and, finally, also to the declaration of independence that was enacted immediately after the October Revolution.

The Finnish independence in 1917, followed by the Civil War between the "reds" and "whites", resulted in a conservative white regime with reciprocal prejudices toward the new Bolshevik Regime. The border between Finland and the Soviet Union was tightly closed and Karelia was divided into two parts. The state border sliced also Viena and the westernmost Finnish villages lost contact with their eastern neighbors, whereas the major core was drawn under Soviet control. This geopolitical solution put an end to the familial relations between Karelia and Finland and defined the rune singers' land as extreme peripheries of the periphery of both the Soviet Union and Finland.

Rural Collectivization in Soviet Viena

The Karelia of the 1920s was a rural world. Human settlement was dispersed in the thousands of villages that made up the country. After the forced collectivization of agricultural production, after the wars and as a result of Soviet forest policies, rural Karelia contained in the early 1990s about 670 villages—of which half lived on the edge of existence.[11] Fifty-five villages disappeared and only four of the old were left in Viena, namely Uhtua (Kalevala), Jyskyjärvi, Vuonninen and Vuokkiniemi, and they served as concentrations of the Soviet system of production. Two new forestry villages, Luusalmi and Kepa, were in addition founded for the needs of the forest industry (Fig. 8.1).

The Soviet reform took place in the form of several dramatic breaks. The first decade under the new regime brought, however, no big changes to Viena and that was much due to its peripheral location. The collective economy of the kolkhozes was introduced in the 1930s to the villages and it finally destroyed the traditions of family farming. The collectivization was obligatory and those unwilling were sentenced to labor camps in Siberia. The change produced a gap between generations. The young people who were integrated into the new regime transformed the orders of the Communist Party into practice and the older generation was simply forced to accept the changes. Cows and pigs were gathered in larger cattle combines and the private fields were collectivized. The first tractors also emerged to the villages.

Concrete signs of progress and efficiency were clearly visible and it was easy to connect the positive development to the new regime. The social and individual suffering of the older generation was considered as a necessary cost of development. Clear division of labor, strict plans of production and economies of scale were seen as solutions to the backwardness of the forest villages.[13]

The Winter War (1939–1940) totally destroyed the Viena villages on the Finnish side of the border. The villages of Rimmi, Hietajärvi and Kuivajärvi

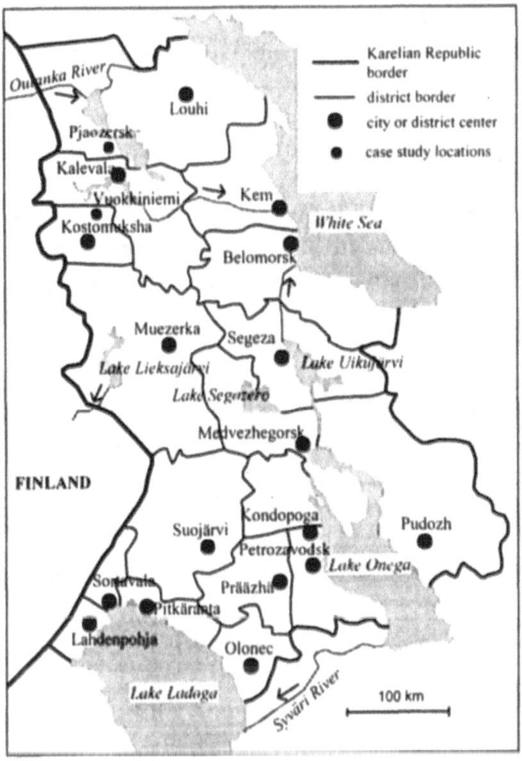

Fig. 8.1. The spatial structure of settlement and administration in the Republic of Karelia.[12]

were evacuated and burned by Finnish troops. The destruction extended over to Soviet Viena during the Continuance War (1941–1944), and most of the villages were evacuated and burned now by the Soviet troops as a response to the Finnish expansion during the early stages of the war. The majority of the Viena Karelians were transported over the White Sea to Arkhangelsk, and only 600 of the 12,000 inhabitants stayed in Viena under the command of Finnish soldiers. Only a few of the evacuated families returned from Arkhangelsk after the wars, which was again a dramatic drawback to Viena Karelian culture.[14]

In Finland, the wartime revitalized the idea of Greater Finland extending to the shores of Lake Onega in the east. All possible scientific evidence was used to construct an argument for the natural size and form of Finland.[15] The definition of nature—the natural covering of uniform bedrock, flora and fauna as well as forest types—was bound to the practical geopolitics of *Lebensraum*. Nature was considered a neutral object and the research was taken as objective and free from societal ambitions. It seemed for a while that it would be possible to recommence the early heroic expeditions in the Karelian wilderness. The footsteps of Elias Lönnrot, I.K. Inha and Jean Sibelius were waiting for followers. Part of

Finland was there, only to be explored and shown to the rest of the world. The war, however, turned out to be a defeat for Finnish ambitions. Most of Karelia, including several national parks founded in 1938, was to be left on the Soviet side of the closed border.

The immediate postwar years witnessed a revival of the kolkhoz economy in Viena. Life was to normalize, by prewar standards, within the separated villages in the Kuittijärvi Lake region. However, the villages were soon put to new trial. In the late 1950s, under the Khrushchev regime, a new wave of collectivization landed in Viena with the establishment of large state farms, sovkhozes. The village kolkhozes were closed and, instead, the sovkhoz of Kalevala was established around the two central villages, Uhtua and Vuokkiniemi. The main buildings from the emptied villages were also transported to the two central villages. The introduction of sovkhozes to Karelia was part of the homogenization of the Soviet Union. Ethnic variation was seen as a hindrance to further industrialization and to the success of the official five-year plans. The Karelian language was prohibited in kindergartens and in village schools as well as in the higher education in Petrozavodsk.[16]

The district administration was reorganized several times during the Soviet years and finally Viena also became divided. The village of Vuokkiniemi was transferred in 1988 from the district of Uhtua to the district of Kostomuksha. Vuokkiniemi, a concentration of 500 inhabitants, was planned to serve as a food-producer for the industrial center, Kostomuksha.

The division of Vuokkiniemi and Uhtua into two different districts was one more drawback for the Viena Karelian culture. The district of Uhtua lost its main village in the south, which meant a significant decrease in the district's population, numbering then approximately 12,000 inhabitants. Vuokkiniemi, with a clear majority of ethnic Karelians,[17] was drawn under the local jurisdiction of an industrial Soviet city. Contacts between the two villages became more laborious because of worsening communicative linkages. The maintenance and development of local bus and telephone networks, for example, favored the district-based administrative system.

Karelia was a newsprint and paper-bag producer in the Soviet division of labor. Viena was defined as a forest reserve whose backwoods resources were tightly tied to the Soviet needs. Large areas of these peripheral forests were, however, left untouched, which was due to long and costly transporting distances. Only the woods close to the main road network were drawn under loggings, which meant large-scale clear-cuttings without any reforestation measures. The backwoods around the old defunct villages of Viena were left alone after the wars and therefore remained quite secure from the Soviet experiments. The forest landscape in Viena became polarized. The unmanaged logging areas soon turned into young deciduous and mixed forests whereas the old-growth backwoods retained a spruce domination and wilderness aspect.

Both forest types are challenging for Western forestry methods that have been introduced to Russian Karelia since the early 1990s by Finnish enterprises. Old-growth forests contain much rotting wood useless to industry, and the young deciduous forests have grown wild with species difficult to process into pulp and paper. Only birch in the younger forests is considered to be valuable and is exported to Finland. The Russian pulp and paper mills cannot use birch as raw material, whereas Finland has been hit by a chronic lack of short fiber from birch.[18]

The federal forestry methods, which are today fueled by the Western demand for cheap timber, are locally repeatedly seen as a continuation to the old colonial practices. The Viena forests are largely under the control of the organizations that date from the Soviet era. This state of affairs leaves the local farmers and forest entrepreneurs quite insecure about their future and the forest villages have in fact continuously suffered from a shortage of wood raw material.[19]

The post-sovkhoz crisis in Viena's economy has freed the rural people from the pressures of forced collectivity but it has left them no alternatives to strive for—to set up on one's own. Family farming without forest resources on which to lean in the beginning, and during the bad times, is not a sustainable alternative in the northern backwoods. The reconstruction of the villages needs much first-class wood material that would in turn provide work for local sawmills. Forestry would give work and local economic incentives if based on premises defined or at least accepted locally. Forestry planning, timber prices, taxation, labor questions, logging methods and local processing *viz-a-viz* export orientation are all questions that have been met in Russian Karelia within the framework of the Federation's chronic need for foreign currency.

The Russian crisis has been taken as a challenge on the Finnish side to widen corporate ranges over the border. The environmental threat from the East (especially airborne pollution) is considered a market potential for the biotech industry. Forest companies purchase cheap timber and sell Western know-how in forestry. Finnish nature conservationists have been actively defining the areas to be preserved in Karelia, which is much easier there, on state-owned land, than in Finland with a dispersed land ownership. Transborder cooperation in the conservation planning is run above the local folks: between companies, conservationists, top officials and scientists.[20]

The new transborder enthusiasm in Finland slightly reminds of the historical motive of Greater Finland. The "return of Karelia" is today made concrete tree by tree, or via conservation decisions. Finnish forest know-how is generally considered to be the solution for the difficulties in Karelian forestry. Nature conservation is to be implemented by founding new national parks and nature reserves in the wilderness that has survived from the Soviet years. Five to ten percent of the total land area of Karelia is to be conserved by drawing the state-owned land under the official control of the conservation administration. The question of economic restructuring and human survival within the Karelian backwoods has been largely ignored.

"Karelien geht an Finnland zurück—per Lastwagen" [21] wrote the conservationists already in the early 1990s, but they could not reflect critically upon their own goals leading in similar direction.

The Karelian ethnicity in Viena is rooted in forests and forest lifemodes on the shores of the lake area of Kuittijärvi. Both elements—forests and lakes—have remained under continuous external threat. The drainage area is threatened by the emissions of the steel industry in Kostomuksha. The forests are under risk of becoming over-harvested by Finnish and Russian companies, or being defined as parks of the Greenbelt.

Forest Villages, Wood Processing and the Greenbelt

During the Soviet years, Karelia was considered to be the "Siberia nearest to Moscow," the place of exile neighboring the capital city.[22] The closing of the western border had made Karelia a marginal land of no interest to the authorities in Moscow. The representatives of the Soviet administration who were "sentenced" up to the Karelian north were often strangers and outsiders not able or willing to build any constructive ties to local residents. Prejudices and fears existed between the rulers and lay communities.

The historical burden also conditions the formulation of development programs for Karelia. The gradual opening of the western border and the joint projects with the Finns are challenging in many ways. Some central questions about this cooperation are summarized below, as lessons from Viena to the developers of the Greenbelt.

First, the degree and form of political independence is of utmost importance for Karelia. The cross-border arrangements under the banner of Moscow will inevitably continue the practices of the Soviet era. Cooperation within the framework of the Republic, that is, with Petrozavodsk, will similarly result in crises at the border settlements. The crucial administrative question is locally tied to the relations between the state's district organizations and the associations of lay people and their representatives, such as village or town committees.

Moscow certainly aims at holding the leading role in the federal governance and this will be guaranteed by tightening the hierarchic system of administration. Petrozavodsk has not been able to construct any forums of disagreeing power (against the Moscow rule), as the Conservatives, most of whom are earlier Communist Party politicians, have been able to keep the majority of seats in the Parliament of Karelia. The dialogue between the regional and federal capitals will undoubtedly keep the local voices in the margins—if not co-strengthened by voices from abroad.

Second, in the longer run the Finnish cooperation with Russian forest industry cannot be leaning exclusively on an outflow of cheap timber from Karelia. Wood-processing in Karelia needs comprehensive renewal that means investments in socially and environmentally-sound technology both in pulp and paper production and in mechanical wood processing. Global markets are increasingly being supplied by fast-growing tropical and temperate tree species, which forces the northern forest industry to re-orient toward production of special articles and careful design by enterprises with flexible management structures. This guides toward high-tech solutions within some fields of special paper production and mechanical wood processing based on particular northern qualifications, as for example densely-fibred pine and curly birch.

The continuance of forest-based development in rural Karelia also requires new combinations of agriculture and forestry leaning on private and local land ownership. The leskhozes that control the local use of state forests have, however, proven rather inflexible toward local potential in agro-forestry. The shortage of wood in the backwoods of Karelia—in the middle of the deep forests—is a problem inherited from the Soviet era. The solving of this paradox needs to be ranked high when sketching future plans in the Greenbelt circumstances.

The historical lessons of colonialism in Russian Karelia clearly demand for a renewal of the rules of socioenvironmental regulation on a multiscale basis. The development of the Greenbelt has turned into a political process where both local co-association and international initiatives have met and questioned the old bilateral model of negotiations between the state neighbors. The local-global networking has thus produced new forms of cooperation and regulation, and this development can be seen as an alternative both to the conservative programs relying on strong federal administration and the post-Soviet search for extreme neo-liberal freedom from any societal regulation.

Finally, the conservation of forest landscapes and traditional wooden architecture in Russian Karelia is of utmost importance in cross-border cooperation. The construction of new infrastructure in the Soviet Union was tied to certain monopolies in the supply of raw materials and production of standard elements. Moreover, the education of planners and architects was strictly bound to certain norms and patterns that could be introduced anywhere. The architect schools produced average architects who could design average buildings all over the country, from Karelia to the Russian Far East.[23] Only the most marginal of the marginal lands could escape the redevelopment according to uniform patterns.

The landscape of wooden houses in Russian Karelia is in danger of disappearing along with the new development strategies. Reforms in housing facilities are desperately needed, and the solutions preferred seem to lean most often on the import of Western models. The Soviet patterns have thus become in large replaced by Western standards. The Finnish postwar experiences from urban and town planning can, however, function as a transborder lesson: the use of standard elements, instead of supporting local resources, skills and traditions, results in dramatic changes in central structures of the landscape and regional identity (see chapter 4).

As an alternative to the scenario above, the Greenbelt of Karelia can also be considered a challenge for new regional design. The primary conditions and codes for the modernization of the wilderness villages and wooden towns can be also drawn from local lifeworlds. Viena Karelia is located centrally in the Greenbelt and it also functions as a good example of a local-global multitude (in the extreme margins) modified, but not entirely destroyed, by the macro-trends of geopolitics. The violent past of the region stands as clear proof that this multitude can only be supported and developed by prioritizing culturally and ecologically sensitive means of cooperation across the border, instead of large-scale industrial, ecological or geopolitical projections controlled from the "outside."

Notes

1. Kirsikka Moring, "Kostamus haastaa Lapualaisoopperan. 70-vuotias Ylioppilasteatteri kertoo yhteisöllistä selviytymistarinaa Kekkosen ja yya:n ajoilta," *Helsingin Sanomat*, 10 November 1996, B1. The quotation is from Esa Kirkkopelto, the coordinator of the play *Kostamus Symphony*. Translated from Finnish by the author.

2. Jorma Korhonen, "Säilyykö Vienan taiga?," *Helsingin Sanomat*, 29 September 1996, D1; Jarmo Pyykkö, ed., *Survey in Russian Karelian Natural Forests in Vienansalo* (Helsinki: WWF Finland, 1996); Jouni Kemppainen, "Ympäristöväki toivoo vihreää vyöhykettä Suomenlahdelta Barentsinmerelle," *Helsingin Sanomat*, 30 July 2002, A10; Riitta Turunen, "Ympäristöväki pelkää Kalevala-puiston suojeluhankkeen puolesta," *Karjalainen*, 19 July 2002, 6.

3. Nikolai Jaakkola, *Pirttijärven rantamilla* (Petrozavodsk: Karjala-kustantamo, 1977); Ortjo Stepanov, *Kotikunnan tarina* (Petrozavodsk: Karjala-kustantamo, 1979).

4. Raimo Heikkilä, Ystävyyden puiston tutkimuskeskus. Unpublished description of the background of the Research Center of the Friendship Park (Kuhmo: Friendship Park Research Center, 2002), mimeo.

5. Tiina Hokkanen, Ympäristöjärjestöt ja kansainvälinen metsäteollisuus kiistakumppaneina Karjalan tasavallassa. Unpublished Master's thesis (Joensuu: University of Joensuu, Department of Geography 1999), 67-9, mimeo; Pilvikki Kause, "Venäjän hallituksen lehti ruoskii Suomea Karjalan talousahdingosta," *Helsingin Sanomat*, 28 October 1999, C5.

6. Jarmo Pyykkö and Rudolf Fenner, "Karelien geht an Finnland zurück—per Lastwagen," *Robin Wood Magazin*, no. 3 (1994), 41-43; Thomas Barow, "Karelische Wälder: Schutz oder Gnadenfrist?," *Deutch-Finnische Rundschau*, no. 92 (1997), 25; Otso Ovaskai-

nen, "Metsäsopu kangertelee Karjalassa," *Helsingin Sanomat*, 23 July 1998, A2 (Vieraskynä); Virpi Sahi, "Kuka hyötyy Karjalan metsistä?," *Helsingin Sanomat*, 25 November 1999), A2 (Vieraskynä).

7. Jevgeni Klementjev, "Autioituneiden kylien ikävä tarina," *Punalippu* 64, no. 2 (1990), 88-96.

8. Klementjev, "Autioituneiden kylien ikävä tarina;" Eira Varis, *The Restructuring of Peripheral Villages in Northwestern Russia* (Helsinki: The United Nations University/WIDER, 1996).

9. *Environmental Priority Action Programme for Leningrad, Leningrad Region, Karelia and Estonia. Synthesis Report* (Helsinki: The Ministry of the Environment in Finland, East Project ,1992); Jaakko Rugojev, "Ennen vedenpaisumusta ja sen jälkeen," *Carelia* 67, no. 5 (1993), 64-89; Jarmo Kortelainen and Juha Kotilainen, "Ownership Changes and Transformation of the Russian Pulp and Paper Industry," *Eurasian Geography and Economics* 44, no. 5 (2003), 392-93.

10. Eino Jutikkala and Kauko Pirinen, *A History Finland* (Helsinki: Weiling+Göös, 1988), 202-11; Ari Aukusti Lehtinen, "Northern Natures," *Fennia* 169, no. 1 (1991), 145-46.

11. Eira Varis, *Karjalan tasavalta tänään* (Ilomantsi: University of Joensuu, Mekrijärvi Research Station, 1993).

12. Markku Nieminen, *Vienan runokylät projekti, II väliraportti* (Kuhmo: Kuhmon Kulttuurikornitsa, 1992).

13. Jaakkola, *Pirttijärven rantamilla*; Stepanov, *Kotikunnan tarina*.

14. Nieminen, *Vienan runokylät projekti*, 15.

15. A Special Issue on Finnish Geopolitics. *Terra* 53, no. 4 (1941); see also Anssi Paasi, "Political Geography around the World VIII. The Rise and the Fall of Finnish Geopolitics," *Political Geography Quarterly* 9, no. 1 (1990), 53-65.

16. Nieminen, *Vienan runokylät projekti*, 16.

17. Ari Aukusti Lehtinen, *The Fall of the Forest Villages: Ecological and Cultural Conflicts in the Russian Taiga* (Uppsala: Uppsala University, Environmental Policy and Society/EPOS, 1993), 20-27.

18. The lack of birch in Finland is a result of forest management practices in the 1960s that labeled birch as waste wood. Birch was an unwanted tree in Finnish forests due to the fact that the wood processing in those days could not make use of it. See Lehtinen, "Northern natures," 103.

19. Nieminen, *Vienan runokylät projekti*, 146-48.

20. Marja Paavilainen, "Suojelualue ainoa keino säilyttää Karjalan uhanalaiset lajit," *Ympäristönsuojelu* 5, no. 2 (1992), 30-33; *Map of Old Growth Forest Areas and Proposals of Russian NGOs on Ecological Optimization of Forest Management in Karelia* (Petrozavodsk: Forest Club of Russian Non-governmental Organizations, 2000). Marjatta Hytönen, ed., *Social Sustainability of Forestry in Northern Europe: Research and Education* (Copenhagen: Nordic Council of Ministers, 2001).

21. Pyykkö and Fenner, "Karelien geht an Finnland zurück—per Lastwagen," ("*Finland gets Karelia Back—By Trucks*").

22. Ulla Vesander, "Siitä puhe mistä puute," (An interview with Sergei Borisovitz), *Maailma ja Me*, no. 12 (1989), 20-22.

23. Ulla Vesander, "Puu vaihtuu betoniin," (An interview with Sergei Katanandov), *Maailma ja Me*, no. 12 (1989), 57-59.

9.

Logging Moratorium: A Tool for Greenbelt Conservation

The worries of the speeded-up disappearance of the old-growth forests in Northwest Russia were confirmed in the mid-1990s when the Biodiversity Conservation Centre in Russia, Greenpeace Russia and the Taiga Rescue Network published first inventories based on forestry maps and satellite images. The environmental organizations soon requested the companies to stop purchasing wood from the old-growth forests designated by the inventories. As a result of a short period of intense public debate, the Finnish forest company Enso announced in 1996 that it will accept the moratorium, a temporary ban on logging or purchasing wood from the disputed old-growth forests in the Republic of Karelia and the Murmansk Oblast. Gradually, in 1997 and 1998, most of the Western forest companies operating in Karelia and Murmansk joined Enso, and it became apparent that the new moratorium initiative had grown into a central tool for forest conservation on the Russian side of the Greenbelt.[1]

The companies agreed not to procure any wood from the old-growth areas until detailed inventories and necessary conservation decisions were made. This solution was historical in many ways, not least that the agreement was made in the negotiations between the environmental organizations and the companies. No governmental bodies were needed in balancing the deviating societal interests. This chapter analyzes the stages that resulted in the moratorium and the subsequent difficulties in maintaining the logging ban (which practically ended in 2001). The administrative problems in turning the agreement into actual conservation decisions are also discussed. The case of Pjaozersky Lespromkhoz— Pääjärvi Forestry District Company—will be introduced as an example of the complicated local-global character of the socioenvironmental tensions attached to the Greenbelt politics.

The Launch: From a Military Zone to a Green Hot Spot

The Forest Committee of the Republic of Karelia made an offer in May 1995 to some Finnish forest companies to start logging at the Finnish-Russian border zone. The invitation was based on the decision of the government of the Russian Federation to open the military security zone for international forestry practices. The decision covered the entire forest belt from the Gulf of Finland up to the Kola Peninsula, and the initial aim of the federal government was to let the companies harvest up to two million cubic meters of timber annually from a zone with a width from 2 to 80 kilometers and with a length of 900 kilometers.[2]

Except for some minor local cuttings, the border zone had been left to heal from the war damage (of the 1940s) and it had largely grown into a zone of old-growth backwoods, especially contrasting to the forest landscape on the Finnish side of the border, mostly consisting of well-managed and even-aged economic forests. The nature conservationists and researchers of the Karelian Science Centre in Petrozavodsk, the capital of the Republic of Karelia, immediately expressed their doubts about the plan of slicing the long zone. The government of the Republic of Karelia soon limited the annual allowable cut down to 190,000 cubic meters.[3]

The Greenbelt had emerged as a challenging target for nature conservation already in the early 1990s when the Karelian Science Centre in Petrozavodsk and the Ministry of the Environment in Helsinki, Finland, agreed upon a research program of the border forests. As a result, several new conservation areas were proposed in 1994, extending from the northern shores of Lake Ladoga up to the surroundings of the already existing Paanajärvi National Park. The idea of the Greenbelt was introduced to the broader public by the representatives of the Karelian Science Centre in January 1994 in a Finnish-Russian environmental meeting in Mekrijärvi, eastern Finland.[4]

Taiga Rescue Network (TRN), which had been founded in 1992 in Jokkmokk, northern Sweden, was also an early protagonist of the Greenbelt of the Finnish-Russian border. TRN and the Russian conservationists soon found the Greenbelt a common challenge that became the key issue of the TRN Workshop in Kostomuksha in October 1995. The workshop took place with participants from several environmental organizations from Northern and Western Europe, such as World Wildlife Fund, Robin Wood, Greenpeace and the Greens in the European Parliament. The organizations wanted guarantees from the forest companies not to get involved in the processing of old-growth timber before the ecological inventories and the following conservation decisions were made in the Republic of Karelia. The reactions of the companies were defensive, but also promises of turning sensitive to the old-growth question were expressed. Greenpeace, Biodiversity Conservation Centre and TRN were able, however, to continuously document breaks between the promises and the actual practices and they started a campaign in Germany by publicly listing the companies involved in the loggings at the Belt and within its extensions eastward in the Republic of Karelia. Enso Gutzeit was especially regarded in the German media as the main actor behind the timber flows from the areas under dispute.[5]

In December 1995, 95,000 supporters of the Greenpeace campaign sent a "Christmas card" to Enso Gutzeit. The card contained a picture of a clear-cut with alarming letters running across it: "*Enso räumt auf!*" ("Enso makes it clear!"). The card contained a demand for withdrawing both from the pristine forests and clear-cut loggings. Enso mailed a letter to all the card senders with a question: "*Wissen Sie, dass...*" ("Did you know that..."). Enso explained that the annual industrial cuttings in Finland cover only 1.8 percent of the forests, thus leaving the remaining 98.2 percent untouched:

> *...1,8 % des finnischen Waldes p.a. wirtschaftlich genutzt werden.*
> *... 98,2 % innerhalb des Wachstums- und Wirtschaftskreislaufes jährlich ungenutzt bleiben.*

The answer did not satisfy the activists due to its misleading information, producing an impression of understating the activists. Christoph Thies, the leader of the Greenpeace campaign, argued that by cutting 1.8 percent of the forests annually it takes only 55 years to complete the whole logging cycle. It is significantly less than the average succession period in the boreal zone which varies between 80–120 years. Succession period is the time needed to get a matured forest after final cuttings.[6]

Enso's reply thus only fueled the Greenpeace campaign. The environmentalists of the Russian Forest Club also contacted the company about its ecological responsibility in the timber trade across the border.[7] The dual attack by environmentalists from Western Europe and Russia made it necessary for Enso to turn from reactive to proactive in its environmental performance. The strategic change took place in a short period in the mid-1990s.

Enso published its own biodiversity strategy in the early winter of 1995 covering both its own forests and the supply forests. Enso, WWF and the city of Kostomuksha cooperated in 1996 in a model project in Viena Karelia aiming to apply seedling-tree methods but the project, being against the Russian Forestry Act, was canceled by the Federal authorities. Enso was also the first company to declare a voluntary logging moratorium at the Greenbelt, starting from 1 January 1997.[8] "We will not be stepping on the minefields on purpose anymore," stated the Vice President Juhani Pohjolainen from Enso in 1996. The company promoted inventories of the remaining old-growth areas in Karelia and also suggested a founding of a working group consisting of all the parties involved, both governmental and non-governmental.[9]

The moratorium was prolonged to the end of 2000. All the main Finnish companies gradually joined it. UPM-Kymmene joined Enso's initiative from the beginning of 1997, and Vapo Timber, Pölkky and Kuhmo announced their participation the following summer. The Swedish Modo also joined then. Vainionpää was the last of the main actors to accept the moratorium in February 1998—after intense environmental pressure. The year 1997 witnessed, however, numerous episodes where environmentalists repeatedly found proof on wood flows form the hot spots to Finland. The licenses for cuttings in the risky areas were sometimes easy to get from the local forestry district companies (lespromkhozes) with acute need of foreign currency. The export of timber was enticing as the foreign companies could pay well. Consequently, the domestic wood-processing plants in the Republic of Karelia largely ran short of raw material.[10]

The federal taxing of forest income is relatively high in Russia and this, in a way, encourages illegal practices. Overloading logging trucks and carrying more wood than is officially declared have been a popular means of diminishing the strain of taxation. Full taxation has also been avoided by barter transactions. As a payment for a logging license, Finnish companies have also supported the construction of public infrastructure, such as schools and churches in the nearby settlement, and this strategy has in some cases secured an increased local return from the logging licenses.[11] The moratorium affected both the local barter practices and federal tax revenue and this turned many in Russia critical toward cross-border environmentalism.

The Case of Pjaozersk

Pjaozersky Lespromkhoz has been among those actors most critical of Greenbelt conservation. The logging center was founded in 1973 as a joint project between Finnish and Soviet partners and it was planned to become a permanent work unit. Most of the logging centers in Karelia were initially founded to serve as short-term work bases with wooden cabins for the loggers (and their families) working nearby. Pjaozersky Lespromkhoz had, however, blocks of flats built by Finnish developers and there were such public facilities as a school and a hospital. Pjaozersk was in 1998 a district of 3300 inhabitants, of whom about one-quarter was employed by forestry-based work such as loggings, timber transport and primary wood processing. The Lespromkhoz has in general gained a reputation of efficiency in the Republic of Karelia and it has been regarded as one of the most important wood suppliers and forest tax payers in the republic.[12]

Most of the wood from Pjaozersk has been exported to Finland. The main purchaser is Stora Enso, which has a pulp plant in Kemijärvi, Finnish Lapland, 270 kilometers northwest of Pjaozersk. The moratorium largely threatened the operations of the Lespromkhoz, and in many local reactions the continuation of the district's forestry and central village was completely put under question. Nevertheless, a satisfactory compromise was reached between the companies, environmentalists and governmental bodies in 2001, promising to save the pristine forests north of Lake Paanajärvi, close to the state border, from logging operations and redirect the logging frontier toward the northeastern parts of the Lespromkhoz.[13] The border area belongs to the upland forests stretching over to the Finnish side and, being mature old-growth, it is challenging for logging tractors. The solution secured a steady flow of wood from Pjaozersk to Kemijärvi. The moratorium thus gave time in Pjaozersk for the stakeholders to find a compromise to guarantee both the continuity of the Belt and the future of the Lespromkhoz.

The episode revealed several historical socioenvironmental tensions that function as central background factors in cross-border cooperation. First, the regional political thinking that is grounded on the idea of a dynamic frontier of logging operations tends in practice to leave behind a landscape of frozen labor divisions: continuation of the initial functions emerges as the *raison d'etre* of maximized forest exploitation. Final cuttings, which are much favored both in Finland and Russia, offer no grounds for continuous harvesting. However, the logging centers, when becoming part of a permanent settlement, have a continuous need for new logging areas. The expanding logging road network and daily commuting distances turn into necessities that make all arguments for non-timber values of forests sound unrealistic—as contrasted with employment issues and rising logistic costs. From a forest-ecological perspective the permanency of the logging centers is thus a threat: while reaching the last remaining old-growth forests at a feasible commuting distance, the risks of unemployment become an important argument against nature conservation. Path-dependency of this type is the underlying dilemma not only in Pjaozersk but in other parts of Karelia and on the Finnish side as well.

From an individual or family point of view, the logging villages often serve as periodic places of paid work but for many the settling down in the backwoods turns into a life-long project. People become rooted to their home area or, alternatively, the poor conditions of living, which worsened in general in the early post-Soviet era, leave no room for escape. Settling permanently in an industrial center such as Pjaozersk, dominated by a single company, offers no realistic alternatives to earn a living on a longer time-span. Families and individual households become by necessity fully dependent on one company.

Second, Pjaozersk has functioned as an important resource frontier for the pulp plant in Kemijärvi in northern Finland, founded in 1968. The motives to locate a pulp plant on the northern side of the Arctic Circle were twofold. On the one hand, the ongoing and planned loggings in Finnish Lapland offered much raw material and, on the other hand, the then popular goals for regional policy favored large industrial projects in the far North. The rising demand for wood in Lapland had turned into overcuttings of pine for decades,[14] and this made it necessary for the Finnish company to aim at extending its supply area across the state border. During the late 1990s, 75–80 percent of the wood logged in Pjaozersk was traded to Finland, Enso and Pölkky being the main purchasers.[15] Enso imports mainly pine from Pjaozersk, whereas birch is the main trade article in the southern parts of the Greenbelt. The role of Pjaozersk for Stora Enso is marginal but locally—in Finnish Lapland—wood supply from the East is crucial, which is partially due to the Wilderness Conservation Programme in Upper Lapland initiated in the early 1990s (see chapter 11).

Third, the moratorium debate demonstrated that the effective and widely-networked formulation of the idea of the Greenbelt was crucial in strengthening the voice of the environmentalists and, in this way, ecological issues became also concrete for the forest companies involved. In Pjaozersk, the Greenbelt emerged as a central tool for founding an ecological buffer zone for Paanajärvi National Park, founded in 1992. The Greenbelt thus functioned as an influential political projection, or a discursive setting, which modified the diverse concerns attached to the moratorium debate. The concerns stretched from the sphere of individual families, suffering from insecurity caused by constraints in logging operations, and extended up to the realms of international environmental and forest-industrial actors competing within their interrelated agendas. The key features of the multilayered formation of the Greenbelt is analyzed below in detail by grouping them into four socioenvironmental tensions running across several spatial scales.

Translocal Logging Community

The loggings of the Pjaozersky Lespromkhoz are the guarantee of human settlement in the northernmost corners of the Karelian Republic. Since its foundation in 1973, the Lespromkhoz has operated in the area that initially covered about 7000 square kilometers of virgin pine and spruce forests, lakes and treeless mountaintops. The establishment of Paanajärvi National Park diminished the area of the Lespromkhoz by about 1000 square kilometers. Moreover, the moratorium in 1996 covered 1500 square kilometers of forest, mostly around Paanajärvi National Park. The Lespromkhoz, which is in charge of the forestry operations and also runs the dominant part of the loggings, operates from within the settlement centers. The centers, of which Pjaozersk (the main village with 500-600 dwellers), Tuhkala and Sofporog are most important, were in the late 1990s home villages for about 3300 persons.[16] Practically all the families were connected to the logging operations of the Lespromkhoz that offered jobs to 900 employees.

The annual loggings in the district, varying between 300,000-500,000 cubic meters in the late 1990s, are practically run by two companies, the Lespromkhoz and SP Paanajärvi. The returns on exports are highly dependent on the customs duties, which tend to fluctuate according to federal decisions. Customs duties cover, with broad annual variation, close to one-quarter of the expenses and an approximately similar share is used for paying both salaries and covering general expenses. The latter refers to costs of technically and logistically running the company but also to costs of supporting local schooling, health care and sport center. When also counting the stumpage fees (5–10 percent, paid to the Karelian Forestry Committee), taxes and other necessary payments, only a minor part of the annual turnover can finally be used in new investments, which clearly is the main long-term challenge for the Lespromkhoz.[17]

The local running of the Lespromkhoz is also conditioned by a dispersed ownership of the company. The employees owned one third (37 percent) of the Lespromkhoz in 1999 but the rest of the owners were translocal: Russian Federation (20 percent), a Moscow-based Korporatsio group of forest and logging dealers (16 percent), privatized Exportles in Moscow (16 percent) and Karellesprom, privatized forest company of the Karelian Republic (10 percent).[18] Logging and export operations are the only source of livelihood for the local employee-owners, which is not the case among the distant owners in Moscow and Petrozavodsk. The latter partners have showed no interest in investing in wood-processing capacity in the northernmost backwoods of Karelia. The Lespromkhoz is for them primarily a logging unit, devoted to "timber-mining."

Some forestry district companies in Russia have attracted foreign owners aiming at participating in the exploitation of the Russian forest resources but also searching for feasible investment targets.[19] The Finnish partners have only minimally utilized the option of investing in wood refining in Pjaozersk as it is much more attractive for them to let the Lespromkhoz serve as a wood supply. The chosen division of labor is both ecologically and socially problematic as it favors a steady flow of raw material from the logging frontiers under the domination of one company. The volume is maximized, at the cost of quality.

Environmentalism Across the Border

Ecological questions and timber trade concerns are thoroughly interlinked in the cross-border operations between Finland and the Republic of Karelia. The former cannot be solved without paying attention to the latter. The conservationists have largely noticed the linkage and only rarely their arguments and proposals are solely grounded on pure ecological facts. The inventory of old-growth forests of boreal Europe[20] by the TRN was narrowly ecological in character but also there the socioenvironmental issues were discussed, especially within the context of Northwest Russia. According to TRN, the current economic model of forest use is oriented mainly toward export of raw materials and cannot provide long-term economic growth for the region. TRN further argues that: "This model, although it may be represented as including ecological considerations, in reality, destroys the last old-growth forests in Russia, which have now become the most threatened natural ecosystems."[21] TRN has also for years emphasized the alternatives of non-motorized tourism, non-timber forest products and certified loggins in the ecologically valuable forests of the Republic of Karelia.[22]

Olli Turunen, a Finnish forest activist who has run nature inventories in the area north of Lake Paanajärvi, expressed his deep "ecological enthusiasm" in the media by picturing in detail the old-growth species he had encountered. But he also had recognized the underlying socioenvironmental tensions: "The village of Pjaozersk is too much dependent on wood export to Finland and the logging operations of one company, the Lespromkhoz." He consequently recommended efforts to broaden the spectrum of local wood-refining and putting emphasis on non-timber values such as berries, mushrooms and nature tourism.[23]

The Finnish companies purchasing wood from Pjaozersk are currently sensitive to international environmental concerns and therefore they actively follow the debate between the Lespromkhoz, the conservationists and the Russian administration. The companies admit that "their voice has an impact but finally the decisions are in the hands of the Russians."[24] The Greenbelt communities in Russia cannot afford to lose contact with their clients in Finland, but the administrative decisions putting forward the initiatives of nature conservation have proceeded slowly. Behind this problem is the tensional relationship between the officers in charge and the conservationists.[25] Ivan Fedchik, the director of Pjaozersk Lespromkhoz, was for example worried about the "greens provoking conflicts between the Lespromkhoz and the Finnish companies." He further argued that "after receiving the maps [results of the ecological forest inventories], the companies tell from where they will not purchase timber."[26]

After examining in detail four international forestry conflicts in Northwest Russia, Maria Tysiachniouk and Jonathan Reisman identified three models of promoting environmental goals in contemporary Russia.[27] The most effective one, in a short run at least, leant on strong individuals of the forest sector who push things forward with their own personal influence. Slower and much more insecure was the model launching and supporting local educational and public activities that aimed at motivating ordinary people in environmental thinking. The model that directed transborder pressure straight onto the Russian administration was the most unsuccessful. In the last case, the results much depended on the position and willingness of foreign forest companies in promoting local environmental goals.

Under the specific circumstances of Pjaozersk, no strategic pro-moratorium links to influential individuals or broader public could be developed by the conservationists but a compromise was, however, reached that secured, at least for a while, the continuation of the forestry work and the Greenbelt. The main reason for the balanced solution was undoubtedly the impact the environmental campaigns had on the foreign companies cooperating with Pjaozersk. The pressure and the decision were thus mainly of translocal origin, lacking any reciprocal links to local key individuals and lay people. No concrete development of the socioenvironmental aspects of transborder cooperation can be identified in the moratorium case concerning Pjaozersk. The compromise was positive only when seen from outside of the local community. The Greenbelt could be protected on the map of Northern Europe, not in the daily life of the villages. The local sense of injustice, put into words by Ivan Fedchik above, will undoubtedly shadow for long the local attitudes on environmental proposals of any kind.

Pjaozersky Les—Made in Europe

Pjaozersk is a minor spot on the forest map of Europe but its location in the debate on the old-growth forests became important in the late 1990s. The northernmost parts of the Lespromkhoz were identified as containing rare and threatened elements of boreal nature and became a critical link in the chain of forests extending from the Gulf of Finland to the Barents Sea. The main method of the conservationists worried about the fate of the forest chain was to raise public debate by direct actions, such as the *"Enso räumt auf!"* campaign, or by local demonstrations at the logistic nodes of wood processing. In August 1996, for example, Greenpeace closed the gate of the Uimaharju pulp mill in North Karelia for a short period to show documents in publicity that Enso, against its promises, still utilized timber from the old-growth forests at the Greenbelt. Greenpeace also demonstrated in October 1996 at the harbor of Lübeck, Germany, while a ship full of Greenbelt timber was unloading its cargo. Then the dispute was focused on the fate of the old-growth forests west of the villages of Viena Karelia.[28]

Activists made also a blockade at the gate of the Vainionpää mill (the Martinniemi sawmill at Haukipudas in Finland) in spring 1997 to raise public concern on the matter that the raw material to the mill originated from the Greenbelt forests planned to become part of a conservation network. In August 1997, consequently, Vainionpää had to sell the chips from its sawmill abroad as the Finnish pulp and paper plants were unwilling to utilize them. They were afraid of the image risks attached to their environmental performance in relation to the Greenbelt. The managing director of Vainionpää was then unwilling to negotiate with any issues related to nature conservation.[29] In February 1998, the company finally relented and joined the moratorium.

The power of forest activists to influence the strategies of the main companies is related to the specific environmental risk-awareness developed among the printing companies and their clients in Western Europe. Certificating the origin of paper was favored already in the early 1990s among the German purchasers of Finnish paper.[30] The printing companies are dependent on the preferences of their primary customers, such as publishers, and the readers and other end-users of paper. An increasing number of customers have learnt to demand and support sustainable products and processes. In addition, the environmental officials regulate the sphere of publishing, both within national frameworks and in the context of the European Union. The EU has also a direct influence on the formation of Greenbelt politics. This has been made concrete through numerous development programs supporting nature and culture conservation, biodiversity management and local sustainability. Both the consumers and the officials follow and respond to the changes in general attitudes and environmental legislation, and it is via this change in cultural norms and customs that environmental activists have aimed at influencing socioenvironmental goal formulation. The forest companies have to adjust to this dynamics if willing to successfully operate in Europe.

The forest industry is increasingly conditioned by discursive regulation taking place through the market and environmental debate.[31] This does not mean that formal legislation and state authorities have disappeared but their arsenal of governance has only become accompanied by "softer" modes of regulation taking place through broader participation. In the case of Pjaozersk and the Greenbelt, one of the primary tensions exists between these two modes of regulation: the governing structures of the Russian Federation meet the multitude of Western co-governance.

Corporate Co-management and Local-Global Responsibility

From inside Stora Enso, Pjaozersk is willingly seen a social and moral issue for the company.[32] Finns have been involved in the development of the Lespromkhoz from the beginning. The project was launched in the early 1970s by an agreement between the Soviet Prime Minister Aleksei Kosygin and Urho Kekkonen, the President of Finland. The aim was to increase wood export from the Soviet Union and strengthen employment in northeastern Finland. The Kemijärvi pulp mill, currently owned by Stora Enso, had been founded in the mid-1960s, and Pjaozersk was regarded as a confirmation of a steady flow of raw material to the mill.[33] The question is thus about regional and social responsibility: Stora Enso is willing to continue operations and considers the risks of unemployment high at the border localities.

Pjaozersk and Kemijärvi are operationally of minimal importance to Stora Enso. The closing of the Kemijärvi mill would not put much strain on the company that is developing its global profile across the oceans in North America, China and Brazil.[34] The intense globalization of the company is, however, the main reason for its sensitivity to local particularities. As was stated above, successful companies have to follow the cultural dynamics of the wider public and they also are able to afford it. In this respect Pjaozersk, and the Greenbelt in general, became a central turning point in Enso's strategies. Global concern was guiding toward and strengthened by concerns of social and environmental responsibility and this link was clearly understood in the company in the mid-1990s.[35]

It was this particular local-global setting that motivated Enso to take the lead in the moratorium debate in October 1996. The proposal that covered about two million hectares of Greenbelt forests gained support from almost all environmental organizations and finally also many of the key officials of the Republic of Karelia accepted the idea, albeit with reservations. The rest of the companies soon followed. The most global of the actors in timber-trade across the border thus had made an offer that no one could refuse. The move was important to the green image of Enso and it also helped the subsequent compromise in the forests north of Paanajärvi National Park.

The Greenbelt is part of the vegetation zone of conifer-dominated forests running through the major regions of Russia and finally encircling the globe. The largest forest companies are gradually extending their operations across the global greenbelt of the conifer-dominated northwoods, accounting nearly half of the world's forest area. The moratorium episode demonstrated how the performance of the companies depends on the discursive practices in which they are embedded. The Greenbelt was, and is, a green projection that linked local issues to broader environmental concerns and it has thus strengthened the articulation and legitimacy of forest conservation. The chain of protected areas gradually gained a high status in the border politics, and the specific model of discursive regulation, based on local-global co-management of socioenvironmental matters, showed its potential. The success of environmentalists deserves to be acknowledged as an example within the broader context of the taiga. The final part of the chapter summarizes the main results of the moratorium in 1996–2001.

Post-moratorium

The debate on the moratorium revealed several important features of the Greenbelt that gradually began to contain an array of symbolic dimensions. The Belt turned into a discursive (local-global) projection with specific ecological and economic values, but it also turned into a battlefield for differing forestry methods and administrative practices. The Greenbelt took shape as the conflict zone between the East and the West, run by forest-industrial actors, the federal administration of Russia and nature conservationists.

The ecological dimension of the Belt fared surprisingly well in the contest. It also became clear in the debate how the ecological and cultural views were conversely interrelated. The opening of the border for human activities had suddenly turned into a threat of closing the border for the species of flora and fauna. The military security zone had functioned as a corridor of nature. The biodiversity of the conservation areas on the Finnish side of the border was, in a way, maintained by the species influx from the Eastern mainland. The environmentalists argued that the species diversity was continuously at risk in the small and scattered islands of Finnish wilderness and a balance could only be secured in the form of imports across the border. The intensified human activity at the border areas of the Republic of Karelia is also responsible for the increased bear population on the Finnish side of the Greenbelt (see chapter 4).

The moratorium demonstrated the strength of transborder environmentalism fueled by rising environmental awareness among the consumers in Western Europe. The leading forest companies had grown big enough to afford to become sensitive to ecological and consumer messages. The moratorium was considered a positive image factor for Enso, the most global of the companies involved, and it was deemed a valuable tool for widening the markets for the end products in Europe. The pros and cons of pulp-processing in Kemijärvi north of the Arctic Circle are repeatedly assessed in the headquarters of Stora Enso, and set in the framework of the globalization contest in which the company is participating.

Most important, the moratorium brought to the surface a new grouping of forest interests. The environmentalists and the companies made the agreement on a periodical withdrawal from the Greenbelt loggings, and the interests of the governments at both sides of the border were largely bypassed. The widely shared view in the Republic of Karelia was critical both of the environmentalists and the foreign companies not paying enough attention to the economic and social consequences of the moratorium. The new environmental grouping brought along practical difficulties in coping with local and federal authorities while running ecological inventories as well as experiments of alternative forestry. The new grouping became also reflected in the slow progression within the federal administration toward legally secured nature conservation. The moratorium initiative needed the support of governmental bodies in order to result in permanent conservation, and the bypassing of the federal administration during the launch of the moratorium was broadly received in Russia as an offensive act.

The intensified international cooperation of the forest industry and environmentalists has profoundly challenged the local and national administrative practices on both sides of the Finnish-Russian border, and the experiences in Pjaozersk should be taken as a course in co-learning. The years of the moratorium debate should serve as an educational episode for the forthcoming projects in transborder environmentalism, both among the popular forums of discursive regulation and within the joint programs coordinated by the European Union and Russia.

Notes

1. Otso Ovaskainen, Minna Pappila and Jyri Pötry, *The Finnish Forest Industry in Russia* (Helsinki: The Finnish Nature League and Taiga Rescue Network, 1999), 8-9; Sarah Lloyd, *Towards Responsible Swedish Timber Trade? A Survey of Actors and Origin of Timber from Russia and the Baltic States* (Jokkmokk: Taiga Rescue Network, 2000); Henna Haapala, *Karjalan tasavallan metsiensuojelukeskustelun retoriikka-analyysi* (Helsinki: Suomen ympäristökeskus, 1999), 10-15.
2. Haapala, *Karjalan tasavallan metsiensuojelukeskustelun retoriikka-analyysi*, 13.
3. Sven Wikström, "Karjala tarjoaa rajavyöhykkeen metsiä suomalaisten hakattaviksi," *Helsingin Sanomat*, 19 July 1995, A9; Haapala, *Karjalan tasavallan metsiensuojelukeskustelun retoriikka-analyysi*, 13.
4. Rauno Ruuhijärvi, "Yhteistyö luonnonsuojelun edistämiseksi Luoteis-Venäjällä," *Ympäristö ja Terveys*, nos. 3-4 (1997), 40-3.
5. Markku Liikamaa, "Kiistely yhtiön raaka-aineen alkuperästä jatkui Uimaharjussa," *Karjalainen*, 23 August 1996, 14; Otso Ovaskainen, "Metsäsopu kangertelee Karjalassa," *Helsingin Sanomat*, 23 July 1998, A2; Dennis Smirnov, "Europe: Finns Break Moratorium," *Taiga News*, no. 37 (2001), <http://www.sll.fi/TRN/TaigaNews/News37/mainarticle/html> (19 Feb. 2002).
6. Final cuttings refer to a harvesting method that exploits larger mature forest stands (of several tens of hectares) by making a clear-cut or, alternatively, a seedling stand. The latter—it is not applied in Russia—is often left to regenerate naturally, with the help of a few seedling trees remaining in the area. The former is followed by tree planting in Finland whereas in Russia the natural regeneration is preferred (see chapter 2).
7. Aleksei Grigoriev, Dimitri Aksionov and Sergei Tsyplenkov, "Glimmers of Hope for Karelia's Old-growth Forests," *Taiga News*, no 20 (1997), <http://www.sll.fi/TRN/TaigaNews/News20/Karelia.html> (18 Feb. 1998).
8. Katri Eronen, "Euroopan kuuluisin kyläkoulu," *Karjalainen*, 2 November 1996, 10.
9. Jake Burbridge, "Enso Declares Moratorium in Karelian Old-growth," *Taiga News* 19 (1996), <http://www.sll.fi/TRN/TaigaNews/News19/enso.html> (18 Feb. 1998); "Enso esittää Karjalan ikimetsien kartoitusta," *Karjalainen*, 23 October 1996, 20.
10. Mikko Keinonen, "Pienet suomalaisyhtiöt nakertavat vaivihkaa Karjalan luonnonmetsiä," *Helsingin Sanomat*, 8 September 1996, B15.
11. Eronen, "Euroopan kuuluisin kyläkoulu;" Grigoriev, Aksionov and Tsyplenkov, "Glimmers of Hope for Karelia's Old-growth Forests."
12. Tiina Hokkanen, Ympäristöjärjestöt ja kansainvälinen metsäteollisuus kiistakumppaneina Karjalan tasavallassa. Master's thesis (Joensuu: Joensuun yliopisto, maantieteen laitos, 2000), 92, mimeo.

13. Raimo Heikkilä, an interview with the author (19 Aug. 2002).
14. Ari Aukusti Lehtinen, "Northern Natures," *Fennia* 169, no. 1 (1991), 99-109.
15. Hokkanen, Ympäristöjärjestöt ja kansainvälinen metsäteollisuus kiistakumppaneina Karjalan tasavallassa, 97.
16. Hokkanen, Ympäristöjärjestöt ja kansainvälinen metsäteollisuus kiistakumppaneina Karjalan tasavallassa, 92.
17. Ivan Fedchik, Forestry at the Pjaozersky District (a speech at a forest meeting in Pjaozersk, 30 May 2000), mimeo; Matti Huuskonen, "Pääjärvellä törmäävät leipä ja luonto," *Helsingin Sanomat,* 10 April 2000, A7; Josif Skadorva, a speech at a forest meeting in Pjaozersk, 30 May 2000, mimeo.
18. Huuskonen, "Pääjärvellä törmäävät leipä ja luonto," A7.
19. Hervé Kempe and Roger Olsson, "French Joint Venture Threatens Unique Forest Reserve. *Taiga News,* no. 8 (1994), 3; Ari Aukusti Lehtinen, "Russian Taiga: Regional Fabrication of the Federal Forest Regime," in *Politics of Forests*, eds. Ari Aukusti Lehtinen, Jakob Donner-Amnell and Bjørnar Sœther (Aldershot: Ashgate, 2004), 92-99.
20. Sarah Lloyd, ed., *The Last of the Last. The Old Growth Forests of Boreal Europe* (Jokkmokk: Taiga Rescue Network, 1999).
21. Lloyd, *The Last of the Last*, 48.
22. Haapala, *Karjalan tasavallan metsiensuojelukeskustelun retoriikka-analyysi*, 41.
23. "Fennoskandian suurin kuusikko," *Helsingin Sanomat,* 10 April 2000, A7 (Translated from Finnish by the author).
24. "Metsäyhtiöt toivovat sopua hakkuualueista," *Helsingin Sanomat,* 10 April 2000, A7. (Translated from Finnish by the author).
25. Maria Tysiachniouk and Jonathan Reisman, "Co-managing the Taiga: Russian Forests and the Challenge of International Environmentalism," in *Politics of Forests*, eds. Ari Aukusti Lehtinen, Jakob Donner-Amnell and Bjørnar Sœther (Aldershot: Ashgate, 2004), 157-75.
26. Huuskonen, "Pääjärvellä törmäävät leipä ja luonto," A7.
27. Tysiachniouk and Reisman, "Co-managing the Taiga: Russian Forests and the Challenge of International Environmentalism," Maria Tysiachniouk and Jonathan Reisman are environmental sociologists specialized in Russia and comparisons between environmental management solutions in Russia and North America.
28. Markku Liikamaa, "Kiistely yhtiön raaka-aineen alkuperästä jatkui Uimaharjussa," *Karjalainen*, 23 August 1996, 14; Hannes Mäntyranta, "Karjalan hakkuut keskeytyivät," *Venäjän aika*, no. 3 (1997), 16-18.
29. Mäntyranta, "Karjalan hakkuut keskeytyivät," 18.
30. Heikki Juslin and Sanna Myrttinen, "Suomalaisen metsäsektorin ympäristöystävällisyys puntarissa. Saksalaisten painotalojen arvioita," *Paperi ja Puu*, nos. 1-2 (1995), 23-24; Hokkanen, Ympäristöjärjestöt ja kansainvälinen metsäteollisuus kiistakumppaneina Karjalan tasavallassa, 42-44.
31. Lehtinen, Donner-Amnell and Sœther, *Politics of Forests*, 275.
32. Hokkanen, Ympäristöjärjestöt ja kansainvälinen metsäteollisuus kiistakumppaneina Karjalan tasavallassa, 97.
33. Huuskonen, "Pääjärvellä törmäävät leipä ja luonto," A7.
34. *Tammi-syyskuun osavuosikatsaus* (Helsinki: Stora Enso, 2003).
35. Teijo Rytteri, *Metsäteollisuusyrityksen luonto* (Joensuu: Joensuun yliopisto, Maantieteen laitoksen julkaisuja, no. 10, 2002), 114-41.

10.

Provincialism and a Frontier Community: The Case of Kuusamo Forest Common

Women's Environmental Network (WEN) arranged in February 1995 a civic demonstration in front of the Finnish Trade Centre in London to appeal to the Finnish Government to stop loggings in the old-growth forests of Kuusamo, north-eastern Finland. The event was part of a wider international forest campaign coordinated by the Taiga Rescue Network and Greenpeace. The target of the demonstration in London was Veitsiluoto, then a state-owned pulp and paper company operating in northern Finland. WEN warned that if the company continued to purchase timber from the disputed forests at the eastern state border, the activists would put pressure on International Publishing Company (IPC) to cancel its trade agreement with Veitsiluoto. IPC was in the mid-1990s the publisher of such journals as *New Scientist*, *Melody Maker*, *Marie Claire* and *Country Life*.[1]

The fate of the old-growth forests in Kuusamo became an issue of intense debate in 1994 when Finnish Nature League discovered there were a few private wildernesses with high ecological value. Findings such as these were no longer thought possible.[2] Romevaara, one of the wildernesses, was under immediate risk to be logged by the owner, the Kuusamo Forest Common (KFC), and the tension soon gained much publicity and political attention. KFC is the largest of the forest commons in Finland, with a land holding of 95,000 hectares and 3830 shareholders.[3]

Despite their marginal location, the backwoods of Kuusamo have functioned for long as the frontier where the aims of the broader society have coalesced. The landscape of the border forests outside the few old-growth remnants is industrial, consisting of large cleat-cuts (up to 500 hectares), planted forests and an extensive logging road network. The relics of wilderness that have not been converted into economic forests have gradually been integrated into the (semi-)protected Greenbelt. This chapter discusses the local cultural features reinforcing and reproducing the local-global dependence structures and keeping these northwoods as marginal lands and resource peripheries.

The forest conflict in Kuusamo is an outcome of specific historical circumstances rooting from the geopolitical construction of the state border and the subsequent confirmation of the border forests as backwoods peripheries. The establishment of the national institution of Forest Commons has also had a strong impact on the formation of the disagreement. KFC has gained a leading position among the forest commons in Finland and therefore the dynamics of the conflict in Kuusamo, including its resolution, was studied with care elsewhere by forest conservationists, the forest industry and landowners. The conflict is analyzed in this chapter by studying the sociohistorical mechanisms favoring expansive and extractive forestry methods resulting in local threats to boreal biodiversity. The difficulties of administering a plausible environmental strategy in the backwoods localities close to the eastern border are also examined.

The analysis begins with a brief elaboration of provincialism as a cultural factor behind the marginalization of Finnish forest peripheries. This is followed by an exploration of the history of the Kuusamo Forest Common. The conclusion aims at rethinking the relationship between environmental and economic issues within the backwoods context. The lessons from Kuusamo are finally rethought within the framework of the provincialism debate in geography.

Provincialism in the Borderland

The recent success of Finnish forest companies abroad has become reflected in the form of lessening production investments in the domestic provinces. Steady outflow of roundwood has been secured but it has not much helped the frontier localities coping with chronic unemployment. The ongoing globalization of the companies has resulted in growing insecurity within provincial economies, both in Finland and internationally.[4] However, this polarization cannot be explained by translocal factors alone, such as actions of the big companies or general economic dynamics. It can, instead, be seen as a logical outcome of the strategies adopted and favored by the provinces. The local vulnerability is partly self-made. It is in particular this feature of provincial mentality, the atmosphere of submission and opportunism under the pressure of globalization, that is examined in this chapter.

Finnish provincialism repeatedly reveals itself in the difficulties in co-promoting local aims in regional development planning. The conditions of translocal division of labor are repeatedly interpreted as necessary adjustments that in practice favor the dominating socioenvironmental order. This discourse leaves no room for feasible alternatives.[5] The provincial attitude manifests itself in those public debates that for example celebrate new records in loggings and export of lumber and pulp without paying any attention to problems related to the low level of local refining.[6] The global success of "our companies" is accordingly considered as a local success and it is also seen as a sign of Finnish competitiveness in the world markets. Costs of company-led globalization, such as unjust economic reorganization, rising social vulnerability, ecological debts and externalization of entrepreneurial risks, have persistently remained unpopular issues within this discursive framework. The signs of globalization that accelerate the marginalization of peripheries are actively excluded from regional strategic thinking.[7]

Provincialism also easily turns to wishful thinking. Despite the lessons from the past, it is firmly hoped that the negative changes in macro-scale would not hit us, here and now. Local debates tend to selectively favor the positive options potentially hidden behind the dependency structures and, accordingly, backlashes of industrial reorganization appear as dramatic local shocks. Provincialism relies on isolated functions of the holding companies and their subcontractors and is therefore insensitive both to the consequences of domination and innovations outside the core operations.

The Finnish forest provinces are suppliers of raw materials and semi-processed goods, such as lumber, board and pulp. Production is highly mechanized and capital intensive and therefore vulnerable to fluctuating demand. The chain of production seems reasonable from the perspective of an export company but is problematic from the point of view of the provinces. The economic landscape of the provinces has grown monotonous as the forests are mostly even-aged economic forests and the level of wood-refining is low. High level of unemployment and outmigration are central characteristics of these regions. Provincialism keeps the local actors satisfied with this situation, and alternatives are often considered as threats.

Forest Commons in Finnish Environmental Policy

The most marginal of the forests in northeastern Finland are dominantly state-owned, whereas company forests, private family forests or jointly-owned common forests prevail in the inner parts of the border provinces. The regional structure of landownership is a result of geohistorical and geopolitical changes that have profoundly influenced and modified the formation of settlement and territorial administration in Finland. The nearness of the state border is the main individual element conditioning the local land and lifescapes in the northeastern provinces, both practically and mentally.[8]

The original idea for founding the forest commons as private cooperatives for rationalizing forest management was developed during the latter half of the 19th century. The main reason was the growing official fear of forest devastation caused by individual peasants with their extractive logging methods. The then ongoing implementation of land reform laid the practical framework for the new initiative. It was thought that joint owning of forests would set limits to the peasants' strive toward maximized short-term returns under the atmosphere of rapidly rising industrial value of timber.

Soon after the establishment of the first forest commons, however, new and more economic and utilitarian motives were introduced and adopted. Forest commons grew into efficient means for intensifying forest management and loggings. It made economic sense to manage larger forest units and the growing demand for wood secured attractive income for the partners. As a reaction to this, the state began to monitor the activities of forest commons more carefully, resulting in regulative acts taking force in the 1920s. This in turn resulted in gradual decline of the importance of forest commons in forestry policy.

The role of forest commons strengthened again in the 1950s as they were integrated in the renewing forest policy favoring the methods of intense industrial forest management. The decades thereafter have witnessed a slowly but steadily growing influence of the forest commons in Finnish forest policy. This has been the case especially in the northern and eastern provinces.

In Kuusamo, a municipality on the Finnish-Russian border in northeastern Finland,[9] the history of the forest commons began in the 1950s. The years after World War II brought remarkable changes to living conditions in Kuusamo. The traditional agrarian mode of living was discarded in favor of the modern industrial one within an incredibly short time-frame. The change resulted in difficult social adjustments. The late implementation of land reform, mechanization of farm work, introduction of chemical fertilizers, commercialization of timber resources and in general the overall infiltration of monetary economics completely reorganized the local sources of livelihood to fit the demand of modernization and export orientation. The past was readily left behind and the promises of a new era were largely welcomed.[10]

The establishment of the Kuusamo Forest Common in 1957 was part of this new turn in economic life and cultural mode of living. The general atmosphere of the time favored expansive utilization of natural resources and only a few voices were heard worrying about losing areas of irrecoverable ecological value.[11] In relation to the establishment of the Kuusamo Forest Common, foundations for three different environmental conflicts were laid, focusing on (i) the future of the Kuusamo rapids; (ii) the question of the Kitkanniemi region; and (iii) the remaining old-growth forests under KFC's ownership.

The fate of Kuusamo rapids became central when initially dividing the lands of KFC. The political solution was a compromise whereby the rapids of Oulanka and Kiutaköngäs remained under the state authority, eventually to become a nature park, while the ownership of the other rapids was assigned to KFC. The two competing electricity companies, Pohjolan Voima and Imatran Voima, had already in the mid-1950s been purchasing private shares in the rapids to build hydroelectric power stations along the Oulankajoki River. Imatran Voima was a state-owned enterprise whereas Pohjolan Voima was governed by forest companies with an aim at securing their energy needs. The speculation on and competition for the rapids intensified in the late 1950s and KFC was able to gain sizeable financial benefits by selling licenses to the rapids.

The negotiations between the companies and landowners, however, delayed the implementation of the plans and consequently gave room for the new factors to modify the entire setting. The regional hydroelectric planning on the Iijoki River, however, prioritized developing the resources that exist west of the municipality of Kuusamo.[12] This emphasis slightly calmed the hydroelectric ambitions in Kuusamo, even though the municipality had put much effort into building power stations inside its own territory. Some influential local voices had also emerged to promote new combinations of nature-based livelihoods and conservation.[13] The final decision in the Finnish Parliament in 1962 was against the hydropower plans. Accordingly, irrespective of the rampant financial speculation and changes in ownership structures, the Kuusamo rapids were left undeveloped and finally became protected by law in 1987.[14]

The Kitkanniemi region, owned by KFC, was included as a conservation area in the national proposal for enlarging the network of national parks and strict nature reserves in 1976.[15] The park proposal faced broad criticism in Finland and it partially served as a medium to unify and strengthen the general political mobilization against nature conservation.[16] The proposal was, however, adopted by environmental officials as a key document coordinating the future conservation of nature in Finland. The implementation of the proposal crucially depended on state budgeting and this made the founding of new parks rather difficult and slow processes.

In spite of and due to the conservation debate, KFC published plans in the early 1980s to start loggings in the Kitkanniemi region. An official committee was immediately appointed and, as a result of long negotiations, the Finnish Government decision of 1986 sided with the existing conservation plan and 5800 hectares of KFC land were annexed for conservation purposes. Compensation for 10,450 hectares of land, partly from the municipality of Suomussalmi south of Kuusamo, was given to KFC. This was in addition to financial reparations of FIM9,170,000, equaling to 1,500,000 euros in today's currency.[17]

The old-growth backwoods of KFC found their way into the national pub-

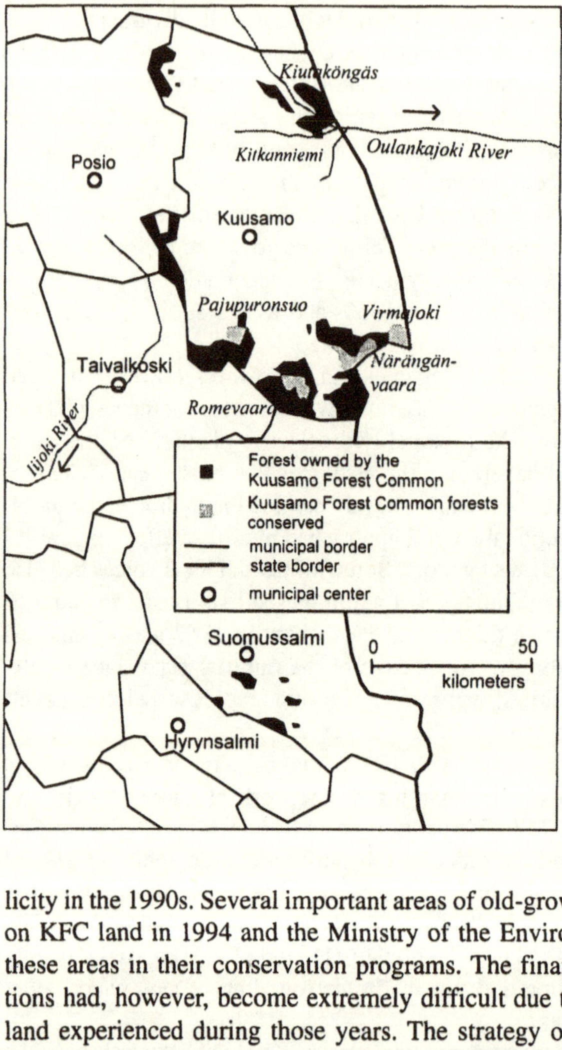

Fig. 10.1. The forests of the Kuusamo Forest Common in autumn 1998.[18]

licity in the 1990s. Several important areas of old-growth forests were identified on KFC land in 1994 and the Ministry of the Environment wanted to include these areas in their conservation programs. The financing of the land acquisitions had, however, become extremely difficult due to the deep recession Finland experienced during those years. The strategy of KFC was now to move from one of these hot spots to another with such speed that the Ministry of the Environment could not afford restriction of loggings (for the period of negotiations), including compensation, in all these areas.

There were three forest areas that attracted the conservationists the most, namely Romevaara, Naranganvaara-Virmajoki and Pajupuronsuo (Fig. 10.1). Romevaara, 4500 hectares, was the case that launched the conflict in autumn 1994 when KFC started building a logging road into the southern part of the forest. KFC had earlier the same year also logged about 100 hectares in the northern part of Romevaara. The largest and most intact of the three areas, Naranganvaara-Virmajoki (14,000 hectares), neighbors the Russian border. No traces of any loggings could be distinguished there. Pajupuronsuo, 4600 hectares, was then in the mid-1990s in no immediate risk of being logged.[19]

Echoing the earlier KFC processes, special working group was appointed and the solution suggested was again favorable to KFC. The conservation of 13,800 hectares of KFC forest was to be compensated by forest property of 26,000 hectares, mostly from the municipality of Kuusamo but also partly (5900 hectares) from the municipality of Hyrynsalmi south of Kuusamo. KFC was also to receive financial compensation of FIM30 million, equaling 5 million euros. KFC rejected the proposal in October 1998 and the state was then forced to use its right of expropriation and simply buy the lands for conservation. The full amount of compensation, covering the land property, damages for operational delays and the jurisdictional costs, amounted to over FIM147 million, thus close to 25 million euros.[20]

Provincialism in Land Speculation and Nature Conservation

The introduction of the concept of shade forests, or shade woods, in the mid-1990s much cleared the debate on the criteria of old-growth status and priorities in nature conservation.[21] Shade woods refer to those rare forests that have never been visibly modified by human action. These backwoods, having remained outside the endeavors of tar producers, slash-and-burn cultivators and industrial loggers, contain such ecological aspects that cannot be found in those old-growth forests that were under intense human utilization in early industrial times. Shade woods contain a high value in forest conservation as they serve as an ecological "time-corridor" to the natural dynamics of postglacial succession. This state of affairs was clearly understood on both sides of the forest debate in Kuusamo.

The Kuusamo Forest Common had learned how to benefit from the high value of the forest areas it had received in the land reform in the 1950s. KFC was also quick to adjust its strategies to the strengthening of conservation demands. Nature conservation became part of the resource politics of the company. The conservation strategy developed by the Kuusamo Forest Common became an early example of bioprospecting in Finnish backwoods. Nature could be saved by aggressively speculating with its value. KFC had a leading role in expanding the private liberty of action within the framework of national conservation programs. The chosen strategy has practically strengthened the translocal control of the backwoods of the Greenbelt. The forests of Kuusamo that were left uncut at the frontier became redefined to match the dominating environmental order strictly dividing forests for industrial actors (under the banner of sustained-yield) and nature conservationists (park planning). The backwoods remained as resource reserves for the development programs designed in the South. This tendency was supported by the Kuusamo Forest Common.

Two questions arise from these experiences. First, local willingness to follow the "imported" environmental order seems to ignore the alternatives that exist beyond the dualistic setting of timber supplies and nature parks. Local opportunism apparently erodes the faith in alternatives that are not in accord with the dominant division of labor. The performance of the local industrial actors in Kuusamo delighted the more conservative wing of the Finnish forest sector, whereas the initially marginal group of local nature conservationists gained support from the (environmental) authorities in Helsinki. Alternative activities within forest-based development or wood refining are easily considered as competitors and the local elites have developed ways of excluding newcomers. From the viewpoint of the local and ignored sectors, these regional blockades, or regimes, seem to function as development hindrances.[22]

Second, the growing international demand for certificates of sustainability forced the wood suppliers of the forest provinces to balance their interest of maximal annual cuttings with the risk of boycotts by the customers abroad. The old project of sustained-yield forestry, aiming at maximal wood utilization and promoting national integration, has faced the discursive risks of globalization, including concerns of socioenvironmental sustainability. The case of KFC demonstrates one route for industrial provincialism to start "greening," and it also shows how the margins of eastern Finland can turn into hot spots of biodiversity planning.

The conflict in Kuusamo suggests that the old model of nature conservation based on human exclusion and expressed in a numerical manner, such as in hectares, regional coverings, rarity values and lists of endangered species, has lost much of its strength. The official financial means to protect parks of "purified" nature are limited. Within the theoretical framework developed in this volume, alternative models of coping with private-public matters of nature conservation can be formulated from within the premises of traditional socioenvironmental knowledge. The layered history of nature-culture of the North, offering for the present generations some examples of ancient shade woods to be conserved, is the cultural capital that has yet only marginally been utilized in nature conservation. The early conservation initiatives in Kuusamo[23] were examples of this type of nature-culture heritage that became later integrated to, and also modified by, the official conservationism. Conserving nature with the help of lay knowledge focuses our socioenvironmental concern on those areas and features of nature that are locally valued high. This emphasis highlights conservation issues that support, and also replace, the practices that exclusively favor universal criteria. The experiments of voluntary forest conservation in southwestern parts of Finland seem to strive toward this direction but also there the dominating ecological knowledge has become prioritized.[24]

The strengthening local-global consensus about the protection of the last remaining shade woods of irreplaceable ecological value is currently largely accepted in Kuusamo, and this seems to be the direction also elsewhere at the Greenbelt. Local solutions vary greatly but in general the preservation of the intrinsic worth of pristine backwoods is gaining support. The model of voluntary socioenvironmental co-management could be worth adopting in cases where general agreement on promoting local-global multitude exists. The episodes in Kuusamo turned into a warning how not to speculate with the value of the shade woods—in the middle of economic forests under different stages of natural-cultural succession.

Nature conservation in the form of land speculation primarily serves the private interests of short sight, but it also keeps conservationists busy with issues that alienate them from the more acute socioenvironmental problems of today. The conservation of the "named nature" of parks and species functioned well during the early years of environmental concern but it has increasingly faced difficulties in social legitimacy. The first summaries of private-public forest conservation on a voluntary basis seem to support this conclusion.[25] Within the theoretical framework of this volume, a gradual shift from conservation of named objects to measures that are sensitive to the multiscale organization of ecological and cultural processes is needed. This approach has to include, and value high, the perspectives of laypersons and their communities, especially those in marginal position.

The debate on biodiversity values is a good example of the need for renewal. The biodiversity perspective has been in general welcomed as a means through which to continue and strengthen conservation based on endangered species, ecosystems and biotopes.[26] The risks of biotic diversity are widely understood as a universal scientific legitimacy for conservation measures, both in the pools of tropical rainforests and in the deserts of the Arctic. In the Finnish North, as in the conifer-dominated North in general, forest nature is largely shaped by the locally specific cultural traditions that have modified biotic diversity throughout centuries. The current biodiversity of the Finnish forest provinces is an artifact: the northwoods are sociohistorically produced landscapes where diversity is human-influenced and in places human-made. Biodiversity is an integral and inseparable part of the cultural land-use history, a legacy prominent in the contemporary landscape of the backwoods. Signs and customs that make up the daily land and lifescapes are seen in this view as the key artifacts of the North. They are the socioenvironmental links—that is: causes, mediums and consequences—from the past to the present. They are also the practical heritage elements to be prioritized in nature-culture conservation. Any conservation proposal derived from the general biodiversity matrixes overlooks the local and regional variations of land-uses and land-beliefs. It easily turns into ecological colonialism. Furthermore, when uncritically accepted and promoted by Finnish conservationists, such a policy indicates provincialism.

Conservation of socioenvironmental variation should not solely be based on purchases of parcels of nature, as was witnessed in the Kuusamo case. Nature should not be given primarily only a financial worth and consequently commodified as pieces of landscape in need of protection. Environmental concern should, instead, be integrated into practical planning and policy measures within different sectors or clusters of society. The administrative means to coordinate private forestry are rather well developed in Finland but in practice the general functional structuring of decision-making, as was illustrated by the Kuusamo case, maintains and reinforces the dualistic setting of exploitation versus conservation.

As is argued in this chapter, the histories of settlement, forest utilization and the institutionalization of forest administration in Finland have co-forged in the eastern provinces a frontier culture where land, and nature in general, is considered a challenge of intensified domination. The practical form of this domination is a strange mixture of orders set from the outside (translocal pressures) and from the inside (from within the realm of daily hardships). The Greenbelt provinces are currently, in the EU Finland, tangled in the financial speculation of nature conservation. Nature conservation is in this setting a finance contest and also a means to direct regional development support to those actors who have learned the rules of the game. The Greenbelt is green gold for some in the backwoods but it is also a cultural fix, a way of reproducing the power relations of the modern past.

Provincialism in Geography

In his influential book on place research in geography, J. Nicholas Entrikin, a geographer from the University of California, remarks how geographers have as a rule valued the provincial as an external object of scientific study. According to him, provincialism has mostly been regarded as a historical remnant in the margins of a cosmopolitan agenda.[27] Entrikin refers not only to geographers but also to a broader companion of the early twentieth-century intellectuals, such as philosopher Josiah Royce, historian Frederick Jackson Turner, ecologist Robert Park, sociologist Howard Odum and geographer Carl Ortwin Sauer, all from the USA, to find the root understanding of provincialism. After examining these sources, he concludes that provincialism in general points to a strong attachment or loyalty to a place and to local community that counters the mobile tendencies of modern society. Entrikin for example shows how Turner understood provincial sectionalism as a means to stabilize the early individualism of the frontier life to a cooperative effort to build a community. The early students of provincialism were attracted by natural social orders of agrarian life and this made them critical of the loss of "authentic" communities as a consequence of modernization.[28]

The US intellectuals of the early 20th century portrayed provincial landscapes with connotations linked to utopian and ideal commemorations of the past, such as agrarian spontaneity, communitarianism, naturalness and antiurbanism. They offered externally constructed romantic and exotic attributes to those remaining in the peripheries.[29] Provincialism has been largely ignored during the later stages of geographical development, which is perhaps due to the academic load the early pioneers had cast on it. Geography has become urban and postmodern in character and this might also have helped to keep provincial features of societal development in the academic margins.[30] The rise and the fall of provincialism (as a geographical concept) are undoubtedly linked to the Anglo-American domination of the geographical renewal discussed in the introductory part of this volume.

The interpretation finds evidence from geographers' growing interest in globalization and geopolitics,[31] which seems to have become indelibly embedded in the still-existing (post)colonial structural networks of the English-speaking *ecumene*. The trend reproduces the sociospatial knowledge and practices of the old Empire[32] and provincialism is non-existent in the current vocabulary. The hegemonic setting, including the silences, is also easily confirmed by those in provincial academic positions following and implementing the "rules" of the Anglophonic wor(l)d order. It is, however, important to recognize that despite the geographical silences in relation to provincialism, empowerment within and among the marginalized peoples and groups has for long been a central theme in geographical research.[33]

Some influential analyses closely related to provincialism can, however, be found outside the geography literature. Tim Ingold's anthropological study on ethnic assimilation problems among the Scolt Lapps and sociologist Thomas Mathiesen's elaboration of the Scandinavian concept *vanmakt* serve as useful guidelines for those with an interest in provincialism.[34] The Scandinavian *vanmakt* refers to a phlegmatic or opportunistic attitude toward the dominating power and it in this way comes close to the Latin root of provincialism that is etymologically related to conceding or submissive features of conquered territories, derived from the Latin *pro vincere*.[35]

Both the translocal and local views of provincial mentality were useful and informative when analyzing the activities of the Kuusamo Forest Common, as was witnessed above. Both approaches guided us toward further specification of the local-global challenges of establishing logging camps and nature parks at the Finnish-Russian border. Greenbelt is an international geopolitical projection based on a translocal motive to defend the last remaining shade woods of the frontier, but it is also an ecological abstraction incapable of taking into consideration local concerns and daily hardships. It therefore serves as an easy target for local criticism about unjust power relations.

The approach that (self-)critically examines the features of submission and opportunism among the provincial actors offers us tools for deepening our understanding of local community dynamics. As became evident in the analysis of Kuusamo, provincial culture tends to support and generate strategies that deepen the translocally conditioned labor divisions. Provincialism takes the shape of standard solutions. The North is standardized into economic forests with even-aged trees, drained peatlands and architecturally monotonous municipal centers. The standard North is also a biodiversity park with only a relatively few species to observe. The striving toward modern standards is motivated by the memories of the past on the frontier. The escape from the backwoods miseries is made concrete by cutting the connection to the past, whence grows the willingness to participate uncritically in "progress."

The participation in the modern is also fueled by short-sighted speculation of the means to maximize the benefit from translocal fluctuations in export demand. Gabriel Bladh's detailed study of 500 years of the frontier history of Värmland, western Sweden, proficiently explicates the main contours of export demand and their impacts on local forest communities.[36] The most "willing ones" largely benefited from the changes while the rest of the locals were more or less ignored. Similar aspects can be distinguished in Kuusamo, even though the change was late and it took place dramatically fast, practically in a few decades. The adjustment was therefore particularly painful and it also took shape as tension between two generations: between those who had grown up during the "old times" before World War II and those who became integrated in the postwar waves of progress. The provincial landscape of Kuusamo turned into an opposite to the one searched after by the intellectual pioneers of academic provincialism. The childhood connection was violently cut in Kuusamo and not much common past was left to commemorate. The pre-war signs of culture-nature are therefore worth valuing, not as romanticized relics from the past but as guidelines for the future on the frontier.

Notes

1. "Kuusamon metsät esillä kansainvälisenä tempauspäivänä," *Karjalainen*, 23 Feb. 1995, 12. "Veitsiluoto—Clear-cutting Kuusamo and Karelia," (Jokkmokk: Taiga Rescue Network's Leaflet, 1995), mimeo.
2. *The Forest Battle in Kuusamo* (Helsinki: Nature League, 1995).
3. The annual harvest of Kuusamo Forest Common was in the mid-1990s settled down to close to 100,000 cubic meters. In 1994, for example, the profit to be divided was FIM8,050,000 (1.3 million euros in today's currency). The large number of shareholders

indicates a wide distribution of economic benefits derived from loggings and this is also reflected in popular opinion against forest conservation.
See Teijo Rytteri, Mikä ihmeen yhteismetsä? Yhteismetsät suomalaisessa metsätaloudessa (Joensuu, Joensuun yliopisto, maantieteen laitos, julkaisematon pro gradu -tutkielma, 1997), 53-4, mimeo.
4. Ari Aukusti Lehtinen, Jakob Donner-Amnell and Bjørnar Sæther, eds., *Politics of Forests* (Aldershot: Ashgate, 2004). 13-19.
5. Jaana Nevalainen, *Tilapelin tiedonpolitiikat—kamppailu kaupunkikeskustan muutoksesta* (Joensuu: Joensuun yliopiston yhteiskuntatieteellisiä tutkimuksia, no. 67 (2004), 273-79.
6. Helena Tahavaninen, "Puoli miljoonaa sellutonnia Joensuun satamasta maailmalle," *Karjalainen*, 24 May 1997, 6; Markku Liikamaa, "Joensuun laivauksen lastauksista liki puolet sellua," *Karjalainen*, 18 September 2004, 14.
7. Matleena Kniivilä, *Euroopan metsämaakunta. Pohjois-Karjalan metsästrategia vuosiksi 1998–2010* (Joensuu: Pohjois-Karjalan liitto, 1998), 3; *Sellua, sivistystä ja sahanpurua. Metsäklusteri Pohjois-Karjalassa* (Joensuu: Pohjois-Karjalan liitto, 1998), 24-33.
8. Anssi Paasi, *Territories, Boundaries and Consciousness: The Changing Geographies of the Finnish-Russian Border* (Chichester: Wiley, 1996); Jouni Häkli, "Manufacturing Provinces. Theorizing the Encounters between Governmental and Popular 'Geographs' in Finland," in *Rethinking Geopolitics*, eds. Gearoid " Tuathail and Simon Dalby (London: Routledge, 1998), 131-51.
9. Kuusamo is a rural town, or a "nature town" ("*luontokapunki*") in the municipality brochures, in the easternmost part of the province of Koillismaa (Northeastern Land) with a population of 18,500 of whom two-thirds live in the municipal center. Sixteen percent of the land area of 5800 square kilometers is covered by forests, and the highest hills rise approximately 500 meters above the sea level. The number of larger lakes is 166. See <http://www.kuusamo.fi > (1 April 2005).
10. Rytteri, Mikä ihmeen yhteismetsä?, 19-30.
11. Elias Savola, *Kuusamon historia 5. Kuusamon isojako* (Kuusamo: Kuusamon kunta, 1993).
12. Jarmo Rusanen, "Role of Local People in the Utilization of Water Resources: A Case Study of the River Iijoki in Northern Finland," *Nordia* 23, no. 3 (1989), 119-208.
13. Reino Rinne, *Olen puhunut. Pohjoista informaatiota* (Helsinki: Alea-kirja, 1973); Reino Rinne, *En ole vaiennut: arkipäivän esseitä* (Helsinki: Alea-kirja, 1976).
14. Rytteri, Mikä ihmeen yhteismetsä?, 55-6.
15. *Kansallispuistokomitean mietintö* (Helsinki: Valtion Painatuskeskus, Komiteanmietintöjä, no. 88, 1976).
16. Ari Aukusti Lehtinen, "Northern Natures," *Fennia* 169, no. 1 (1991), 81.
17. *The Forest Battle in Kuusamo* (Helsinki: Nature League, 1995).
18. *Niin metsä vastaa kuin sinne huudetaan* (Kuusamo: Kuusamon Yhteismetsän tiedote, 1996); *Yhteismetsä hylkäsi tarjouksen Kuusamossa* (Helsinki: Suomen Tietotoimiston tiedote, 6 October 1998).
19. Matti Ikonen, Sari Kuvaja and Roger Olsson, *Hot Spot: Kuusamo, Finland* (Jokmokk: Taiga Rescue Network's Fact Sheet, 1995).
20. Tapio Mainio, "Kuusamon vaihtomaista syntyi sopu," *Helsingin Sanomat*, 31 January 1997, A8; Pekka Virtanen, "Operaatio Kuusamo onnistui," *Vihreä Lanka* 31, 31 July 1997), 6-7. Eero Kaakinen, Pohjois-Pohjanmaan ympäristökeskus, personal information, 6 September 2004.

21. See about shade forests (*katvemetsät*), Heikki Simola, "Land-use History Explains the Value of the North Karelian Biosphere Reserve in Preserving the Old-growth Forest," in *Karelian Biosphere Reserve Studies*, eds. Timo J. Hokkanen and E. Ieshko (Joensuu: University of Joensuu, Biosphere Studies, 1995), 15-20.

22. Ari Jokinen, "Metsänomistajien osallisuus ja puunkasvun politiikka," in *Leipäpuusta arvopaperia*, eds. Ari Aukusti Lehtinen and Pertti Rannikko (Helsinki: Metsälehti Kustannus, 2004) 162-66; Nevalainen,*Tilapelin tiedonpolitiikat—kamppailu kaupunkikeskustan muutoksesta*, 276-79.

23. Rinne, *En ole vaiennut: arkipäivän esseitä.*

24. Jokinen, "Metsänomistajien osallisuus ja puunkasvun politiikka," 166-72.

25. Jokinen, "Metsänomistajien osallisuus ja puunkasvun politiikka," 166-72.

26. Yrjö Haila and Jari Kouki, "The Phenomenon of Biodiversity in Conservation Biology," *Ann. Zool. Fennici* 31, no. 1 (1994), 5-18; Juha Kotilainen, "Between the Global and the Local in Environmental Politics," *Nordisk Samhällsgeografisk Tidskrift*, no. 23 (1996), 61-68.

27. J. Nicholas Entrikin,*The Betweenness of Place* (Baltimore: The Johns Hopkins University Press, 1991), 3.

28. Entrikin, *The Betweenness of Place*, 33-37.

29. Entrikin, *The Betweenness of Place*, 66-78; Häkli, "Manufacturing Provinces,"132.

30. Roger Hayter, Trevor J. Barnes and Michael J. Bradshaw, "Relocating Resource Peripheries in the Core of Economic Geography's Theorizing: Rationale and Agenda," *Area* 15, no. 1 (2003), 15-23.

31. Peter J. Taylor, "On the Nation-state, the Global, and Social Science," *Environment and Planning A* 28 (1996), 1917-28; Gearóid Ó Tuathail, *Critical Geopolitics. The Politics of Writing Global Space* (London: Routledge, 1996); Andrew Herod, Gearóid Ó Tuathail and Susan M. Roberts, eds., *Unruly World? Globalization, Governance and Geography* (London: Routledge, 1998); Steven Flusty, *De-coca-colonization. Making the Globe from Inside Out* (London: Routledge, 2004).

32. Andrew D. King, "Opening up the Social Sciences to the Humanities: A Response to Peter Taylor," *Environment and Planning A* 28 (1996), 1954-59; Michael Hardt and Antonio Negri, *Empire* (Cambridge, Ma.: Harvard University Press, 2000); Gunhild Setten, "Naming and Claiming Discourse," in *European Rural Landscapes: Persistence and Change in a Globalizing Environment*, eds. Hannes Palang, Helen Sooväli, Marc Antrop and Gunhild Setten (Dordrecht: Kluwer, forthcoming).

33. David Harvey, "On the History and Present Condition of Geography: An Historical Materialist Manifesto," *Kulturgeografiske Hæfter* 30 (1986), 5-19; Richard Peet and Michael Watts, *Liberation Ecologies. Environment, Development, Social Movements* (London: Routledge, 1996); Steve Pile and Michael Keith, eds., *Geographies of Resistance* (London: Routledge, 1997).

34. Thomas Mathiesen,*Makt och motmakt* (Göteborg: Korpen, 1982); Tim Ingold, *The Scolt Lapps Today* (London: Cambridge University Press, 1976).

35. Colin Gordon, ed., *Power and Knowledge. Selected Interviews and Other Writings by Michel Foucault, 1971-77* (New York: Pantheon, 1980), 69.

36. Gabriel Bladh, *Finnskogens landskap och människor under fyra sekler* (Karlstad: Högskolan i Karlstad, Forskingsrapport, no. 11, 1995). Bladh works as a researcher and university lecturer (*lektor*) in geography at the University of Karlstad, Sweden.

11.

Quel che Resta di una Foresta: Wilderness Politics and *Erämaa* Practices in Anár, Sápmi

On 16 March 2005, Greenpeace activists demonstrated their worry about the disappearance of the last old-growth forests and natural reindeer pastures in northern Finland by spreading a truckload of wood chips in front of the headquarters of the United Nations's Food and Acriculture Organization, FAO, in Rome. "*Quel che resta di una foresta*" was written on a poster on the chips, and the main banderol above the entrance door insisted on a discontinuation of the loggings in the pasture forests in the Sámi homeland, Sápmi, in Upper Lapland. Matti Vanhanen, Prime Minister of Finland, participated during the same day in a forest meeting in FAO and he also opened an exhibition marketing Finnish forestry and wood processing in the building.[1]

The episode in Rome was part of a heated confrontation in Paadarskaidi and Njellim, Upper Lapland, between Greenpeace and local reindeer herders on the one side and the Finnish State Forest Service and lumbermen on the other. Stora Enso, the prior purchaser of wood from Upper Lapland, had been involved in the debate a week earlier by expressing its hope for a halt in loggings at the hot spots in question. The company also asked for a compromise and wanted the Finnish State Forest Service, the main landowner in Upper Lapland, to work for reaching it.[2] The compromise would be a relief for the company worried about the signals from the paper markets.

The Greenpeace demonstration in Rome and the confrontation in Paadarskaidi are events in a long chain of disputes about the land-use in Upper Lapland. The actions of conservationists root from the 1980s when the industrial logging frontier finally reached the northernmost pine forests. The extension of loggings and the question of land rights are complicated in the Finnish North and they are thoroughly linked to the unjust historical configuration of life conditions and political space in the North. The valley of Anár is located centrally in the eastern Sápmi and it is the primary home land of Anár Sámi and Scolt Lapps (Fig. 11.1.)

The aim of this chapter is to analyze how local, national and international wilderness interests have met and coalesced in Upper Lapland and resulted in the establishment of a new nature conservation regime under the banner of wilderness management. The meeting of local and translocal motives in the establishment and governance of the areas with a wilderness status will be examined. The particular view adopted here emphasizes the strengthening articulation of environmental justice issues both within local politics (in Anár and Upper Lapland) and in the practices of international environmental actors and the forest industry. This finally leads toward a preliminary outlining of postcolonial alternatives gradually taking shape in Finnish wilderness politics.

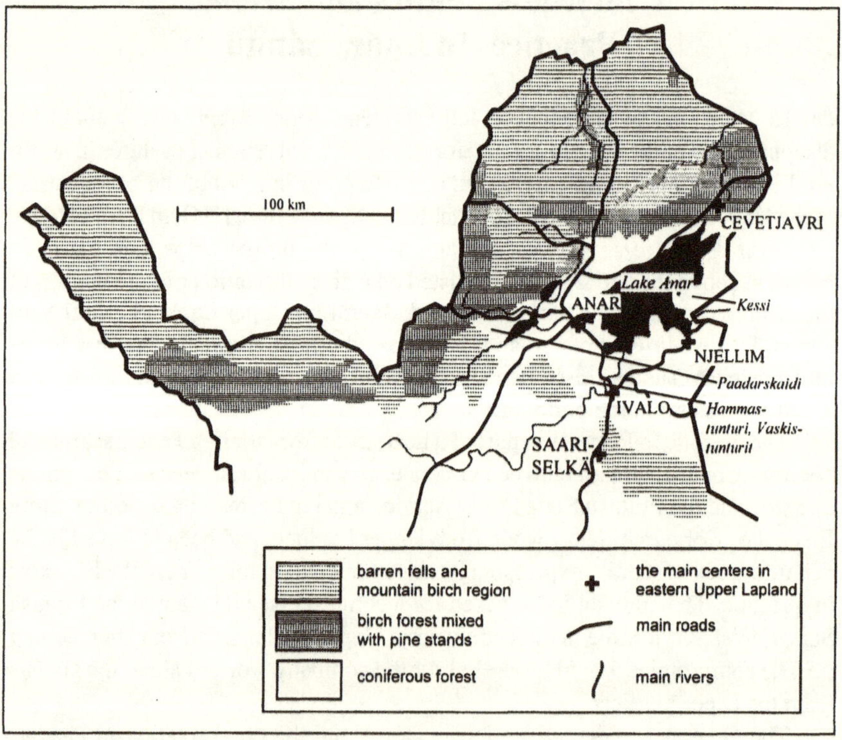

Fig. 11.1. Anár in Upper Lapland[3]

Logging the Far North

"The traditional Lappological research has not regarded the Sámi as subjects but objects—they have been taken as objects adapting to the interests of other nationalities," argues Veli-Pekka Lehtola,[4] a literary researcher from Oulu, northern Finland, and criticizes the dominating portrayal of the Sámi as victims who were robbed, destroyed and imposed on under foreign rule. The history of Lapland is abundant with layers where the North has been modified to meet the standards of the South. The first decade of the new wilderness policy in Upper Lapland (1991–2001) was no deviation from this historical setting. The practical management of the wilderness in Upper Lapland has faced serious problems in coping with the local traditions that have regarded the wilderness areas as part of the everyday.[5]

The forest-based development in Finnish Lapland followed during the post-World War II decades the needs of the national forest sector. The northern provinces grew hand in hand with forestry and wood processing, and this period finally integrated the most marginal of the backwoods into industrial forestry. In fact, within circumpolar comparisons, the northernmost experiments of industrial forestry have so far been run in Upper Lapland.[6]

The northerning of industrial forestry principally occurred along with enlarging pulp capacity. The existing forest resource base was considered insufficient for the demands of the forest industry, which was reflected in occasional regional over-cuttings, in wood import from southern Finland and Russia, and in loggings within the upper shelterwoods. As a whole, the contradiction between the capacity for wood processing and the provincially sustainable loggings effectively shadowed the worries of viability within the traditional domestic sources of livelihood. This was the case particularly in regard to reindeer herding.[7]

The rising demand for wood motivated loggings up to the northernmost limits of the continuous pine forests in Lapland. One of the most extreme regions to be included in the logging program was the forest area east of Lake Anár, neighboring the Russian and Norwegian borders. Through publicity, this forest area was to be known as the backwoods of Kessi, or *Kessin kaira* in Finnish.[8] The logging plan, published in 1982, was immediately received with broad disagreement. First, critical voices grew from inside the official working group behind the plan: Forest researcher Yrjö Norokorpi expressed doubts about the size of the individual areas of final cuttings reaching up to 20 hectares. He favored the methods derived from the experiences of rational thinning and shelterwood cuttings.[9] The Sámi Parliament also participated in the debate by emphasizing the open question of land rights in the domestic region of the Sámi. The Parliament referred to the immemorial rule over the common lands by Sámi Siidds (villages), while the forest-industrial interest, it was argued, rooted from the forest act of

1886 declaring the common backwoods as state property.[10]

Nature conservationists in Lapland also participated in the debate from the beginning.[11] They were in general fearful for the future of the existing wilderness forests and particularly for the ecological vulnerability of the backwoods of Kessi. The regeneration of the forests at the arctic forest-tundra zone after industrial-scale loggings was doubted. In addition to the ethnic and environmental arguments, the public discussions in Lapland encompassed local employment needs, the threats to and potentials for reindeer herding aside industrial forestry, and possible future alternatives for the village of Njellim near the conflict area.[12]

Local opinion was broadly in favor of the road construction across the backwoods of Kessi up to northern Norway.[13] The old and still existing road connection northward via Pechenga was closed after World War II, which left Njellim isolated in a blind alley. Every sign of opening corridors northward from Njellim has therefore been heartily welcomed. Forest-industrial developers also referred to the option of extending the logging road up to Kirkenes in Norway. The breakdown of the Soviet Union in 1991 suddenly modified the geopolitical position of the Kola Peninsula and offered a chance for re-opening the old Pechenga road running via Njellim, but this has not yet resulted in any practical outcome.

The opinion on the future of Kessi was extremely diversified in Njellim, reflecting economic, political and social relations in the village. At one end, the local reindeer herders argued against full-scale wood exploitation while, at the other end, the local state lumbermen demanded employment security. By 1986, the debate over the backwoods east of Lake Anár reached an impasse. Despite the widespread polemic against the logging plan, there was no sign of official rethinking, and the forestry road construction and loggings were to start. The limits of the political space of the main critics, the Sámi Parliament and the nature conservationists, had been reached and there seemed to be no way to stop the logging machinery.

In the fall of 1986, a new phase was launched by environmentalists (from Helsinki, southern Finland) who had become worried about the waning debate around Kessi. A country-wide network of contacts was established. Strategy formulation was shaped in a twofold manner. The importance of continuing and further developing the political lobbying was widely accepted but its limits, already proven, were also understood. Broadening public discussion by the means of direct action was seen necessary.

Both of these strategies were realized in a rather dramatic way in spring 1987. In March, the group of environmentalists from Helsinki briefly visited Anár. The local interest was discovered to be extremely ambivalent and the northern suspicion on southern-led re-opening of the conflict was faced as well. Tension between socioenvironmental and nature conservationist strategies also emerged inside the ranks of activists. Despite this, a demonstrative action was held in April on the bridge, then under construction, over the Paatsjoki River. A figure of a bleeding reindeer and the slogans "*Kessi itkee*" ("Kessi is crying") and "*Kenen maa?*" ("Whose land?") were painted on the bridge structures. The paintings were printed on the front pages of the provincial newspapers and the demonstration was made public nationally by the prime time TV News on Saturday, 11th April. The Kessi debate was thus re-opened.

The April demonstration was documented in a diary form by Veikko Haakana, one of the best-known contemporary wilderness novelists in Finnish Lapland. Haakana's diary of hiking in the forests east of Lake Anár and north of the Paatsjoki River guides the reader both in the backwoods of Kessi and into the public debate concerning the feasibility of loggings in the area. Haakana describes how the bridge was built across the river in 1987, in order to get logging tractors, trucks and other vehicles of lumbermen over to the other shore. He also writes how a handful of activists, drew the slogans and the bleeding reindeer on the bridge structures in the late hours of 10 April 1987. Veikko Haakana concludes then that: "Both slogans were cleaned in a hurry, to avoid broader public attention. The question was thought better forgotten, because answering it would be more than annoying."[14]

The conflict deepened later in spring 1987 when 87 of the 200 members of the Finnish Parliament sent a written question to the Finnish Government concerning the reasonableness of the loggings in Kessi, and whether the Government of Finland had any intentions of canceling the planned loggings.[15] The local municipal authorities in Anár immediately acted in the name of the whole municipality and labeled the parliamentary intervention as "childish nonsense." They also said that the further conservation of the North on southern conditions was over and done with.[16]

The strong reactions by the local elite were received with confusion by the lay people in Anár. Widely shared disbelief and mistrust toward the leaders even resulted in a small local action group in the early summer of 1987. This move contradicted the official stereotyping of the one-sided southern activism and gave a new setting for environmentalism.

Many of the southern burdens of environmentalism were further eliminated in June 1987 by a working camp "*Puuta & heinää*" ("Wood and Hay") in Njellim, mainly organized by the local action group. For two weeks, collective *talkoo* work was done in small farms by day and the evenings were devoted to forest debates opened by invited experts. All this confirmed the existence of realistic alternatives for industrial wood exploitation at the arctic forest tundra. Close to one hundred participants were gathered together from all over the country. The meeting of the lay people of the village and the activists from the North and the South cut across the stereotypes produced by the local authority. Those from the caricatures in the provincial newspapers turned in fact into ordinary people with rather reasonable arguments.[17]

Kessi gradually became an essential part of national environmental discourse, with its mixed societal and symbolic values. The Minister of the Environment, Kaj Bärlund, raised in the late summer of 1987 his political profile through the conflict by questioning the rationale for the cuttings in Kessi. He expressed his willingness to start negotiations with the representatives of the Finnish forest administration. The conflict of Kessi reached its broadest public attention during the fall of 1987. The public polemic for and against industrial forestry in Kessi and in the other wilderness forests nearby flourished. The interest groups involved in the debate represented a wide spectrum from almost all possible spheres of society, stretching from the main political parties to several key corporations and associations, all having a word to say about Kessi.[18]

In December 1987, the Government of Finland saw it necessary to ease the conflict by appointing a committee to clarify the wilderness question. The Wilderness Committee was asked to map the sites, the size and importance of the existing wilderness regions in northern Finland, and thereafter to formulate an outline for future land-use in the defined regions. The composition of the Committee was planned to include all central interest groups, and even a representative of the "Kessi Movement" was invited. The representatives directly linked to the forest sector occupied, however, seven of the eighteen Committee seats.[19] The northern forest conflict consequently turned into a wilderness issue, and forest-industrial needs were secured through the Committee's composition.

Politics of Wilderness

The opening challenge for the Wilderness Committee was the definition of the basic concept expressed in the name of the Committee. The etymology of wilderness was explicitly related in the Committee work both to the economic history of Finland and the broader Anglo-American debates (behind the wilderness enactments since the 1960s). The latter, regarding the wildernesses as areas mostly untrammeled by man and managed in such a way that they appear to have been affected primarily by the forces of nature,[20] markedly guided the Committee's final proposal published in 1988.[21] The official wilderness areas of Upper Lapland were to be established in order to secure the natural or natural-like state of the selected areas. Extensive use of the land was suggested to be allowed, including natural-like, or nature-imitating loggings in certain areas. The practical governance of the wildernesses was planned to be administered by the Finnish State Forest Service.

The traditional *meachhi* (or *erämaa)*,[22] i.e. the outer lands of the villages under seasonal hunting and gathering practices, was in other words redefined as wild nature in need of protection and zoning, including nature-imitating management. This paradoxical dualism (of wild but managed) was confirmed by the Committee by finally dividing the proposed wilderness regions into areas to remain in a natural state and areas of natural-like state. The latter definition referred to the regions with forest cover most acceptable for logging and left, in fact, the doors open for rather intensive forestry. The areas that had functioned as actual sites for the initial environmental dispute were included mostly in the category of natural-like forestry, if not left as economic forests as was the case with Kessi.

Due to the permission to carry out intensive loggings in the wildernesses, and as an effect of the Committee's composition, the interests of forestry were underlined in such a manner that it was easy to consider the other interests as secondary matters mainly producing hindrances to loggings. It was the forest sector that was to suffer if forced to make compromises with the rest of society. When making compromises, the weakening of the employment options offered by forestry was emphasized. The other interests, such as reindeer herding, gathering economies and tourism, were the ones to be faced with this primary viewpoint. No calculations of the impacts of the economic restrictions on the other sources of livelihood caused by the expansion of forestry were made. In contrast, the causes of reductions made from the hypothetical level of maximal mobilization of wood were put at the forefront.[23]

Despite the numerous statistics in the Wilderness Report sensitive to regional variations, few outlines were built on the basis of the regional economic particularities of Sápmi or Upper Lapland. The provincial perspective favored the framework of Lapland as one uniform unit and was projected into Anár as local compromises due to wilderness management, instead of reflecting the (provincially) marginal sources of livelihood gaining more importance and in practice even exceeding the economic benefits of forestry in the northernmost communities. No serious outlines favoring local processing alternatives for reindeer meat and saw-milling were formulated.[24]

The biases expressed above influenced the identification of wildernesses in a confusing way. The strong voice in the Committee belonged to forest professionals, even though the main spatial focus was finally limited beyond the forested regions. This bias was reflected in the outlines as exclusions of several central wilderness forests from any preservation status. These exclusions later found their way to international agenda, for example in Germany and Britain (chapter 6) as well as in the FAO meeting in Italy referred to at the beginning of this chapter.

Accordingly, in the initial Report from 1988, 7000 hectares of wilderness forests previously regarded as economic forests were finally left in a natural state and 57,500 hectares were to be integrated into industrial forestry by the softer methods of nature-imitating forestry. Most of the wilderness forests introduced by the Committee as wilderness reservations were actually forests already under conservation (80,000 ha) or beyond any possibilities of potential felling (25,000 ha). Considering them as wilderness forests to be left in a natural state only confirmed the conservation—and gave a reason for the Committee to note the change as a reduction in hypothetic felling potentials.

Fourteen percent (112,000 of the 1,488,500 hectares) of the total area included in the wilderness program could be regarded as forests left outside industrial forestry.[25] The northern forest question was turned into one of conserving the tundra. For the public, the maps showing the areas as well as the statistics that revealed the enormous number of hectares to be conserved were to sharpen the local reactions against everything that was related to nature conservation.

According to the Committee proposal, the areas that had functioned as initial symbols for the conflict were to stay under the pressure of industrial forestry. The southern part of the backwoods of Kessi was defined as an economic forest under normal utilization pressure and the northern part was to be treated with softened natural-like forestry methods. The wilderness of Hammastunturi was integrated into industrial forestry via the areas accessible to financially profitable logging. The slopes of the Vaskistunturit were planned to be exploited up to the existing tree line.

The Committee also formulated a proposal for a Wilderness Act which would confirm the position of the outlines set when facing new demands on resource utilization. The legalization of wilderness conservation in Finland had been one of the aims of the civil servants in charge since the US Wilderness Act took effect in 1964. This aim had appeared in several of the official working papers and committee reports[26] with the results referred to above. The long period of preparation motivated the civil servants of the Ministry of the Environment to integrate the revitalized civic demands of the 1980s into the institutional efforts and in this way revitalize the official wilderness conservation stranded in administration. The socioenvironmental alternatives formulated were thus absorbed into the institutionalized (Anglo-American) idea of wilderness conservation.

The debate held after the publication of the Report was a lively and critical one, with a wide spectrum of demands for re-evaluating the wilderness proposals. However, the conclusions made in the Ministry of the Environment from the public hearing one-sidedly favored the outlines suggested in the Report.[27] The rush to legalize the long-awaited official wilderness visions motivated the interpretation, which reflected a minimal willingness for re-evaluation on the basis of the critical statements received.

Finally, the proposal for the Wilderness Act was delivered to the Finnish Government with no essential changes in content. Thereafter, in spring 1990, the Wilderness Act was presented to the Parliament by the Minister of the Environment, then accepted by the Parliament in November and finally put into effect 1 February 1991. The era of wilderness governance was to begin in Upper Lapland, taking the form of detailed nature inventories and zonal co-management experiments, and finally resulting in plans for land use. The plans have been prepared by the Finnish State Forest Service and the final approval is in the hands of the Ministry of the Environment in Helsinki.

Municipal Drama in Anár: The Rise of the Independents

One specific challenge of wilderness governance in Upper Lapland is rooted to the well-known history of colonialism in the North. The present land and lifescapes carry the traces of politico-economic dependencies and they are therefore loaded with suspicion and skepticism in regard to any change demands coming from the South. The local sense of justice has been violated too many times. Due to this skepticism, the older layers of dependency are easily preferred locally when challenged with new ones. The question is also about local power relations. The local administrative regime favored the location of official wilderness areas beyond the main forested areas of Upper Lapland, that is: beyond the hot spots of the forest debate. The political elite was not willing to reconsider the setting and this paved the road for the rise of a new political force in municipal politics in Anár, namely the Independents. The local lay people with a critical eye on the way things were progressing expressed their view rather dramatically in the municipal polls of the 1990s.

The political field in Anár, as in Upper Lapland in general, has been traditionally dominated by one party with rural roots, Finland's Centre (Centre Party), which has for long kept 30-60 percent of the seats in the municipal councils as their mandates. The Social Democrats, the Conservatives and the left-wing parties have stayed far behind the Centre Party. The Sámi representatives have mainly expressed their voices via the main parties. Within national comparisons, the voting activity has remained persistently high in Upper Lapland, which is an indication of broad respect for the political sphere. It also is an expression of a clear division between the political and everyday spheres: voting is regarded as a duty, and it often seems to free from worrying about politics in between the polls. Political interests are seen as different from the rest of the social interests. The municipal administration is a model for decision-making that has been imported from the South and it is run by the parties integrally linked to the power contestation within the national sphere. Lay people of the North are unfamiliar with the party apparatus and therefore it is not easy to rely on the importance of one's own worries in the realm of the official municipal decision-making.[28]

Despite all this, the candidates independent of the dominating party coalitions received broad support in the elections of 1992 in Anár by gathering 1008 votes from the total of 4345 (Fig. 11.2). This was a clear turn upward: in 1988 the Independents got 244 votes from the total of 4195. The most dramatic change took place in 1996 when the group of independent candidates got 1430 votes from the total of 3953. This made them the largest political group in Anár, having ten seats of the total 27 in the Council of Anár. The upswing was conversely relational to the loss of support to Finland's Centre. The Centre Party got 1050 votes in 1996, which was a serious fall from the 1680 votes in 1988. In addition, Teuvo Niemelä, one of the most visible local environmentalists during the years of the Kessi conflict, became the popular draw of the elections, leading the Independents into a key political position in Anár. In the period of 1996–2000, Niemelä, however, felt himself isolated within his group and jumped over to the ranks of Finland's Centre. This move brought the Centre Party back in the dominant position in the poll of 2000: 14 seats in the Council whereas Niemelä's earlier group got only 3 representatives. His personal support rose now up to a record of 363 votes, which was three times the number of votes of his nearest rival. The municipal poll in 2004 resulted also in the victory of the Centre Party, and the return to the old political order was confirmed.

The strong upswing of the Independents during the early 1990s was a result of their profile across the established settings and due to their fresh articulation of key matters. The group aimed to integrate environmental issues into the local politics but they also emphasized general social and ethnopolitical questions. The wilderness debate undoubtedly had an impact on the local political turn. During the conflict of Kessi, several of the latent strains of the dominant political culture surfaced and in this way Kessi functioned as a catalyst for the generational shift in the local politics and, partially, also within the Centre Party.[29]

The loggings hence reached the backwoods of Kessi that were not given an official wilderness status and also Vätsäri, the wilderness region north of Kessi, later got a logging plan.[30] The Wilderness Act could not protect the forest areas of the forest tundra and the conservationists broadly regarded this as a major weakness of the Wilderness Act and its implementation.[31] Despite this backlash in the process, a slight socioenvironmental turn could be identified, both in municipal politics in Anár[32] as well as in the operations of the Finnish State Forest Service.[33] At least two new political trends took shape, the first one in the form of interdiscursive openings across the borders of local municipal administration versus forest and wilderness management and the second one within the more cultural sphere of humanity versus wilderness interrelations. These shifts were clearly identifiable locally even though they may have come too late, after the loss of irreplaceable forest-ecological and cultural values in Upper Lapland and at the cost of growing bitterness among those whose sense of justice was deeply

Fig. 11. 2. The results of the municipal elections in Anár 1980-2004; respective seats in the council of 27 representatives.[34]

	1980	*1984*	*1988*	*1992*	*1996*	*2000*	*2004*
Finland's Centre (Suomen Keskusta)	*11*	*11*	*12*	*10*	*7*	*14*	*10*
The Conservative Party (Kokoomus)	*6*	*5*	*4*	*3*	*3*	*3*	*4*
The Social Democratic Party (SDP)	*2*	*3*	*2*	*2*	*2*	*2*	*3*
The Rural Party of Finland (Suomen Maaseudun Puolue)		*1*	*2*				
The left-wing parties (SKDL, DeVa, Vasemmistoliitto)	*8*	*7*	*6*	*6*	*5*	*5*	*6*
The rest (Sámi associations, the Greens, and the Independents)			*1*	*6*	*10*	*3*	*4*

wounded. They also seemed to be too weak to ease the local-global confrontation in wilderness matters, as has been argued by local reindeer herders, environmental activists, and German and British consumers of northern paper.

The local political upheaval in Anár revealed the problematic relationship between the local community and the forest sector. The wilderness issue was the arena where the forest sector had to face the signs of changing political culture.[35] The old model of expansive forestry had moved the logging frontier over to the extreme forest tundra, and this was not only a question of reaching the extreme physical limit. The limits of local tolerance surfaced earlier than the limits of forestry. However, after the politically exceptional years of the late 1990s, the local opposition has remained too weak to concretely stop the forestry machinery. A more profound change seems to need strong international support from the paper consumers and environmentalists, including cooperative efforts from the leading industrial operator in the area, Stora Enso.

The temporary changeover in Anár in the 1990s was a clear symptom of the tolerance limits faced. The rise of the Independents was a sign of widely-shared willingness to renew the political routines. Disappointments of the past resulted in remarkable changes in the framing of the municipal decision-making, both in terms of the mode of making politics and, especially, in terms of substance matters. The deep economic recession of the 1990s in Finland also reformulated the local political agenda. All the municipalities had to face the question of prioritized costs during the era of diminishing financial space. The question of justice in local welfare politics became heated when facing the demand of cuts in municipal practices.[36] The new political order in Anár could reflect better (than the old administration) the local multiethnic lifeworld but it faced difficulties while trying to maintain the welfare functions in the era of chronic fiscal crisis.

The municipal decision-making in Anár could construct in the 1990s an axis between ethnic and ecological issues. The problems of reindeer herding, which is broadly in the hands of the Sámi in Anár, were discussed more openly: overgrazing, erosion of the pasturing grounds as well as the difficulties in meat marketing gathered increasing attention. The shifts in forestry and tourism also surfaced as municipal issues.[37] Local coordination of the individual sectors is, however, difficult, and the municipality is not strong enough for the task—when facing the powerful translocal sectors of governance with their respective southbound dependencies.

The realization of the ideal of local-global co-management is primarily conditioned by the willingness of the forest sector to loosen its hold on the logging options in the forest tundra. On the other hand, the success of exporting forest products, including forest know-how, is crucially dependent on the credibility of the whole chain of actors involved in paper processing. One cannot disregard the question of reindeer herders and the Sámi at the primary end of paper processing. The rising socioenvironmental awareness among the paper consumers in Western Europe has already had an impact on the performance of the leading forest-industrial companies in Finland. In the case of "wrong moves" in official wilderness politics, the most critical comments will undoubtedly be stated from within the international setting to which the companies are linked. Bad news from the North evokes proactive responses in the headquarters of the companies, as was clearly witnessed in the case of the logging moratorium (chapter 9). The decision was due to a heated international environmental debate concerning the fate of the old-growth forests at the border zone.[38]

Rethinking Wilderness Governance: Three Conclusions

The description above documented a significant broadening of the field of nature conservation during the early years of the wilderness conflict. The protection of the backwoods in the forest tundra was reasoned by various combinations of ecological, ethnic and regional economic worries. Reforestation was known to be difficult after large-scale loggings but the impacts of industrial forestry on living conditions in the northern villages were also reconsidered. The problems were both local and translocal: local reforestation was part of circumpolar ecology, the Scolt Lapps in Njellim were a local ethnic minority group but also a group member of the Fourth World of stateless indigenous peoples. Local wood processing was in parallel bound to the ongoing transnationalization within the Nordic forest industry.

The broadening of the wilderness question was far from a natural extension of earlier politics. New formulations were also regarded as a threat by those belonging to the establishment of nature conservation in Finland. Some drawbacks could also be noticed and willingness to return to traditional questions of nature conservation was repeatedly expressed. The initiative to move from forest-political questions to wilderness issues was in fact a partial return to old labor divisions between conservationists and resource users. By excluding the forest hot spots from the official wilderness program, the Wilderness Committee secured the completion of the task addressed by the Finnish Government. Focusing on forests issues in Upper Lapland would have added tensions and schedule delays to Committee meetings. The composition of the Committee paved the chosen path.

The official ignoring of the forest question in the North soon resulted in an emergence of new local forest conflicts in northern and eastern Finland, followed by wide monitoring of old-growth forests. The new setting confirmed the gradual broadening of the conservation debate: forest-ecological issues were interconnected to cultural and artistic initiatives in Talaskangas in central Finland,[39] landscape aesthetic values were related to geomorphologic specialties in Koli in North Karelia[40] and new economic incentives were introduced as tools for forest conservation in Kuusamo (chapter 10). The new element in these interdiscursive openings was the departure from spatial restrictions to more general elaboration of the interfaces between the polarities of local-global and culture-nature. Conservation had still much to do with named entities (areas, species, etc.) and factual justifications but it became increasingly informed by the coalescense of perspective-bound layers of interests and values under constant contestation. Nature conservation turned into reciprocal recognition of multicultural natures, environmental justice issues were introduced, and models of environmental co-management were adapted.

The debate on the wildernesses and old-growth forests in Finland is in general linked to the emotional sphere of national identity narrations, which is due to the heritage-like awareness of the northern backwoods in the Finnish past. The internationally-spread media images of clear-cut forests and the alarmingly-long red lists of endangered species have challenged the Finnish self-image based on the belief of self-made know-how to cope with the North. The self-respect that comes from the long history of survival in the deep northern backwoods is taken as proof of sound know-how. "We have lived here from the beginning and, as you all see, there still is much worth conserving. No advice from outside is needed", argue those annoyed by the negative publicity.[41] This defense is popular in the villages in the frontier regions and only occasionally do the doubts against the domestic model of expansive control of nature surface.[42]

The model of expansive utilization of wildernesses has its roots in the pioneering colonization of the northwoods. The current phase is only confirming the strength of the model: even the most distant corners of the northern wildernesses have been drawn under human domination. The model reached its limits when forced to meet the changing culture of local politics, as was witnessed in Anár during the 1990s. The model has also been questioned in the context of international trade politics gradually taking notice of the social and ecological costs of production. The setting is difficult in Finland. The intergenerational routines of culture-nature in the North have landed in an era where their continuity is at serious risk. Paradoxically, the last scattered remnants of wildernesses have surfaced as central constituents of new local-global citizenship, as became clear in the upheaval of the Independents in Ánar. The marginal has been re-located in the center.

The current re-configuration of culture-nature is no longer based on the conflict between the users and the defenders of nature, and this seems to be true even in the most distant corners of pristine nature. Instead, the last fringes of wildernesses have emerged as a question of cultural self-reflection and regeneration. This turn has had an impact on wilderness conservation, which was witnessed also in the Greenpeace demonstration in Rome, Paadarskaidi and Njellim in 2005: international environmentalists were concerned about reindeer herding in Upper Lapland. Signs of environmental renewal can be identified at least in three different spheres of articulation.

First, the politics of wilderness conservation based on ecological arguments stand at center stage. The first decade of wilderness management in Upper Lapland has confirmed that the motive for expansive domination of nature cannot be solely regarded as a privilege of resource exploitation. It is also linked to the scientifically justified monitoring and management of ecologically defined zones and areas. It has become evident that wilderness management focusing solely on scientific grouping and naming of the different elements of pristine nature ignores the question of multicultural wilderness.[43] The wilderness areas that have been thoroughly mapped and divided into different land-use categories are fundamentally paradoxical constructions: they are wildernesses under human domination. Ecological wilderness conservation is thus in practice at risk of continuing and completing the project of domination it was initially launched against. Industrial resource allocations have merely turned into ecological inventories. The Finnish wilderness debate was able to re-address the ecological challenge for a while and, despite the drawbacks faced, this opening can be seen as the most innovative of the elements in the long process. The Independents of Anár could occasionally formulate important ethnoecological arguments that found broad support within the local community. Geographically speaking, the postcolonial alternative emphasizing the need to become sensitive to the multicultural voices attached to the overlapping layers of culture-natures was widely debated locally and even voted into the political lead in 1996—which was, at least in the Finnish context, a brave and pioneering launch.

Second, and accordingly, the difficulties of running culturally sensitive politics of wilderness were soon faced in Anár and this emphasized the contingent nature of the different local-global settings and solutions. Promoting the multitude of culture-nature in a local-global setting is an alluring challenge, or vision, but difficult to make concrete in a particular political arena. So far, only a few comparable analyses of similar type of openings exist. Within the European Union, the regional forest cultures have proved incompatible with more profound policy coordination.[44] Trans-Atlantic comparisons confirm that multicultural historical contingencies are decisively conditioning the conflict configurations,[45] which has also been witnessed by the Nordic forest companies with transcontinental operations. Finnish forest know-how has also proved culturally ignorant in the context of tropical timber trade[46] and this observation has forced the actors in charge to become sensitive to varying cross-cultural tensions between and within local ethnic groups, forest-industrial companies and transnational conservation agencies.[47]

The local-global re-scaling of culture-nature has also redefined the northern forests and wildernesses as forums of contested international steering. The culture-nature of the European North is today a deeply multilayered and ethnic question that demands new vocabulary from the conservationists. This change has been linked to the change in the sphere of languages. Paradoxically, again, the anglophonic dominance has secured a basis for intercultural sensitivity. The Finnish language, and more broadly the Finno-Ugric ways of viewing the world, can only with great difficulty be translated to match the anglophonic wor(l)d order and this controversy has caused additional thresholds in internationalization. The Finnish *erämaa* refers to Anglophonic wildernesses only where a programmatic vision of coordinative unification of marginal natures takes place. Biodiversity, which is so well entrenched in describing the qualitative aspects of nature at the tropical and middle latitude zones, describes only a minor part of the variation of northern nature.

Third, broader societal dimensions have also caused trouble for the conservationists and wilderness managers. Traditionally thinking, no clear connection can be found between the macro-spheres of politico-economic reorganization and the premises of wilderness politics. Societal issues have, however, been practically linked to wilderness discourse on several forums: e.g. within the contested calculations of the economic costs of conservation decisions, a debate that in fact appeared as a major issue during the early 1990s in Finland as part of the debate on old-growth forests. The speeded-up internationalization of resource trade has in general forced the conservationists and environmental managers to rethink the connection between resource exploitation and processing and their societal costs. The socioenvironmental evaluation of the product chains based on utilizing wilderness resources has gained popularity, and some analyses of the macro-circuits of the politico-economic sphere running the wilderness exploitation have been published.[48] The main challenge for wilderness politics is related to the difficulty of producing and constantly updating the main moments of politico-economic reorganization crucial to conservation. The macro-scale debate has primarily leaned on myriads of evaluation matrices and certification models that seem to live their own lives far above the actual reorganization. The contested matrix and model production has turned into a green developmentalism[49] that often seems to regard the main industrial actors of globalization as "black boxes," that is: abstract economic units becoming only concrete when causing socioenvironmental harm. It thus remains an open and acute question whether the knowledge of the dominant actor-spaces connecting the most marginal of the marginal lands into local-global trade practices will ever be considered important among the deep ranks of the conservation movement.

The remark by Veikko Haakana in the early part of this chapter regarding the question painted in the bridge over the Paatsjoki River in Anár that was scrubbed out in a hurry due to the annoying nature of the question refers to those anxieties within the land and lifescapes in the North that have not received enough self-reflective elaboration. This chapter has a similar message. The most difficult of the land right issues have to be solved before Finland can present herself as a country with certified and credible wilderness politics. The question "Whose land?" is still as actual as it was in April 1987. The currently painful hot spots in Upper Lapland are annoying for the processors of northern pulp and paper but they are equally annoying for the consumers of Finnish paper in Western Europe, not to mention anything about the confusing uneasiness among the ordinary Northerners.

Notes

1. Silja Nikkanen, "Ylä-Lapin hakkuukiistaa ratkotaan ensi viikolla," *Karjalainen*, 17 March 2005, 12.
2. Jaakko Tahkolahti, "Ylä-Lapin metsäkiistassa yritetään neuvotteluja," *Helsingin Sanomat*, 8 March 2005, A10.
3. Ari Aukusti Lehtinen, "Northern Natures," *Fennia* 169, no. 1 (1991), 112.
4. Veli-Pekka Lehtola, "Kansain välit—monikulttuurisuus ja saamelaishistoria," in *Beaivvi Mánát. Saamelaisten juuret ja nykyaika*, ed. Irja Seurujärvi-Kari (Helsinki: Suomalaisen Kirjallisuuden Seura), 187. Translated from Finnish by the author.
5. Pertti Veijola, *Suomen metsänrajametsien käyttö ja suojelu* (Kolari: Metsäntutkimuslaitoksen tiedonantoja, no. 692, 1998); Jarkko Saarinen, ed., *Erämaapolitiikka* (Rovaniemi: Metsäntutkimuslaitoksen tiedonantoja, no. 827, 2002), 135-41.
6. Veijola, *Suomen metsänrajametsien käyttö ja suojelu*, 17.
7. Tim Ingold, "Land, Labour and Livelihood in Salla, Northeastern Finland," in *The Social Implications of Agrarian Change in Northern and Eastern Finland*, ed. Tim Ingold, (Helsinki: Transactions of the Finnish Anthropological Society, no. 22, 1988), 121-39.
8. *Paatsjoen metsätaloustyöryhmän mietintö* (Helsinki: Maa- ja metsätalousministeriö, 1982).
9. Yrjö Norokorpi, "Eriävä mielipide Paatsjoen metsätaloustyöryhmän mietintöön," in *Paatsjoen metsätaloustyöryhmän mietintö* (Helsinki: Maa- ja metsätalousministeriö, 1982), 50-56.
10. Lausunto Maa- ja metsätalousministeriölle Paatsjoen siltatyöryhmän mietinnöstä (Sámi Parlamenta, 16 March 1983), mimeo; Metsän hakkuiden rajoittaminen ja hakkuualueiden puhdistuksesta saamelaisten kotiseutualueella. Kirje Metsähallitukselle (Sámi Parlamenta, 13 January 1986), mimeo. Sámi Parlamenta served as the highest decision-making forum for the Sámi in Finland in 1973-1995. Thereafter, Sámediggi (Saamelaiskäräjät) has continued as the main representative body of the Sámi, elected every fourth year. Sámediggi with its 21 members coordinates the matters of cultural autonomy of the Sámi, explicated in the Constitution of Finland, see <www.samediggi.fi> (23 March 2005).
11. Kirjelmä Maa- ja metsätalousministeriölle (Lapin luonnonsuojelupiiri, 22 March 1983), mimeo.
12. Njellim is a small village southeast of Lake Ánar and close to the Russian border. Approximately half of the 200 inhabitants of the village are Scolt Lapps, World War II immigrants from the Pechenga valley on the Russian side of the border. See Lehtinen, "Northern Natures," 126.
13. Liisa Itkonen, Kessin hakkuiden sosiaaliset vaikutukset. Unpublished seminar presentation (Helsinki: University Helsinki, Department of Social Policy, 1988), mimeo.
14. Veikko Haakana, *Inarilta itään, Paatsjoelta pohjoiseen* (Hämeenlinna: Karisto, 1989), 14. Translated from Finnish by the author.
15. Kirjallinen kysymys tiestön laajentamisen ja hakkuusuunnitelman toteuttamisen keskeyttämiseksi Kessin erämaassa Inarinjärven itäpuolella Eduskunnan Herra Puhemiehelle (Helsinki: Eduskunta, 8 May 1987), mimeo.
16. "Vain kunnanmiehet kärtysivät luonnonsuojelijoille. Inarin metsien käsittelystä sopukeskustelu," *Lapin Kansa*, 23 May 1987), 3.

17. Lehtinen, "Northern Natures," 117.
18. Lehtinen, "Northern Natures," 166-67.
19. *Erämaakomitean mietintö* (Helsinki: Valtion Painatuskeskus, Komiteanmietintöjä, no. 39, 1988).
20. Roderick Nash, *Wilderness and the American Mind* (New Haven: Yale University Press, 1967), 5.
21. *Erämaakomitean mietintö.*
22. Audhild Schanche, "Horizontal and Vertical Perceptions of Saami Landscapes," *Diedut*, no. 3(2004), 5. The closest translations of wilderness are *meachhi* in Northern Sámi and *erämaa* in Finnish. However, *meachhi* is linguistically close to Finnish *metsä*, forest. *Metsästää* in Finnish, that is, to go hunting, is not limited to hunting in forests, and can thus be applied both in treeless tundra and forested taiga.
23. *Erämaakomitean mietintö*, 58, 77, 85-9; Maire Puikko, "Eriävä mielipide," in *Erämaakomitean mietintö*, 143, 151.
24. Puikko, "Eriävä mielipide," 151-53, *Erämaakomitean mietintö*, 73-85.
25. *Erämaakomitean mietintö*, 57, 86.
26. *Virkistysaluekomitean mietintö* (Helsinki: Valtion Painatuskeskus, Komiteanmietintöjä, no. 143, 1973); *Kansallispuistokomitean mietintö* (Helsinki: Valtion Painatuskeskus, Komiteanmietintöjä, no. 88, 1976); *Alueiden käyttö Suomessa.* (Helsinki: Sisäasiainministeriön kaavoitus- ja rakennusosaston tiedotuksia, no. 4, 1982); Rolf Oinonen, Erämaaselvitys (Helsinki: Maa- ja metsätalousmininisteriö, 1983), mimeo.
27. Pekka Salminen, Yhteenveto Erämaakomitean mietinnöstä annetuista lausunnoista (Helsinki: Ympäristöministeriö, 1989), mimeo.
28. Lehtinen, "Northern Natures," 125-42; Samu Pehkonen, *"Tänne, muttei pidemmälle!" Alta-kamppailu ja Pohjois-Norjan monikulttuurinen maisema* (Tampere: Rauhan- ja konfliktintutkimuslaitoksen tutkimuksia, no. 88, 1999); Sarah Lloyd, *The Emergent Forest Landscape in Sweden: A Case Study of Relationships Between Socio-economic and Ecological Space in Jokkmokk* (Uppsala: Swedish University of Agricultural Sciences, Department of Rural Developments Studies, Master's Thesis, no. 13, 2001).
29. Arja Pehkonen, Suojeluaste on korkea, sille ei tavallaan voi mitään. Inarilaisten kunnanvaltuutettujen ja lukiolaisten ympäristöasenteet (Joensuu: Joensuun yliopisto, maantieteen laitos, julkaisematon pro gradu -tutkielma, 1999), 37-39, mimeo.
30. Tapio Tynys, *Vätsäri—erämaa järven takana* (Helsinki: Edita, 2000).
31. Susan Heikkinen, "Kessimistit," *Helsingin Sanomat*, 12 August 2001, D5.
32. Pehkonen, Suojeluaste on korkea, sille ei tavallaan voi mitään.
33. Esa Väliverronen, *Ympäristöuhkan anatomia. Tiede, mediat ja metsän sairaskertomus* (Tampere: Vastapaino, 1996); Ville Hallikainen, *The Finnish wilderness experience* (Rovaniemi: Metsäntutkimuslaitoksen tiedonantoja, no. 711, 1998); Veijola, *Suomen metsänrajametsien käyttö ja suojelu*; Jarkko Saarinen, ed., *Erämaapolitiikka* (Rovaniemi: Metsäntutkimuslaitoksen tiedonantoja, no. 827, 2002).
34. Pehkonen, Suojeluaste on korkea, sille ei tavallaan voi mitään, 112; Suomen tilastokeskus, vaalipalvelu <http://kuntavaalit.html> (23 March 2005).
35. Veikko Väänänen, "Moskovaan siirtyvä Ylä-Lapin luonnonhoitoalueen johtaja Pertti Veijola: On vain uskottava, että maaoikeusvalta luo myös vastuuta," *Lapin Kansa*, 1 November 2001, 10.

36. Ilkka Lehtola, *Palvelujen muutos ja syrjäkyläläisen arki* (Joensuu: Joensuun yliopisto, yhteiskuntatieteellisiä tutkimuksia, no. 50, 2001), 118-45.
37. Pehkonen, Suojeluaste on korkea, sille ei tavallaan voi mitään.
38. Tiina Hokkanen, Ympäristöjärjestöt ja kansainvälinen metsäteollisuus kiistakumppaneina Karjalan tasavallassa (Joensuu: Joensuun yliopisto, maantieteen laitos, pro gradu - tutkielma, 2000), mimeo; Teijo Rytteri, *Metsäteollisuusyrityksen luonto* (Joensuu: Joensuun yliopisto, maantieteen laitoksen julkaisuja, no. 10, 2002), 133-55.
39. Hannele Nykänen and Timo Järvikoski, "Matkalla maan ääriin—Talaksen ystävien toimintamotiivit," in *Pasilasta Vuotokselle. Ympäristökamppailujen uusi aalto*, eds. Ari Aukusti Lehtinen and Pertti Rannikko (Helsinki: Gaudeamus, 1994), 55-71.
40. Erkki Sankari, "Koli kolikoiksi vai kansallisomaisuudeksi?," in *Pasilasta Vuotokselle. Ympäristökamppailujen uusi aalto*, eds. Ari Aukusti Lehtinen and Pertti Rannikko (Helsinki: Gaudeamus, 1994), 48-53.
41. Ari Aukusti Lehtinen, "Tales From the Northern Backwoods: Fairy Tales and Conspirators in Finnish Forest Politics," in *Approaching Nature from Local Communities*, ed. Anders Hjort af Ornäs (Linköping: Linköping University, Research Programme on Environmental Policy and Society/EPOS, 1996), 48-53.
42. Minna Tanskanen, *Näkyvän takana. Tutkimus metsäojitetun suomaiseman kulttuurisuudesta* (Joensuu: Joensuun yliopisto, maantieteen laitoksen julkaisuja, no. 10, 2000), 8.
43. See some parallel findings: John Rennie Short, *Imagined Country* (London: Routledge, 1991); Yrjö Haila, "Wilderness and the Multiple Layers of Environmental Thought," *Environment and History*, no. 3 (1997), 129-48; David Demeritt, "Scientific Forest Conservation and the Statistical Picturing of Nature's Limits in the Progressive-era United States," *Society and Space* 19 (2001), 431-59; Sarah Whatmore, *Hybrid Geographies. Natures, Cultures, Spaces* (London: Sage, 2002).
44. Cecil Hazley, *Forest based and Related Industries of the European Union* (Helsinki: ETLA Publications, no. B 160, 2000).
45. Thomas Beckley, "Social Sustainability of Forestry in Northern Regions: Linking Canada to Nordic and North-west Russian Social Forestry Research," in *Social Sustainability of Forestry in Northern Europe*, ed. Marjatta Hytönen (Copenhagen: Nordic Council of Ministers, 2001), 97-112; Eeva Hellström, *Conflict Cultures—Qualitative Comparative Analysis of Environmental Conflicts in Forestry* (Helsinki: The Finnish Society of Forest Science, Silva Fennica Monographs, no. 2, 2001).
46. Sari Kuvaja, Marko Ulvila and Thomas Wallgren, eds., *Tropiikin vihreä kulta. Pohjolan pojat Kaakkois-Aasian sademetsissä* (Helsinki: Like, 1998).
47. Marcus Colchester, *Sustaining the Forests: The Community-based Approach in South and South-East Asia* (Geneva: United Nations Research Institute for Social Development, UNRISD Discussion Papers, no. 35, 1992); David Sonnenfeld, "Vikings and Tigers: Finland, Sweden, and the Adoption of Environmental Technologies in Southeast Asia's Pulp and Paper Industries," *Journal of World-System Research* 5, no. 1 (1999), <http://csf.colorado.edu/wsystems/jwsr.html> (18 May 2001); Maria Åkerman, "Investointi ympäristöpoliittisena toimintana: UPM-Kymmenen ja kansalaisjärjestöjen välinen määrittelykamppailu," in *Ympäristöpolitiikka*, eds. Yrjö Haila and Pekka Jokinen (Tampere: Vastapaino, 2001), 100-16.

48. L. Anders Sandberg and Sverker Sörlin, eds., *Sustainability the Challenge* (Montréal: Black Rose Books, 1998); Bjørnar Sæther, *Regulering og innovasjon: miljöarbeid i norsk treforedlingsindustri 1974-1998* (Oslo: University of Oslo, Department of Sociology and Human Geography, Doctoral dissertation, 1999).
49. Kathleen McAfee, "Selling Nature to Save It?," *Environment and Planning: Society and Space* 17 (1999), 133-54.

12.

Re-scaling the Northwoods: Finnish Paper Industry in the Age of Globalization

This chapter concentrates on the internationalization of Finnish forest companies. The profiles of the leading companies are analyzed by grouping the changes in the forest industry into three spatial scales: the articulation of Finnish (national) forest interest is related to the strategic openings of the Finnish forest companies within European (continental) and global (transcontinental) contexts. The analysis covers both the active exporting of the Finnish model and the following new location of Finland in the networks of international actors. Both material and symbolic dimensions of the process are highlighted, and the slow dynamics of the paper production is set against the current fluidity of societal demands fed by intensifying competition between the leading companies, profit "hunting" among the shareholders, and active steering of globally aware environmentalists and consumers. Attention is finally paid to the socioenvironmental consequences of this type of globalization by concentrating on the most debated signs and signals: size ranking of the companies, profit maximizing, image and identity politics, as well as product certifications.

Material and Symbolic Forests

The intense internationalization of the forest industry in the 1990s and during the first years of the 21st century has thoroughly rearranged the interrelations between the leading companies and their respective suppliers and customers. The governance of the companies has also been under reorganization as shareholder motives increasingly condition the decision-making of the managers in charge. The whole societal setting of the forest industry has therefore changed, both at the level of material production as well as in terms of financial performance and image profiles. This chapter outlines the elementary features of forest-industrial reorganization in connection to the rise of symbolic and speculative values in paper production.

The goal is to analyze the socioenvironmental interdependencies and consequences of globalizing forest industry and trade related to the growing demands of profit maximizing on the one hand and to widening sustainability and justice concerns on the other. In theoretical terms, the question is about the contested rearticulation of local-global interfaces and nature-culture relations, both shaped by conceptual refocusing on the interrelations between the material and symbolic spheres of production and consumption. The empirical material is limited to the Finnish forest-industrial companies currently re-working their historical embeddedness in Finnishness and Finnish forest resources. The analysis covers the period 1990–2005, but earlier material is also included when necessary.

The starting point leads toward an evaluation of the links between the ongoing industrial reorganization and the local-global reconfiguration of socioenvironmental problems, debated under such umbrellas as global environmental change (climatic transformation, biodiversity erosion, etc.) and new translocal division of production. The talk about "China phenomenon" (*"Kiina-ilmiö"*) in Finland is a central part of the question, focusing on the persistently high level of domestic unemployment *vis-á-vis* the new investment programs in the countries with lower costs of raw material and labor.[1] Socioenvironmentalism offers a way to combine the ecological and social concerns but it also underlines our incapability to deal with purely objective ecological problems and formulating solutions based on facts derived directly from the material reality "out there." Ecological concerns and imperatives are human derivations and therefore loaded with varying affiliated societal motives. There is no way back to the modern worldview based on solid divisions between us and them, the internal and the external, or the human and non-human entities, as was explicated already in the introductory part of this volume.

The human influenced bio-geo-physical erosion of the natural sphere continues—locally and globally—and a considerable part of humankind has serious difficulties in fulfilling the basic needs. Over 800 million individuals, one-seventh of the global population, are undernourished.[2] This darker side of modernization (the so-called ecological debt[3]), once ignored by the economic mainstream, cannot be excluded from today's local-global decision-making. It is here, in between and across the dominating ways of knowing (in economic, welfare and environmental thinking), that new openings and radical socioenvironmental inclusions are needed.

The task is challenging, as it aims at breaking the dominating thought routines of the Modern Era. Nature and culture can no longer be divided into separate entities and the same is true in terms of environmental "goods and bads," or values and facts. Critical voices emerge from experiences of alarming material shortcomings but, while aiming at integrating them into trade routines as expenses or guiding rules, they turn into qualitative attributes. Sustainability, green certificates, organic farming and just forestry are models and ideals that aim at changes in human practices but they are also signals in the market that more or less measure the viability of the production process and the value of the end product. Forest-industrial actors, for example, are today increasingly forced to integrate image aspects into their production and trading profiles, and the direction of this qualitative change is under heated contestation. The researcher's work here is to provide information and viewpoints that help assessing the validity of the translation process where the material questions turn into qualitative criteria (and back again). The task is to identify and evaluate the signals of the actors and target groups and, furthermore, to check that even the most marginal(ized) but concerned voices will become audible and influential in the translation.

The ongoing qualitative turn in the forest industry and trade is taking place in the negotiations concerning the central criteria of credibility and the indicators of sustainability. The macro-level merger logic follows the size and credibility rankings of the key actors, the stock markets are sensitive to the moves of the companies, and the markets respond to the credibility labels of the suppliers. New and contested measures of forest certification have been introduced at the same time, and the publishers and media houses are today willing to confirm the sound background of the paper used.[4] The consumers are inundated by diverging guarantees of sustainability. The leading forest actors are thus thoroughly embedded in the (more or less public) negotiations of credibility that, while surfacing as economically significant, turn into forums of hegemonic competition. The competition is about the formulation of the primary form and content of the negotiations, including the subsequent optional distribution of loads and benefits due to agreements possibly made. We have examples of negotiation processes where the initial socioenvironmental worries have turned into a game of relational positions and benefits, and resulting in an illusion of strengthening sustainability.[5] The researchers' task is to identify and document the changing conditions and rules of the game. This includes an evaluation of the correspondence between the announced goals and actual performances of the key actors, and clarifications of the possible decoupling[6] of the two profiles. It is also important to identify the cases where ethical arguments are made economically convincing.

The forest-industrial operations and negotiations are documented in this chapter with the help of geographical scaling. The Finnish model of forest-based modernization is briefly described as a historical context whereupon the Europeanization (since the mid-1980s) and the later globalization (since the mid-1990s) have developed as new phases of activity for Finnish companies—all, however, integrally characterized by strong interdependencies across the dominating spatial scales and marked by rapidly evolving discursive contents. The multiscale approach helps to distinguish the sociospatial processes and mechanisms by which the forest-industrial actors and activities are ranked as successes or failures. Continental European companies are often seen less successful if compared with global companies and this makes a difference, e.g. in merger negotiations. This tends to confirm and legitimate the hegemonic tendency and, moreover, the direction of reach: globalization becomes the primary goal and even the guiding ideological discourse. The scaling appears as a construction of reference fields (for the competing actors), and it proceeds through merit and status assessments. Cosmopolitan Europe is for example different from the "Fortress Europe". Europe thus varies according to the discursive field it is integrated into, as does Finland: "Nokia Land" can hardly hide its Finno-Ugric roots (as was debated in chapters 2 and 3). There seems to be a continuous ideological contest between and within the dominant sociospatial scales.

Concretely, illustrating the role of the "inter-scaling" in forest-industrial practices, the Finnish model successfully exported during the early years of current globalization seemed to essentially change the model that was exported. The forest provinces became for example part of the Greenbelt of Northern Europe. Similarly, the European Union looked significantly different—more bureaucratic and regulative—from the inside than from the outside, as was strongly argued in the mid-1990s by Casimir Ehrnrooth[7], the then leading spokesman for Finnish forest industries. The global reach of the forest industry suddenly also turned into concern about local sensitivity. The companies grew big with their transcontinental operations but they were confused by culture variations and local particularities they had to learn to respect.[8]

The following analysis of Finnish forest-industrial firms is organized according to this type of multiscale framework. The phases (export phase, Europeanization, globalization) of internationalization are examined and evaluated as challenges to Finland and the companies, as well as to the new actors and arenas of the contest.

Exporting Finland

Finland became integrated during the 20th century into the globalizing economy as an exporter of forest-industrial products. The process was intensified in the 1920s and 1930s and continued in the post World War II decades, only to be questioned by the rapid rise of information technology industries during the last years of the century. The share of forest products in total exports fell from 37.6

percent (1990) to 28.9 percent in 1997 and 29.4 percent in 1999. However, in international comparison, the Finnish export profile was still exceptionally forest-dominated in the late 1990s. In other northern countries with parallel forest-industrial histories, the level of forest dependency has stayed below 20 percent. The respective figures were 14.9 percent in Sweden and 16.7 percent in Canada in 1996.[9]

Forest-industrial production has principally been limited to the domestic markets throughout the world. As the main deviation to this, Finland has oriented toward export trade and here especially toward the core countries of the European Union: France, Germany and Great Britain. In 1999, about 90 percent of the paper produced in Finland was exported, and only Sweden could achieve almost the same export level, namely 84 percent. The export share reached up to 75 percent in Canada, while in the rest of the paper-producing countries the respective figures stayed much lower: slightly below 50 percent in France and Germany and below one-tenth of production in the USA and Japan. South Korea was able to reach the export level of 32 percent in 1999.[10]

The "Finnish deviation" is partially a matter of scaling. In the framework of the European Union, export and import activities between the EU countries can be considered as part of the internal domestic trade. The broader spatial view brings up new questions of trade, and it modifies the coding of forest statistics. It also makes comparisons with federal jurisdictions, such as Canada and the USA, more reasonable. The EU scaling brings along several important changes in forest strategy formulations. For example, when Sweden, Austria and Finland became members of the EU in 1995, the Union turned into a net exporter of forest products, and this raised the status of forest-industrial policy within the Union. Finnish forest experts have also developed Pan-European Forest Certification (PEFC) criteria for forest management, and this has strengthened the "continental scaling" of forest-based trade.[11]

The Finnish forest industry has been internationalized by expanding its production and ownership abroad, especially in Western Europe but also transcontinentally. In 2000, 43 percent of the paper and board production capacity of the Finnish companies still existed in Finland, whereas 44 percent was based in the rest of Europe. Nine percent of the production took place in the USA. In comparison, the production capacity abroad was about 10 percent in 1980.[12] The rapid internationalization was due to industrial reorganization that had raised three forest-industrial companies from Finland to the ranking list of the twelve biggest companies in the world (Fig. 12.1).

International Paper, USA	*16 900*
Stora Enso, Finland	*15 000*
UPM-Kymmene, Finland	*8 600*
Smurfit-Stone Container, USA	*8 100*
Oji Paper, Japan	*7 000*
Georgia-Pacific, USA	*6 900*
Abitibi-Consolidated, Canada	*6 800*
Nippon Paper, Japan	*6 000*
Asia Pulp & Paper, Indonesia	*5 700*
SCA, Sweden	*5 200*
Weyerhaeuser; USA	*5 000*
Metsä-Serla (M-real), Finland	*5 000*

Fig. 12. 1. The world's largest paper and board producers in 2000, per capacity, thousands of metric tons.[13]

The rapid expansion and the top ranking of the major Finnish companies owe much to the national subsidies during the years before the EU membership. The success was made possible by numerous collaborative linkages and risk-sharing mechanisms within the nation-state context, which strengthened the competitiveness of the companies. The companies themselves were also dynamic enough to create a successful outward-looking path. They could integrate forward from pulp and newsprint to more upgraded products such as coated papers, liquid packaging board and specialty papers. This unique state-company combination—the Finnish model—was the background recipe for the global launch during the late 1990s.[14]

Simultaneously, as part of the expansion, the structures of company ownership went through a major transformation. Global investors, seeking for maximal profit, emerged as influential actors of forest trade. The company investments became more actively followed by the shareholders and professional risk evaluators, and this brought a new layer of sensitivity to the decision-making. The companies have for example faced the signal to slow down the speed of capital allocation. The pressure for that has come from international investors who easily react to risky moves of the firms by selling their shares. This, in turn, causes a fall in the stock prices. The setting is crucial to an industry that is capital intensive and in which over-investment has been a repeatedly-faced problem. Periods of over-capacity become reflected as fluctuations in price levels and profitability and they are worrying investors. This is contrary to the earlier Finnish national context which less critically supported expansive investment strategies.[15]

As is evident, the current competitive internationalization is in a state of discord. The big companies are searching for firm (long-term) market positions and even leading roles in selected product groups through mergers and by investing in renewal of capacity, but every move is evaluated by the investors as possible signs of eroding (short-term) profitability. The companies thus need to take care of both the material and symbolic dimensions of paper-making. They have to take risks in order to keep or gain the firm ground in the markets but simultaneously they have to look like attractive global corporations with market power. The risks of a rapid fall in the markets are numerous and, as a key sign of our age, often emerging from the speculative side of trading.

Today, as the result of speeded outward orientation, the international sphere of speculation is a remarkable element behind the Finnish forest-industrial policy, and an integral part of the company dynamics. The share of foreign—that is, non-Finnish—ownership was for example the following for the three biggest Finnish-based companies: for Stora Enso 72 percent, for UPM 67 percent and for M-real 35 percent in 2003. It is evident that the American type of shareholder ideology has arrived in European economies, and this has put much pressure on the companies to improve their financial attractiveness and short-term profitability.[16]

Finnish Companies in Europe

The above clearly indicates that the leading Finnish forest companies were actively stretched and pushed forward into international competitive positions. The societal support was considered necessary among those involved in national forest sector politics. The companies became consequently a part of the European Union ahead of Finland. The initial connection was, of course, due to the Finnish export orientation but the actual contextual change took finally place during the 1980s in the form of expansive continental ownership of production capacity.

The Europeanization was not an easy process for the Finnish companies. The northern newcomers were considered outsiders that played with unfair rules, for example by gaining benefits from the devaluations of the Finnish mark and by keeping the domestic production costs, i.e. wood and energy prices and employer expenses, at an artificially low level. The most heated debate, however, was related to overcapacity issues. The supply of fine paper and magazine papers as well as lumber had greatly exceeded the demand for several years in the early 1990s and this had resulted in serious reductions in price levels and in unused capacity of the mills. The French paper producers and sawmills for example felt that their economic space was unjustly eroded, and the Finnish "invaders" faced protectionistic governmental reactions. The main Finnish forest exporters were therefore invited into negotiations with the EU in 1994 in order to solve the serious structural overcapacity problem in fine paper.[17]

The setting changed in 1995 when Finland became part of the European Union. The era of the domestic devaluations of the Finnish mark was left behind and the EU became a self-sufficient exporter of paper. The EU founded a central office for the coordination of the forest-industrial benefits and, moreover, cleared the role of forest-based industries as one of the trading policy emphases that could benefit from structural funds and internal research programs.[18]

The leading Finnish forest companies achieved a firm hold in Continental Europe, and for a while it seemed that the Finnish strategy was exclusively Western European, with strong regional concentrations in Germany, Great Britain and France (Fig. 12.2). This was especially true till 1997. In Europe, outside Finland, UPM-Kymmene (United Paper Mills-Kymmene Inc.) had become an important producer of coated magazine paper in Wales and Scotland, whereas in northern Germany the operations were limited to fine-paper production. The company had also grown into an important producer in France, concentrating on pulp, newsprint and fine paper grades. However, and as a partial consequence of the above-mentioned trade confrontation between Finland and France, UPM-Kymmene's "French strategy" faced serious drawbacks, and a withdrawal in 1997 from magazine paper production near Rouen thereafter lessened the visibility of the company in the country.

Enso (Enso Gutzeit Inc.) merged with the Swedish company Stora (Stora Kopparberg Inc.) in 1999, and the new company immediately won a place among the three leading paper and board producers in the world. Both companies were already before the merger on the top ten list of the world's biggest forest companies. In Europe, Stora Enso has a strong position in Finland, Sweden and Germany. Enso had actively invested in Germany before the merger: in 1994, a newsprint unit, supplied by recycled fiber, was opened in eastern Germany and another one, producing both newsprint and magazine paper (near Karlsruhe), was bought a few years later. Stora Enso also owns a remarkable fine-paper unit in the Netherlands. Sawing has traditionally been a key element in Enso's domestic strategies, and this is also true in Central Europe: Austria is an important sawing area for the company. The company has also activities in the Baltic countries and Russia: Pakenso has invested in cellular board production in Tallinn and Riga, as well as in Palapanovo south of Moscow. Stora Enso has also joint operations with the partners in the Karelian Republic: Ladenso is an important purchaser of wood for the pulp and paper plants in eastern Finland.

Stora Enso inherited the earlier operations of Stora in Europe, including eight major paper or board plants in Sweden and five large pulp, paper or board units outside Sweden, namely in Germany, Belgium and France. The pulp production at Stora Celbi in Portugal has to be considered strategically important. The supply of wood for Stora Celbi is based on eucalyptus plantations.[19]

M-real (Metsä-Serla Inc.) has become an important fine-paper producer in Europe and, after the purchase of Swedish Modo Paper in 2000, it has even reached the position of a continental market leader in the grade. Modo Paper has large fine-paper units in Sweden, Germany, France and Austria. The merger was originally accompanied by a plan to sell the production of tissue papers to the Swedish SCA (Svenska Cellulosa Aktiebolag), but this was prevented by the EU Commission: the market share of SCA in tissue papers would have grown too large in Europe. The setback caused serious liquidation problems for M-real and it also forced the company to rethink its magazine paper strategies in southern Germany. M-real had achieved in the latter half of 1990s a visible role in the production of coated magazine papers in Germany, which was due to a period of intense cooperation with Finnish Myllykoski Paper. Myllykoski Paper, a family-owned company from southern Finland, has succeeded in keeping the ownership in the hands of the Björnberg family and this has secured some entrepreneurial freedom and elasticity: decisions are made according to managerial aims, not for attracting broader ranks of shareholders.[20] In comparison, M-real is greatly dependent on Metsäliitto, the cooperative organization of Finnish forest owners, which aims at keeping the major shareholders' voice in the company.[21]

Finally, strikingly deviating from the volume-based strategies of the above-mentioned companies, Ahlstrom Industries has a highly focused production profile and a well-established transcontinental production network. In Europe, Ahlstrom owns notable paper units in Germany and northern Italy, producing industrial filter papers, package covers and some other special paper grades.[22]

The Europeanization was in general a rather natural and necessary step for the Finnish companies. New limits and risks were soon, however, faced and this was primarily due to the emerging stronger regulative interests of the European Union. In the eyes of the forest industry, the Union had become a bureaucratic unit not fully developing its competitive advantages within the global spatial division of labor.[23] The last years of the 20th century witnessed, therefore, a clear activation of the transcontinental relations and operations.

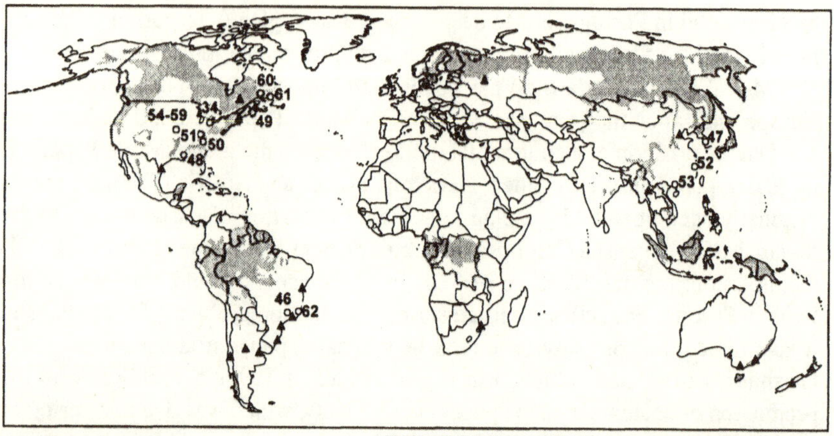

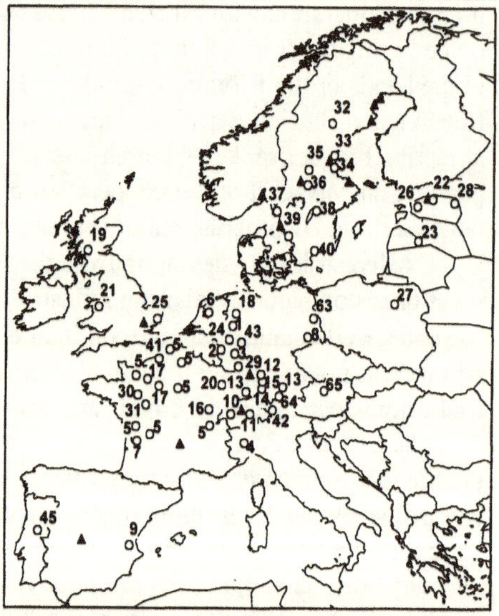

1. Kämmerer, Germany (a)
2. Ferd Jagenberg, Germany (a)
3. Homburger Papierfabrik, Germany (a)
4. Bosso Carte Speciali, Italy (a)
5. Sibille-Dalle, France (a)
6. Berghuizer, Netherlands (se)
7. Soustre & Fils (Corenso), France (se+u)
8. Sachsen Papier, Germany (se)
9. Enso Espanola, Spain (se)
10. Biberist, Switzerland (mr)
11. Utzenstorf, Switzerland (my)
12. Maxau and Wolfsheck, Germany (se)
13. MD Lang Papier, Germany (my)
14. MD Albbruck Papier, Germany (mr+my)
15. MD Plattling Papier, Germany (mr+my)
16. Papeteries de Docelles, France (u)
17. Chapelle Darplay, France (u)
18. Nordland Papier, Germany (u)
19. Caledonian Paper, Scotland (u)
20. Stracel, France (u)
21. Shotton Paper, Wales (u)
22. Pakenso Eesti, Estonia (se)
23. Pakenso Baltika, Latvia (se)
24. Papierwerke Halstrick, Germany (mr)
25. New Thames and Sittingbourne, England (mr)
26. Neopac-Elkson, Estonia (mr)
27. Warszawskie Zaklady Papierniche, Poland (mr)
28. Walki Paberisto, Estonia (u)
29. E. Holtzmann, Germany (se)
30. Alizay, France (mr)
31. Pont-St-Maxence, France (mr)
32. Wifsta and Husum, Sweden (mr)
33. Norrsundet, Sweden (se)
34. Skutskär, Seden (se)
35. Kvarnsveden, Sweden (se)
36. Fors, Sweden (se)
37. Gruvön, Swden (se)
38. Skogshall, Sweden (se)
39. Hylte, Sweden (se)
40. Nymölla, Sweden (se)
41. Corbehem, France (se)
42. Baienfurt, Germany (se)
43. Reisholz und Kabel, Germany (se)
44. Langerbrugge, Belgium (se)
45. Celbi, Portugal (se)
46. Nicolaus Papéis, Brazil (a)
47. Ahlstrom Korea, South Korea (a)
48. Ahlstrom Filtration, USA (a)
49. Madison Paper, USA (my)
50. Chicago (Alsip), USA (my)
51. Blandin Paper, USA (u)
52. Changshu Paper, China (u)
53. Suzhou Paper, China (se)
54. Stevens Point, USA (se)
55. Duluth, USA (se)
56. Biron, USA, (se)
57. Niagara, USA (se)
58. Kimberley, USA (se)
59. Whiting, USA (se)
60. Port Hawkesbury, Canada (se)
61. Repap Hawkesbury, Canada (u)
62. Aracruz, Brazil (se)
63. Schwedt, Germany (u)
64. Augsburg und Schongau, Germany (u)
65. Steyermühl, Austria (u)

Fig. 12.2. Globalization and the Finnish forest sector. The central locations of the leading companies in Europe and on other continents in 2002: Ahlstrom (a), Jaakko Pöyry (triangle), M-real (mr), Myllykoski (my), Stora Enso (se), UPM (u). Shaded area refers to existing forest cover.[24]

Transcontinental Operations

Even though the active phase of the globalization of the Finnish companies is a matter of a decade, it was not launched in a vacuum. Numerous contacts and experiments in transcontinental production had already been established. The experiences of the past also had a significant influence on the later moves.

The above-mentioned overseas success of Ahlstrom Industries was due to strict concentration on special papers, mainly industrial filters, and the strategy was based on flexible customer orientation. This recipe has proved useful not only in Europe but also in Brazil, South Korea and the USA. Among the rest of the Finnish companies, only Myllykoski has had longer-lasting experience in overseas operations. Myllykoski bought in 1980 a paper mill—Madison Paper in Maine—on the eastern cost of the USA, following then the client's needs. *The New York Times*, after accidentally discovering the special quality of Myllykoski's magazine paper, sought closer cooperation. Myllykoski seized the opportunity and the company became the local supplier to the newspaper's sunday issues. After two decades of low profile in the USA, Myllykoski announced a new move in 2000: Madison Paper bought an old (recycled fiber based) newsprint unit in Chicago that was only recently run into bankruptcy. The aim was again, as was the case in Maine, to replace the old machinery and invest in the production of coated magazine papers.[25]

Enso was, however, initially the first from Finland to start trans-Atlantic cooperation in wood processing. The project, begun already during the 1960s, gradually turned into Enso's major ownership of Eurocan Pulp & Paper in British Columbia, Canada. The company concentrated on sawmilling and kraft paper production. After economic and political setbacks, Enso was forced to withdraw from British Columbia during the early 1990s. The difficulties were mostly economic but also partly relating to the growing local environmental concerns against the clear-cuts run by the company.[26] Nevertheless, the merger with Stora in 1999 brought Enso back to trans-Atlantic paper processing: Stora has long experience in Eastern Canada.[27] The new Stora Enso soon expanded to the US markets by purchasing Consolidated Paper (in 2000), an influential actor in the lake area of the United States. At the time of the merger, the combined enterprise was announced to be the world's largest producer of paper and board by capacity, reaching 15 million metric tons per year, mainly in magazine papers.[28]

Stora Enso naturally inherited the activities of the former separate companies, including Stora's footholds in Canada, Brazil and China, and Enso's orientation to Indonesia. Enso led a 25-year project of tree plantations, mainly Acasia, utilizing the logged areas of previous rain forests on the island of Borneo. The cooperation was organized as a joint venture, PT Finnatara Intiga, owned by Inhutani III, the state company of Indonesia (40 percent of the shares), Gudang

Garamin with a Chinese background (30 percent of the shares) and Enso (30 percent of the shares). Their aim was to establish a pulp plant there in the near future, but the project was run down in 2004 without any broader public reflection of the backlash. The politically and economically insecure conditions in Indonesia—after the decades of dictatorship—have undoubtedly much to do with the withdrawal. The freezing of the Indonesian project, on the other hand, became reflected in the new investment decisions in South America. Stora Enso had for long been a minor partner in Aracruz, Brazil, and in 2003 a decision for building a global-scale pulp unit in Aracruz in cooperation with Veracel, a local forest-industrial actor, was announced. This cooperation was a signal of the rising global importance of pulp production in South America.[29]

The globally most active and visible of the Finnish forest companies has in recent years been UPM (UPM-Kymmene), the company that had no significant overseas operations before 1997. Due to limited experience, perhaps, the leaps over to South-East Asia and the USA have resulted in partial drawbacks, and the real transcontinental breakthrough has not yet (in 2005) taken place. The North American strategy was initiated by purchasing a paper mill—Blandin Paper—in Minnesota in 1997. This move, although expensive and loaded with risks due to old machinery, low profitability and supply problems, strengthened the company's leading global ranking in the production of coated paper for magazines. More important, however, UPM became an internal actor in the US markets.[30]

The landing of UPM in the USA was soon planned to be followed by a merger with Champion International, a company not much smaller than the Finnish partner. The merger, already agreed by the boards of both companies, became seriously contested by International Paper, a company from the United States that has led for long the global size ranking of forest-industrial enterprises. What was even more serious, the shareholders and the mill localities expressed their worries over the merger with a European company. Finally, after a few dramatic weeks in spring 2000, International Paper could make a better offer, and soon afterward the meeting of the shareholders of Champion International rescinded the earlier agreement of the boards. The widely published merger plan, including the symbolically significant change of the name of the company—UPM was to become Champion International—turned into a serious backlash for the Finnish company.[31]

The backlash did not have deep impacts on UPM's trans-Atlantic strategy even though subsequent steps have been less ambitious. The aim has, however, remained the same: to win a secure position in North America. This was confirmed in the early fall of 2000 when UPM-Kymmene announced a purchase of Repap in New Brunswick, Canada. Repap was a deeply indebted company that had been for sale for years. Repap's main product, magazine paper, corresponded well with the profile of the purchaser. The first years of UPM governance in

New Brunswick have been difficult, as both the forest conservationists and the mill workers have criticized the authoritarian culture of decision-making. Conservationists expressed their worry about forest management that, according to them, one-sidedly favors fir trees and makes the province's forest landscape monotonous in character. The mill workers have been especially disappointed about the culture of administration but also about the reorganization of working conditions and lessening employment, and the disagreement led to a long strike in winter 2004-5.[32]

UPM also initiated its Southeast Asian operations in 1997. The company announced a cooperation plan with Asia Pacific Resources International (April) in fine-paper production and marketing. The initial plan, which included a joint foundation of a paper unit close to a pulp mill in Riau in Sumatra, Indonesia, was, however, soon rejected due to the economic recession into which Indonesia, as most countries of Southeast Asia, fell during the last years of the 20th century. The plan was also severely criticized by a network of local and global rainforest conservationists[33] and this might also have had an effect on the withdrawal. The April cooperation finally resulted in UPM's ownership in a fine-paper mill close to Shanghai, China, which is expected to become an economic success in the future. The success is, of course, highly dependent on the political stability of China under the Communist Party.

The Southeast Asian project has tied UPM into economic cultures and resource policies that deviate from the Western ones. This makes the company vulnerable to risks arising from the cultural differences. The most worrying questions are related to undemocratic political practices and the human rights situation, as well as to the continuing exploitative devastation of rain forests. This means entrepreneurial risks but also new marketing problems for a Western company due to the rising global awareness of the consumers.

UPM's withdrawal from Indonesia led to investment decisions in South America in a manner similar to Stora Enso. UPM announced together with Metsäliitto and M-real a plan in 2004 to build a large pulp mill in Uruguay, supplied by eucalyptus plantations. The announcement was received with ambivalence in Finland, as both companies have actively searched for cost minimization in their domestic mills by freezing investments in new production capacity and diminishing the number of employees. The move to Uruguay seems also an especially high risk to M-real, the company with deep financial problems in Europe. The South American project is, however, a decades-long project for UPM; it has since the 1980s prepared for the mill plan by experiments in eucalyptus plantations

The most global of the Finnish forest companies is Jaakko Pöyry International, specializing in forest-industrial consulting. The company has offices in 35 countries, with regional clusters of consultation in South America, Europe, South-East Asia and the USA.[34] Jaakko Pöyry has concentrated on country or area specific Forest Sector Master Plans covering consultancy from forestry practices, wood processing and logistics to market and management development with an aim at expansive pulp and paper production. The Master Plans are programs for intensifying wood exploitation and paper production in the client countries. During the most recent years, e.g. Brazil, Nepal and Russia, as well as many of the countries in South-East Asia, have ordered Master Plans. The programs have practically functioned as tools for introducing Finnish expertise to the clients. The Finnish companies focused on different branches of forest expertise—from reforestation and tree plantations to the whole chain of forest-industrial machinery (forest tractors, and entire plant units and integrates)—have in many cases become initially introduced to the target countries as subcontractors of the Master Plans. Both the United Nations Development Program (UNDP) and the Finnish development cooperation agency (FINNIDA) have financially supported this type of forest cooperation.[35]

Local and Global Finland

The gradual globalization of the forest sector is loaded with risks and drama, at least while observed from Finland, a country with a strong historical forest dependency. The Finnish know-how spreads in different parts of the world and the Finnish model is applied to joint projects. The overseas success and visibility of Finnish forest companies are undoubtedly key elements of the Finnish globalization. Forest-based modernization is supported in many parts of the world by Finnish expertise.

The forest-based globalization also has its darker side. The leading companies no longer can integrate any local or national premises into their strategies, as was earlier the case.[36] Now it would affect their competitiveness. Similarly, Finland's position has also changed in the networks of paper production. In the new spatial division of labor, Finland has still kept its role as a home base for the key companies, and it also seems to remain an important supply and production area for them. Finland will evidently exist on the world map of the companies as a resource base and an area of mass production, a supplier of virgin fiber and selected paper grades. The setting is framed by Finland's geographical location in the conifer-dominated zone, providing markets with long-fibered pulp. Finland is also part of the northern wildernesses of the European Union, as well as a bridge to the forest resources of Northwest Russia.

The wilderness role of EU Finland has added a new dimension to the local-global dynamics. The environmental regulation of the European Union increasingly functions as a risk signal to the companies and they therefore invest abroad, beyond Europe. This brings along the risk of slower modernization rates in domestic production technology and raises the problem of stagnation in wood-processing design. However, the companies still hold a key position in national forest economic policy, which tends to keep Finnish forest-industrial activities deeply integrated in the international division of paper production. The export orientation is thus structurally determined, and especially the forest provinces of the country maintain their vulnerability to fluctuations in pulp and paper markets.

This type of translocalization is not only a question of the changing roles within a broader spatial division of labor. It is also loaded with symbolic moves. Precise identification of the biggest forest companies has for example become difficult, which is due to the fluid character of globalization. It appears today to be misleading to talk about Finnish companies when referring to those companies from Finland that are largely owned by professional US investors and whose central production capacity is located abroad. This confusion is obvious when thinking about the names of the companies and the contested renaming during mergers and acquisitions. The purchaser often swallows the purchased one and the minor name or trademark simply disappears from the markets. Sometimes, however, we learn to use new complicated combinations or compromises of names that more or less carry the past of the unified companies. Stora Enso has a Swedish-Finnish background and even particular localities can be distinguished behind the names: Stora Kopperberget originates from a mining locality in central Sweden and Enso is an industrial town in the "Old Finland" ceded to the Soviet Union after World War II and renamed Svetogorsk.[37]

UPM—then still known as UPM-Kymmene—was ready to take the name of the North American company, Champion International, during the negotiations of the merger in spring 2000. The change was already accepted in the boards of both companies, only to be overruled by the intervention of International Paper before the decisive meeting of the shareholders of Champion International. The re-naming was (only) seen a question with symbolic significance, and ignored when set against hard economic benefits. "Kymmene" relates, however, the company to its Finnish roots as the river valley of Kymi, Kymmene in Swedish, is a central part of Finland's forest industrial history. The Swedish translation reminds us about the Finnish-Swedish forest capital behind the original company. It was unified with the Finnish forest capital in 1995, when UPM-Kymmene was established. The merger was a historical one and it wiped away the confrontations between the two leading private forest-industrial groups in Finland.[38]

The rest of the global forest actors from Finland also carry similar pasts in their names: Ahlstrom is a name of a family, as is Jaakko Pöyry, and Myllykoski is also related to family ownership. M-real (earlier Metsä-Serla) has partly roots in Serlachius, a family company that was integrated into Metsäliitto's forest-industrial operations in 1986. Metsäliitto is a cooperative organization for the

Finnish forest owners founded at the beginning of the 20th century. In winter 2001, soon after Metsä-Serla's reorientation toward fine-paper production, the company announced its new name, M-real, which can be seen a symbolical disengagement from the past. Among the older consumers in Northern Europe, "Serla" is first of all connected to tissue papers, and there especially to our washroom conveniences, whereas the new M-real is a key actor in fine paper in Europe. In addition, *metsä*— forest in Finnish, whereas Metsäliitto means Forest Union—is a general word connecting Finland to its eastern Finno-Ugric past.

Both the initial localities and founding patrons have been important for the forest companies throughout their histories. This underlines the value of the symbolic dimension, including cultural continuity, within forest-industrial reorganization. Most of the symbolic bridges have, however, disappeared in the mergers. Only a few of the localities are still "honored" and thus represented in company names whereas earlier, during the era of the national forest sector, the company names were, as a rule, closely related to their main operational localities. The companies often carried the names of the towns: Oulu had Oulu Inc., Kajaani had Kajaani Inc. and even Nokia, the world-wide actor in telecommunications business, has its roots in a mill town of Nokia close to Tampere. Nokia Inc. ran in the beginning a small forest company in Nokia.

The local and family pasts of the companies are also loaded with memories not so willingly recalled. Towns with only one significant industrial employer were often paternalistic communities and sometimes the companies, local elites and townspeople behaved as single-minded actors.[39] Public disagreeing was more or less forbidden. The North American lessons of UPM have been important in this respect. It was the meeting of the shareholders of Champion International that canceled the decision of the board. The shareholder interest overcame the managers in charge. The patrimonial tradition was challenged.

The rules of global financial speculation have during the recent years emphasized the role of shareholders, at the cost of the leading managers, and this has had an effect on the company identification. Today, as was argued above, the managers are keenly steered by the owners, and strategic moves get rapidly reflected in the form of shifts in the stock markets. Often the owners seek for the best short-term options, which can run counter to the benefits of the company, a least in the long run. This shift can, however, be regarded as an opening toward more participatory decision-making in the forest-industrial policy. Even the small-owners have a vote, though a minor one, in the meetings and, accordingly, critical issues can be brought to the agenda. All this can be considered positive, at least if set against the old patrimonial model of decision-making in the one-company towns.

Depending on the shareholder profiles, the current reorganization of the forest companies can take radically differing paths; toward more accountable and polyphonic practices or, which seems more likely, toward increasingly aggressive private profit maximizing. The former alternative can only surface with the help of non-governmental organizations (NGOs) and intergovernmental regulations.[40] The ethical dimension needs to be brought into the forefront and in this way finally—via discursive regulation and actor-specific negotiations—made a routine measure of forest trade. Some preliminary steps toward this direction have in fact been taken already in the shareholder meetings of UPM and Stora Enso: the most prominent of the environmental activists have raised their voices as minor owners of the companies and directed the shareholder debate toward ethical and socioenvironmental challenges. The professional shareholders have, however, tended to bypass the ethical issues by considering them as purely managerial and strategic challenges and thus unsuitable for shareholder meetings. This interpretation, if becoming a rule, is a serious drawback to the democratization of company administration. [41]

Forest Trade and Green Image

Globalization has, in a way, brought environmental values into forest trade. In order to secure their share of markets, companies need to take care of their environmental performance and profile. This is also true for the Finnish companies. They have become cautious of the risks of loggings in the old-growth forests. The value preferences turn to market questions for the forest companies via their customers: leading newspapers, journals, producers and media houses. They have an interest over their circulation and profit, and the new environmental risk is, of course, willingly minimized. The forest-industrial strategies are thus increasingly conditioned by reader responses and boycott risks.[42]

The transnational companies, while becoming bigger than ever, have not been able to free themselves from the intensifying competition. They are subjected to changes in their operational contexts and networks. This makes the transnational companies vulnerable to varying contextual shifts—and to their own strategies. Wrong moves in global competition turn easily into falling profit options and losses in the stock markets and even difficulties within the markets of the end products. The global economy seems to turn more and more fragile in this process.

The fate of the last old-growth forests also shapes the local-global linkages of the Finnish forest industry. As seen from Central Europe, the last old-growth forests are the remaining natural areas of the whole continent. The consumers of Finnish paper are aware of this and, consequently, the most marginal lands of the North have occasionally emerged as hot spots of consumer politics. Similarly, the broader social and ethical questions, concerning the legitimacy and justice dimensions of paper production, have been introduced to the companies as critical aspects of globalization. The problems of uneven and unjust development have emerged both in Finnish domestic settings as well as within the overseas projects, and now the question is not only about the green image of the companies. Instead, the role of the whole of Finland is weighed, as well as the national credibility in the global division of labor.

The problem of credibility has also become entangled in the question of forest certifications. Forest certification was initially introduced as a means to guarantee that sustainability and biodiversity concerns were respected in economic forests and, moreover, that certain areas of old-growth forests will be left untouched. Later, however, it has been debated whether the scope should also be extended to cover social criteria by highlighting the wealth of logging communities and forest workers and, in general, the socioenvironmental viability of the whole chain of forest-based production and consumption. This is a contested process that has brought several difficult and yet unresolved questions into the forest-based globalization.[43]

The Pan-European Forest Certification model (PEFC), which is an intergovernmental forest certification process guided by Finnish expertise, concentrates on forest management and aims to guarantee the sound origin of paper and other wood products. Changes in forest covering and health, timber production, non-timber values, diversity and conservation issues as well as the socioeconomic aspects of forest management are highlighted. In comparison, Forest Stewardship Council (FSC), which is supported by several international environmental organizations, has included several social factors in their certification procedure and, especially, the participatory dimension of forest planning and wood processing is emphasized. The long-term socioeconomic wellbeing of forest workers and local communities is required to be confirmed via negotiations and consultations with people and groups directly involved in and affected by the operations. In the case of loss or damage affecting the legal or customary rights of local people, a fair compensation mechanism is also demanded.[44]

PEFC and FSC are the two competing systems of forest certification in Northern Europe. FSC is the more proactive one of the two systems, basically concerned about forests and forest-dependent communities, whereas PEFC proceeds more reactively, emphasizing the certification as a means of marketing.[45] It seems that the ecological concern has become widely accepted as a conditioning factor of the forest trade while the broader socioenvironmental dimension is still causing confusion. The ongoing debate is intensive even though the result seems for the most part clear already: the broader socioenvironmental criteria are to be implemented in the assessments of the sustainability of wood-processing and refining.[46]

As has become clear, the debate on certification has emerged as a central element in the current reorganization of the forest industry and trade. The forestry practices and production processes are keenly followed, and demands of accountability and broader participation have become difficult to ignore. For the forest companies, this means adjustment to the changing rules of the game: the previously excluded costs of production are now becoming part of the business. This might appear as a threat for some but it can also be regarded as a means to expand over to new markets.

Toward New Wood Order

The above analysis underlines the necessity to include the previously ignored socioenvironmental costs of economic reorganization in the calculations of actor and product-specific credibility. The forest industry is part of this reorientation. However, the main forest companies—as the key actors of change—have also become embedded in a global ranking competition that tends to keep the new socioenvironmental openings in the margins.

We are therefore left with some critical questions. Volume-based expansion through mergers has become the guiding principle for the forest-industrial companies but not without obvious deviations. There still is life behind the big actors of the global stock markets, and also some entrepreneurial creativity, as has become evident in the profiles of Ahlstrom and Myllykoski. How to secure the variation in the future, if the smaller companies with some financial attractiveness are, as a rule, to be eaten by the big ones? The question is also important to peripheral forest resource communities, such as the provinces of Forest-Finland: What is left of the regional (horizontal) dynamics when the provinces become thoroughly integrated in the companies with global vertical power and, accordingly, effectively located in the "new wood order" as a producer of pulp and bulk?

On the other hand, the growing shareholder interest in forest-industrial operations can also be seen as an alternative to the older managerial model of decision-making, as was witnessed in the UPM-Champion International case in spring 2000. This episode was an important lesson for the Finnish partners and it highlighted the practical power of shareholders. It made the managers of the Finnish-based companies more sensitive to the voices of the new shareholder-owners. The lesson can be taken as a sign of strengthening sociocultural pressure—shareholder democracy—in the forest-industrial goal formulation. The floor is at least open to broader representativeness, including socioenvironmental views, as has been witnessed in the meetings of the shareholders of both UPM and Stora Enso.

The managers of the Finnish forest industry—as the forest sector in general—have much to learn from the experiences gathered during the first decade of intense globalization. However, as was argued earlier, the Finnish model undoubtedly contains much that is worth exporting. The long history of society-company negotiations and environmental pressure have left their mark on the domestic forest know-how, and these experiences should decidedly be integrated into the current global learning process. It is evident that along the globalization the Finnish model—or the Nordic model in general—is more and more challenged by the North American and "Southern" models that significantly deviate from the regulative norms and measures to which the Nordic countries have become accustomed. Not much debate has, however, emerged about the comparative pros and cons between the models. We do not have any clear idea to what degree the Finnish companies are "exporting" their model across the seas and continents and to what degree they are adopting the models and cultures of the target countries. We do not know much about the actual compromises of the competing models.[47]

Nevertheless, the intensive globalization of the Finnish forest companies forces us to face the transcontinental comparative settings. The process simultaneously expands and shrinks our world and demands us to take a stance on the local-global dynamics and socioenvironmental transformations. From a geographical point of view, this is an especially challenging view.

Notes

1. Ari Aukusti Lehtinen, "Kiina-ilmiö metsäalalla Suomen globalisaatiohaaste," *Helsingin Sanomat*, 3 November 2004, A2 (vieraskynä).
2. Lori Brown and Christopher Flavin, "Uusi vuosisata—uusi talousmalli," in *Maailman tila 1999*, ed. Linda Starke (Helsinki: Gaudeamus, 1999), 13-32.
3. Joan Martinez-Alier, *The Environmentalism of the Poor* (Cheltenham: Edward Elgar Publishing, 2002), 13.
4. Wolfgang Fürstner, The publishers' View on Eco-certification. A paper presented at the Annual Conference of the Finnish Forestry Association, Helsinki, 26 March 1996, mimeo.
5. Kathleen McAfee, "Selling Nature to Save It? Biodiversity and Green Developmentalism," *Environment and Planning D: Society and Space* 17 (1999), 133-54; Juhani Tirkkonen, *Ilmastopolitiikka ja ekologinen modernisaatio. Diskursiivinen tarkastelu suomalaisesta ilmastopolitiikasta ja sen yhteydestä metsäsektorin muutokseen* (Tampere: Acta Universitatis Tamperensis, no. 781, 2000).
6. About decoupling, see Mika Kuisma, *Ympäristöjohtamisen käytäntöjen ja poliitikkojen erisuuntainen muutos* (Helsinki: Helsingin kauppakorkeakoulu, 2004); Ari Aukusti Lehtinen, Jakob Donner-Amnell and Bjørnar Sæther, eds., *Politics of Forests* (Aldershot: Ashgate, 2004), 267-68.
7. Casimir Ehrnrooth, "Euroopassa tarvitaan täysin uusia kasvun ja työllisyyden strategioita. Työttömyyden perussyy on liian heikko kilpailukyky," *Helsingin Sanomat*, 5 February 1995, B9.

8. Alf Hornborg, "Mi'kmaq Environmentalism: Local Incentives and Global Projections," in *Sustainability the Challenge. People, Power and the Environment*, eds. L. Anders Sandberg and Sverker Sörlin (Montréal: Black Rose Books), 202-12; Otso Ovaskainen, Minna Pappila and Jyri Pötry, *The Finnish Forest Industry in Russia. On the Thorny Paths towards Ecological and Social Responsibility* (Helsinki: The Finnish Nature League, 1999); Otso Miettinen and Tove Selin, *Harkittu riski. UPM-Kymmene Indonesian sademetsissä* (Helsinki: Vihreä Sivistysliitto, 1999).
9. *Avain Suomen metsäteollisuuteen* (Helsinki: Metsäteollisuus ry, 1998).
10. *Forest Industry Statistics* (Helsinki: Forest Industries Finland, 2000) <http://www.forestindustries.fi/tilastot> (15 Jan. 2001).
11. Colin Hazley, *Forest-based and Related Industries of the European Union—Industrial Districts, Clusters and Agglomerations* (Helsinki: The Research Institute of the Finnish Economy/ETLA, 2000).
12. Markku Lammi, *Metsäklusteri Suomen taloudessa* (Helsinki: The Research Institute of the Finnish Economy/ETLA, 2000), 33; *Forest Industry Statistics.*
13. *Forest Industry Statistics.*
14. Juha Näsi, Pasi Ranta and Pasi Sajasalo, *Metsäteollisuuden megamuutos. Pelinäkökulmainen analyysi suomalaisen metsäteollisuuden kehkeytymisprosesseista vuosina 1985-1996* (Jyväskylä: Jyväskylän yliopiston taloustieteellinen osaston julkaisuja, no. 114, 1998); Tarmo Koskinen, "The Forest Cluster: Economic Order and Societal Integration in Finland," in *The Green Kingdom. Finland's Forest Cluster*, eds. Aarne Reunala, Ilpo Tikkanen and Esko Åsvik (Helsinki: Otava and Metsämiesten Säätiö, 1999), 201-07; Eli Moen and Kari Lilja, "Constructing Global Corporations: Contrasting National Legacies in the Nordic Forest Industry," in *The Multinational Firm: Organizing across Institutional and National Divide*, eds. Glenn Morgan, Peer Hull Kristensen and Richard Whitley (Oxford: Oxford University Press, 2003), 145-68.
15. Moen and Lilja, "Constructing Global Corporations."
16. Ari Aukusti Lehtinen, "Vastuu- ja oikeudenmukaisuuskysymykset globalisoituvassa metsäyhteistyössä," in *Leipäpuusta arvopaperia,* eds. Ari Aukusti Lehtinen and Pertti Rannikko (Helsinki: Metsälehti Kustannus, 2004), 263.
17. Lehtinen, "Globalisation and the Finnish Forest Industry," 241.
18. Hazley, *Forest-based and Related Industries of the European Union—Industrial Districts, Clusters and Agglomerations.*
19. *Stora Environmental Report 1997* (Falun: Stora Kopparberg's Bergslags Aktiebolag, 1998).
20. Jyrki Iivonen, "Myllykoski maksaa vanhasta tehtaasta USA:ssa 268 miljoonaa," *Helsingin Sanomat*, 14 April 2000, D6.
21. Lehtinen, "Globalisation and the Finnish Forest Industry," 242.
22. <http://Ahlstrom.corporate.governance> (1 April 2005).
23. Ehrnrooth, "Euroopassa tarvitaan täysin uusia kasvun ja työllisyyden strategioita. Työttömyyden perussyy on liian heikko kilpailukyky."
24. Ari Aukusti Lehtinen, "Globalisation and the Finnish Forest Industry," *Fennia* 180, nos. 1-2 (2002), CD-ROM map. The map is republished by the permission of the Finnish Geographical Society.
25. Jyrki Iivonen, "Myllykoski rakentaa Saksaan uuden sanomalehtipaperikoneen," *Helsingin Sanomat*, 23 December 2000, D3.

26. Anne Brax, "Enso-Gutzeit haluaisi hakata intiaanien pyhän erämaan," *Vihreä Lanka*, no. 25 (1991), 4 (26 June 1991).
27. Hornborg, "Mi'kmaq Environmentalism."
28. Lasse Lindberg, "Finnish Forest Cluster Links Global Markets," *Paper and Timber* 82, no. 3 (2000), 146-48.
29. Anu Nousiainen, "Enso haluaa Borneoon sellutehtaan," *Helsingin Sanomat*, 29 September 1996, B 14; Sari Kuvaja, Marko Ulvila and Thomas Wallgren, eds., *Tropiikin vihreä kulta* (Helsinki: Like, 1998); *Forest Industry Statistics* (Stockholm: Forest Industries Sweden, 2001), <http://www.forestindustries.se/eng/fakta> (15 Jan. 2001); Ari Aukusti Lehtinen, "Vastuu- ja oikeudenmukaisuuskysymykset globalisoituvassa metsäyhteistyössä," in *Leipäpuusta arvopaperia*, eds. Ari Aukusti Lehtinen and Pertti Rannikko (Helsinki: Metsälehti Kustannus, 2004), 245-70.
30. Lehtinen, "Globalisation and the Finnish Forest Industry," 242.
31. Lehtinen, "Globalisation and the Finnish Forest Industry," 243.
32. "Luonnonsuojelijat huolissaan UPM:n hakkuista Kanadassa," *Helsingin Sanomat*, 20 March 2003, D7; "UPM:n Kanadan-tehtaan lakosta tulossa ennätysmäisen pitkä," *Helsingin Sanomat*, 4 March 2005, B5.
33. Kuvaja, Ulvila and Wallgren, eds., *Tropiikin vihreä kulta*; Miettinen and Selin, *Harkittu riski.*
34. Alexander Mather, "Foreword," in *Politics of Forests*, eds. Ari Aukusti Lehtinen, Jakob Donner-Amnell and Bjørnar Sæther (Aldershot: Ashgate, 2004), xiii.
35. Marko Ulvila, "Indonesiasta löytyy halpaa kuitua ja joustava lainsäädäntö. UPM-Kymmene sijoittaa sademetsien hävitykseen," *Ydin*, no. 7 (1997), 5-8; Ari Aukusti Lehtinen, "Metsäsektori ja maailmantalous," in *Suomen kartasto 1999*, eds. John Westerholm and Pauliina Raento (Helsinki: Wsoy and Suomen Maantieteellinen Seura, 1999), 156-59.
36. Koskinen, "The Forest Cluster: Economic Order and Societal Integration in Finland; Jarmo Kortelainen, "Forest Industry Communities—In the Light or Shadow of the Mill?," in *The Green Kingdom. Finland's Forest Cluster*, eds. Aarne Reunala, Ilpo Tikkanen and Esko Åsvik (Helsinki: Otava and Metsämiesten Säätiö, 1999), 208-13.
37. Björn Axelsson, Sune Berger and Jan Hogdal, *Vikmanshyttan: lära för framtida bruk. En bok om studiearbete, frigörelser och Stora Koppparberg* (Uppsala: Verdandi, 1980); Jarmo Kortelainen and Juha Kotilainen, "Svetogorsk Revisited: On the Impacts of the Border on a Russian Forest Industrial Locality," A paper presented at the 2nd Workshop of Border Research Network in Aabenraa, Denmark, 25-27 May 2000, <http://www.crossborder.ifg.dk/workshop> (12 Oct. 2001).
38. Näsi, Ranta and Sajasalo, *Metsäteollisuuden megamuutos.*
39. William Solecki, "Paternalism, Pollution and Protest in a Company Town," *Political Geography* 15, no. 1 (1996), 5-20; Kortelainen, "Forest Industry Communities—In the Light or Shadow of the Mill?."
40 Ari Aukusti Lehtinen, Jakob Donner-Amnell and Bjørnar Sæther, eds., *Politics of Forests* (Aldershot: Ashgate, 2004), 275.
41. Lehtinen, "Globalisation and the Finnish Forest Industry," 245-46; "Stora Enso merkitsi tiedoksi Greenpeacen Lapin-huolet," *Helsingin Sanomat*, 23 March 2005, B3.
42. Fürstner, The publishers' View on Eco-certification; see also chapter 6 in this volume.
43. Thomas Beckley, "Pluralism by Default: Community Power in a Paper Mill Town," *Forest Science* 42, no.1 (1996), 35-45; Mary Rees, "Jobs Talk: Retreating from the Social Sustainability of Forestry Communities," *The Forestry Chronicle* 75, no. 5 (1999), 755-63.

44. Sarah Lloyd, "The Emerging Socio-economic and Ecological Forest Landscape in Sweden," in *Socio-economic Sustainability of Forestry in Northern Europe*, ed. Marjatta Hytönen (Copenhagen: Nordic Council of Ministers, 2001), 277-94.

45. "Suomi tyrkyttää kiinalaisille asiantuntijoille hyvän metsänhoidon tunnustaan," *Helsingin Sanomat*, 24 March 2005, B3.

46. As an illustrative episode of the certification contest, WWF Europe and several other environmental civic organizations published in April 2000 the following claims addressed to PEFC: First, according to them, PEFC has to convince that it actually leads toward a better forest management and not only into a confirmation—i.e. "greenwashing"—of the differing national and local practices already in use. Second, PEFC has to follow the Local Agenda 21 directions, agreed by the meeting of the United Nations' Conference on Environment and Development (Earth Summit) in Rio de Janeiro in 1992, and include demands of broader participation in their criteria. This claim is related to the accused dominance of industrial and private forest owners' interests in PEFC-based cooperation. Third, PEFC has to look beyond Europe and include global forest issues in their views. The European scope, as the critics of PEFC say, should necessarily be linked to Eurasian and trans-Atlantic questions, as well as to global North-South relations. Source: Arja Asunta, "Ympäristöjärjestöt eivät pidä PEFC-sertifiointijärjestelmää uskottavana," *WWF metsätiedote*, no. 1-2 (2000), 4.

47. See, however, Lehtinen, Donner-Amnell and Sæther, eds., *Politics of Forests*, as a preliminary comparison of the forest-industrial models between the countries of the conifer-dominated North.

13.

On the Edge: Barents Region and the North of *N66*

"The further to the North, all objects and beings are shedding their firm forms and contours. The strictly organized cosmos is defused. The Universe is losing its [spatial] and time boundaries. The space is melting away and disappears," formulates Nikolaj M. Terebikhin, Professor of History at Pomor University in Archangel, and derives his view from the historical experience of the Northern peoples. Terebikhin further argues that the time also slows down in the extreme North, and finally stops and turns into eternity. He concludes thereafter that the North in the worldview of Scandinavian and Russian nations was never a proper geographical category.[1]

Terebikhin's North is part of the Barents Region, which is the frame along which many of the new initiatives of the European North have been formulated. The new framework emerged in the early 1990s, soon after the collapse of the Soviet Union. The arctic part of Northwest Russia could now be more easily and directly contacted from the centers of the Nordic North-Calotte, and the Barents region could be defined as the northernmost Europe stretching from the Lofoten Islands in western Norway to Novaya Zemlya in northernmost Russia.

The Barents Region is in the Western European eyes the extreme northern edge of the inhabited world, far beyond the limits of the central logistic maps of the continent. No essential reorientation has yet taken place to this mental setting due to Sweden and Finland's memberships in the European Union in 1995. The Barents Region still functions as an area of resource exploitation in the international economic programs. It also carries traces and memories from the military geopolitics as an interface between NATO and Russia. The colonial setting has not disappeared but, instead, become articulated in a more delicate manner. The acute social and environmental problems are reflected on and criticized, and this is clearly an outcome of the comparative setting the cooperation across the borders has enabled.

The Barents framework cannot, however, solely be regarded as a tool for development critique. Rather, it has been established as an arena for formulating economically feasible alternatives to the (post)colonial spatial division of labor. The regional emphasis is a sign of renewal primarily taking place in the politico-economic sphere but it is also formulated as a cultural and communicative process within a particular spatial framework. The way out from the current societal shortcomings is sketched and based on the shared experiences from the past: from the experiences of marginalization and (post)colonial exploitation but, moreover, from within the deeper spheres of cultures and everyday life in the far North. Schooling and education, literary and publishing cooperation, performance activities of various type as well as research initiatives have taken shape across the old geopolitical curtains, and with the help of new electronic networks of communication. The northern space—given the physical constraints and distances of the Barents Region—is increasingly present and represented in the www world. One essential sign of this cultural turn of the North was *N66—Culture in the Barents Region*, a journal and cultural forum that developed the options provided by the new multimedia age. *N66*, referring to the latitudinal degree crossing the Region, was launched in 1997. The process initially concentrated around the journal but it was gradually developed into a www-based multimedia forum supporting the multitude of the North. Sixteen issues of the journal were published during the six-year period of 1997–2002.

Arctic Land and Lifescape

Kenneth Mikko, the editor in charge of the journal, outlined that *N66* is an invitation to participate in the reunion of the Arctic North "by making room for writers, artists, photographers, scholars and culture workers from the whole region—and give all the readers the possibility to take part in thoughts and feelings, visions and nightmares in the region."[2] The first issues of the journal concentrated on the historical and cultural diversification of the Northern peoples, dispersed and divided according to streams of settlement and jurisdictional reorganizations. Paradoxically, as part of the gradual differentiation and fragmentation, the collective historical land and lifescapes, based on shared and similar customs, attitudes and experiences, were identified. Ancient interdependencies, including similarities in archaic beliefs and interlingual links, were introduced on the pages of the journal as events and phenomena present in everyday life practices. The drama of seasonal changes, life in the middle of the wide open landscapes and the low light of the long winter months formed in *N66* the basis of shared identification, northern identity and belonging.

The common difficulties caused by the peripheral colonial location have been accumulated in the Northern cultures and landscapes. The invaders and exploiters have, repeatedly, come from the South and brought with them the religions, economic models and political patterns of their own—to be adopted by the Northerners. There is distrust toward the South but it was reconstructed on the pages of *N66* as a source for cooperation. The North is seen by the journal as an alternative to the modern South.

N66 concentrated on the mythopoetic dimension of the North: the "edge phenomenon"—the lived world of the extreme Arctic—is elaborated on within the renewal in literature, music, visual arts and multi-media performances and in connection to various ethno-religious reformulations. Photography was central to *N66*'s northern approach. The photographs grew into stories of land and life—and they also served as a common language in the multilingual Barents region. Northern cultures and people stand in the photographs in their own lands, they breath within their own landscapes. The "lived edge" seemed to reconnect the present of *N66* to the ancient past: all generations were located under the influence of the same edge. This archaic connection was seen significantly deeper than the shared experience of the historical (post)colonialism led from the South.

The complementarity of languages became the specialty of *N66*. Most of the articles were accompanied with a translation to one of the neighboring languages, and often an abstract in English was attached. The multilinguality is a sign of pluralism and richness, which characterized both the journal and the corners of world of which it became part. Through centuries, the social world has been constructed in the North by necessity as an arena of several co-existing languages, further enriched by numerous sociospatial dialects and lingual mixtures. This is, the journal argued, inevitably the most concrete cultural outcome of the historical forms of (post)colonial domination and submission. For an individual, this has brought an option for a multilingual identification, which is, undoubtedly, a strength of the Northern peripheries. You had to learn to become sensitive to other wor(l)d orders and different modes of perceiving the world.

N66 took multilingualism as a natural and characteristic feature of the North. It was also developed into art. The frequent crossings of lingual borders deepen the understanding of the lands and lives of the Northerners. Moreover, the question was not only about languages but about identification: how we define the North as part of ourselves. Northern cultural awareness, distinctiveness and self-respect, emerging from the pages of *N66*, turned into a generative regionalistic movement. The past was not a record of intrusions from the South but, instead, a source of inspiration. A view to indigenous cultures was opened, despite the humiliating processes of submission, or sometimes even due to the shared experiences, related to them. The North emerged as a multilayered land and lifescape, simultaneously existing on several levels of collective awareness and identity.

N66—Culture in the Barents Region was for a while an important programmatic vision and, as such, a contact field for numerous diverging ambitions. One cannot avoid the question: How to represent the vast Barents area and its cultures by a macropolitical tool derived from the regional strategic renewal in Northern Europe? How natural a regional unit is the Barents area, when seen in a historical context or from the point of view of local cultures? *N66* undeniably looked "from above," from a certain elite position down to everyday life circumstances and exciting local pasts. The journal could also be occasionally caught exoticizing the unknown post-Soviet East of the Barents region. The collaborative network was based on the new technology, it was stretched as electric links between the main nodes. The fluid space of high-tech communication is not a familiar world for everyone in the North and, therefore, several of the cultural spheres became underrepresented or even excluded from the networking. The journal thus seemed to face a risk to become abstracted from the "real" lands and lives of the North, in a similar manner to most northern excursions of academic geographers, as was argued in the introductory part of this volume.

The problem of representation seems to appear unavoidable in this type of multicultural and experiential collaboration across cultural borders. Programmatic initiatives turn into authoritarian outlines of the content. Coordination emerges as unification. Regionalistic actions are often at risk of becoming either provincial adjustments to messages "from above," or territorial groupings of lands and lives of the people "down there."[3] *N66* offered, however, regionalism which was sensitive to the problems of representation and domination. Therefore, in this chapter, the message of *N66* is primarily read as an inspiration to geographers, and scholars of the relating sciences, with an interest in the North. The question simply is: How to receive the challenge of multicultural geographies emerging on the pages of *N66*? The answers to this question will be shaped by textual examinations of the topographies of dwelling, border-crossings of different type, reciprocal mappings and the edge cultures of the Arctic illustrated and developed by *N66*. It will be also asked whether the multilayered North could be regarded as a "geographical category," despite the argument by Nikolaj Terebikhin in the first issue of *N66* in 1997, quoted at the beginning of this chapter.

Topography of Dwelling

> In every village the church rose above all other buildings. The bell tower with its blue domes was the highest building in the village and its white-stone walls with the green roof could be seen from a long distance. Near the church there were public buildings: schools, the house of village gatherings, the library.[4]

The above *N66* excerpt was originally published in Pitirim Sorokin's autobiographical memoirs under the title *A Long Journey*. In this book, Sorokin (1889-1968), a well-known Russian-American sociologist, writes about his childhood in the Komi village of Turja by recalling the memory traces of the physical and symbolic landscape of his initial home region. Turja is the embryonic place he is part of and it is the place he carried with him across the Atlantic. Dmitri Nesanelis and Victor Semjonov, researchers from the University of Syktyvkar in Komi, base their article in *N66* (no. 10) on Sorokin's memories, and explicate further the symbolic dimension of dwelling in Komi. For them, both the traditional villages and houses presented an organized microcosmos. They were thus social places of symbolic signs and arrangements that reflected the shared worldview. The symbolic order was an expression of laws, customs and traditions, reproduced via generations.[5]

The interiors of Komi houses were encircled around the stove and the corner of icons as layers representing the family life and broader social relations. The symbolic organization of the houses, divided into different sections for members of the family, visiting relatives and strangers, became especially significant in such rituals as weddings and burials. These rituals were the most important events within the families, as they implied significant changes in the family structures as well as in the organization and use of the house interiors. The yard around the house correlated with the sacred extension: household buildings, saunas, wells, chapels, crosses and worshipped springs all together constituted both the practical and religious realm of daily life. The indoors and outdoors were concretely arranged as horizontal and vertical layers of family life and these layers also functioned as gates to the symbolic and sacral worlds. The larger neighborhood units were built along rivers and tracks as compact settlements connecting the past to the present. New buildings were designed with respect to the will of ancestors and their spirits because these still had a connection to their earthly home. The village topography became in this way the visual manifestation of the cosmic exchange between the present and the eternal, gradually landscaped into a spatial narration, or a collection of architectural forms as shared memories across the generations.[6]

Lauri Anttila, a Finnish architect and artist, describes in *N66* (no.10) in a parallel manner the lifestyle and traditions of the nomadic Innu people in Labrador, Canada. The traditional Innu tent is a product of the land and life in the North; it is, according to Anttila, a "summary" of inherited customs and knowledge of surviving within the conditions of the extreme North. Anttila notes that the variation in the steepness of the coneshaped tent is connected to the latitude. The more northern tents are lower and less steep, giving better heating economy to the building. The nomadic Innu lifestyle is an expression of dwelling in which "the whole landscape and nature is their living room, and that their life view is holistic—the people and the nature are one."[7]

The layered interpretation of dwelling comes close to humanistic geographies of the lived and perceived worlds. Pauli Tapani Karjalainen, a geographer from Oulu, northern Finland, reads Bo Carpelan's *Urwind*, a diary, or a collection of weekly letters by Daniel Urwind to his wife (who has gone faraway from home) during one year, and finds three different ways of reading them. Mimetic reading aims at constructing a physical map of the letters, whereas hermeneutic reading sketches the contours of the person and his spatial extensions; the map of the mind constitutes of such metaphoric oppositions as internal and external, past and present, winter and summer as well as cellar and attic. Finally, textual reading focuses on the changing relations between the letters and the reader. The author, or subject, is replaced by a continuous re-creation by the reader. Here, the reader, or the geographer, is invited to return to a nomadic, mobile position.[8]

This type of orienteering and mapping, or circular return to the threshold between the familiar and the unfamiliar, are part of the nomadism between such modern polarities as awakening and fall, creation and erosion, dawn and edge, known and unknown. Inger Birkeland, a Norwegian geographer, finds the same rhythmicity and in-betweennes in the particular context of Northern traveling. Her heterogeneous subject, constituted by semiotic and symbolic dispositions, travels from home—that is, from *khōra*—to the outer boundaries of the subject and society. *Khōra* is the beginning, the initial home, reached by spatial intuition and semiotic elements, and it comes before the entry to the symbolic world. According to her, "for a woman traveler the journey starts with a departure from home with the separation from the mother, to the discovery of the father, associated with language, the Phallus and the symbolic world."[9]

Birkeland also argues that it is possible to see the journey from home to the North as a discovery of the mythical projections. The unfamiliar is made familiar by repeating the creation myths of the home land by the rituals awakening the consciousness of the new land. The northern mythology, beyond the patriarchal monoteism of Judeo-Christian religion, is according to Birkeland an expression of polytheism that took gradually shape during the risky habitation of the North, as part of the struggles against darkness, coldness and winter. The Northern sun stands at the center of this eternal struggle between light and dark. The sun is associated with fertility, creation, and healing. From here rises the magnetic experience of the midnight sun. This deviates from the pre-Christian sun of the peoples from the more Southern latitudes, often taking the shape of an authoritarian eye of the universe, holding the powers of superior will.[10]

The cosmology of the Komi villages, the traditional tents of the Innu people, the intimate layers of *Urwind* as well as the poetic nomadism of *khōra* invite us to look at the layered co-existence of lands and lives of the North. Instead of fixed positions and panoptical perspectives, the heterogeneous subject finds difference in archaic repetition and continuity in variation. The actual co-existence of layered and shared spheres of the Arctic questions the horizontal and vertical fixations (e.g. in geopolitical thinking), and it also aims at deepening the understanding of indigenous nativity as an integral part of the Arctic. It asks us to critically reflect upon the various scientific ecologies offered from the South as guarantees of sustainability in Northern development programs.

A Gate to Other Side: Pendulum

"The theme of swinging in a traditional world view can be considered as one of the methods of overcoming fatal indefinition and unpredictability", argue V.E. Shaparov and D.A. Nesanelis in *N66* (no. 2). The researchers (from the University of Syktyvkar) summarize that the act of swinging in the Northern folk cultures and shamanism can be interpreted in several ways. It is seen as the symbol of cyclical time, or a central element in a ritual of purification. Swinging has also been connected to agricultural cults and even to symbolic banishment of evil forces. It has been one of the forms of traditional amusement and, undoubtedly, an imitation of a sexual act.[11]

Shaparov and Nesanelis have examined the role of swinging in wedding and funeral rituals among the Komi people and found parallels to their traditions of Easter swing. The construction of the Easter swing—originally stretched between two living trees—correlates with the image of gates and, consequently, the act of swinging becomes a symbolic crossing of the border between two worlds. The archaic ceremonial acts of swinging in the wedding games or by coffin swaying in funeral procession were often linked to rituals of creation, birth and rebirth, or to deny final death. The pendulum, rooted to shared rhythmicity and repetition, functioned as the gate to layered timescapes, a connection between self and other, here and there, motion and emotion.

The sensitivity to the layered presence of humanity and nature or past and present is part of the respect to the forces that work beyond the reach of our senses. It also grows from scepticism toward geoscientific constructions solely based on measured entities. For example, we can ask: How "real" are the archaic beliefs—perhaps still remarkably conditioning our ways of thinking and being—in comparison with those explanations and arguments about ourselves that have become established through exact testing and professional dispute? Evidently, no proof exists that the geoscientific view currently accepted as the firm ground of mainstream geographical thinking—the shared *khōra* of geoscience—would not one day become uncovered as one more cultural narration rooted to belief systems we do not fully recognize yet. Therefore, in order to save us from such disappointments, we (geographers) could develop our sensitivity toward the layered presence of the human world, characterized by a complete rhythmicity of earthly lands and lives. We could in this way also get closer to understanding the immanent forces of humanity and nature. By learning to listen to the rhythms beyond the individual self and behind exclusive hereness, we might also learn to respect the variations of earthly rhythms in the different timescapes in which we are inevitably enveloped.

The geographies of co-existence link our corporeal rhythms—nature closest within—into broader socioenvironmental timescapes. In the North, daily routines are shaped by dramatic seasonal variations, which in turn are dependent on the geohistories of climatic change. Post Ice Age drama of the millenniums is today challenged by the human-influenced athmospheric warming that has a direct impact for example on the annual extension and variation of snowscapes. The advent of snow cover, the dawn of the snowlight, is awaited and debated every fall in the North, *Aurora Borealis* decorates the clear-dark winter skies beyond the city lights and the return of the sun above the horizon marks the opening of spring. Tensions between the traditions and modern innovations characterize for example city planning. The Southern model of winter cities guides toward indoor spaces and thus aims at freeing the humanity from the seasonal rhythmicity, whereas the traditional Northern model is based on the adaptation and utilization of seasonal variation, exemplified in architecture, transportation and individual clothing.[12]

N66 (no. 10) amusingly introduced kick sleds as part of the winter cities development, debated in winter conferences in Luleå and Kiruna in spring 2000. The journal reported that in Jukkasjärvi, northern Sweden, kick sleds had partially replaced local busses, and are provided to the citizens for free. The journal thereafter describes how the kick-sled reduces the ground friction to a minimum. The kick-sled rider is pictured in good contact with the soil while hovering over it: "The short thrust with one leg—the concentrated and firm contact with the ground—is then rewarded with a long period of relaxation, a lustful cancellation of the inevitable inertia of the natural forces."[13] This interpretation is an excellent example of the layered geography of winter.

Alternative Mappings

> It can happen, suddenly, unexpectedly, and most frequently in the half-light-of-glimpses, that we catch sight of another visible order which intersects with ours and has nothing to do with it. Our customary visible order is not the only one: it coexists with the other orders. Stories of fairies, sprites, ogres were a human attempt to come to terms with this co-existence.[14]

The pages of *N66* can be read as an introduction to alternative ways of mapping. The insert above is a good example of the epistemic leaps from one system of mapping to another debated in *N66*. The journal referred often to hunters who are continually aware of the parallel maps and so can read signs most people cannot. Children are also mentioned in this connection to feel several "levels" of signs intuitively. Animals, with their sharp senses and specific memory systems, are also presented as natural frontier experts between various world orders.

N66 speaks also about experiences, both positive and negative, in applying the tools of topographic cartography in northern mapping and orienteering. Examples of logistic and thematic maps were regularly published in *N66* and, even, satellite images from the Esrange Space Center, Kiruna. A special collection of maps of the Barents region "from above"—*Barents från ovan*—was published in *N66* (no. 7). The narration starts by Abraham Ortelius' map on Biarmia from 1570, illustrated by a sea monster in the Arctic Sea, and continues through decenniums up to the currently ongoing digitalization of a common geographical database to be monitored online on the internet. An article on ethnic mapping by Hans Ragnar Mathisen, an artist from Tromsdalen, northern Norway was also included. Mathisen has used Sámi names in his cartographical and cosmological artworks.[15]

Mathisen stated in *N66* (no. 4) that using maps as we know them is not common among the Sámi but, instead, the maps became concrete in their language and common memory: "The topographic names of the Sámi are very detailed, and give a lot of specific information about a place and its qualities—height, vegetation, landscape forms etc."[16] He also underlines that Sámi shamans could construct maps of both their spiritual and real worlds, and these were imprinted on their sacred drums. Drawing these maps is for Mathisen a way of showing the invisible history and culture of the Sámi.

The cartography of the North has in academic geographical practices always been loaded with the tension of mapping-as-expansive-controlling versus mapping-as-mutual-learning. Väinö Tanner (1881–1948), one of the first cultural geographers from Finland with an interest in Sámi cultures, experienced this tension while leading the field research of the Commissions of Reindeer Herding—*Renbeteskommissioner*, 1910–1917—and, later, in his geological surveys in Petsamo during 1924–1931. Tanner repeatedly extended the official geo-surveys of the North to cover the indigenous Scolt Lapps and their ways of living, even though this was criticized in the Annual Reports of the Geological Commission. It also caused trouble for Tanner when his scientific merits were evaluated for higher academic posts. Tanner, however, argued that the cartographers should not focus their interest solely on the physical terrain but, with a similar enthusiasm, on the indigenous place names and their symbolic and aesthetic meanings. Tanner received a chair in geography at the University of Helsinki in

1931, but with merits other than his "philological-sociological" interest in the Scolt Lapps, which was then weighed as non-geographical.[17]

This philological-sociological dimension is still on open and painful question in geography. Practical mapping of the Barents Region "from above" has become easy with the help of satellites and GIS technology, but the invisible landscapes of the North, only comprehensible "from inside," have been mostly left outside the mainstream studies, or they have received only limited theoretical concern. The geographical approach cannot possibly be expanded to reach all the spheres of humanity and nature of the North, but the task to deepen geographical understanding could be most easily started by critically reflecting upon the academic ignorance in the face of the apparent cultural domination and bias caused by the expansive mapping technologies. We again face a variation of the same root question, initially formulated in the introduction of this volume: How to became aware of and free ourselves from the (post)colonial manners inherently hidden in the practices and narrations of institutional geography? Given the disciplinary past, it is demanding to learn to respect the various modes of mapping we humans have constructed in different times and places. During the five years it was published, *N66* sketched several alternative solutions to these academic dilemmas.

Wounds on the Edge

"[We] have been screaming for ten years: in front of the Arctic Sea, at the Finnish president's reception, at the opening of the Olympic Games, outside the Eremitage in S:t Petersburg," recalled Petri Sirviö, the conductor of the *Huutajat* from Oulu, and mentioned the impromptu performance at the Arctic Ocean as one the highlights of their tours.[18] The concert without an audience aroused strong emotions among the choir: Thirty rather young men, dressed in formal, dark suites with rubber ties, filling their lungs with fresh air, then letting it out with tremendous force and screaming hard traditional folklore, worker songs, children's songs and new experimental compositions.

The scene painted in front of our eyes by *N66*—a choir of formally dressed men facing the vast polar sea masses, screaming the lores of the North—is loaded with paradoxical drama: humanity against and within nature. Strange performers standing proudly at the edge, clearly not belonging there and, therefore, separate from the harsh surroundings but, simultaneously, becoming one with the forces of the North. Extreme human voices drowning in the emptiness. "The Arctic is most likely silence. Why should we violate the prohibition and talk about it?," asked Ilya Kabakov,[19] an artist from Dnepropterovsk in Russia, and formulated the same paradoxical remark about the multilayered co-existence of humanity and nature, felt so concretely and thoroughly at the edge. Words are (only) derivations from the already known; in emptiness, shouting turns to whisper.

"It is precisely in the North that the continents are anchored to the space of the boundless white ice, where everything ceases in the face of total absence, lifeless emptiness, White Nothingness. It is precisely in the North that the Earth touches the Sky", formulate the artists Sergei Bukaev, Viktor Samokhvalov, Vladimir Kulikov and Sergei Anufriev,[20] and join the *Huutajat* choir. The North emerges here as a gate to the other world, a "place of power," and grows into a condition for our natural-cultural heritage, a framework to our earthly existence and identification. It becomes a zone beyond human reach and a source of renewal. It functions as a source of inspiration, the focal point of circular re-creation and continuous return—at least till the day it has lost all its secrecy in our minds. Until it has become thoroughly mapped and tamed and thus made a finite entity: the end of the earth.

In the Nenets tongue, according to Bruce Forbes, an arctic researcher from Rovaniemi, northern Finland, Yamal translates roughly as the end of the earth and it is an apt description. "The Yamal Peninsula juts out several hundred kilometers into the Kara Sea just east of Novaya Zemlya and is underlain by frozen ground, or permafrost, at depths which range up to 300 meters in places," described Bruce Forbes in *N66* (no. 3).[21] The same article showed how the homeland of the Yamal Nenets is undergoing a large-scale industrial development phase due to its newly found oil and gas resources. According to Forbes, slightly over half of the 9000 indigenous people of the Yamalskii Raion still lead a nomadic or semi-nomadic lifestyle under the control of three large state farms (sovkhozes). In Yamal, the era of petroleum and gas explorations started in the late 1970s and it has already—before the actual oil and gas production—completely transformed the lands and lives of the Nenets people. Drill pads, road and railway constructions, geological surveys, off-road vehicle traffic and quarrying for gravel and sand have turned into euthrophication of waterways, sand and dust blows, and they have changed the land-use patterns of reindeer herders.[22]

Not all Nenets have, according to Forbes, condemned the industrial development. It has brought along modern alternatives to traditional modes of living, e.g. paid work, schools, health care, and faster transportation. The circles of life have enlarged. The life is, however, at the edge again: How will the extreme North—already markedly modified by nomadic life modes and overgrazing by reindeer sovkhozes—react to the expansive industrial activities? Could it still in the future be regarded as a source of cultural renewal? Forbes himself concluded that any future changes should be made according to the choices of the people themselves, for whom their culture is at stake, and not imposed by remote government bureaucracies, petroleum companies, or well-wishing scientists.[23]

Both the traditional and modern communities of the North face the same condition: the challenge of circumpolar nature. The North is full of contrasts. It is characterized by unexpected changes, but within the variation already known, including spasmodic bursts from within periods of calm and radical difference in complete indifference. Everything can change rapidly, for example with the sudden rise of the Northwind and, just as quickly, return to the calm. According to Pavel Limerov, an ethnologist from the University of Syktyvkar in Komi, the wind (from the North) exists in the backround of the "mythological topography" of the Komi, determining the land of the dead to be situated in the North. The Northwind was traditionally considered as punishment for the violation of some prohibitions, emerging from the "next world." It could freeze crops and bring disease, corresponding to the transition from the realm of life into the world of death. The Northwind is the movement of the souls of the cursed and missing people; it carries the forces of abduction and it contaminates the lands and lives of the people by drawing them into the next world, permanently or temporarily.[24]

The peoples of the North have undoubtedly learned the intensive here-and-thereness of the environing nature; the painful memory of the events and accidents when some of us have been overtaken by the Northwind is shared. When in pain you could only cry northward. This sense of belonging is easily turned into a kind of fatalism, or submissive surrendering under the pressure "from above." Life has become tenable by carefully listening to the signs of sudden change. You needed to know the breaks in weather beforehand. During storms, you had to learn to wait. Traditionally, the North was something to listen to, adapt to and shelter oneself from. The minds of the newcomers from the modern South were, however, often too impatient to learn to listen and wait. The modern North was primarily defined by Southerners as the storehouse of valuable resources and there was no apparent need to develop sensitivity toward the more layered North. The South had developed the worldview, and a self-legitimacy, where the indigenous North was understood as the primitive other to be civilized. It was the white zone on the map, to be found and named according to Southern standards. The Northerners knew already how to adapt, now under the pressure from the South. They were prepared for an external invasion.

This is the same process that Kirsten Hastrup, professor of anthropology at the University of Copenhagen, has described as the emergence of *Uchronia*, a nowhere-land. The two histories of Iceland meet where the measured time of modernity overcomes the orally transmitted *Sagas* out of time; where the linear crashes with the eternally returning; where the modern timescapes slice the layered memories of local communities. Hastrup writes about the North where the past that was familiar and always present becomes strange even to the Northerners themselves. She formulates the process of internal alienation initiated "from outside," which gradually replaces the mnemonic past which used to keep the generations in touch with one another. From here emerges the modern Other—

the Other that now refers to the denied self: the externalization of the Icelandic *Sagas*.[25]

The North is the modern Other that has replaced—Othered—the indigenous lived worlds in Iceland, in Biarmia, in Sápmi and Komi as well as in the Nenets' Yamal. It is easy to conclude on the basis of these historical interpretations that there never was one indigenous North up there. The North is there only from a certain perspective, that is: from the South. The North disappears when seen from inside, from here. Accordingly, as Markku Heikkilä remarks in the introductory book to a photograph exhibition *Pohjoinen valokuva* (Northern Photograph) in Oulu, "Pure geography disappears and turns into a relational one when we return into the mental world. The North becomes dependent on the mindscapes of the individuals and communities of which they are part."[26] This dimension of the North, which is "independent of the laws of gravitation," as Nikolaj Terebikhin put it in *N66* (no 1),[27] summarizes well the geoscientific dilemma; the apparent ignorance of the layered existence of human lands and lives. The North is different, and this difference is invisible from outside. It seems that we can only learn to sense it by respecting the difference and in this way gradually perhaps abandon the whole concept of the North by using the more detailed and intimate georeferences shared by the Northern communities.

It becomes evident from the pages of *N66* that the sensitivity to the difference can only be approached by turning to myths, beliefs and metaphoric vocabularies attached to the lay communities of the lived North. There seems to be no other way to restrain the dramatic Othering of individual and collective selves. This forces us to relocate ourselves, as geographers of the lands and lives of the North, to a new position toward the "processes" we are studying. Then we might find ourselves completely embedded in the networks we have initially identified as our research fields. The North speaks through us and we speak through the North. The communities of the North become one with the geographies of the lived North.

This transformation from modern geoscience to multilayered geographies seems, paradoxically again, inevitable—and unlikely, which is due to geography's indelible embeddedness in the early colonial modernization, where science was originally defined as the tool for de-mythicizing the false beliefs of humanity. On the other hand, along the rising postcolonial awareness, the modern scientific conceptualization of the arctic North "as the laboratory to collect empirical material or to test theories"[28] will certainly face increasing criticism from the communities under "testing"—and from the side of humanities in general.

From Geoscience to Geographies

As was witnessed, *N66* reflected and further developed a wide variety of alternative Northviews that have parallels to the ongoing renewal of academic geographies. Both discourses are profoundly linked to the streams of broader society and reflect upon the same trends and circumstances. They cannot avoid overlapping. *N66*, however, developed a multicultural profile and it also mirrored a broader cultural reorientation that cannot be ignored by the academic geographers of the North. On the contrary, *N66* can be seen as a place of learning and, even, a moment of unlearning the (post)colonial maneuvers of geography. The following themes introduced by *N66* can be read as signals of the need for geographical updating.

First, the layered existence of the North questions the self-satisfaction of the cultural geographers attracted by postmodern or "transhuman" approaches. The North of *N66* is a land and lifescape that vary within numerous historical scales: archaic, traditional and modern timescapes emerge side by side. The time-dimensions are not understood as chronological periods but as co-existing layers of our local-global world. The archaic dimension is well illustrated by *N66* and, apparently, no corresponding elaboration can yet be found within the current academic geographies. Some important views on psychohistorical geographies have been sketched (see chapter 3) but not in the context of the extreme North.[29]

Second, the North of *N66* is indeed a strange combination of marginality and centrality. The extreme edge magically turns into a source of regeneration: the barren lands appear rich in narrations and beliefs. The marginal places and zones of the North have attracted geographers and colleagues in the relating disciplines from the "beginning"—as the white areas on the map to be found, named and developed. Only a few works can be found emphasizing the immanent being of the marginal(ized) North, for example in the spirit of Väinö Tanner during his field work among the Scolt Lapps. The geographical landscape has become repeatedly established by an authoritarian and universalizing eye cast from the South and "from above." The sociospatial fixations built on the exclusive strive for correspondence between the physically real and its representation are thoroughly criticized within today's geographies but the practical interconnection between the lived "reals" and their intersubjective variations are broadly ignored. The North could be a perfect subject of studies that focus on the renewal of cultural belonging through societal and psychohistorical practices in the everyday.

Third, the culture of mutual learning is starkly present in *N66*. In comparison, the academic geographical practices are still dominantly based on abstractions constructed according to scientific motives and this tends to distance the phenomena studied from their socioenvironmental contexts. The focusing on scientifically identified slices of humanity or nature decisively limits the options for reciprocal learning. The identification and representation of these "geographical islands" only confirm the continuation of (post)colonial domination from the South. The study objects are defined as laboratories of land and life, or "interesting cases" of theory testing. The question here is whether there will be imagined a study praxis that is free enough from the academic dependencies (derived e.g. from paradigmatic constraints, intertextual nihilism, meritocratic contestation and rules of publishing) so that it will settle down in a setting where the messages from inside the study focus can gain value of their own. This kind of immanency would naturally confuse the relations between the study subjects and objects.

Fourth, the North of *N66* took a shape of lived communities embedded in their local-global life worlds. Traditional villages and modern centers of settlement met the network communities of artists and researchers. The journal supported the formation of local-global communities but it also carefully listened to the traditional local voices and even developed new network relations on the experience of the local communities. The locals were central actors and innovative members of the networking, respected as experts of their own land and lifescapes. On the contrary, academic geography seems to follow a more individualistic and transhuman orientations by enthusiastically elaborating theories of fluid spaces built upon translocal or nonlocal lived worlds, becoming perhaps true only in the great sprawling cities of the South.[30]

Fifth, geographers of the North no longer can exclude or purify themselves from the symbolic and geopolitical contestation between the regimes of the North. *N66* is part of the redefinition of the North from the South, as are geographers, with their varying southern dependencies. Both the North and the geographers of the North face the same pressure of submissive adjustment under the current ideological discourse on globalization. *N66* was, however, developed into a multilingual forum sensitive to the multitude of the Barents Region. This format can be seen as an alternative to the trends of lingual homogenization in today's local-global world. Multilingualism was a starting point for the journal and it became a tool for arguing against provincial divisions of labor. Multilingualism could and perhaps should similarly be taken as the guideline to geographers working with sosioenvironmental variations in humanity and nature.

Finally, *N66* was able to articulate the stratified character of the North in a manner which is rare among geographers. The communities and people of the North were represented with respect, and much room was devoted to socioenvironmental differences. This type of sensitivity to difference celebrates the emotional dimensions of community-building, which are incomprehensible from any universalizing points of view. The universal truths even seem to turn into strange and marginal endeavors when conceived from within a context of a particular local-global community. The layered North of *N66* thus invites geographers to reflect upon the "science myths" in which geography as an academic discipline has been immersed.

Notes

1. Nikolaj M. Terebikhin, "Bjarmaland. Spiritual Culture in the Barents Region," *N66. Culture in the Barents Region*, no. 1 (1997), 21.
2. Kenneth Mikko, "Dear Reader!," *N66. Culture in the Barents Region*, no. 1 (1987), 2.
3. Tim Ingold, *The Scolt Lapps Today*, (Cambridge: Cambridge University Press, 1976); Ari Aukusti Lehtinen, Kalottipolitiikka ja saamelainen regionalismi," *Terra* 99, no. 1 (1987), 13-18.
4. Dmitri Nesanelis and Victor Semjonov, "The Village Universe," *N66. Culture in the Barents Region*, no. 10 (1999), 15.
5. Dmitri Nesanelis and Victor Semjonov, "The Village Universe," 14-16.
6. Dmitri Nesanelis and Victor Semjonov, "The Village Universe."
7. Lauri Anttila, "Tents and Fireplaces in Labrador," *N66. Culture in the Barents Region*, no. 8 (1999), 8-9.
8. Pauli Tapani Karjalainen, "Elämä tässä talossa: lähikartoitusta kirjallisuuden kautta," *Alue ja Ympäristö* 24, no. 2 (1995), 15-24. Bo Carpelan, born in 1926 in Helsinki, is one of the most translated of Finnish writers and widely known in the Nordic countries and in Continental Europe.
9. Inger Birkeland, "The Mytho-Poetic in Northern Travel," in *Leisure/Tourism Geographies*, ed. David Crouch (London: Routledge, 1999), 26.
10. Birkeland, "Mytho-Poetic in Northern Travel," 28-30.
11. V.E. Sharapov and D.A. Nesanelis, "The theme of Swinging in Shamanism and Folk Culture," *N66. Culture in the Barents Region*, no. 2 (1997), 2.
12. Jorma Mänty and Neil Pressman, eds., *Cities Designed for Winter* (Tampere: Tampere University of Technology, 1988); Jaana Nevalainen, "Ikuisesta kesästä talvikaupunkiin—vuodenajat suomalaisessa kaupunkiympäristössä," *Alue ja Ympäristö* 24, no. 2 (1995), 6-14.
13 Kenneth Mikko, "Just Kicking Around," *N66. Culture in the Barents Region*, no. 10 (2000), 4.
14. John Berger, "It can happen," *N66. Culture in the Barents Region*, no. 1 (1997), 28.
15. Kenneth Mikko, "Hans Ragnar Mathisen. Samernas kartograf," *N66. Culture in the Barents Region*, no. 4 (1998), 2-4.
16. Mikko, "Hans Ragnar Mathisen. Samernas kartograf," 4.
17. Väinö Tanner, "Petsamon alueen paikannimiä. I. Lappalaisia paikannimiä," *Fennia* 49, no. 2:1 (1929), 1-36; Väinö Tanner, "Antropogeografiska studier inom Petsamo-området. I. Skolt-lapparna," *Fennia* 49, no. 4:1 (1929), 1-518; Paulo Susiluoto, "Suomen ajan ihmismaantiedettä Petsamosta," in *Väinö Tanner. Ihmismaantieteellisiä tutkimuksia Petsamon seudulta I. Kolttalappalaiset*, ed. Paulo Susiluoto (Helsinki: Suomalaisen Kirjallisuuden Seura, 2000), 9-31.
18. Kenneth Mikko, "Screaming all over the World," *N66. Culture in the Barents Region*, no. 4 (1998), 6-7.
19. Ilya Kabakov, "Questions," in *Strangers in the Arctic. 'Ulthima Thule' and Modernity*, ed. Marketta Seppälä (Pori: Pori Art Museum, 1996), 152.
20. Sergei Bukaev, Viktor Samokhvalov, Vladimir Kulikov and Sergei Anufriev, "Vorkuta," In *Strangers in the Arctic. 'Ulthima Thule' and Modernity*, ed. Marketta Seppälä (Pori: Pori Art Museum, 1996), 125.

21. Bruce Forbes, "Wounds on the Tundra," *N66. Culture in the Barents Region*, no. 3 (1997), 16.
22. Forbes, "Wounds on the Tundra," 18.
23. Forbes, "Wounds on the Tundra," 18.
24. Pavel Limerov, "When the Northern Wind Begins to Blow," *N66. Culture in the Barents Region*, no. 4 (1998), 20.
25. Kirsten Hastrup, "Uchronia and the Two Histories of Iceland," in *Strangers in the Arctic. 'Ulthima Thule' and Modernity*, ed. Marketta Seppälä (Pori: Pori Art Museum, 1996), 36-49.
26. Arja Maunuksela, "Kuvia pohjoisesta identiteetistä," *Helsingin Sanomat,* 3 August 2000, B8. A review on a photography exhibition *Pohjoinen valokuva—identiteettien dokumentti* in Oulu, summer 2000, including an introductory book by Jukka Järvinen, Arja-Liisa Räisänen, Pirkko Siitari and Jussi Vilkuna, eds., *Pohjoinen valokuva—dokumenttivalokuvaus Pohjois-Suomessa* (Oulu: Pohjoinen valukuvakeskus and Kustannus-Puntsi, 2000). Translated from Finnish by the author.
27. Terebikhin, "Bjarmaland," 21.
28. Lassi Heininen, *Euroopan pohjoinen 1990-luvulla* (Rovaniemi: Lapin yliopisto, Arctic Centre Reports, no. 30, 1999), 25; see also Lassi Heininen, "The International Situation and Cooperation in Change," in *The Snowbelt*, ed. Leo Granberg (Helsinki, Kikimora Publications, 1998), 25.
29. The only psychogeographical excursion toward the Arctic as far as I am aware of is Birkeland, "Mytho-Poetic in Northern Travel." The article is based on her Doctoral thesis: Inger Birkeland, *Stories from the North. Travel as Place-Making in the Context of Modern Holiday-Travel to North Cape, Norway* (Oslo: University of Oslo, Department of Sociology and Human Geography, Rapport 2, 2002).
30. The term fluid spaces is derived here from a Los Angeles geographer Edward W. Soja, *"Thirdspaces. Journeys to Los Angeles and Other Real-and-Imagined Places* (Oxford: Blackwell, 1996), which is an inspiring and influential example of the geographical *avant-garde* concentrating on the multilayered scenes of the postmodern city. Soja "re-opens the voyages of discovery" (p. 12) inside and outside the "postmetropolises" (p. 23) and developes a personal urban vocabulary of fluid cities under such signs as "flexcities," "cosmopolises," "exopolises" and "simcities." On the other hand, by individualistic orientations in geography I refer, for example, to Steven Flusty's programmatic elaboration of the globe "from inside out." Flusty, a geographer from Los Angeles and Toronto, has developed individual geographies of globalization where multiple perspectives and cultural expressions constantly interact, influence, inform and contend one another. The approach seems to systematically ignore the main economic and political actors conditioning the life worlds of marginal people and communities in different corners of the world. See Steven Flusty, *De-Coca-Colonization. Making the Globe from Inside Out* (London: Routledge, 2004). See discussion about Flusty's book: Ari Aukusti Lehtinen, "Kohti monimuotoista ja minäkeskeistä globalisaatiota, *Terra* 116, no. 2 (2004), 116-17.

Part III. Conclusions

14.

Respecting the Difference: Geographies of the Multitude

The introduction of this volume sketched a particular Nordic interpretation of human geography, focusing on the hybrid configuration of both societal vs. cultural and natural vs. human-influenced changes in Northern European land and lifescapes. The Nordic approach was seen as critically responding to and further developing the Anglo-American and Continental European debates on socioenvironmental discrimination and empowerment. It was also emphasized that Nordic geographers have developed an array of research orientations for studying the specific local-global questions of the European North and taken an ethically active role in formulating the "northern dimension" in Europe and globally, for example in North-South dialogues.[1]

The Nordic formulation of human geography guided us (i) to critically reflect upon the practical societal distribution of the "goods and bads" or pros and cons of socioenvironmental development and governance. It became also evident that this type of research demands certain sensitivity (ii) to recognize cultural and community-bound variations in the development of the sense of justice. Furthermore, the task to learn (iii) to identify the historical and layered constitution of socioenvironmental ethics, stretched in myriads of ways within the local-global axes, arose as a central issue.

In the light of the historical lessons explicated in the case studies, it seems almost impossible to imagine any community, local, (inter)national or global, that could benefit in the long run from systematically ignoring or silencing some of its members. It is therefore important to reflect upon how familiar we are with the daily measures along which we renew the memberships of our communities and confirm the division between us and them, and how we extend the ethical thinking beyond those we recognize as nearest to us. The Western past provides evidence of a gradual, if painful and contested, spreading of ethical circles—originating from the free men at the agoras of the Greek poleis up to the activists of the Animal Liberation Front—and it also reveals the fate of the totalitarian and univalent regimes as unfortunate and appalling sidesteps of humanity.

The case studies of this volume provided evidence of an East-West dialogue where the Nordic (Scandinavian) practices of participation and welfare distribution meet the Russian techniques of patrimonial governance. The Greenbelt communities took the shape of an anomaly between the two regimes, carrying signs from both models. The Nordic approaches in human geography offered a framework wherein to compare the Finnish and Northwest Russian recipes in coping with socioenvironmental matters. The comparative setting helped in recognizing the weaknesses of governance among the Finnish and Russian actors. The lack of respect toward the land and lifescapes of the past was noticeable in the border communities. Wooden towns and old-growth forests have mostly disappeared on the Finnish side of the border and a similar trend, if not so a thoroughgoing, could be documented in Russia. The political space of the multitude was also strikingly limited in the Greenbelt communities. The tension between the demands of accountability on the one hand and the practices that favor authoritarian and single-minded solutions on the other hand was witnessed in several case studies, especially in North Karelia, Viena, Pjaozersk and Kuusamo.

The case studies also showed that the direct application of the Nordic "model" to the Belt conditions causes serious problems. It became clear that any measures for promoting favorable development of the Belt communities need to be applied to the particular local-global conditions varying case by case. The history of the border is present in the way the indigenous and immigrant communities react to initiatives from "the outside," and this has to be respected in development projects. The local histories are signposted by memories from the periods of imperial aggression both from the East and the West (see Fig. 3.2), but the case studies confirmed that northern colonialism is not merely something that characterizes the past. No clear break between the colonial past and (post)colonial present could be identified. The practices of domination were seen as becoming more indirect and nuanced in time, emerging primarily in the form of discursive pressure that stresses the necessities of international competitiveness and export trade. The most telling examples of imperial domination were, however, documented in interlingual relations: landscapes and *landskaps* emerged as tools of homogenization in the Barents context, and similar processes could be identified in wilderness and *erämaa* politics in Upper Lapland. Ethnic Karelians and their languages were also documented to have become marginalized in their own lands due to the geopolitical confirmation of the state borders.

The Greenbelt cases provided insights to the practices of the communities and networks that have ambitions in developing the conditions of the Finnish-Russian border zone. The views of the backwoods traditionalists, cultural minorities, industrial modernizers and wilderness conservationists were interpreted as part of the overall envisioning of the local-global change. The local studies engendered two general socioenvironmental conclusions that seem to characterize more generally the relations between indigenous and imported innovations. The first underlines the worth of the traditional values that guided in minimizing the human impact on the natural realm and avoided large-scale transformation of the physical environment. The second concerns the fate of minor lingual groups, including their socioenvironmental knowledge, under the pressure of global-local homogenization.

The indigenous northerners developed their nomadic cultures by minimizing the physical changes in the surrounding nature. This was difficult due to the harsh and vulnerable environment. For example, wild reindeer largely disappeared in the 19th century as a result of over-exploitive hunting methods and the need for firewood often caused local disappearance of forest cover.[2] The principle of minimal impact was understood as the only means of surviving in the long run in the extreme North. The newcomers, such as Finns, later developed a model of environmental expansion and enlarging control (chapter 4). The indigenous ideal was the initial version of sustainability thinking but it could not be defended against the land demands of the immigrants. Without permanent landmarks and structures, it was difficult for the nomadic groups to prove their ownership to the land they had utilized for centuries. The settlers established farms, and thus through occupancy acquired land ownership.

The principle of minimal impact has eroded in modernization and resulted in compromises with lack of respect toward the past land and lifescapes. The tension between the indigenous sustainability thinking and the imported concern on deepening resource control has, however, remained both in cosmological matters (chapter 13) and in land-use conflicts. The early "model" saw humans in a minor role in the North, whereas the latecomers aimed at strengthening the signs of human governance. The motive of taming the land turned into massive ecological transformation of forests and peatlands, and the frontier of modernization culminated in urban concentrations, such as Murmansk at the Arctic Sea coast with its 300,000 inhabitants.

The new era brought monuments of progress to the North to exist side by side with the earlier monuments of sacred stones, mountains, waters, islands and forests. The new era also introduced wilderness parks and outdoor recreation centers as monuments of nature conservation. The entire Greenbelt can also be regarded as a huge natural-cultural monument developed by those who look for historically impressive solutions. Greenbelt planning has taken place through a dialogue between industrial developers and conservationists, and this setting is in opposition to the indigenous sustainability thinking, based on the coexistence of nature-culture without human traces of governance.

From the viewpoint of the Finno-Ugric minorities of the North (see Fig. 3.1), the Greenbelt concern for ecological corridors and biodiversity centers shows serious ignorance of the living conditions on the fringes of Northern Europe. Biodiversity programs appear for the small and scattered ethnic groups as one-sided means for promoting sustainability. They also carry traces of environmental discrimination, and racism, when excluding the socioenvironmental values of the ethnic multitude of the North. The minority languages in Northern Europe are currently under a serious risk of becoming extinct, but this has not raised public attention to the extend that biodiversity concerns have.[3] From a socioenvironmental perspective, however, the lingual multitude is a guarantee for ecological multitude.

According to expert scenarios, up to 90 percent of all human languages on earth are at risk of disappearing during the present century.[4] This is a highly dramatic view, both ethnoculturally and socioenvironmentally, and it also threatens our future means of learning the wisdoms of traditional ecological knowledge. Most of the Finno-Ugric languages, including Livonian, Votic and four (of the total nine) Sámi languages, are doomed to disappear soon, as there are only a few elderly persons capable of speaking them today. The losses are not natural outcomes of development but results of the route we have chosen.

The Greenbelt—Case by Case

The routes of modernization have varied in Russia and the Nordic Countries, and the zone in between has grown into a historical mixture of the two regimes. The Nordic model became characterized by a division between state-owned and private lands, whereas the eastern model was forged by conditions of exclusive state ownership.

The popular family forestry on the Finnish side of the Greenbelt has secured a fragmented and varying forest landscape but the particular application of sustained-yield thinking resulted in the domination of homogeneous and species-poor stands. No wider areas of primeval forests have been left to secure the living conditions of old-growth species in Finland. The case studies of North Karelia and Kuusamo illustrated two views on private forestry. The attitudes of North Karelians (chapter 6) are proof of deep resentment toward any new initiatives for environmental regulation from the South. The confidence in the traditional knowledge of earning one's living in the North without destroying the resource basis is high and other forms of nature conservation are regarded unrealistic. The voice of private forest-owners in North Karelia is surprisingly high in matters concerning the conservation of the state forests, as the surrounding forests are in general regarded as part of the local usufruct. This attitude roots back to the old traditions of common access explicated in the introduction of this volume.

The study on Kuusamo (chapter 10) presented a particular type of activism of private forest-owners. The Kuusamo Forest Common, an enterprise with a diverse local shareholder representation, had become an effective vehicle to run the logging operations; only by intensive pressure applied by the environmental authorities could the last local remnants of primeval nature be left outside commercial loggings. The Forest Common was, however, quick to learn the new rules of green developmentalism and it could gain significant financial benefits from the Greenbelt enthusiasm. Some parts of the logging frontier turned into bricks of the Greenbelt, but the decades-long confrontation eroded the local trust in land (*maausko* in Finnish). Outmigration is currently high in Kuusamo, as it is throughout the Finnish side of the Greenbelt, and no feasible employment alternatives to industrial forestry have been developed.

Finnish state forestry was examined in the case study on the Sámi in Upper Lapland. This case illustrated the deep historical tension between the indigenous groups (the Northern Sámi, the Anár Sámi and the Scolt Lapps) and Finnish settlers, and it also revealed the incapability of the Finnish State Forest Service to cope with the Sámi question. The state authorities have learned to behave as the patrons of Upper Lapland and only slowly, with extensive local-global pressure, the state forestry practices have adopted measures that take the multicultural demands into consideration. The conflict between reindeer herding and state forestry has remained unsolved for decades, and the solution in this respect seems to need a signal from the globalizing forest industry. Stora Enso is the primary consumer of wood from Upper Lapland and, as was witnessed in chapters 9 and 12, the company has become increasingly involved in questions of socioenvironmental responsibility.

In Russia, on the other hand, the state ownership of lands and forests has led to complicated speculation on logging rights. This is also the case at the Greenbelt. The Russian model has furthermore resulted in a wide dispersion of logging income across the Federation's administration levels, diminishing the investment opportunities in local production capacity. In Viena (chapter 8), the oldest inhabitants of the villages still remember the days when private farming was the way to earn their living and the Soviet experiments of collectivization are painful memories for them. The tensions across generations were common, as were the tensions between the ethnic Karelians and the settlers from different parts of the Soviet Union. Ethnic and intergenerational disagreements were, however, swept under the patrimonial rule of the Soviet state. The post-Soviet era has not rendered much relief to the local communities that are still living on the edge of existence, suffering from historical discontinuities in agricultural production and from shortage of wood material—in the middle of deep backwoods.

The study on Pjaozersk (chapter 9) concentrated on the history of industrial logging in cooperation between the Finnish and Russian partners. The villages were founded only for the purpose of logging operations and, therefore, no deeper (ethno)historical concern was developed in the region. The forest conservationists were repeatedly referring to the short history of settlement in order to strengthen their ecological argument. For them, the long natural history of the primeval northwoods needs to be prioritized when comparing the ecological and cultural values of the region. A partial compromise was found in Pjaozersk, and an important factor behind the solution was the presence of Finnish forest companies. Stora Enso is there also, as in Upper Lapland, the single most important purchaser of wood and the company has to take care of its ranking in the international image markets.

Stora Enso connects in many ways several of the local case studies in this volume. The company is the leading forest-industrial actor in the Greenbelt and it is a concrete link between local efforts and the pressure of globalization. Chapters 7 and 12 described the diverging paths of Finnish and Russian forest industries but, when comparing them, the similarities of the two forest regimes become apparent. Stora Enso is thus not the only link between the two regimes. This is a conclusion worth highlighting here: despite the deep historical contrasts, the East and the West of the European North are growing closer and closer to each other. Northern Europe, extending from the Atlantic shores to the Ural Mountains, has in many respects become a single arena for local-global forest cooperation. This is in particular true in industrial operations and forest conservation.

Proof of such a conclusion can be found not only in intensified official and lay cooperation across the border but also in the changes in the structures of company ownership and in the performance of environmental organizations. Western investments in the forest industry in Northwest Russia have steadily grown both in the border locations and in the more faraway parts of the country. On the other hand, Greenpeace, Taiga Rescue Network and World Wildlife Fund have all spanned their activities across the forests of Northern Europe. For them, the question of old-growth forests connects and unifies the Eastern and Western sides of the European North. The Greenbelt is a symbolic and practical (geo)political element in this unification. The apparent wideness of the cultural and political gaps between the two regimes should thus not blind us to the fast co-development of certain sectors.

The still-ongoing Finnish debate of the "return of Karelia," or the parts of Karelia that were ceded to the Soviet Union after World War II, is in this view only maintaining the old geopolitical polarizations and ignoring the profound transformations that have taken place in the cross-border operations in economic and socioenvironmental spheres.

The more acute question for the people and forests of Northern Europe is bound to changes in global North-South cooperation in the forest industry. The biggest of the companies have already become active in Southeast Asia and South America and the leading managers underline today the options of fast-growing Eucalyptus and Acacia trees in Southern plantations. The forestry in Northern Europe has learned to live with the geophysical limits of the North, but the new setting forces an active search for alternatives to producing wood primarily for paper. The future of the pulp and paper plants in the North also much depends on the growth of pulp production in the South. This is of particular concern in the Nordic countries where the prices of wood and labor are high, but undoubtedly Russia will also face the tightening competition with the global South.

This being the case, the forest actors of the European North need to carefully examine the new signals in forest trade, emerging in the form of green developmentalism and new tourism entrepreneurship. The case studies of Kuusamo and North Karelia sketched the contours of a new era of immaterial trade, based on the idea of conducting business without altering the physical characteristics of forests. Old-growth forests are valued high in the urban centers of Western Europe and there is no reason to believe the concern is only limited to nature conservation. The old-growth forests of the North are tourist attractions and future targets for the urban Europeans searching for second homes in primeval nature. In addition, the various forms of indigenous and traditional knowledge of the Belt communities can be seen as an alternative to the polarized contest between industrial loggings and conservation. This alternative can become concrete for example by examining the pre-industrial modes of livelihood and revitalizing them with the help of the innovations of the telecommunication age (see chapter 13).

The limits of forest-industrial growth have been met in Finland in the form of lessening employment in forestry areas and mill communities. The forests on the Russian side of the border still contain several large areas of primeval forests, and the Finnish past should function there as a place of learning: by exporting raw material, without any serious measures of local refining, the frontiers will in a few decades turn into land and lifescapes lacking potential for new forms of economic or socioenvironmental development.

The emergence of the global South as a factor on the forest-industrial scene forces the Northern Europeans to rethink the physical and symbolic extensions of the Greenbelt. The more globally-oriented case studies of this volume (chapters 7 and 12) show that the impression of the Greenbelt as a narrow zone between Finland and Russia has become outdated. The Belt is, instead, thoroughly local-global today. It is reasonable to identify the Greenbelt as a network of socioenvironmental actors and factors co-linked by shared or colliding interests. The Belt extends from Pjaozersk and Upper Lapland to the Russian Far East and stretches its "fingers" to Southeast Asia and also to the Amazon basin. The Belt is a matter of negotiations among industrial developers and consumers, local and union activists, indigenous networks, landless groups and nature conservationists in different parts of the world. Changes in one part of the network have impacts on the other parts. Greenbelt geographies refer now to the lived spaces, territorial practices and network topologies of the communities sharing and dividing the limited forest resources, both local and global.

This conclusion is not, however, an objective deduction, or result, from the excursions into Nordic and Greenbelt geographies. It was developed by identifying and assessing those aspects of Nordic human geography that were seen as pertaining to similar questions that are central to this research (see the questions in chapter 1). The conclusion was also developed via personal and subjective interpretations of the Belt cases. They are thus part of my Greenbelt travelogue. Several methodological weaknesses and difficulties were observed and they are treated here in a summarizing manner. This is done by critically relating the key findings of the case studies to the renewal of Nordic human geography explicated in the introduction. The criticism can be grouped into two general sets of remarks, namely the concern for societal escapism, or *vanmakt*, in human geography and the unease about the weakening sense on socioenvironmental variation in the current international reorganization of geography.

Escapism in the Academia: Just Geography

Anne Buttimer, when receiving an honorary doctorate at the University of Joensuu in 1999, critically assessed the threat of geography becoming too sophisticated to be able to deal with the central topics of our global and local worlds.[5] Doreen Massey's thought-provoking discussion on the powerlessness of academic geography is an expression of a similar type of concern. It is not only the "others" that are to be blamed if the surrounding society finds it difficult to read us.[6] The sensitivity to endlessly fragmented practices of biopower can be regarded, as I do here, a welcome step forward in activating human geography in contemporary socioenvironmental matters. The biopolitical renewal remains, however, elitist if not translated and extended into societal practices. The most critical of our referees stay beyond the academic circles and there is no reason to ignore their messages. Massey argued that "changing discourses is part of changing the world," and she looks forward to influential societal involvements.[7]

We could call this an invitation to move from the cartography of biopolitics toward more participatory studies of biopower and (in)justice or, alternatively, a leap from intertextual choreogeographies to emancipatory research profiles. The questions are: How much do we geographers identify ourselves as activists in the biopolitics of our daily lives? How do we define today the "thirdspaces" between action and research? Olli Tammilehto,[8] a veteran activist and ecophilosopher from Finland, was once worried about the popularity of environmental research among the younger social scientists. He thought they had turned to environmental research due to personal conviction: they believed the environmental questions were important. "But why don't they have anything more pressing to do with these questions then," he continued. Tammilehto's provocative question is loaded with scepticism toward scientific work, but it can also be interpreted as an invitation to critically and repeatedly examining our own research motives. Is it just geography we are engaged in? For whom are we making our analyses?

The societal relevance of research depends on its capability to cope with the social and environmental factors constraining and conditioning the action spaces of the subject groups. Acute environmental questions emerge from this viewpoint as questions that are both shaping, as well as becoming shaped by, the shifting content of the actualized representations of environmental problems. While focusing on biopolitics and environmental discrimination in this volume, it was easy to highlight those socioenvironmental processes and projections that remarkably modify the most marginal(ized) of the lands and people of Northern Europe. This task directed our attention to those historical mechanisms of exclusion and inclusion that have been, and still are, dominating the practices and experiences of our lived spaces in the Nordic peripheries, including, if possible, the voiceless groups of the North.

The processes of discrimination and marginalization were further particularized by examining both the physical-ecological and sociocultural concerns of the Greenbelt actors. Peripheries, both social and spatial, were seen as biopolitically defined attributes and entities: they are land and lifescapes characterized by (post)colonial resource utilization, provincial adjustments and cultural-lingual assimilation—which all are identifiable as traces in the local-global practices of culture-nature. The clear boundary between ecological and societal concerns became useless. The erosion of the sense of justice and the erosion of the physical environment were seen as profoundly interrelated.

The decades-long re-thinking of the interrelations of culture-nature in Nordic human geography has only occasionally resulted in cooperation across the subdisciplinary divide between physical and human geographies.[9] The hybrid approach can, however, be formulated as a challenge to physical geographers to offer material for human geographers to rework their understanding of the physical-ecological foundations of social life. This type of interdisciplinary co-development is taking place within the new subdisciplines of environmental sociology and policy as well as in environmental history.[10] It seems that the disciplinary history of Nordic *samhällsgeografi* prevents us from seriously engaging in concrete ecological matters and overcoming the distance between human and physical geographies, both within disciplinary practices as well as in relation to the world "out there," beyond the academic circles.[11] The setting is strange, keeping in mind both the institutional structure of the discipline, stretching across physical and human faculties, and the long-lived emphasis of *samhällsgeografi* of culture-nature, focused on the material foundations of human life. The setting is strange when compared with the conditions of land and life in the extreme North where physical-ecological and sociocultural factors emerge in a thoroughly overlapping manner as practical combinations in the sphere of daily life and where the human existence completely depends on the skills of communities and individuals in reading and quickly reacting to the changes in physical conditions.

The case studies brought about the conclusion that the way out from the current societal invisibility of human geography could, and should, be broken by radically strengthening the link between the physical and human subdisciplines. The case analyses also revealed that this link should be made via the "lived worlds" of the communities, both local and global.

The Annihilation of the North

The northern question constructed in this volume represents only a few branches of Nordic human geography. In general, individual choices of Nordic human geographers have during the cultural and environmental turns resulted in a division of labor that has tended to weaken the elaboration of the Nordic and northern aspects of geography. This is especially true in theoretical renewal. It has become a routine measure in Nordic geography to value the individual research profiles according to the visibility in anglophonic publications. One symptom of this change is the fact that inter-Nordic conferences of *samhällsgeografi* have increasingly been held in English after the earlier favoring of Scandinavian languages. This lingual turn has also become reflected in reference practices: it is not rare today to find Nordic contributions in geography that almost in a programmatic manner ignore colleagues from the neighboring universities.[12]

The abandonment of the specific view from the European North will, if it were to continue, inevitably leads to the weakening of the sensitivity to geographical variation. Nordic human geography will become one of the homogenizing tools of globalization. The Nordic countries are part of the northernmost zone of the inhabited world and this setting calls for continuous (self-)reflection. The spaces of culture-nature are different in the North and this difference has repercussions on geographical practices. The urban life of the North has a dynamics of its own, as has the rural North, and this needs repeated updating and re-conceptualization in geography. We cannot stay indifferent to the difference of the North.

The key words of geography that seem to lead to fruitful approaches within the urban centers of Continental Europe and the trans-Atlantic West cannot directly be translated into concepts suitable for the urban-rural North. The critical sensitivity to the various forms of biopolitical annihilation of the North needs therefore to be extended to cover also our own arguments: How often have we undermined and ignored in our research programs the concerns of the lay communities of which we are part while joining the anglophonic renewal, or used the North merely as an interesting case for theory-testing?

Nordic geographers cannot free themselves from the symbolic and geopolitical contestation between the regimes of the European North. Human geography is an indelible part of the redefinition of the North, and today—as throughout the known history—this re-naming has taken place under conditions introduced and adopted from the South and the West. Both the North and the geographers of the North face the same pressure of submissive adjustment under the ideological discourse on globalization, emerging among the ranks of geographers and in the form of general societal changes. The call of globalization has had an inevitable impact on geographical thinking but it has also become a painful reminder of our own dependence on the fluid networks of (post)colonial homogenization, often becoming concrete in the tightening pressure to adopt English as the one and only common lingual framework.

The uneasiness in this respect grows from the findings of the case studies in this research which confirmed that the anglophonic North is different from the Scandinavian North, which in turn is different from the Norths of the various Finno-Ugric and Slavic peoples. Multiperspectivity, or the layered existence of land and lifescapes, is not alien to Nordic human geographers, even though the approaches from within the Nordic North and from within the East have been primarily shadowed by Western (Southern) innovations. The balancing of perspectives would, however, help us to free ourselves from the remnants of (post)colonialism in geography, and it could also be taken as a natural extension of Nordic *samhällsgeografi* during and after the cultural and environmental turns.

The Nordic North is a land and lifescape that varies within numerous geohistorical scales: archaic, traditional and modern (including late modern) timescapes emerge side by side and, thus, not as chronological periods but as coexisting layers of contemporary land and lifescapes. The linking of the layers has, however, not been favored by the key promoters of the cultural turns in geography and that is due to often well reasoned skepticism toward broad historical narrations and fear of transhistorical generalizations. These reservations have, however, partly turned into strict academic limitations where all the local-global traces of intergenerational or cultural dependencies have been ignored.[13] This stance has weakened the overall sensitivity to the practical time-space relations between the lived "realities" and their intersubjective variations. The socioenvironmental conditions of the extreme North clearly challenge geographers to take seriously the expressions of collective cultural belonging through rituals and routines.[14] The North would be a perfect subject of studies that aim at understanding[15] the dimensions and senses of human land and lifescapes.

Academic geographical practices are still dominantly based on abstractions constructed according to scientific traditions and, as was argued in chapter 13, this tends to tear the phenomena studied apart from their natural biohistorical contexts. The slicing of cultures and natures decisively limits the geographical scope in coping with the multitude of lay geographies. It constrains our ability to renew ourselves as researchers in dialogue with the subjects in study focus, as was stated in chapter 3 while referring to Juha Siltala's critical view on the general discursive turn in social sciences. The research and documentation of the North by restricting the study focus exclusively according to scientific criteria tend to confirm the continuation of the (post)colonial domination of the North from the South. The study objects are merely defined as interesting cases for theory-testing.

While keeping in mind the risks, fears and commitments disclosed above, I finally sketch a summary and grouping of the most encouraging traditions of human geography with a sensitivity to socioenvironmental matters. The view is three-dimensional and rooted to the oldest of the geographical traditions in the Western world, namely the classical formulations in the Ancient Greece, but primarily utilizing the Nordic formulations dealt with in this volume.

Studying *Khōra*: Place-making and Geography

Most of the local case studies of this volume contained analyses of communities that defended their own lifemode against the offers and demands from the outside. The local reactions were linked to traditional values and customs but also, especially in my interpretation, seen as outcomes of earlier compromises between local and translocal pressure. The home areas of the Belt communities were regarded and defended as places where the cultural-natural heritage has throughout the past been protected by the decisions of the locals. The southern conservationists of culture or nature were in most cases seen as intruders incapable of distinguishing the worth of the local way of conserving nature; not by establishing monuments of nature-culture but by living in such a way that the physical surroundings are kept in satisfactory condition.

The study of home places is among the oldest in Western geographical traditions. Some Nordic human geographers, such as Inger Birkeland and Kenneth Olwig,[16] end up with the Greek *khōra* while searching for the initial formulations of their research questions, and here they start with Plato and his identification of *khōra* in *Timaeus* as one of the foundational forms of existence. It was for him an initial and embryonic state wherein the material and visible comes into being.[17]

Plato distinguished three elementary forms of existence in *Timaeus*. The first is the realm that functions according to universal laws and is under the scrutiny of reason, whereas the second is the realm that is within the reach of senses. The third is *khōra,* and it offers the initial condition and principle for material existence. It is the container and receptacle of the materializing things.[18] *Khōra* thus appears in *Timaeus* as the motive that signifies the relations between the present and its origin. It is for Plato the source of identity and life connected to motherhood and birthing. Etymologically *khōra* roots, among other related things, to the Greek place, and home place or village in particular.[19]

The Greek *khōra* did not contain the practical values to become a central concept for the early geographers of the Roman Empire. On the contrary, it turned into a nuisance for the imperial administrators while serving as the emotional source of inspiration for the local opposites on the Aegean Islands critical to the rule of Rome. Olwig argues that Roman geography became established as a tool for expansion and governance, which meant an emphasis on geometric thinking and chorological mapping.[20] He mentions Claudius Ptolemaeus (87–165 AD) as the founder of chorological geography. Ptolemaeus was a Greek astronomer and geo-mathematician whose *Geographike hyphegesisi* developed mapping projections inspired by the "cosmic principles" of geometry. He paid no attention to spatial differentiation or variation in human cultures. The chorological model was forgotten in Medieval Europe, only to be rediscovered in the 15th century. Then it became part of the revolution in natural sciences, which gradually eroded the key principles of geocentric cosmology. The chorological model became applied in colonial mapping and it also inspired the later development of spatial analysis and geoinformation sciences.[21]

Plato's *khōra* was, however, included in the humanistic rethinking of the relations between place and space in the 1970s, and during the cultural turns in geography. The renaissance of the Platonic concept was primarily influenced by innovations in French philosophy: Julia Kristeva interpreted *khōra* as the feminine origin that comes before the symbolic and masculine ordering of things,[22] whereas Jacques Derrida linked *khōra* with community and "affinity of birth," which exist prior to all naming. Derrida's *khōra* is the condition beyond memory; it can be sensed in the concerns for architectural, textual and organic composition.[23]

Birkeland criticizes Derrida and Kristeva for their inability to develop the understanding of *khōra* through a positive self-definition: *khōra* is for both of them a premise to logocentric thought.[24] Derrida, argues Birkeland, destroys the positive potential of *khōra* by reorganizing and reducing it under the logic of lingual communication. Kristeva leans, according to Birkeland, too faithfully on Plato's interpretation which tends to restore both place and women as unconscious, repressed or unspoken foundations for philosophy and Western thinking. She formulates on the basis of this criticism a personal interpretation of *khōra*, to be applied in her study on nature tourism and place-making by traveling in the extreme North. Birkeland shapes *khōra* as the medium that enables us to cross the divide between the known and the unknown. It thus turns into place-making in the dialogues between presence and absence, traveling and return. Place is the "outcome" of home-making by journeying, both emotional and symbolic, where the sensible and the reasonable become one, both in thoughts and feelings as well as in embodied experiences and memories.

The debate on *khōra* offers geography a central role in developing our understanding of the motives and premises of those who defend their home areas and living conditions under the pressure of uncontrollable change. Studies on *khōra* can also help us to identify the layered motives of traveling and tourism, both in terms of travelers and those who serve as targets of tourism. The legitimacy of environmental planning, as was argued in chapter 1, has been grounded on chorological thinking, favoring natural scientific expertise, and only occasionally the expertise that has been developed by lay persons through their daily routines has gained a decisive role in environmental governance. On the contrary, cases where local views have been regarded as a hindrance to ecologically correct solutions or even as tools for unsustainable development are common.[25]

Sensitivity to the dimensions of *khōra* in socioenvironmental research brings along solutions where local lay appreciation of environmental change gains a central role in research documentation. In nature conservation, for example, "inventories" of local opinions would gradually lead to calming down the tensions between local people and environmentalists. The first experiments in voluntary nature conservation in southern Finland have been promising in this respect, though also loaded with risks of becoming poor compromises resulting in practices that tend to benefit those locals who speculate with short-term financial returns (see chapter 10).

Local protectionism that turns into provincial opportunism cannot be bypassed when coping with the lay geographies of *khōra*. Local reactions and proactions are often formulated against and within broader societal changes, both on the Aegean Islands as in the northwoods of the Greenbelt. In this volume, the tension between indigenous and immigrant interests, and thus a dialogue between the known and the unknown, became a key question. It became an inseparable part of the human community-building. The overcoming of indigenous values was witnessed in many case studies of the Belt but, in addition, the disregard of those immigrants who had come later was also seen as a symptom of cultural discrimination. The ranking of communities according to their degree of aboriginality, for example when formulating strategic coalitions in nature conservation or when officially distinguishing indigenous from non-indigenous groups, appeared as a tool for sharpening the local historical disagreement. This was especially the case in Upper Lapland.

When understanding geographical work as motivated by a need to make sense of the daily dialogues between the known and the unknown, or us and them, it becomes easier to formulate the constructive assessment of the "goods and bads" of the local compromises. The above-explicated links between geographical research and the traditions of *khōra* clearly support the conclusion that socioenvironmental geographies could, and perhaps also should, be developed toward a subdiscipline that would help us to identify the premises of lay communities for the local-global decision-making, balancing and correcting the informational basis drawn by the experts of special fields.

Politics of Identity: Studying Socioenvironmental Discrimination

As was argued in chapter 2, the concerns of environmental justice assist us in shaping the societal mechanisms that divide those who benefit and those who suffer from the societal and environmental changes prioritized or regarded as necessary. Socioenvironmental tensions are issues that easily become instruments of identity politics. This is especially the case when deciding the criteria according to which individuals and communities are included in or excluded from decision-making on matters that affect them. The slow and contested extensions of the culture of participation—the spreading of ethical communities—in the Western past stand as historical proof of the link between practices of participation and politics of identity.

This link has only occasionally drawn attention in geographical studies. This is strange, keeping in mind the geographical lessons from the colonial past. In the 1920s and 1930s, Carl Ortwin Sauer examined in detail the ethnoenvironmental consequences of the European colonization of the "new world." He was concerned about the crimes of ethnic reorganization of the land and lives of the indigenous Americans but he also paid attention to the loss of ecological values under the progression of the white frontier. One of the key motives for Sauer was to show alternatives to those geographical formulations that favored environmentally deterministic interpretations. In his most influential methodological formulations Sauer attacked those geographical views, then also promoted in European geography, where physical natural conditions were seen as explaining the variation in the spreading of civilization.[26]

Some deterministic views have survived surprisingly well in environmental and ecological thinking throughout the 20th century. Genetic or physical-environmental variations are repeatedly regarded as central factors that explain the differences in human development, and here the notes on variation often derive from estimated deviations from Western standards.[27]

Ethnic discrimination in natural scientific practices has also had a profound impact on the historical orientation in nature conservation. Racism in nature conservation became acute in the 1870s when the first national parks were founded in Yosemite and Yellowstone (in the USA). The parks that have often been mentioned as the beginning of nature conservation in the West were established by evacuating the indigenous first nations that happened to have settled inside the border of the proposed parks.[28] The parks, as monuments of nature, served as instruments for writing and confirming European supremacy in North America, and no traces of other histories were allowed to contest the new order.

Larry Lohman, a well-known environmental researcher and activist, has argued that the wilderness parks that were cleansed from traces of indigenous cultures have served as useful symbols for the national elites in the USA, as in other parts of the world under European colonialism. The white Europeans were able to distinguish such values from the wildernesses that were seen as justifying the evacuations. Selected wilderness areas were first culturally purified into "white areas" that could thereafter be developed into national parks for the amusement of the white middle class.[29]

The Greenbelt studies in this volume showed that environmental racism and discrimination are not only unfortunate episodes in the Western past. Signs of similar thinking are prevalent in contemporary industrial programs and park planning in Northern Europe. Overlooking ethnic values takes place for example when concerns of biodiversity shadow the ongoing extinction of lingual minorities. Questions of discrimination arise when environmental changes are justified and promoted within "non-Western" land and lifescapes by models that prioritize Western values and interpretations.

In the discursive context of this volume, it is not difficult to sketch geographical approaches that link socioenvironmental changes with identity politics. The case studies of the Belt provided methodological examples of how to proceed when aiming at identifying communities, and their values, that are part of the local-global politics of inclusion and exclusion. The case studies also showed how to focus on the societal mechanisms that produce and maintain the divisions between those who benefit and those who suffer from the decisions. In general, no universal rules could be sketched but, instead, each case was seen as deserving a study approach of its own. This methodological solution facilitated the appreciation of the multitude of the border geographies.

Studying Biopolitics

The fate of oppressed communities lies also in the core of biopolitical research. The biopolitical approach links socioenvironmental decisions with measures of population policy. The prefix "bio" guides us to concerns of life and conditions of land and life. Main socioenvironmental changes, and changes in attitudes toward them, are seen in this view as causing profound alterations in the living conditions of individuals, communities and social strata. Within this framework, socioenvironmental governance is inseparable from demographic governance.

Biopolitical research pays also attention to the activity, or passivity, of individuals and communities amidst societal changes. The erosion of local land and lifescapes is not regarded as a direct outcome of societal reorganizations (extended as necessities from "the outside") but as a result of choices in the intimate sphere of the communities themselves. The Greenbelt communities were, therefore, examined by paying attention to spatio-technical, aesthetic and metaphoric dependencies between general societal pressure and particular cultural adjustments.

The border zone between Finland and Russia provided a window to provincial biopolitical transformations where the success of the local communities is highly dependent on the success of the leading export actors. This was a societal condition forged by past decisions and it was also the dominant cultural interpretation of the present and future room to manoeuver. The belief in this type of positive linkage between local and translocal successes was contested during the economic and political crises of the early 1990s in Finland and Russia. In Finland, the rapid rise of the translocal actors from the recession, accompanied by signs of the "China phenomenon," further questioned the old routines of formulating success recipes. The simultaneous emergence of a new economic elite and the accelerating confrontations among central financial groups resulted in similar doubts in Russia.

In this volume, these changes at the interface of the micro and macro spheres of society highlighted the need to further develop the aspects of critical biopolitical research. However, the task to identify and analyze the connections between the two spheres turned out to be difficult and demanding in the case studies on the Greenbelt, and this experience was confirmed by the discovery how few examples of similar endeavors could be found in research literature. Nordic human geography undoubtedly has weaknesses here but the problem is more general in nature.

The weaknesses at least partially root from the orientation of Nordic human geography toward hybrid innovations, such as time-geographies, bodily interspaces, choreographies of life and rural-urban interfaces,[30] which have value as descriptive tools when analyzing the everyday sceneries of land and life. Nordic human geography has developed a particular sensitivity in crossing borders of many types but it seems to have largely left the societal connections between local communities and translocal communities unexamined. This has taken place by exclusively prioritizing the links between personal research ambitions and academic universalisms.

The reasons for this state of affairs are manifold, but we cannot ignore the inspiration of Bruno Latour and his hybrid thinking, explicated in chapter 3. The limits of hybrid thinking were planned to overcome in this study by applying biopolitical views in critical globalization research. Michael Hardt and Antonio Negri's *Empire* helped much in sketching a satisfactory approach. The combination of the two discourses seemed reasonable, especially as it was supported by a few similar endeavors from within the Nordic circles.

These type of epistemic leaps are, however, always risky. Latour has attacked such leaps by arrogantly criticizing the taken-for-granted acceptance of social forces in biopolitical globalization research: "Take the example of Hardt and Negri's *Empire* if you want an example of the emptiness of what critique has become, that's the best case: because they claim to look behind the appearances and reveal the hidden forces, they take away the critical attention, they add a world of beyond to the only real world of practices."[31] Latour is afraid of *Empire*-type research because it looks critical and radical but only guides people to the "non-existing afterworld."

The results of the Greenbelt research lead to an opposite conclusion. By excluding the social forces, i.e. the macro sphere, from our studies and by selectively focusing on "appearances" we take the risk of contributing to the erosion of the critical scope and societal credibility of research. Our study subjects are treated as interesting cases for theory-testing or as pure laboratories of land and life. We are in danger of losing the opportunities of building reciprocal relationship between the subject partners of research and perhaps even begin to imagine ourselves as honored members of a particular academic elite, consciously ignoring the changing societal conditions of the lay reality of the everyday. The Nordic and Greenbelt studies in this volume stand as proof of the necessity to cross the border between the societal and the cultural in socioenvironmental research. This aim characterizes the gradual development of Nordic *samhällsgeografi* and there is no reason to allow any short-sighted interpretations of the cultural and environmental turns to make us bypass the main trends of the ongoing reorganization of our local-global land and lifescapes.

Notes

1. The question of the North was reconstructed in the EU in 1995 when Finland and Sweden became members of the Union. The promoters of the northern dimension have suggested that the special conditions of the North, such as cold climate, sparse population and proximity to Russia, should be given due consideration in EU politics. They have also underlined the potential of intensified cross-border cooperation in the Barents Region and across the Baltic Sea. See Paavo Lipponen, "The Northern Dimension of Europe," in *Europe's Northern Dimension: The Bear Meets the South*, eds. Lassi Heininen and Richard Langlais (Rovaniemi: University of Lapland, Publications of the Administrative Office, no. 39, 1997), 29-35; Pertti Joenniemi, "Can Europe be Told from the North? Tapping into the EU's Northern Dimension," in *Encountering the North. Cultural Geography, International Relations and Northern Landscapes*, eds. Frank Möller and Samu Pehkonen (Aldershot: Ahhgate, 2003), 221-60. The northern focus of Nordic geographers has been less restricted in the framework of the European Union, which has in turn enabled a more varied and cross-cultural understanding of the North, especially in connection to the North Atlantic and Northwest Russia.
2. See formulations of the principle of minimal impact among the Sámi: Tvyr Ivar Bergsmo, *Boazojahki* (Oslo: Pantagruel Forlag, 2001), 9-13; Veli-Pekka Lehtola, *Nickul, rauhan mies, rauhan kansa* (Jyväskylä: Kustannus-Puntsi, 2000), 58-64. See also a reference to the ecological problems of traditional Sámi culture, Lehtola, *Nickul, rauhan mies, rauhan kansa*, 52.
3. Kaisa Häkkinen, *Nykysuomen etymologinen sanakirja* (Helsinki: Wsoy, 2004), 6-16; Jani Kaaro, "Kun kieli katoaa," *Tiede*, no. 2 (2005), 34-36.
4. Kaaro, "Kun kieli katoaa," 34.
5. Ari Aukusti Lehtinen, "Anne Buttimer Joensuun yliopiston kunniatohtoriksi," *Terra* 111, no. 4 (1999), 234-35. Buttimer is a Professor of Geography at University College Dublin.
6. Doreen Massey, "Geography on the Agenda," *Progress in Human Geography* 25, no. 1 (2001), 5-17. Massey is a Professor of Geography at the Open University, London.
7. Massey, "Geography on the Agenda," 10.
8. Olli Tammilehto, "Tutkijankammio ympäristökriisin myllerryksessä," in *Ympäristökysymys*, eds. Ilmo Massa and Rauno Sairinen (Helsinki: Gaudeamus, 1991), 212.
9. A few serious attempts can, however, be found: see for example Michael Jones, "The Elusive Reality of Landscape," *Norsk Geografisk Tidsskrift* 45 (1991), 229-44; Perttu Vartiainen and Heikki Vesajoki, "Ekologisen maantieteen haasteista," in *Saimaalta Kolille. Karjalan tutkimuslaitos 1971-1991*, eds. Pekka Hakamies, Väinö Jääskeläinen and Ilkka Savijärvi (Joensuu: Joensuun yliopisto, Karjalan tutkimuslaitos, 1991), 169-95; Gabriel Bladh, *Finnskogens landskap och människor under fyra sekler* (Karlstad: Högskolan i Karlstad, Forskningsrapport 11, 1995).
10. Timo Myllyntaus and Mikko Saikku, eds., *Encountering the Past in Nature* (Athens: Ohio University Press, 2001); Yrjö Haila and Chuck Dyke, eds., *How Nature Speaks: The Dynamics of Human Ecological Condition* (Durham: Duke University Press, 2005).
11. Tina Hansen and Keld Buciek, "Landskabet som samfundsmæssig forestilling," *Nordisk Samhällsgeografisk Tidskrift* 31 (2000), 73 express the challenge most clearly: "To

see the cultural values and social, economic and political processes that emerge in our experience and representation of landscape is a central element of the new cultural geography. Therefore, it is not relevant to study the processes of nature in the landscape." Translated from Danish by the author.

12. Jan Öhman and Kirsten Simonsen, eds., *Voices from the North. New Trends in Nordic Human Geography* (Aldershot: Ashgate, 2003).

13. See Tuija Pulkkinen, *Postmoderni politiikan filosofia* (Helsinki: Gaudeamus, 2003), published also in English: *The Postmodern and the Political Agency* (Helsinki: University of Helsinki, Department of Philosophy Publications, 1998).

14. Paul Connerton, *How Societies Remember?* (Cambridge: Cambridge University Press, 1989); Simon Schama, *Landscape and Memory* (London: Fontana Press, 1995); Brian Graham and G.J. Ashworth, eds., *A Geography of Heritage* (London: Arnold, 2000).

15. The varying realms the translations of "to understand" refer to indicate cross-cultural differences in cosmological views: "to understand" locates the observer below the object contacted, whereas "*att förstå*" (in Swedish) and "*zu verstehen*" (in German) refer to a subject that stands in front of the object. Finnish "*ymmärtää*" confuses the division between subject and object by guiding the subject to surround the thing in mind.

16. Kenneth Robert Olwig, "Landscape as a Contested Topos of Place, Community and Self," in *Textures of Place: Geographies of Imagination, Experience, and Paradox*, eds. Steven Hoelscher, Paul C. Adams and Karen E. Till (Minneapolis: University of Minnesota Press, 2001); Inger J. Birkeland, *Stories from the North. Travel as Place-Making in the Context of Modern Holiday-Travel to North Cape, Norway* (Oslo: University of Oslo, Department of Sociology and Human Geography, Report no. 2, 2002).

17. Platon, *Teokset V (Sofisti, Valtiomies, Timaios, Kritias ja Filebos)* (Helsinki: Otava, 1999), 193.

18. Platon, *Teokset V (Sofisti, Valtiomies, Timaios, Kritias ja Filebos)*, 197.

19. Julia Kristeva, *Revolution in Poetic Language* (New York: Columbia University Press, 1984), 25; Olwig, "Landscape as a Contested Topos of Place, Community and Self," 97-101.

20. Olwig, "Landscape as a Contested Topos of Place, Community and Self," 98.

21. Ari Aukusti Lehtinen, "Modernization and the Concept of Nature: On the Reproduction of Environmental Stereotypes," in Timo Myllyntaus and Mikko Saikku, eds. *Encountering the Past in Nature* (Athens: Ohio University Press, 2001), 29-37.

22. Kristeva, *Revolution in Poetic Language*, 29.

23. Jacques Derrida, *On the Name* (Stanford: Stanford University Press, 1995), 106, 126.

24. Birkeland, *Stories from the North. Travel as Place-Making in the Context of Modern Holiday-Travel to North Cape, Norway*, 289-90.

25. Ari Aukusti Lehtinen and Pertti Rannikko, *Oikeudenmukaisuus ja ympäristö* (Helsinki: Gaudeamus, 2003), 234-37.

26. John Leighly, ed., *Land and Life. A Selection From the Writings of Carl Sauer* (Berkeley: University of California Press, 1963).

27. David Harvey, *Justice, Nature and the Geography of Difference* (Oxford: Blackwell, 1996), 366-402; Eeva Berglund, "Finland as Information Society," *Suomen Antropologi* 28, no. 4 (2003), 2-16; Michael Hardt and Antonio Negri, *Empire* (Cambridge, Ma.: Harvard University Press, 2003), 134-36.

28. Yrjö Haila, "'Wilderness' and the Multiple Layers of Environmental Thought," *Environment and History* 3, no. 2 (1997), 133-37.
29. Larry Lohman, "Mitä rasismilla on tekemistä meidän kanssamme?," *Muutoksen kevät* 23 (2001), 24.
30. Jan Öhman and Kirsten Simonsen, eds., *Voices from the North. New Trends in Nordic Human Geography* (Aldershot: Ashgate, 2003).
31. Yrjö Haila and Turo-Kimmo Lehtonen, "Iconoclash: Two Years After. An Interview with Bruno Latour," *Framework,* no. 2 (2004), 20.

Index

www.ingramcontent.com/pod-product-compliance
Lightning Source LLC
LaVergne TN
LVHW091920140926
847999LV00012B/73
9780761834175